CONNECTIONIST
PSYCHOLINGUISTICS

CONNECTIONIST PSYCHOLINGUISTICS

Edited by
Morten H. Christiansen
and Nick Chater

ABLEX PUBLISHING
Westport, Connecticut • London

Library of Congress Cataloging-in-Publication Data

Connectionist psycholinguistics / edited by Morten H. Christiansen and Nick Chater.
  p.   cm.
  Includes bibliographical references and index.
  ISBN 1–56750–594–5 (alk. paper)—ISBN 1–56750–595–3 (pbk. : alk. paper)
  1. Psycholinguistics. 2. Connectionism. I. Christiansen, Morten H., 1963– II. Chater,
 Nick.
  BF455.C677   2001
  401′.9—dc21   00-052555

British Library Cataloguing in Publication Data is available.

Library of Congress Catalog Card Number: 00–052555
ISBN: 1–56750–594–5 (hc.)
       1–56750–595–3 (pbk.)

First published in 2001

Ablex Publishing, 88 Post Road West, Westport, CT 06881
An imprint of Greenwood Publishing Group, Inc.
www.greenwood.com

Printed in the United States of America

The paper used in this book complies with the
Permanent Paper Standard issued by the National
Information Standards Organization (Z39.48–1984).

10 9 8 7 6 5 4 3 2 1

Contents

Preface

Connectionist modeling has had a vast impact throughout cognitive science, and has been both highly productive and highly controversial in the area of natural language processing and acquisition. The decade and a half after the publication of David Rumelhart and Jay McClelland's seminal *Parallel Distributed Processing* volumes has seen an explosive growth of connectionist modeling of natural language. During this period the field has matured and is moving away from abstract "existence-proof" models toward making close contact with a range of psycholinguistic data. This book offers the first comprehensive treatment of this emergent area of research, demonstrating the current state of the art (Part I) and appraising the prospects for future development (Part II) of "connectionist psycholinguistics."

The book is based on a special issue of *Cognitive Science*, "Connectionist models of human language processing: Progress and prospects," Vol. 23, no. 4, edited by Morten H. Christiansen, Nick Chater, and Mark S. Seidenberg. The papers in the special issue were solicited from an outstanding group of connectionist language researchers, specifically to address the key subareas in connectionist language research and to discuss the future prospects of connectionist psycholinguistics. For the purpose of this book, each paper has been updated, including the addition of a descriptive list of further readings. In most cases the papers have also been substantially revised.

Part I, The State of the Art, brings us to the forefront of current connectionist modeling of psycholinguistic processing, with individual chapters on speech perception, morphology, sentential recursion, sentence processing, language production, and reading, beginning with an in-depth perspective on the breadth and variety of work in connectionist modeling of language. Part II, Future Prospects, provides a multifaceted discussion of the prospects for future research within connectionist psycholinguistics.

Each chapter is written by leading researchers who are defining the current state of the art within the connectionist approach to language. The book should therefore provide both a summary of where the field stands and a stimulus to future research in connectionist psycholinguistics. More generally, the book is aimed at researchers, scholars, and advanced students in psychology, linguistics, psycholinguistics, cognitive neuroscience, cognitive science, philosophy, or computer science with interest in the psychology of language and in computational approaches to the understanding of psycholinguistic processing.

1

Connectionist Psycholinguistics: The Very Idea

Morten H. Christiansen and Nick Chater

What is the significance of connectionist models of language processing? Will connectionism ultimately replace, complement, or simply implement the symbolic approach to language? Early connectionist models attempted to address this issue by showing that connectionist models could, in principle, capture aspects of language processing and linguistic structure. Little attention was generally paid to the modeling of data from psycholinguistic experiments. However, we suggest that connectionist language processing has matured and that the field is now moving forward into a new phase in which closer attention is paid to detailed psycholinguistic data. This book provides the first comprehensive overview of work within the emergent field of "connectionist psycholinguistics," connectionist models that make close contact with psycholinguistic results.

But how are we to assess the models within this emerging new area of research? We suggest that computational models of psycholinguistic processing, whether connectionist or symbolic, should attempt to fulfill three criteria: (1) data contact, (2) task veridicality, and (3) input representativeness (Christiansen & Chater, 2001). Data contact refers to the degree to which a model provides a fit with psycholinguistic data. We distinguish here between primary and secondary data contact. Primary data contact involves fitting results from specific psycholinguistic experiments (e.g., reaction-time data), whereas secondary data contact involves fitting general patterns of behavior (e.g., experimentally attested developmental changes in language processing) rather than specific results. Task veridicality refers to the degree of match between the task facing people and the task given to the model. Although a precise match is typically difficult to obtain, it is important to minimize the discrepancy. For example, much early work on modeling the English past tense suffers from low task veridicality (e.g., Rumelhart & McClelland, 1986, but see, e.g., Hoeffner, 1997, for an exception) because models are trained to map verb stems to past-tense forms, a task unlikely to be relevant to children's language acquisition. Input representativeness refers to the degree to which the information given to the model reflects what is available to a person or child. For example, the computational modeling of morphology suffers from the lack of good training corpora of high input representativeness with which to train the models. This problem is most serious for non-English morphology, making it problematic to make a priori conclusions about the feasibility of connectionist accounts in the area (e.g., Berent, Pinker, & Shimron, 1999).

It is also important to take stock of where symbolic models stand on our three criteria for computational psycholinguistics. Interestingly, few symbolic models make direct contact with psycholinguistic data. Most of the exceptions are within the study of sentence processing, where some comprehensive models of word-by-word reading times exist (e.g., Gibson, 1998; Just & Carpenter, 1992) and have a reasonable degree of task veridicality. More generally, however, symbolic models appear to pay little attention to task veridicality. Indeed, the rule-based models of the English past tense (e.g., Pinker, 1991) involve the same stem-to-past-tense mappings as the early connectionist models, and thus suffer from the same low task veridicality. Input representativeness is often ignored in symbolic models, in part because learning plays a minimal role in the performance of these models, and in part because symbolic models tend to be focused on more abstract fragments of language, rather than the more realistic language input that some connectionist models can handle. Low input representativeness may, for these reasons, actually inflate performance for many types of symbolic models, whereas the opposite tends to be true of connectionist models.

Currently, then, connectionism appears to provide a better framework for detailed psycholinguistic modeling than the symbolic approach. For many connectionists the advantages of this framework for doing computational psycholinguistics derive from a number of properties of the connectionist models.

Learning. Connectionist networks typically learn from experience, rather than being fully prespecified by a designer. By contrast, symbolic computational systems, including those concerned with language processing, are typically, but not always, fully specified by the designer.

Generalization. Few aspects of language are simple enough to be learnable by rote. The ability of networks to generalize to cases on which they have not been trained is thus a critical test for many connectionist models.

Representation. Because they are able to learn, the internal codes used by connectionist networks need not be fully specified by a designer, but are devised by the network so as to be appropriate for the task. Developing methods for understanding the codes that the network develops is an important strand of connectionist research. While internal codes may be learned, the inputs and outputs to a network generally use a code specified by the designer. These codes can be crucial in determining network performance. How these codes relate to standard symbolic representations of language in linguistics is a major point of contention.

Rules versus Exceptions. Many aspects of language can be described in terms of what have been termed "quasi-regularities," regularities that are usually true but admit some exceptions. According to the symbolic descriptions used by modern linguistics, these quasi-regularities may be captured in terms of a set of symbolic rules and sets of exceptions to those rules. Symbolic models often incorporate this distinction by having separate mechanisms that deal with rule-governed and exceptional cases. It has been argued that connectionist models provide a single mechanism that can pick up general rules while learning the exceptions to those rules. While this issue has been a major point of controversy surrounding connectionist models, it is important to note that attempting to provide single mechanisms for rules and exceptions is not essential to the connectionist approach; one or both separate mechanisms for rules and exceptions could themselves be modeled in connectionist terms (Coltheart, Curtis, Atkins, & Haller, 1993; Pinker, 1991; Pinker & Prince, 1988). A further question is whether networks really learn rules at all, or whether they simply approximate rulelike behavior. Opinions differ concerning whether the latter is an important positive proposal, which may lead to a revision of the role of rules in linguistics (Rumelhart & McClelland, 1986; see also Smolensky, 1988), or whether it is a fatal problem with connectionist models of language processing (Marcus, 1998; Pinker & Prince, 1988).

These four properties all play important roles in the models described in Part I of this volume, as well as in the appraisals of connectionist psycholinguistics presented in Part II.

ORGANIZATION OF THIS VOLUME

Part I of this volume, The State of the Art, presents the current state of the art in connectionist psycholinguistics with specific models from five key areas: speech processing, morphology, sentence processing, language production, and reading aloud. Part II, Future Prospects, then provides three contrasting perspectives on the field from leading researchers working on computational models of human natural language processing.

Part I begins with Chapter 2, Connectionist Psycholinguistics in Perspective, by Morten H. Christiansen and Nick Chater. This chapter provides an in-depth introduction to the field of connectionist psycholinguistics, and sets the context for the rest of the volume. The historical roots of the connectionist approach to language processing are traced and key themes that arise throughout different areas of connectionist psycholinguistics are highlighted. The chapter also provides a detailed review of the five key empirical areas described in the chapters comprising the rest of this part of the book, highlighting the interplay between connectionist modeling and empirical research. This review indicates that connectionist psycholinguistics has already had a significant impact on the psychology of language, and suggests that connectionist models are likely to have an important influence on future research. With this review in place, the subsequent chapters in this part of the book present central recent developments in the field.

Chapter 3, Simulating Parallel Activation in Spoken Word Recognition, by M. Gareth Gaskell and William D. Marslen-Wilson, concerns the connectionist modeling of speech processing. A critical property of the perception of spoken words is the transient ambiguity of the speech signal. Speech information is spread out across time, and early on in the processing of a word the speech information will be compatible with more than one lexical item. In localist models of speech perception this property is captured by allowing the parallel activation of multiple independent lexical representations. Gaskell and Marslen-Wilson examine how this property can be accommodated in a distributed model of speech perception, in which word representations are not independent. In this case an approximation to the activation of more than one representation is possible by activating a "blend" of the different distributed representations. Statistical analyses of vector spaces show that coactivation of multiple distributed representations is inherently noisy, and depends on parameters such as sparseness and dimensionality. Furthermore, the characteristics of coactivation vary considerably, depending on the organization of distributed representations within the mental lexicon. This view of lexical access is supported by analyses of phonological and semantic word representations, which provide an explanation of a recent set of experiments on coactivation in speech perception (Gaskell & Marslen-Wilson, 1999). More generally, this work illustrates a tight interplay between connectionist psycholinguistic modeling and experimental psycholinguistic research. Thus, the model provides for a good primary data contact and reasonable input representativeness, but suffers from a relatively poor task veridicality because of the abstract nature of the simulations.

Chapter 4, A Connectionist Model of English Past-Tense and Plural Morphology, by Kim Plunkett and Patrick Juola, concerns what has been one of the most controversial domains to which connectionist research has been applied: morphological processing. Theorists advocating a symbolic perspective have frequently taken morphology as a paradigmatic case of a "rule + exception" mapping. A rigid symbolic rule, which specifies a regular morphological mapping, is presumed to be supplemented with a set of explicit exceptions, which are assumed to be processed by a very different mechanism. In line with much connectionist work in this area, Plunkett and Juola make the opposite assumption, that a single mechanism explains both rule and exception cases in morphological processing. Specifically, they model the acquisition of English noun and verb morphology using a single connectionist network. The network is trained to produce the plurals and past-tense forms for a large corpus of monosyllabic English nouns and verbs. The developmental trajectory of network performance is analyzed in detail and is shown to mimic a number of important features of the acquisition of English noun and verb morphology in young children. These include an initial error-free period of performance on both nouns and verbs followed by a period of intermittent overregularization of irregular nouns and verbs. Errors in the model show evidence of phonological conditioning and frequency effects. Furthermore, the network demonstrates a strong tendency to regularize denominal verbs and deverbal nouns and masters the principles of voicing assimilation. Despite being dealt with by a single network, nouns and verbs exhibit some important differences in their profiles of acquisition. Most important, noun inflections are acquired earlier than verb inflections. The simulations generate several empirical predictions that can be used to further evaluate the suitability of this type of cognitive architecture in the domain of inflectional morphology, thus pointing the way for close links between computational and empirical research. The model has good secondary data contact and decent input representativeness, but the task veridicality is poor because the task of mapping noun and verb stems to plural and past-tense inflections is not likely to play a large role in language acquisition.

Chapter 5, Finite Models of Infinite Language: A Connectionist Approach to Recursion, by Morten H. Christiansen and Nick Chater, deals with another theoretical issue that has been seen as strongly supporting a symbolic, rather than a connectionist, approach to language processing: natural language recursion. Since the inception of modern linguistics there has been considerable emphasis on the importance of recursive phenomena in natural language, and the assumption that any approach to sentence processing must allow for unbounded recursion. Indeed, the existence of different kinds of recursion has had important implications on the choices of symbolic formalisms (e.g., different kinds of generative grammars, different classes of parser and generator) that have been used to explain natural language. From this perspective, natural language recursion presents a difficult challenge to any nonsymbolic account of natural language processing.

A range of connectionist approaches have been put forward that attempt to deal with recursion in natural language, although they have not typically achieved the unbounded character of natural language recursion that linguists typically assume. Christiansen and Chater note, though, that the proposition that natural language allows unbounded applications of recursion may make an inappropriate target for connectionist modeling. Instead, they argue that a more appropriate goal for connectionism is to account for the levels of performance that people exhibit when exposed to recursive constructions—to address recursion as a purely psycholinguistic phenomenon, rather than as a linguistic abstraction. It is important to note that people's ability to process recursive constructions is quite limited. People produce only a very limited number of complex recursive constructions in naturally occurring speech, and this is reflected in the empirically documented difficulties that people experience when processing such structures.

Christiansen and Chater present a connectionist model of human performance in processing recursive language structures, based on Elman's (1990) simple recurrent network (SRN). The model is trained on simple artificial languages inspired by Chomsky (1957). They find that the qualitative performance profile of the model closely matches human behavior, both on the relative difficulty of center-embedded and cross-dependency, and between the processing of these complex recursive structures and right-branching recursive constructions. Christiansen and Chater analyze how these differences in performance are reflected in the internal representations of the model by performing discriminant analyses on these representations both before and after training. The model has good primary data contact and reasonable task veridicality, but the input representativeness is low because of the abstractness of the artificial languages. More generally, this work suggests a novel explanation of people's limited recursive performance, without assuming the existence of a mentally represented grammar allowing unbounded recursion.

Chapter 6, Dynamical Systems for Sentence Processing, by Whitney Tabor and Michael K. Tanenhaus, like the previous chapter, addresses the question of natural language processing at the level of the sentence, using input patterned on natural language rather than the more abstract structures used by Christiansen and Chater. Tabor and Tanenhaus suggest that the theory of dynamical systems, originated in the physical sciences, provides a revealing general framework for modeling the representations and mechanisms underlying sentence processing. Recent work in sentence processing (e.g., McRae, Spivey-Knowlton, & Tanenhaus, 1998) suggests that parsing biases change fairly continuously over the course of processing the successive words of a sentence. Connectionist networks are good at fitting graded data, and their dynamical properties are naturally suited to modeling continuously changing quantities. But the connectionist network that has been most successful in modeling natural language syntax (Elman's SRN, which is used by Christiansen and Chater in the previous chapter) does not explicitly model processing times. They argue that, like many connectionist models at the present time, the SRN is analytically opaque: It is difficult to see the principles underlying its solutions to complex tasks. And it is relativistic—no categorical distinctions are made between grammatical and ungrammatical strings—so it is hard to use linguistic structural insights, which make heavy use of such distinctions, to get past the opaqueness. They suggest that dynamical systems theory, through its insight into the relationship between quantitative and topological properties of systems, offers a solution to these shortcomings.

As in their previous work (Tabor, Juliano, & Tanenhaus, 1997), Tabor and Tanenhaus add a postprocessor to the SRN that has explicit dynamics, thus introducing potentially useful dynamical systems concepts: attractors, basins, saddle points, trajectories. They call this the Visitation Set Gravitation (VSG) model. Trained on a simple formal language that shares certain key properties with English, the model predicts the important reading-time contrasts in a recent study of the real-time evolution of parsing biases (McRae et al., 1998).

Further examination of the VSG model reveals that a standard structural contrast in dynamical systems—between saddle points and attractors—maps onto the fundamental linguistic contrast between ungrammatical and grammatical strings, thus helping to bridge the gap between connectionist models and linguistic theory. And without further modification of the model, a behaviorally accurate analysis of semantically strange sentences falls out: They are grammatical sentences that involve long trajectories in the state space of the dynamical system and thus have long processing times. This insight helps move work on formal language learning in the much-needed direction of addressing semantic structure.

Overall, the Tabor and Tanenhaus model has good primary data contact and decent task veridicality, but the input representativeness is low because of the simplicity of their formal language. The results suggest that dynamical-systems theory is a promising source of ideas for relating the flexible, real-time behavior of the human language processor to its overarching, relatively static, categorical organization. This application of dynamical-systems ideas is part of a larger movement within cognitive science (e.g., Kelso, 1997; Port & van Gelder, 1995; Thelen & Smith, 1994), which seeks to understand cognition in dynamical terms. Language processing provides a challenging test case for the application of the dynamical approach, because language has traditionally been conceived from a symbolic perspective. It is interesting, too, to wonder to what extent connectionist researchers will follow Tabor and Tanenhaus in using ideas from dynamical-systems theory to construct and understand connectionist systems. If this does occur, it might represent a substantial departure from the current technical literature on connectionist networks, which is grounded in probability, information theory, and statistical mechanics, rather than dynamical ideas (Bishop, 1995; Frey, 1998).

Chapter 7, Connectionist Models of Language Production: Lexical Access and Grammatical Encoding, by Gary S. Dell, Franklin Chang, and Zenzi M. Griffin, moves the focus from how language is understood to how it is produced. Language production, like language understanding, has frequently been characterized as involving the operation of symbolic processes on a generative grammar, and a specification of the message to be produced, in terms of a symbolically encoded underlying "logical form" or "conceptual representation." In contrast to this kind of account, there has also been a long tradition of connectionist theorizing about language production. Indeed, Dell's (1986) "spreading activation" model of speech production was one of the most important models in the revival of interest in connectionist models of psychological processes, which began in the early to mid-1980s. In their chapter, Dell et al. describe the most recent developments in this approach to modeling speech production. Specifically, they outline the issues and challenges that must be addressed by connectionist models of lexical access and grammatical encoding, and review three recent models. The models illustrate the value of a spreading activation approach to lexical access in production, the need for sequential output in both phonological and grammatical encoding, and the potential for accounting for structural effects on phonological errors and syntactic priming. These models account for a broad range of data on speech production, from the analysis of speech errors, to the performance of aphasic patients, to results from syntactic priming studies. Indeed, in speech-production research the interplay between connectionist modeling and the gathering of empirical data that we view as constitutive of connectionist psycholinguistics is particularly well developed.

Dell et al. consider several specific models, rather than attempting a single overarching model of speech production. Individually, the models have good primary or secondary data contact and good task veridicality, but all models suffer from relatively low input representativeness because the models only cover small language fragments. An important question for future research concerns the degree to which models of specific aspects of speech production can be integrated in a cohesive way, an issue that also arises in relation to the models of speech and language processing described in earlier chapters of this book.

The chapters described so far have focused on the comprehension and production of speech, rather than how written language is processed. The reading of single words has, in particular, been an area of intense connectionist research. Chapter 8, A Connectionist Approach to Word Reading and Acquired Dyslexia: Extension to Sequential Processing, by David C. Plaut, outlines a new model of reading, building on the long research tradition. Plaut begins by discussing some general principles of the connectionist approach to word reading—of which he is a leading proponent—including distributed representation, graded learning of statistical structure, and interactivity in processing. These principles have led to the development of explicit computational models that account for an impressively broad range of data, from the interaction of word frequency and spelling-sound consistency in normal skilled reading to analogous effects in the reading errors of surface dyslexic patients and the co-occurrence of visual and semantic errors in deep dyslexia.

Plaut notes, though, that there have been recent empirical challenges to these models, and the approach in general, relating to the influence of orthographic length on the naming latencies of both normal and dyslexic readers. For instance, the models account for relatively little variance associated with individual words in large databases of naming latencies, partly due to insufficient sensitivity to orthographic length. The models also underestimate length effects in the naming latencies for nonwords. This kind of empirical challenge is an illustration of the productive interaction between connectionist modeling and empirical research—predictions of connectionist models have had a crucial impact in directing the search for relevant empirical confirmation or disconfirmation.

Plaut addresses this challenge by presenting a new model that generates sequential phonological output in response to written input. He trains an SRN (Elman, 1990) to produce sequences of single phonemes as output when given position-specific letters as input. The model was also trained to maintain a representation of its current position within the input string. When the model found a peripheral portion of the input difficult to pronounce, it used the position signal to refixate the input, shifting the peripheral portion to the point of fixation where the model has had more experience in generating pronunciations. In this way the model could apply the knowledge tied to the units at the point of fixation to any difficult portion of the input. Early on in training, the model required multiple fixations to read words, but as the model became more competent it eventually read most words in a single fixation. The model could also read nonwords about as well as skilled readers, occasionally falling back on a refixation strategy for difficult nonwords. The model exhibits an effect of orthographic length and a frequency-by-consistency interaction in its naming latencies. When subject to peripheral damage, the model exhibits an increased length effect that interacts with word frequency, characteristic of letter-by-letter reading in pure alexia. The model thus has a good primary data contact and good task veridicality, but input representativeness suffers somewhat because the model is only trained on monosyllabic words. Plaut notes that the model is not intended as a fully adequate account of all the relevant empirical phenomena. But the model provides a compelling demonstration of how connectionist models may be extended to provide deeper insight into sequential processes in reading.

Plaut's chapter concludes the first part of the book, which reviews current models of connectionist language processing. The second part of the book consists of three insightful perspectives on the significance, interpretation, and utility of connectionist psycholinguistics by eminent researchers in the cognitive science of language processing.

Chapter 9, Constraint Satisfaction in Language Acquisition and Processing, by Mark S. Seidenberg and Maryellen C. MacDonald, sets out the most radical connectionist agenda, seeing connectionism as potentially undermining classical symbolic theorizing in linguistics and psycholinguistics. In particular, they see connectionist psycholinguistics as part of a larger theoretical framework focusing on probabilistic constraints on language processing and language acquisition (Seidenberg, 1997). This probabilistic framework offers an alternative viewpoint on language and language use to that found in generative linguistics. The generative approach attempts to characterize knowledge of language (i.e., competence grammar) and then asks how this knowledge is acquired and used. Seidenberg and MacDonald's probabilistic approach is performance oriented: The goal is to explain how people comprehend and produce utterances and how children acquire this skill. From a probabilistic perspective, using language is thought to involve exploiting multiple probabilistic constraints over various types of linguistic and nonlinguistic information. Children begin accumulating this information at a young age. The same constraint-satisfaction processes that are central to language use in adulthood also serve as the bootstrapping processes that provide entry into language in childhood. Framing questions about acquisition in terms of models of skilled language use has important consequences for arguments concerning language learnability and holds out the possibility of a unified theory of acquisition and use.

Seidenberg and MacDonald put forward a vigorous case for opposition between connectionist and symbolic approaches to language. But this is, of course, by no means the only possible viewpoint. Language might instead be viewed as emerging from a mixture of linguistic rules, which can be specified in symbolic terms, and probabilistic factors that determine how language is used in specific contexts; and, indeed, symbolic linguistic rules need not, perhaps, be quite as rigid as is typically assumed. Thus, a more conciliatory line between connectionist psycholinguistics and symbolic, generative linguistics may be imagined.

Chapter 10, Grammar-Based Connectionist Approaches to Language, by Paul Smolensky, outlines a specific conception of how connectionist and symbolic theorizing about language might be integrated, rather than set against each other. In particular, Smolensky argues that connectionist research on language can and must involve the development of grammar formalisms rather than merely producing connectionist computer models. From formulations of the fundamental theoretical commitments of connectionism and of generative grammar, it is argued that these two paradigms are mutually compatible: The commitments of connectionism concern computational principles, and those of generative grammar concern explanations of certain fundamental empirical characterizations of human language. Integrating the basic assumptions of the two paradigms results in formal theories of grammar that centrally incorporate a certain degree of connectionist computation. Two such grammar formalisms—Harmonic Grammar (Legendre, Miyata, & Smolensky, 1990) and Optimality Theory (Prince & Smolensky, 1997)—are briefly introduced to illustrate grammar-based approaches to connectionist language research. The strengths and weaknesses of grammar-based research and more traditional model-based research are argued to be complementary: Grammar-based research more readily allows explanations of general patterns of language, while model-based research more readily allows exploration of the full richness and power of connectionist computational mechanisms. This complementarity of strengths suggests a significant role for both strategies in the spectrum of connectionist language research.

Smolensky's standpoint provides a counterweight to the view that connectionist psycholinguistics should attempt to overturn previous theorizing about language and language processing. Moreover, the synthesis of principles from connectionism and generative grammar that he outlines gains considerable credibility from its very widespread influence in modern linguistics. Indeed, optimality theory is widely viewed within linguistics as one of the central theoretical developments within the field. Smolensky's approach may not, however, satisfy more radical connectionists, who may see the move from specific and implementable connectionist models of psychological processes (such as are described in the first half of this book) to abstract connectionist principles as too great a departure from the original aims of the connectionist paradigm.

Chapter 11, Connectionist Sentence Processing in Perspective, by Mark Steedman, presents an outsider's perspective on the project of connectionist psycholinguistics. Steedman has been associated with symbolic approaches to language, and has been involved in pioneering novel linguistic formalisms, such as categorial grammar, as well as carrying out highly influential computational and experimental work on human language processing. Steedman focuses on connectionist sentence processing, a topic discussed in Chapters 5 and 6 of this book. Steedman argues that the emphasis in the connectionist sentence-processing literature on distributed representation and emergence of grammar from such systems seems to have prevented connectionists and symbolic theorists alike from recognizing the often close relations between their respective systems. He argues that SRN models (Elman, 1990) are more directly related to stochastic Part-of-Speech taggers than to parsers or grammars as such, while recursive auto-associative memory of the kind pioneered by Pollack (1990) and incorporated in many hybrid connectionist parsers since may be useful for grammar induction from a network-based conceptual structure as well as for structure building.

These observations suggest some interesting new directions for connectionist sentence-processing research, including more efficient devices for representing finite-state machines, and acquisition devices based on a distinctively connectionist-grounded conceptual structure. Thus, Steedman, like Smolensky, argues for an integration of connectionist and symbolic views of language and language processing. But Steedman and Smolensky differ concerning the nature of the integration. Whereas Smolensky argues that connectionist principles should be integrated into grammar formalisms, Steedman sees connectionist networks as integrating with symbolic language-processing mechanisms to produce a hybrid computational account of language processing and acquisition. And both Smolensky and Steedman differ from the more radical agenda of Seidenberg and MacDonald, which aims to replace, rather than interconnect with, previous theories of language processing and structure. Clearly, only the future development of connectionist research will decide which of these perspectives, each of which is persuasively argued, proves to be the most fruitful.

THE SIGNIFICANCE OF
CONNECTIONIST PSYCHOLINGUISTICS

Current connectionist models involve important simplifications with respect to real natural language processing. In some cases these simplifications are relatively modest. For example, models of reading aloud typically ignore how eye movements are planned and how information is integrated across eye movements; they also tend to ignore the sequential character of speech output, and typically deal only with short words. In other cases the simplifications are more drastic. For example, connectionist models of syntactic processing involve vocabularies and grammars that are vastly simplified. However, it is important to note that symbolic models in many cases have lower task veridicality and input representativeness than their connectionist counterparts. Furthermore, many symbolic models may give the appearance of good data contact simply because they have not yet been implemented and have therefore not been tested in an empirically rigorous way, in contrast to the connectionist models.

The present breadth and significance of connectionist psycholinguistics, as evidenced by the chapters in this volume, suggests that the approach has considerable potential. Despite some attempts to argue for a priori limitations on connectionist language processing (e.g., Pinker & Prince, 1988; Marcus, 1998), connectionist psycholinguistics has already had a major impact on the psychology of language.

First, connectionist models have provided the first fully explicit and psychologically relevant computational models in a number of language-processing domains, such as reading and past-tense learning. Previous accounts in these areas consisted of "box-and-arrow" flow diagrams rather than detailed computational mechanisms. Whatever the lasting value of connectionist models themselves, they have certainly raised the level of theoretical debate in these areas by challenging theorists of all viewpoints to provide computationally explicit accounts.

Second, the centrality of learning in connectionist models has brought a renewed interest in mechanisms of language learning (Bates & Elman, 1993). While Chomsky (e.g., 1986) has argued that there are "universal" aspects of language that are innate, the vast amount of information specific to the language that the child acquires must be learned. Connectionist models provide mechanisms for how (at least some of) this learning might occur, whereas previous symbolic accounts of language processing have not taken account of how learning might occur. Furthermore, the attempt to use connectionist models to learn syntactic structure encroaches on the area of language for which Chomsky has argued innate information must be central. The successes and failures of this program thus directly bear on the validity of this viewpoint.

Third, the dependence of connectionist models on statistical properties of their input has been one contributing factor in the upsurge of interest in the role of statistical factors in language learning and processing (MacWhinney, Leinbach, Taraban, & McDonald, 1989; Redington & Chater, 1998). This renewed interest in the statistical properties of language and statistical methods of analysis is, of course, entirely compatible with the view that language processing takes account of structural properties of language, as described by classical linguistics. But more radical connectionists have, as we have noted, also attempted to encroach on the territory of classical linguistics.

Finally, connectionist systems have given rise to renewed theoretical debate concerning what it really means for a computational mechanism to implement a rule, whether there is a distinction between "implicit" and "explicit" rules (see, e.g., Davies, 1995, for discussion), and which kind should be ascribed to the human language-processing system.

The potential implications of a realistic connectionist approach to language processing are enormous. If realistic connectionist models of language processing can be provided, then the possibility of a radical rethinking not just of the nature of language processing, but of the structure of language itself, may be required. It might be that the ultimate description of language resides in the structure of complex networks, and it can only be approximately expressed in terms of structural rules, in the style of generative grammar (Seidenberg & MacDonald, Chapter 9, this volume). On the other hand, it may be that connectionist models can only succeed to the extent that they build in standard linguistic constructs (Smolensky, Chapter 10, this volume), or fuse with symbolic models to create a hybrid approach (Steedman, Chapter 11, this volume). We suggest that the only way to determine the ultimate value of connectionist psycholinguistics is to pursue it with the greatest possible creativity and vigor, as exemplified by the chapters in this volume.

NOTE

We are grateful to the Cognitive Science Society for allowing us to put this book together based on papers that appeared in *Cognitive Science*. All the chapters except one are revised and updated versions of earlier solicited papers found in the special issue, "Connectionist models of human language processing: Progress and prospects," vol. 23, no. 4, 1999, edited by Morten Christiansen, Nick Chater, and Mark Seidenberg. Chapter 5 is a substantially revised version of an article that appeared in vol. 23, no. 2, 1999. We would like to thank the contributors for updating and revising their papers for this book, and to the reviewers for helping to ensure a very high quality of papers throughout.

This work was partially supported by the Leverhulme Trust and by European Commission grant RTN–HPRN-CT-1999-00065 to Nick Chater.

REFERENCES

Bates, E. A., & Elman, J. L. (1993). Connectionism and the study of change. In M. J. Johnson (Ed.), *Brain development and cognition* (pp. 623–642). Cambridge, MA: Basil Blackwell.

Berent, I., Pinker, S., & Shimron, J. (1999). Default nominal inflection in Hebrew: Evidence for mental variables. *Cognition, 72*, 1–44.

Bishop, C. M. (1995). *Neural networks for pattern recognition*. New York: Oxford University Press.

Chomsky, N. (1957). *Syntactic structures*. The Hague: Mouton.

Chomsky, N. (1986). *Knowledge of language: Its nature, origin, and use*. New York: Praeger.

Christiansen, M. H., & Chater, N. (2001). Connectionist psycholinguistics: Capturing the empirical data. *Trends in Cognitive Sciences, 5*, 82–88.

Coltheart, M., Curtis, B., Atkins, P., & Haller, M. (1993). Models of reading aloud: Dual-route and parallel-distributed-processing approaches. *Psychological Review, 100*, 589–608.

Davies, M. (1995). Two notions of implicit rules. In J. E. Tomberlin (Ed.), *Philosophical perspectives: Vol. 9. AI, connectionism, and philosophical psychology*. Atascadero, CA: Ridgeview.

Dell, G. S. (1986). A spreading activation theory of retrieval in language production. *Psychological Review, 93*, 283–321.

Elman, J. L. (1990). Finding structure in time. *Cognitive Science, 14*, 179–211.

Frey, B. J. (1998). *Graphical models for machine learning and digital communication*. Cambridge, MA: MIT Press.

Gaskell, M. G., & Marslen-Wilson, W. D. (1999). *Representation and competition in the processing of spoken words*. Manuscript submitted for publication.

Gibson, E. (1998). Linguistic complexity: Locality of syntactic dependencies. *Cognition, 68*, 1–76.

Hoeffner, J. (1997). *Are rules a thing of the past? A single mechanism account of English past tense acquisition and processing*. Unpublished doctoral dissertation, Carnegie Mellon University, Pittsburgh.

Just, M. A., & Carpenter, P. A. (1992). A capacity theory of comprehension: Individual differences in working memory. *Psychological Review, 98*, 122–149.

Kelso, J.A.S. (1997). *Dynamic patterns: The self-organization of brain and behavior*. Cambridge, MA: MIT Press.

Legendre, G., Miyata, Y., & Smolensky, P. (1990). Harmonic grammar—a formal multi-level connectionist theory of linguistic well-formedness: Theoretical foundations. In *Proceedings of the Twelfth Annual Conference of the Cognitive Science Society* (pp. 388–395). Hillsdale, NJ: Lawrence Erlbaum.

MacWhinney, B., Leinbach, J., Taraban, R., & McDonald, J. (1989). Language learning: Cues or rules? *Journal of Memory and Language, 28*, 255–277.

Marcus, G. F. (1998). Rethinking eliminative connectionism. *Cognitive Psychology, 37*, 243–282.

McRae, K., Spivey-Knowlton, M. J., & Tanenhaus, M. K. (1998). Modeling the influence of thematic fit (and other constraints) in on-line sentence comprehension. *Journal of Memory and Language, 38*, 282–312.

Pinker, S. (1991). Rules of language. *Science, 253*, 530–535.

Pinker, S., & Prince, A. (1988). On language and connectionism: Analysis of a parallel distributed processing model of language acquisition. *Cognition, 28*, 73–193.

Pollack, J. B. (1990). Recursive distributed representations. *Artificial Intelligence, 46*, 77–105.

Port, R. F., & van Gelder, T. (Eds.). (1995). *Mind as motion: Explorations in the dynamics of cognition*. Cambridge, MA: MIT Press.

Prince, A., & Smolensky, P. (1997). Optimality: From neural networks to universal grammar. *Science, 275*, 1604–1610.

Redington, M., & Chater, N. (1998). Connectionist and statistical approaches to language acquisition: A distributional perspective. *Language and Cognitive Processes, 13*, 129–191.

Rumelhart, D. E., & McClelland, J. L. (1986). On learning the past tenses of English verbs. In J. L. McClelland & D. E. Rumelhart (Eds.), *Parallel distributed processing: Explorations in the microstructure of cognition. Vol. 2: Psychological and biological models* (pp. 216–271). Cambridge, MA: MIT Press.

Seidenberg, M. S. (1997). Language acquisition and use: Learning and applying probabilistic constraints. *Science, 275*, 1599–1603.

Smolensky, P. (1988). On the proper treatment of connectionism. *Behavioral and Brain Sciences, 11*, 1–74.

Tabor, W., Juliano, C., & Tanenhaus, M. K. (1997). Parsing in a dynamical system: An attractor-based account of the interaction of lexical and structural constraints in sentence processing. *Language and Cognitive Processes, 12*, 211–271.

Thelen, E., & Smith, L. B. (1994). *A dynamic systems approach to the development of cognition and action*. Cambridge, MA: MIT Press.

PART **I**

THE STATE OF THE ART

2

Connectionist Psycholinguistics in Perspective

Morten H. Christiansen and Nick Chater

Connectionist approaches to language have been, and still are, highly controversial. Some have argued that natural language processing from phonology to semantics can be understood in connectionist terms; others have argued that no aspects of natural language can be captured by connectionist methods. And the controversy is particularly heated because of the revisionist claims of some connectionists: For many, connectionism is not just an additional method for studying language processing; it also offers an alternative to traditional theories, which describe language and language processing in symbolic terms. Indeed, Rumelhart and McClelland (1987, p. 196) suggest "that implicit knowledge of language may be stored among simple processing units organized into networks. While the behavior of such networks may be describable (at least approximately) as conforming to some system of rules, we suggest that an account of the fine structure of the phenomena of language and language acquisition can best be formulated in models that make reference to the characteristics of the underlying networks." We shall see that the degree to which connectionism supplants, rather than complements, existing approaches to language is itself a matter of debate. Finally, the controversy over connectionist approaches to language is an important test case for the validity of connectionist methods in other areas of psychology.

In this chapter we aim to set the scene for the present volume on connectionist psycholinguistics, providing a brief historical and theoretical background as well as an update on current research in the specific topic areas outlined later. First we describe the historical and intellectual roots of connectionism, then introduce the elements of modern connectionism and how it has been applied to natural language processing, and outline some of the theoretical claims that have been made for and against it. We then consider five central topics within connectionist psycholinguistics: speech processing, morphology, sentence processing, language production, and reading. We evaluate the research in each of these areas in terms of the three criteria for connectionist psycholinguistics discussed in Chapter 1: data contact, task veridicality, and input representativeness. The five topics illustrate the range of connectionist research on language discussed in more depth in the other chapters in Part I of this volume. They also provide an opportunity to assess the strengths and weaknesses of connectionist methods across this range, setting the stage for the general debate concerning the validity of connectionist methods in Part II of this volume. Finally, we sum up and consider the prospects for future connectionist research, and its relation to other approaches to the understanding of language processing and linguistic structure.

BACKGROUND

From the perspective of modern cognitive science, we tend to see theories of human information processing as borrowing from theories of information processing in machines (i.e., from computer science). Within computer science, symbolic processing on general-purpose digital computers has proved to be the most successful method of designing practical computational devices. It is therefore not surprising that cognitive science, including the study of language processing, has aimed to model the mind as a symbol processor.

Historically, however, theories of human thought inspired attempts to build computational devices, rather than the other way around. Mainstream computer science arises from the intellectual tradition of viewing human thought as a matter of symbol processing. This tradition can be traced to Boole's (1854) suggestion that logic and probability theory describe "Laws of Thought," and that reasoning in accordance with these laws can be conducted by following symbolic rules. It runs through Turing's (1936) argument that all human thought can be modeled by symbolic operations on a tape (the Turing machine), through von Neumann's motivation for the design for the modern digital computer, to the development of symbolic computer programming languages, and thence to modern computer science, artificial intelligence, and symbolic cognitive science.

Connectionism (also known as "parallel distributed processing," "neural networks," or "neurocomputing") can be traced to a different tradition, which attempts to design computers inspired by the structure of the brain.[1] McCulloch and Pitts (1943) provided an early and influential idealization of neural function. In the 1950s and 1960s Ashby (1952), Minsky (1954), Rosenblatt (1962), and others designed computational schemes based on related idealizations. Aside from their biological origin, these schemes were of interest because they were able to learn from experience, rather than being designed. Such "self-organizing" or learning machines therefore seemed plausible as models of learned cognitive abilities, including many aspects of language processing (although Chomsky, 1965, among others, challenged the extent to which language is learned). Throughout this period connectionist and symbolic computation stood as alternative paradigms for modeling intelligence, and it was unclear which would prove to be the most successful. But gradually the symbolic paradigm gained ground, providing powerful models in core domains such as language (Chomsky, 1965) and problem solving (Newell & Simon, 1972). Connectionism was largely abandoned, particularly in view of the limited power of then current connectionist methods (Minsky & Papert, 1969). But more recently, some of these limitations have been overcome (e.g., Hinton & Sejnowski, 1986; Rumelhart, Hinton, & Williams, 1986), reopening the possibility that connectionism constitutes an alternative to the symbolic model of thought.

So connectionism is inspired by the structure and processing of the brain. What does this mean in practice? At a coarse level of analysis, the brain can be viewed as consisting of a very large number of simple processors, neurons, which are densely interconnected into a complex network. These neurons do not appear to tackle information processing problems alone. Rather, large numbers of neurons operate cooperatively and simultaneously to process information. Furthermore, neurons appear to communicate numerical values (encoded by firing rate), rather than passing symbolic messages, and, to a first approximation at least, neurons can be viewed as mapping a set of numerical inputs (delivered from other neurons) onto a numerical output (which is then transmitted to other neurons). Connectionist models are designed to mimic these properties: Hence, they consist of large numbers of simple processors, known as *units* (or nodes), which are densely interconnected into a complex network, and which operate simultaneously and cooperatively to solve information-processing problems. In line with the assumption that real neurons are numerical processors, units are assumed to pass only numerical values rather than symbolic messages, and the output of a unit is usually assumed to be a numerical function of its inputs.

The most popular of the connectionist networks is the *feed-forward network*, as illustrated in Figure 2.1. In this type of network the units are divided into "layers" and activation flows in one direction through the network, starting at the layer of input units and finishing at the layer of output units. The internal layers of the network are known as hidden units (HU). The activation of each unit is determined by its current input (calculated as

Figure 2.1
Feed-Forward Network

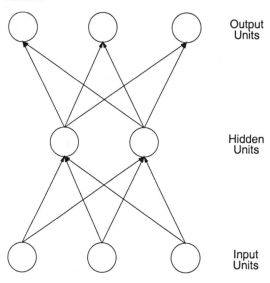

Information flows entirely bottom-up in these networks, from the input units through the
hidden units to the output units, as indicated by the arrows.

the weighted sum of its inputs, as before). Specifically, this input is
"squashed," so that the activation of each unit lies between 0 and 1. As the
input to a unit tends to positive infinity, the level of activation approaches 1;
as the input tends to negative infinity, the level of activation approaches 0.
With occasional minor variations, this description applies equally to almost
all feed-forward connectionist networks.

Feed-forward networks learn from exposure to examples, and learning is
typically achieved using the back-propagation learning algorithm (Rumelhart
et al., 1986; prefigured in Bryson & Ho, 1975; Werbos, 1974). When each
input is presented, it is fed through the network and the output is derived.
The output is compared against the correct "target" value and the difference
between the two is calculated for each output unit. The squared differences
are summed over all the output units to give an overall measure of the
"error" that the network has made. The goal of learning is to reduce the
overall level of error, averaged across input–target pairs. Back-propagation
is a procedure that specifies how the weights of the network (i.e., the strengths
of the connections between the units) should be adjusted in order to decrease the error. Training with back-propagation is guaranteed (within certain limits) to reduce the error made by the network. If everything works
well, then the final level of error may be small, meaning that the network
produces the desired output. Notice that the network will produce an output

not only for inputs on which it has been trained, but for any input. If the network has learned about regularities in the mapping between inputs and targets, then it should be able to generalize successfully (i.e., to produce appropriate outputs in response to these new inputs).

Back-propagation may sound too good to be true. But note that back-propagation merely guarantees to adjust the weights of the network to reduce the error; it does not guarantee to reduce the error to 0, or a value anywhere near 0. Indeed, in practice, back-propagation can configure the network so that error is very high, but changes in weights in any direction lead to the same or a higher error level, even though a quite different configuration of weights would give rise to much lower error, if only it could be found by the learning process. The network is stuck in a *local minimum* in weight space, and cannot find its way to better local minima, or better still, to the optimal weights that are the global minimum for error. Attempting to mitigate the problem of local minima is a major day-to-day concern of connectionist researchers, as well as being a focus of theoretical research. The problem of local minima can be reduced by judicious choice among the large number of variants of back-propagation, and by appropriate decisions on the numerous parameters involved in model building (such as the number of hidden units used, whether learning proceeds in small or large steps, and many more). But the adjustment of these parameters is often more a matter of judgment, experience, and guesswork than it is a product of theoretical analysis. Despite these problems, back-propagation is surprisingly successful in many contexts. Indeed, the feasibility of back-propagation learning has been one of the reasons for the renewed interest in connectionist research. Prior to the discovery of back-propagation, there were no well-justified methods for training multilayered networks. The restriction to single-layered networks was unattractive, since Minsky and Papert (1969) showed that such networks, sometimes known as "perceptrons," have very limited computational power. It is partly for this reason that hidden units are viewed as having such central importance in many connectionist models; without hidden units, most interesting connectionist computation would not be possible.

A popular variation of the feed-forward network is the simple recurrent network (SRN; Elman, 1988, 1990) (see Figure 2.2). This network is essentially a standard feed-forward network equipped with an extra layer of so-called context units. At a particular time step an input pattern is propagated through the hidden-unit layer to the output layer (solid arrows). At the next time step the activation of the hidden-unit layer at the previous time step is copied back to the context layer (dashed arrows) and paired with the current input (solid arrows).[2] This means that the current state of the hidden units can influence the processing of subsequent inputs, providing a limited ability to deal with integrated sequences of input presented successively.

Whereas simple recurrent networks can be trained using the standard back-propagation learning algorithm, fully recurrent networks are trained using more complex learning algorithms, such as discrete back-propagation

Figure 2.2
Simple Recurrent Network

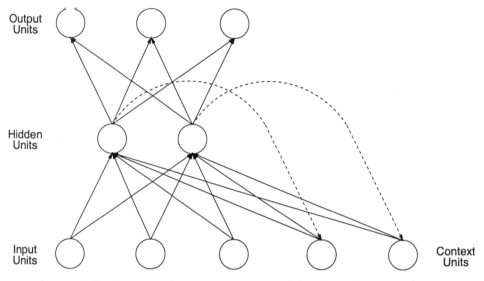

At a particular time step an input pattern is propagated through the hidden-unit layer to the output layer (solid arrows). At the next time step the activation of the hidden-unit layer at the previous time step is copied back to the context layer (dashed arrows) and paired with the current input (solid arrows).

through time (Williams & Peng, 1990) and continuous back-propagation (Pearlmutter, 1989). This type of network architecture is shown in Figure 2.3. Through the recurrent links (circular arrows), current activation can affect future activations similarly to the simple recurrent network, but in a more fine-grained manner and potentially reaching further back in time.

Another popular network architecture is the interactive activation network, shown in Figure 2.4. This type of network is completely prespecified (i.e., it does not learn). It consists of a sequence of unit layers. Units in the first layer typically encode fine-grained features of the input (e.g., visual or phonetic features). Units in the subsequent layers encode elements of increasingly higher levels of analyses (e.g., letters → words or phonemes → words). Units are connected using bidirectional links that can be either excitatory (arrows) or inhibitory (filled circles). This style of connectivity allows for activation to flow both bottom-up and top-down, reinforcing mutually consistent states of affairs and inhibiting mutually inconsistent states of affair.

The behavior of individual units in interactive activation networks is somewhat more complex than in the network architectures we have described so far, because it depends not only on the current input but also on the previous

Figure 2.3
Fully Recurrent Network

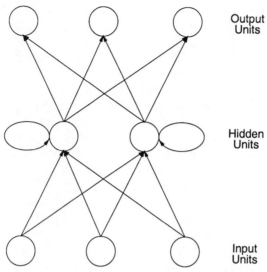

Recurrent links (circular arrows) allow activation at the current time step to affect activations for many future time steps.

Figure 2.4
Interactive Activation Network

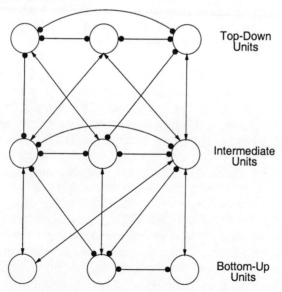

The links are bidirectional and can be either excitatory (arrows) or inhibitory (filled circles). Activation in this network flows both bottom-up and top-down.

level of activity of the unit. If the input to a unit is 0, then all that happens is that the level of activity of the unit decays exponentially. The input to the unit is, as is standard, simply the weighted sum of the outputs of the units that feed into that unit (where the weights correspond to the strengths of the connections). If the input is positive, then the level of activity is increased in proportion both to that input and to the distance between the current level of activation and the maximum activation (conventionally set at 1); if the input is negative, the level of activity is decreased in proportion to the input and to the distance between the current level of activation and the minimum activation (conventionally set at −1).

While this behavior sounds rather complex, the basic idea is simple. Given a constant input, the unit will gradually adjust to a stable level where the exponential decay balances with the boost from that input: Positive constant inputs will be associated with positive stable activation, negative constant inputs with negative stable activation; small inputs lead to activations levels close to 0, while large inputs lead to activation values which tend to be 1 or −1. If we think of a unit as a feature detector, then an activation level near 1 corresponds to a high level of confidence that the feature is present; an activation level near −1 corresponds to a high level of confidence that it is not.

With respect to the relationship between connectionist models and the brain, it is important to note that none of the connectionist architectures that we have described amount to realistic models of brain function (see, e.g., Sejnowski, 1986). They are unrealistic at the level of individual processing units, where the models not only drastically oversimplify, but knowingly falsify, many aspects of the function of real neurons, and in terms of the structure of the connectionist networks, which bear little if any relation to brain architecture. One avenue of research is to seek increasing biological realism (e.g., Koch & Segev, 1989). In the study of the areas of cognition in which few biological constraints are available, most notably language, researchers have concentrated on developing connectionist models with the goal of accurately modeling human behavior. They therefore take their data from cognitive psychology, linguistics, and cognitive neuropsychology, rather than from neuroscience. Thus, connectionist research on language appears to stand in direct competition with symbolic models of language processing.

As noted earlier, the relative merits of connectionist and symbolic models of language are hotly debated. But should they be viewed as in opposition at all? After all, advocates of symbolic models of language processing assume that symbolic processes are somehow implemented in the brain. Thus, they too are connectionists at the level of implementation. But symbolic theorists assume that language processing can be described at two levels: at the psychological level, in terms of symbol processing, and at the implementational level, in neuroscientific terms (to which connectionism is a crude approximation). If this is right, then connectionist modeling should proceed by taking symbol-processing models of language processing and attempting to implement these in connectionist networks. Advocates of this view (Fodor & Pylyshyn, 1988; Marcus, 1998; Pinker & Prince, 1988) typically assume that it implies that symbolic modeling should be entirely autonomous from connectionism; symbolic theories set the goalposts for connectionism, but not the other way round. Chater and Oaksford (1990) have argued that even according to this view there will be two-way influences between symbolic and connectionist theories, since many symbolic accounts can be ruled out precisely because they could not be neurally implemented. But most connectionists in the field of language processing have a more radical agenda: not to implement, but to challenge, to varying degrees, the symbolic approach to language processing. Part II of this book will illustrate a variety of contemporary viewpoints on the relationship between connectionist and symbolic theories of language.

With these general issues in mind, let us now consider the broad spectrum of connectionist models of language processing.

SPEECH PROCESSING

Speech processing in its broadest sense encompasses a broad range of cognitive processes, from those involved in low-level acoustical analysis to those involved in semantic and pragmatic interpretation of utterances. Here we shall focus much more narrowly, on the processes involved in segmenting and recognizing spoken words from input that is represented in a linguistic form (e.g., as sequences of phonetic features or phonemes). Thus, we will not be concerned with connectionist research on the enormously complex issues involved in dealing with the complexity, variability, and noisiness of acoustic representations of speech (see, e.g., Salmela, Lehtokangas, & Saarinen, 1999, for a typical application of connectionist methods to speech technology). We also shall not deal with higher-level aspects of linguistic processing. Nonetheless, as we shall see, even given these restrictions, the problem of understanding human speech processing is still formidable.

Naïvely, we might imagine that the speech processor has to do two jobs, one after the other. First, it has to segment speech input into units corresponding to words (i.e., it has to find word boundaries); second, it has to recognize each word. But on reflection, this viewpoint seems potentially problematic, because it is not clear how the speech processor can determine where the word boundaries are until the words are recognized. And conversely, word recognition itself seems to presuppose knowing which chunk of speech material corresponds to a potential word. Thus, segmentation and recognition appear to stand in a chicken-and-egg relationship—each process seems to depend on the other.

One approach to resolving the paradox is to assume that segmentation and recognition are two aspects of a single process, that tentative hypotheses about each issue are developed and tested simultaneously, and mutually consistent hypotheses are reinforced. A second approach is to suppose that there are segmentation cues in the input that are used to give at least better-than-chance indications of what segments may correspond to identifiable words. So the question is this: Does speech processing involve dedicated segmentation strategies prior to word recognition?

Developmental considerations suggest that there may be specialized segmentation methods. The infant, initially knowing no words, seems constrained to segment speech input using some method not requiring word recognition. Moreover, infant studies have shown that prelinguistic infants may use such methods, and are sensitive to a variety of information that is available in the speech stream and potentially useful for segmentation, such as phonotactics and lexical stress (Jusczyk, 1997).

Connectionist models have begun to address questions of how effective different kinds of segmentation cues might be. For example, Cairns, Shillcock, Chater, and Levy (1997) explore a model of segmentation based on predictability. They note that language is less predictable across, rather than between, words. They trained a recurrent network on a large corpus of phonologically transcribed conversational speech, represented as a sequence of bundles of binary phonetic features. The network was trained to predict the next bundle of features along with the previous and current feature bundles, based on the current input material. Where prediction error was large, it was assumed that a word boundary had been encountered. This model captured some aspects of human segmentation performance. For example, it spontaneously learned to pay attention to patterns of strong and weak syllables as a segmentation cue. However it was able to reliably predict only a relatively small proportion of word boundaries, indicating that other cues also need to be exploited. While the Cairns et al. model uses just a single cue to segmentation, Christiansen, Allen, and Seidenberg (1998) showed how multiple, partial constraints on segmentation could yield much better segmentation performance. They trained an SRN to integrate sets of phonetic features with information about lexical stress (strong or weak) and utterance boundary information (encoded as a binary unit) derived from a corpus of child-directed speech. The network was trained to predict the appropriate values of these three cues for the next segment. After training, the network was able to integrate the input such that it would activate the boundary unit not only at utterance boundaries, but also at word boundaries inside utterances. The network was thus able to generalize patterns of cue information that occurred at the end of utterances to cases where the same patterns occurred within an utterance. This model performed well on the word-segmentation task while capturing additional aspects of infant segmentation, such as the bias toward the dominant trochaic (strong–weak) stress pattern in English, the ability to distinguish between phonotactically legal and illegal novel words, and having segmentation errors being constrained by English phonotactics.

This model shows how integrating multiple segmentation cues can lead to good segmentation performance. To what extent does it provide a model of how infants process speech? Christiansen, Conway, and Curtin (2000) used the trained model, without any additional modifications, to fit recent infant data. These data are of particular interest, because they have been claimed to be incompatible with a purely connectionist approach to language processing, and to require the language processor to use "algebraic" or symbolic rules (Marcus, Vijayan, Rao, & Vishton, 1999). Marcus et al. habituated infants on syllable sequences that followed either an AAB or ABB pattern (e.g., *le-le-je* versus *le-je-je*). The infants were then presented with sequences of novel syllables, either consistent or inconsistent with the habituation pattern, and showed a preference for the inconsistent items. Christiansen et al. suggested that statistical knowledge acquired in the context of learning to segment fluent speech provided the basis for these results, in much the same way as knowledge acquired in the process of learning to read can be used to perform experimental tasks such as lexical decision. Their simulation closely replicated the experimental conditions, using the same number of habituation and test trials as in the original experiment (no repeated training epochs) and one network for each infant. Analyses of the model's segmentation performance revealed that the model was significantly better at segmenting out the syllables in the inconsistent items. This makes the inconsistent items more salient and therefore explains why the infants preferred these to the consistent items. Thus, Christiansen et al.'s results challenge the claim that the Marcus et al. infant data necessarily require that the infant's language-processing system is using algebraic rules. Moreover, these infant data provide an unexpected source of evidence for the Christiansen et al. model, viewed as a model of infant segmentation.

Segmentation cues are potentially important in guiding the process of word recognition. But even if such cues are exploited very effectively, segmentation cues alone can achieve only limited results. A definitive segmentation of speech can only occur after word recognition has occurred. Speech is frequently locally ambiguous: To use an oft quoted example, it is difficult to distinguish "recognize speech" from "wreck a nice beach" when these phrases are spoken fluently. These interpretations correspond to very different segmentations of the input. It is therefore clear that bottom-up segmentation cues alone will not always segment the speech stream into words reliably. In such cases of local ambiguity, a decisive segmentation of the input can only be achieved when the speaker has recognized which words have been said. This theoretical observation ties in with empirical evidence that strongly indicates that during word recognition in adulthood multiple candidate words are activated, even if these correspond to different segmentation of the input. For example, Gow and Gordon (1995) found that adult listeners hearing sentences involving a sequence (e.g., *two lips*) that could also be a single word (*tulips*) showed speeded processing of an associate of the second word (*kiss*) and to an associate of the longer word (*flower*), indicating that the two conflicting segmentations were simultaneously entertained. This would not occur if a complete segmentation of the input occurred before word recognition was attempted. On the other hand, it is not clear how these data generalize to word segmentation and recognition in infancy before any comprehensive vocabulary has been established. How segmentation and recognition develop into the kind of integrated system evidenced by the Gow and Gordon data remains a matter for future research.

Gow and Gordon's (1995) result also suggests that word recognition itself may be a matter of competition between multiple activated word representations, where the activation of the word depends on the degree of match between the word and the speech input. Indeed, many studies point toward this conclusion, from a range of experimental paradigms. Such competition is typically implemented in connectionist networks by a localist code for words (the activation of a single unit represents the strength of evidence for that word, with inhibitory connections between word units). Thus, when an isolated word is identified, a "cohort" of words consistent with that input is activated; as more of the word is heard, this cohort is rapidly reduced, perhaps to a single item.

While competition at the word level has been widely assumed, considerable theoretical dispute has occurred over the nature of the interaction between different levels of mental representation. Bottom-up (or "data-driven") models are those in which less abstract levels of linguistic representation feed into, but are not modified by, more abstract levels (e.g., the phoneme level feeds to the word level, but not the reverse). We note, however, that this does not prevent these models from taking advantage of suprasegmental information, such as in the inclusion of lexical stress in the Christiansen et al. (2000) segmentation model, provided that this information is available in a purely bottom-up fashion (i.e., no lexical-level feedback). Interactive (also "conceptually-driven" or top-down) models allow a two-way flow of information between levels of representation. Figures 2.1 and 2.4 provide abstract illustrations of the differences in information flow between the two types of models. Note that bottom-up models allow information to flow through the network in one direction only, whereas interactive models allow information to flow in both directions.

The bottom-up versus interactive debate rages in all areas of language processing, and also in perception and motor control (e.g., Bruner, 1957; Fodor, 1983; Marr, 1982; Neisser, 1967). Here we focus on putative interactions between information at the phonemic and the lexical levels in word recognition (i.e., between phonemes and words), where experimental work and connectionist modeling has been intense.

The most obvious rationale for presuming that there is top-down information flow from the lexical to the phoneme level stems from the effects of lexical context on phoneme identification. For example, Ganong (1980) showed that the identification of a syllable-initial speech sound, constructed to be between a /g/ and a /k/, was influenced by lexical knowledge. This intermediate sound was predominantly heard as a /k/ if the rest of the word was -iss (*kiss* was favored over *giss*), but heard as /g/ if the rest of the word was -ift (*gift* was favored over *kift*).

The early and very influential TRACE model of speech perception (McClelland & Elman, 1986) attempts to explain data of this kind from an interactive viewpoint. The model employs the standard interactive activation network architecture already described, with layers of units standing for phonetic features, phonemes, and words. There are several copies of each layer of units, standing for different points in time in the utterance, and the number of copies differs for each layer. At the featural level, there is a copy for each discrete "time slice" into which the speech input is divided. At the phoneme level, there is a copy of the detector for each phoneme centered over every three time slices. The phoneme detector centered on a given time slice is connected to feature detectors for that time slice, and also to the feature detectors for the previous three and subsequent three slices. Hence, successive detectors for the same phoneme overlap in the feature units with which they interact. Finally, at the word level there is a copy of each word unit at every three time slices. The window of phonemes with which the word interacts corresponds to the entire length of the word. Here, again, adjacent detectors for the same word will overlap in the lower-level units to which they are connected. In short, then, we have a standard interactive activation architecture, with an additional temporal dimension added, to account for the temporal character of speech input. TRACE captures the Ganong effect because phoneme and lexical identification occur in parallel and are mutually constraining. TRACE also captures experimental findings concerning various factors affecting the strength of the lexical influence (e.g., Fox, 1984), and the categorical aspects of phoneme perception (Massaro, 1981; Pisoni & Tash, 1974). TRACE also provides rich predictions concerning the time course of spoken word recognition (e.g., Cole & Jakimik, 1978; Marslen-Wilson, 1973; Marslen-Wilson & Tyler, 1975), and lexical influences on the segmentation of speech into words (e.g., Cole & Jakimik, 1980).

TRACE provides an impressive demonstration that context effects can indeed be modeled from an interactive viewpoint. But context effects on phoneme recognition can also be explained in purely bottom-up terms. If a person's decisions about phoneme identity depend on both the phonemic and lexical levels, then phoneme identification may be lexically influenced, even though there need be no feedback from the lexical to the phoneme level. For example, the Ganong effect might be explained by assuming that the phoneme identification of an initial consonant that is ambiguous between /g/ and /k/ is directly influenced by the lexical level. Thus, if *gift* is recognized at the lexical level, this will influence the participant to respond that the initial phoneme was a /g/, but if *kiss* is recognized, this will influence the participant to respond that the initial phoneme was a /k/.

A substantial experimental literature has attempted to distinguish TRACE from bottom-up models, indicating the importance of connectionist modeling in inspiring experimental research. One line of attack was that the interactive character of TRACE causes word-level context to have too abrupt an effect in modulating phoneme perception. Massaro (1989) had people listen to phonemes on the continuum between /r/ and /l/ in syllables in which they were immediately preceded by /t/ or /s/. In normal English these preceding phonemes are highly informative about the ambiguous /r/–/l/. With an initial /t/, the next item must be an /r/, because /t/ followed by /l/ is not permissible according to the phonotactics of English (i.e., the constraints on legal phoneme sequences). Conversely, with an initial /s/, the next item must be an /l/, because /s/ followed by /r/ is not phonotactically permissible.

When TRACE is applied to these stimuli, there is a relatively abrupt switch from the one interpretation of the ambiguous phoneme to the other. For example, in the context of an /s/, TRACE adopts the context-appropriate interpretation that the ambiguous phoneme is an /l/ until the ambiguous phoneme is perceptually very strongly biased toward /r/, at which point the model switches sharply to the opposite interpretation. The opposite pattern was observed in the context of a /t/. But this sharp crossover was not consistent with the human data that Massaro (1989) collected. Instead, people required less perceptual bias to override word-level context, but the transition between judging the ambiguous phoneme to be an /r/ or an /l/ was also much more gradual over the /r/–/l/ continuum. Massaro concluded that the interactive activation approach was flawed, because it allowed more distortion of the perceptual stimulus by contextual factors than is actually observed. Massaro further showed that a bottom-up model, based on his Fuzzy Logic Model of Perception (FLMP), could account for the empirical data more accurately. FLMP involves a simple linear combination of cues from the perceptual stimulus and surrounding context: It can be viewed as equivalent to a single-layer connectionist network (with noise added, so that the network is merely biased toward producing one response more than the other, rather than producing the same output deterministically).

McClelland (1991) showed, however, that adding noise to the units in TRACE could also produce a more graded pattern of responding. Intuitively, adding noise to any decision-making system will inevitable blur the boundary between the inputs that typically give rise to one decision and the inputs that typically give rise to another. Massaro and Cohen (1991) responded that there are other aspects of the data that McClelland's revised interactive model does not capture. On the other hand, McClelland's model provides a much more detailed computational mechanism than is provided by FLMP, so a fair comparison between the two is not straightforward.

Another potential difficulty for TRACE in relation to data on phoneme perception is that the influence of lexical factors on phoneme perception appears to be quite variable. In some experiments substantial lexical influences on phoneme judgments are observed; but in others, often differing only slightly, the effects disappear. For example, Cutler, Mehler, Norris, and Segui (1987) found lexical effects when participants were asked to monitor for initial phonemes of monosyllabic targets only when the filler items varied in syllabic length, and McQueen (1991) found lexical influences on the categorization of ambiguous word-final fricatives (on the continuum between /s/ and /ʃ/) only when the stimuli were perceptually degraded by low-pass filtering them at 3kHz. These and other studies (see Pitt & Samuel, 1993, for a review) present a confusing picture for any theoretical account.

Opponents of the interactive character of TRACE argue that some of these data can be understood by assuming a bottom-up model in which phoneme judgments are jointly influenced by a phonemic level of representation and a lexical level of representation. According to this view, the direct influence of the lexical level of representation on phoneme judgments (although not on the level of phoneme representation) is the source of context effects, and these effects can be turned on and off to the degree that the task demands encourage participants to attend to the lexical level. Thus, if the filler and target items are monosyllabic, they may become monotonous and discourage attention at the lexical level; if targets are perceptually degraded, this may encourage attention to the lexical level, because perceptual representations are not sufficiently reliable to be used alone. Thus, critics of TRACE have argued that it is limited by having only one "route" by which phonetic judgments can be made—this route depending directly on the representations at the phoneme level. By contrast, in order to capture context effects, bottom-up models necessarily allow two routes that can influence phonemic judgments, via phonemic and lexical representations. Various models, both nonconnectionist (Cutler & Norris, 1979) and connectionist (Norris, McQueen, & Cutler, in press), have been proposed in opposition to TRACE. These models exploit two routes, and hence allow for the possibility of "attentional" switching between them.

Despite the considerable empirical and theoretical interest that these issues have attracted, it seems unlikely that the instability of lexical influences will be decisive in determining whether speech perception is viewed as bottom-up or interactive. This is because the simple expedient of allowing that phonemic judgments can depend on the activations of both the phonemic and lexical level in TRACE immediately give the interactive account precisely the same explanatory latitude as bottom-up models. There is no reason why interactive models cannot also assume that a variety of levels of representations may be drawn upon in performing a specific task. Nonetheless, although this theoretical move is entirely viable for advocates of the interactive position, it is unattractive on the grounds of parsimony. This is because the resulting model would have two routes by which contexts effects could arise, one due to the direct influence of high-level representations on task performance (specifically, the influence of word-level representations on phoneme judgment tasks), and the other due to the indirect, top-down impact of higher levels on lower levels (specifically, the top-down links from the word to the phoneme level). If a bottom-up account can explain the same data using just one mechanism—the direct influence of higher-level representations on phoneme judgments—then this viewpoint has a considerable advantage in terms of parsimony.

One key experimental result (Elman & McClelland, 1988), derived as a novel prediction from TRACE, appeared to be particularly persuasive evidence against bottom-up connectionist models. In natural speech the pronunciation of a phoneme will to some extent be altered by the phonemes that surround it, in part for articulatory reasons. This phenomenon is known as "coarticulation." Listeners should therefore adjust their category boundaries depending on the phonemic context. Experiments confirm that people do indeed exhibit this "compensation for coarticulation" (CFC; Mann and Repp, 1980). For example, given a series of synthetically produced tokens between /t/ and /k/, listeners move the category boundary toward the /t/ following a /s/ and toward the /k/ following a /ʃ/. This phenomenon suggests a way of detecting whether lexical information really does feed back to the phoneme level. Elman and McClelland considered the case where compensation for coarticulation occurs across word boundaries. For example, a word-final /s/ influences a word-initial phoneme ambiguous between /t/ and /k/ to be heard as a /k/ (as in *Christmas capes*). If lexical-level representations feed back onto phoneme-level representations, the compensation of the /k/ should still occur when the /s/ relies on lexically driven phoneme restoration for its identity (i.e., in an experimental condition in which the identity of /s/ in *Christmas* is obscured, the /s/ should be restored and thus compensation for coarticulation should proceed as normal). Elman and McClelland confirmed TRACE's prediction experimentally. Recognition of the phoneme at the start of the second word was apparently influenced by CFC, as if the word-final phoneme in the first word had been "restored" by lexical influence.

Surprisingly, bottom-up connectionist models can also capture these results. Norris (1993) provided a small-scale demonstration, training an SRN to map phonetic input onto phoneme output, for a small (twelve-word vocabulary) artificial language. When the network received phonetic input with an ambiguous first word-final phoneme and ambiguous initial segments of the second word, an analog of CFC was observed. The percentages of /t/ and /k/ responses to the first phoneme of the second word depended on the identity of the first word, as in Elman and McClelland (1988). But the explanation for this pattern of results cannot be top-down influence from word units, because there are no word units. Moreover, Cairns, Shillcock, Chater, and Levy (1995) scaled up these results using a similar network trained on phonologically transcribed conversational English. How can an autonomous computational model, where there is no lexical influence on phoneme processing, mimic the apparent influence of word recognition on coarticulation? Cairns et al. argued that sequential dependencies between the phoneme sequences in spoken English can often "mimic" lexical influence. The idea is that the identification of the word-final ambiguous phoneme favored by the word level is also typically favored by transitional probability statistics across phonemes. Analyzing statistical regularities in the phoneme sequences in a large corpus of conversational English, Cairns et al. showed that this explanation applies to Elman and McClelland's experimental stimuli. If these transitional probabilities have been learned by the speech processor, then previous phonemic context might support the "restoration" of the ambiguous word-final phoneme, with no reference to the word in which it is contained. Pitt and McQueen (1998) tested between these two explanations experimentally. They carefully controlled for transitional probabilities across phonemes, and reran a version of Elman and McClelland's experiment: Compensation for coarticulation was eliminated. Moreover, when transitional probabilities are manipulated in nonword contexts, compensation for coarticulation effects were observed. This pattern of results suggests that compensation for coarticulation is not driven by top-down lexical influence, but by phoneme-level statistical regularities.

Against this, Samuel (1996) argues that the precise pattern of phoneme restoration does indicate the existence of small but discernible top-down effects. He conducted a statistical analysis of people's ability to discriminate whether a phoneme has been replaced by a noise in a word or nonword context from the case where the phoneme and noise are both present. The logic is that to the extent that top-down factors "restore" the missing phoneme, it should be difficult to tell whether or not the phoneme is actually present, and hence people's discrimination between the two cases should be poorer. Hence, phoneme present–absent discrimination should be poorer in word contexts than for nonword contexts, because top-down factors should be stronger. This prediction was confirmed experimentally (Samuel, 1996). However, this pattern of data also follows from bottom-up models, to the extent that the judgment concerning whether the phoneme is present is determined not only by phonological but also lexical representations. Accordingly, in a word context, judgments will be potentially biased by the word-level representation signaling that the missing phoneme is present (because a word in which that phoneme normally occurs has been recognized). This line of evidence, therefore, does not seem to provide a strong way of distinguishing between bottom-up and top-down accounts, and there are connectionist models compatible with Samuel's data that operate in each way (McClelland & Elman, 1986; Norris et al., in press).

Another recent study by Samuel may pose a more difficult challenge to bottom-up accounts. Samuel (1997) uses the fact that hearers adapt their classification of speech continua, such as the continuum between /b/ and /d/, after hearing a word beginning with a speech sound at one end of the continuum. For example, after hearing *bird*, a hearer's category boundary shifts toward /b/ on the /b/–/d/ continuum. The logic of Samuel's study was to investigate whether adaptation can occur to a word in which the key initial phoneme is perceptually restored, rather than actually presented. Thus, Samuel presents words in which the initial phoneme (/b/ or /d/) is replaced by noise, as in a typical phoneme-restoration study. As expected, he found that participants restored the "missing" phoneme, even though it was not present. But crucially, he also found that these words did indeed produce an adaptation effect with respect to the categorization of ambiguous phonemes on the continuum from /b/ to /d/. The effect did not occur where the deleted phonemes were replaced by silence rather than a burst of noise, and hence there was no perceived phoneme restoration. Samuel argues that this pattern of results indicates that the phoneme representations are being affected by the lexical level, and that this leads to the adaptation. Norris et al. (in press) note that it remains to be shown that the adaptation effect is itself mediated by the phoneme level: If, for example, adaptation effects for phonemes could be caused directly by the lexical level, then this would provide a possible account of Samuel's data. Nonetheless, if Samuel's result does prove to be robust, it could be extremely difficult for bottom-up accounts to deal with, except by using rather ad hoc explanations.

Finally, additional evidence for the ability of bottom-up models to accommodate apparently lexical effects on speech processing was provided by Gaskell, Hare, and Marslen-Wilson (1995). They trained an SRN model to map a systematically altered featural representation of speech onto a canonical representation of the same speech, and found that the network showed evidence of lexical abstraction (i.e., tolerating systematic phonetic variation, but not random change). More recently, Gaskell and Marslen-Wilson (1997) have added a new dimension to the debate, presenting an SRN network in which sequentially presented phonetic inputs for each word were mapped onto corresponding distributed representations of phonological surface form and semantics. Based on the ability of the network to model the integration of partial cues to phonetic identity and the time course of lexical access, they suggested that distributed models may provide a better explanation of speech perception than their localist counterparts (e.g., TRACE). An important challenge for such distributed models is to accommodate the simultaneous activation of multiple lexical candidates necessitated by the temporal ambiguity of the speech input (e.g., /kæp/ could be the beginning of both *captain* and *captive*). The coactivation of several lexical candidates in a distributed model results in a semantic "blend" vector. Through statistical analyses of these vectors, Gaskell and Marslen-Wilson (Chapter 3, this volume) investigate the properties of such semantic blends, and apply the results to explain some recent empirical speech-perception data.

The theoretical debate concerning segmentation and word recognition has been profoundly influenced by connectionist psycholinguistics. We have considered various streams of research arising out of the TRACE model of speech perception to illustrate the interplay between connectionist modeling and experimental studies, and there are many other important areas of research we have not considered for lack of space (e.g., recent work on an apparent interaction between phonetic mismatch and lexical status, which has triggered a subtle and important strand of research; Marslen-Wilson & Warren, 1994; McQueen, Norris, & Cutler, in press). Connectionist models are now the dominant style of computational account, even for advocates of very different positions (as we have seen in relation to the bottom-up–interactive debate). Attempts to test between the predictions of competing models have generated experimental advances that have in turn informed how models develop. However, this progress has yet not resulted in a resolution of the fundamental debate between proponents of bottom-up and interactive approaches to speech processing, though Norris et al. (in press) may provide some advantage for the opponents of top-down lexical effects.

Overall, these studies indicate how connectionist models of speech processing have been able to make good contact with detailed psycholinguistic data and been important in motivating experimental work. Input representativeness is also generally good, with models being trained on large lexicons and sometimes corpora of natural speech. Task veridicality may perhaps be questioned, however, by the use of abstract representations of the input (e.g., phonetic or phonological representations) that may not be computed by the listener (Marslen-Wilson & Warren, 1994), and that also bypass the deep problems involved in handling the physical variability of natural speech.

MORPHOLOGY

One of the connectionist models that has created the most controversy is Rumelhart and McClelland's (1986a) model of the learning of the English past tense. The debate has to a large extent focused on whether a single mechanism may be sufficient to account for the empirical data concerning the developmental patterns in English past-tense learning, or whether a dual-route mechanism is necessary. Here we provide an overview of the current debate, as well as pointers to its wider ramifications.

Can a system without any explicit representation of rules account for rulelike behavior? Rumelhart and McClelland's (1986a) model of the acquisition of the past tense in English was presented as an affirmative answer to this question. The English past tense is an interesting test case because children very roughly appear to exhibit U shaped learning, traditionally characterized as having three stages. During the first stage, children only use a few verbs in past tense and these tend to be irregular words—such as *came, went,* and *took*—likely to occur with a very high frequency in the child's input. These verbs are, furthermore, mostly used in their correct past-tense form. At the second stage, children start using a much larger number of verbs in the past tense, most of these of the regular form, such as *pulled* and *walked*. It is important that children now show evidence of rulelike behavior. They are able to conjugate nonwords, generating *jicked* as the past tense of *jick*, and they start to overgeneralize irregular verbs, even the ones they got right in stage one; for example, producing *comed* or *camed* as the past tense of *come*. During the third stage the children regain their ability to correctly form the past tense of irregular verbs while maintaining their correct conjugations of the regular verbs. Thus, it appears that children learn to use a rule-based route for dealing with regulars as well as nonwords and a memorization route for handling irregulars. But how can such seemingly dual-route behavior be accommodated by a single mechanism employing just a single route?

Rumelhart and McClelland (1986a) showed that by varying the input to a connectionist model during learning, important aspects of the three stages of English past-tense acquisition could be simulated using a single mechanism. The model consists of three parts: a fixed encoding network, a pattern-associator network with modifiable connections, and a competitive decoding–binding network. The encoding network is an (unspecified) network that takes phonological representations of root forms and transforms them into sets of phonetic feature triples, termed wickelfeatures (after Wickelgren, 1969, who employed triples in modeling memory for sequential material).[3] In order to promote generalization, additional incorrect features are randomly activated, specifically those features that have the same central feature as well as one of the two other context features in common with the input root form.

The pattern-associator network, which is the core of the model, has 460 input and output units, each representing a wickelfeature. This network is trained to produce past-tense forms when presented with root forms of verbs as input. During training the weights between the input and the output layers are modified using the perceptron learning rule (Rosenblatt, 1962) (the back-propagation rule is not required for this network, since it has just one modifiable layer). Since the output patterns of wickelfeatures generated by the association network most often do not correspond to a single past-tense form, the decoding–binding network must transform these distributed patterns into unique wickelphone representations. In this third network, each wickelphone in the 500 words used in the study was assigned to an output unit. These wickelphones compete individually for the input wickelfeatures in an iterative process. The more wickelfeatures a given wickelphone accounts for, the greater its strength. If two or more wickelphones account for the same wickelfeature, the assigned "credit" is split between them in proportion to the number of other wickelfeatures they account for uniquely (i.e., a "the rich get richer" competitive approach). The end result of this competition is a set of more or less nonoverlapping wickelphones that correspond to as many as possible of the wickelfeatures in the input to the decoder network.

By employing a particular training regime, Rumelhart and McClelland (1986a) were able to obtain the U-shaped learning profile characteristic of children's acquisition of the English past tense. First, the network was trained on a set of 10 high-frequency verbs (8 irregular and 2 regular) for 10 epochs. At this point the network reached a satisfactory performance, treating both regular and irregular verbs in the same way (as also observed in the first stage of human acquisition of past tense). Next, 420 medium-frequency verbs (about 80% of these being regular) were added to the training set and the network was trained for an additional 190 epochs. Early on during this period of training the net behaved as children at acquisition stage 2: The network tended to regularize irregulars while getting regulars correct. At the end of the 190 epochs, network behavior resembled that of children in stage 3 of the past-tense acquisition process, exhibiting an almost perfect performance on the 420 verbs. The network appears to capture the basic U-shaped pattern of the acquisition of English past tense. In addition, it was able to exhibit differential performance on different types of irregular and regular verbs, effectively simulating some aspects of similar performance differences observed in children (Bybee & Slobin, 1982; Kuczaj, 1977, 1978). Moreover, the model demonstrated a reasonable degree of generalization from the 420 verbs in the training set to a separate test set consisting of 86 low-frequency verbs (of which just over 80% were regular); for example, demonstrating that it was able to use the three different regular endings correctly (i.e., using /t/ with root forms ending with an unvoiced consonant, /d/ as suffix to forms ending with a voiced consonant or vowel, and /d/ preceded by an unstressed vowel (schwa) with verb stems ending with a *t* or a *d*).

The merits and inadequacies of the Rumelhart and McClelland (1986a) past-tense model has been the focus of much debate, originating with Pinker and Prince's (1988) detailed criticism (and to a lesser extent Lachter & Bever's 1988 critique). Since then the debate has flourished across the symbolic–connectionist divide (e.g., on the symbolic side, Kim, Pinker, Prince, & Prasada, 1991; Pinker, 1991; and on the connectionist side, Cottrell & Plunkett, 1991; Daugherty & Seidenberg, 1992; Daugherty, MacDonald, Petersen, & Seidenberg, 1993; MacWhinney & Leinbach, 1991; Seidenberg, 1992). Here we focus on the most influential aspects of the debate.

The use of wickelphones–wickelfeature representations has been the subject of much criticism (e.g., Pinker & Prince, 1988). Perhaps for this reason, most of the subsequent connectionist models of English past tense (both of acquisition, e.g., Plunkett & Marchman, 1991, 1993, and diachronic change, Hare & Elman, 1995) therefore use a position-specific phonological representation in which vowels and consonants are defined in terms of sets of phonetic features. Another, more damaging criticism of the single-route approach is that the U-shaped pattern of behavior observed in the model during learning essentially appears to be an artifact of suddenly increasing the total number of verbs (from 10 to 420) in the second phase of learning. Pinker and Prince (1988) point out that no such sudden discontinuity appears to occur in the number of verbs to which children are exposed. Thus, the explanation of U-shaped learning suggested by the model is undermined by the psychological implausibility of the training regime.

More recently, however, Plunkett and Marchman (1991) showed that this training regime is not required to obtain U-shaped learning. They trained a feed-forward network with a hidden-unit layer on a vocabulary of artificial verb stems and past-tense forms, patterned by regularities of the English past tense. They held the size of the vocabulary used in training constant at 500 verbs. They found that the network not only was able to exhibit classical U-shaped learning, but also had learned various selective micro U-shaped developmental patterns observed in children's behavior. For example, given a training set with a type and token frequency reflecting that of English verbs, the network was able to simulate a number of subregularities between the phonological form of a verb stem and its past tense form (e.g., *sleep → slept, keep → kept*).[4] In a subsequent paper, Plunkett and Marchman (1993) obtained similar results using an incremental and perhaps more psychologically plausible training regime. Following initial training on 20 verbs, the vocabulary was gradually increased until reaching a size of 500 verb stems. This training regime significantly improved the performance of the network (compared with a similarly configured network trained on the same vocabulary in Plunkett & Marchman, 1991). This approach also suggested that a critical mass of verbs is needed before a change from rote learning (memorization) to system building (rulelike generalization behavior) may occur, the latter perhaps related to the acceleration in the acquisition of vocabulary items (or "vocabulary spurt") observed when a child's overall vocabulary exceeds around fifty words (e.g., Bates, Bretherton, & Snyder, 1988). Plunkett and Juola (Chapter 4, this volume) find a similar critical-mass effect in their model of English noun and verb morphology. They analyzed the developmental trajectory of a feed-forward network trained to produce the plural form for 2,280 nouns and the past tense form for 946 verbs. The model exhibited patterns of U-shaped development for both nouns and verbs (with noun inflections acquired earlier than verb inflections), and also demonstrated a strong tendency to regularize deverbal nouns and denominal verbs.

Another criticism of the connectionist models of past-tense acquisition is that they may be too dependent on the token and type frequencies of irregular and regular vocabulary items in English. Prasada and Pinker (1993) have argued that the purported ability of connectionist models to simulate verb inflection may be an artifact of the idiosyncratic frequency statistics of English. The focus of the argument is the default inflection of words; for example, the *-ed* suffixation of English regular verbs. The default inflection of a word is assumed to be independent of its particular phonological shape and occurs unless the root form corresponds to a specific irregular form. According to Prasada and Pinker, connectionist models are dependent on frequency and surface similarity for their generalization ability. In English, most verbs are regular—that is, regular verbs have a high type frequency but a relatively low token frequency—allowing a network to construct a broadly defined default category. Irregular verbs in English, on the other hand, have a low type frequency but a high token frequency, the latter permitting the memorization of the irregular past tenses in terms of a number of narrow phonological subcategories (e.g., one for the *i–a* alternation in *sing → sang*, *ring → rang*, another for the *o–e* alternation in *grow → grew*, *blow → blew*, etc.). Prasada and Pinker showed that the default generalization in Rumelhart and McClelland's (1986a) model was dependent on a similar frequency distribution in the training set. They furthermore contended that no connectionist model can accommodate default generalization for a class of words that have both low type frequency and low token frequency. The default inflection of plural nouns in German appears to fall in this category and would therefore seem to be outside the capabilities of connectionist networks (Clahsen, Rothweiler, Woest, & Marcus, 1993; Marcus, Brinkmann, Clahsen, Wiese, & Pinker, 1995). If true, such lack of cross-linguistic validity would render connectionist models of past-tense acquisition obsolete.

However, recent connectionist work has addressed the issue of minority default mappings with some success. Daugherty and Hare (1993) trained a feed-forward network (with hidden units) to map the phonological representation of a stem to a phonological representation of the past tense given a set of verbs roughly representative of very early Old English (before about A.D. 870). The training set consisted of five classes of irregular verbs plus one class of regular verbs, each class containing twenty-five words (each represented once in the training set). Thus, words taking the default generalization *-ed* formed a minority (i.e., only 17%) of the words in the training set. Pace Prasada and Pinker (1993) and others, the network was able to learn the appropriate default behavior even when faced with a low-frequency default class. Indeed, it appears that generalization in connectionist networks may not be strictly dependent on similarity to known items. Daugherty and Hare's results show that if the nondefault (irregular) classes have a sufficient degree of internal structure, default generalization may be promoted by the lack of similarity to known items. These results were corroborated by further simulations and analyses in Hare, Elman, and Daugherty

(1995). Moreover, Forrester and Plunkett (1994) obtained similar results when training a feed-forward model (with hidden units) to learn artificial input patterned on the Arabic plural. In Arabic, the majority of plural forms—called the Broken Plural—are characterized by a system of subregularities dependent on the phonological shape of the noun stem. In contrast, a minority of nouns take the Sound Plural inflection that forms the default in Arabic. Forrester and Plunkett's net was trained to map phonological representations of the noun stems to their appropriate plural forms represented phonologically. Their results also indicate that connectionist models can learn default generalization without relying on large word classes or direct similarity.

Finally, rulelike and frequency-independent default generalization may not be as pressing a problem for connectionist models as Clahsen et al. (1993) and Marcus et al. (1995) claim. Reanalyzing data concerning German noun inflection (in combination with additional data from Arabic and Hausa), Bybee (1995) showed that default generalization is sensitive to type frequency and does not seem to be entirely rulelike. This pattern may fit better with the kind of default generalization in connectionist nets rather than the rigid defaults of symbolic models. Moreover, Hahn and Nakisa (in press) outline problems for the dual-route approach. They compared connectionist and other implementations of rule and memorization routes against a single memorization route on a comprehensive sample of German nouns and found that performance was consistently superior when the rule route was not used.

The issue of whether humans employ a single, connectionist-style mechanism for rulelike morphological processing is far from settled. Connectionist models can provide an impressive fit to a wide range of developmental and linguistic data. Even detractors of connectionist models of morphology typically concede that some kind of associative connectionist mechanism may explain the complex patterns found in the irregular cases (e.g., Pinker, 1991). The controversial question is whether a single connectionist mechanism can simultaneously account for both regular and irregular cases, or whether regular cases can only be generated by a distinct route involving (perhaps necessarily symbolic) rules.

Most of the connectionist models of morphology only make contact with secondary empirical data. Many of the models suffer from low task veridicality because they are trained to map verb stems to past-tense forms (e.g., Plunkett & Marchman, 1991, 1993; Rumelhart & McClelland, 1986a; but see, e.g., Hoeffner, 1997, for an exception), a task unlikely to be relevant to children's language acquisition. However, rule-based morphology models (e.g., Pinker, 1991) also involve stem to past-tense mappings as the connectionist models, and thus suffer from the same low task veridicality. Input representativeness, on the other hand, is reasonable; Plunkett and Joula (Chapter 4, this volume) provide a good example in this respect. The future is likely to bring further connectionist modeling of cross-linguistic data concerning morphology, as well as a closer fitting of developmental micro patterns and distributional data to such models. As we shall see next, the question of whether language processing can be accounted for without the explicit representation of rules also plays an important part in connectionist modeling of sentence processing.

SENTENCE PROCESSING

Syntactic processing is arguably the area of natural language that has the strongest ties to explicit rules as a means of explanation. Since Chomsky (1957), grammars have been understood predominately in terms of a set of generative phrase-structure rules (often coupled with rules or principles for the further transformation of phrase structures). In early natural language research the central status of rules was directly reflected in the Derivational Theory of Complexity (Miller & Chomsky, 1963). This theory suggested that the application of a given rule (or transformation) could be measured directly in terms of time it takes for a listener–reader to process a sentence. This direct mapping between syntactic rules and response times was soon found to be incorrect, leading to more indirect ways of eliciting information about the use of rules in the processing of syntax. But can syntactic processing be accounted for without explicit rules? Much of the recent connectionist research on sentence processing aims to show that it can.

Sentence processing provides a considerable challenge for connectionist research. In view of the difficulty of the problem, much early work "hand-coded" symbolic structures directly into the network architecture; starting with Small, Cottrell, and Shastri's (1982) first attempt at connectionist parsing, followed by Reilly's (1984) connectionist account of anaphor resolution, and later, for example, by Fanty's (1985) connectionist context-free parser, Selman and Hirst's (1985) modeling of context-free parsing using simulated annealing, Waltz and Pollack's (1985) interactive model of parsing (and interpretation), McClelland and Kawamoto's (1986) connectionist model of case-role assignment, and, more recently, Miyata, Smolensky, and Legendre's (1993) structure-sensitive processing of syntactic structure using tensor representations (Smolensky, 1990) as well as Kwasny and Faisal's (1990) deterministic connectionist parser. Such connectionist reimplementations of symbolic systems might have interesting computational properties and even be illuminating regarding the appropriateness of a particular style of symbolic model for distributed computation (Chater & Oaksford, 1990). But most connectionist research has a larger goal: to provide alternative accounts of sentence processing in which networks learn to form and use structured representations rather than simply implement symbolic representations and processes.

Two classes of models potentially provide such alternatives. Both classes of model learn to process language from experience, rather than implementing a prespecified set of symbolic rules. The less ambitious class presupposes that the syntactic structure of each sentence to be learned is more or less given; that is, each input item is tagged with information pertaining to the syntactic role of that item (e.g., the word *cat* may be tagged as "singular noun"). In this class we find, for example, connectionist parsers, such as PARSNIP (Hanson & Kegl, 1987) and VITAL (Howells, 1988), the structure-dependent processing of Pollack's (1988, 1990) recursive auto-associative memory network subsequently used in Chalmers's (1990) model of active-to-passive transformation and in a model of syntactic processing in logic (Niklasson & van Gelder, 1994), Sopena's (1991) distributed connectionist parser incorporating attentional focus, and Stolcke's (1991) hybrid model deriving syntactic categories from phrase-bracketed examples given a vector-space grammar. Typically, the task of these network models is to find the grammar (or part thereof) that fits the example structures. This means that the structural aspects of language are not themselves learned by observation, but are built in. These models are related to statistical approaches to language learning, such as stochastic context-free grammars (e.g., Brill, Magerman, Marcus, & Santorini, 1990; Charniak, 1993; Jelinek, Lafferty, & Mercer, 1990), in which probabilities of grammar rules in a prespecified context-free grammar are learned from a corpus of parsed sentences. Another approach within this class of connectionist models—sometimes referred to as "structured connectionism"—involves the construction of a modular system of networks, each of which is trained to acquire different aspects of syntactic processing. For example, Miikkulainen's (1996) system consists of three different networks: one trained to map words onto case-role assignments, another trained to function as a stack, and a third trained to segment the input into constituent-like units. Although the model displays complex syntactic abilities, the basis for these abilities and their generalization to novel sentence structures derive from the configuration of the stack network combined with the modular architecture of the system, rather than being discovered by the model.

The second, more ambitious class of models, which includes Christiansen and Chater (Chapter 5, this volume) as well as Tabor and Tanenhaus (Chapter 6, this volume), attempts the much harder task of learning syntactic structure from sequences of words, with no explicit prior assumptions about the particular form of the grammar. These models have only recently begun to provide accounts for empirical sentence-processing phenomena. This may explain why the more ambitious connectionist attempts at syntax learning have not caused nearly as much debate as the earlier-mentioned model of English past-tense acquisition (Rumelhart & McClelland, 1986a), and the model of reading aloud discussed later (Seidenberg & McClelland, 1989). Nevertheless, these models may potentially have a great impact on the psychology of language because they bear the promise of language learning without a priori built-in linguistic knowledge (pace, e.g., Chomsky, 1965, 1986; Crain, 1991; Pinker, 1994; and many others).

The most influential approach of this kind is due to Elman (1991, 1993), who trained an SRN to predict the next input word for sentences generated by a small context-free grammar. This grammar involved subject noun–verb agreement, variations in verb argument structure (i.e., intransitive, transitive, optionally transitive), and subject and object relative clauses (allowing multiple embeddings with complex long-distance dependencies). Elman's simulations suggested that an SRN can acquire some of the grammatical regularities underlying a grammar. In addition, the SRN showed some similarities with human behavior on center-embedded structures (Weckerly & Elman, 1992). Christiansen (1994, 2000) extended this work, using more complex grammars involving prenominal genitives, prepositional modifications of noun phrases, noun-phrase conjunctions, and sentential complements, in addition to the grammatical features used by Elman. One of the grammars, moreover, incorporated cross-dependencies, a weakly context-sensitive structure found in Dutch and Swiss-German. Christiansen found that SRNs could learn these more complex grammars, and, moreover, that they exhibit the same qualitative processing difficulties as humans do on similar constructions (see also Christiansen & Chater, Chapter 5, this volume). The nets moreover showed sophisticated generalization abilities, overriding local word cooccurrence statistics while complying with structural constraints at the constituent level (Christiansen & Chater, 1994).

Current models of syntax typically use "toy" fragments of grammar and small vocabularies. Aside from raising questions about how well the results will scale up, this makes it difficult to provide detailed fits with empirical data. Nonetheless, some attempts have recently been made toward fitting existing data and deriving new empirical predictions from the models. For example, Tabor, Juliano, and Tanenhaus (1997) provide a two-component model of ambiguity resolution, combining an SRN with a "gravitational" mechanism. The SRN was trained in the usual way on sentences derived from a grammar. After training, SRN hidden-unit representations for individual words were placed in the gravitational mechanism, which was then allowed to settle into a stable state. Settling times were then mapped onto word-reading times. Using their two-component model, Tabor et al. were able to fit data from several experiments concerning the interaction of lexical and structural constraints on the resolution of temporary syntactic ambiguities (i.e., garden-path effects) in sentence comprehension. Tabor and Tanenhaus (Chapter 6, this volume) extend the two-component model to account for empirical findings reflecting the influence of semantic role expectations on syntactic-ambiguity resolution in sentence processing (McRae, Spivey-Knowlton, & Tanenhaus, 1998).

In a different strand of research concerned with relating connectionist networks to psycholinguistic results, Christiansen and Chater (1999) developed a measure of grammatical prediction error (GPE) that allowed network output to be mapped onto human performance data. GPE scores are computed for each word in a sentence and reflect the processing difficulties that a network is experiencing at a given point in a sentence. Averaging GPE across a whole sentence, Christiansen (2000; Christiansen & Chater, Chapter 5, this volume) fitted human data concerning the greater perceived difficulty associated with center-embedding in German compared to cross-serial dependencies in Dutch (Bach, Brown, & Marslen-Wilson, 1986). Christiansen was able to derive novel predictions concerning other types of recursive constructions, and these predictions were later confirmed experimentally (Christiansen & MacDonald, 2000). MacDonald and Christiansen (in press) mapped single-word GPE scores directly onto reading times, providing an experience-based account for human data concerning the differential processing of singly center-embedded subject and object relative clauses in human participants with different levels of reading comprehension ability.

Some headway has also been made in accounting for data concerning the effects of aphasia on grammaticality judgments. Allen and Seidenberg (1999) trained a recurrent network to mutually associate two input sequences: a sequence of word forms and a corresponding sequence of word meanings. The network was able to learn a small artificial language successfully; it was able to regenerate the word forms from the meanings and vice versa. Allen and Seidenberg simulated grammaticality judgments by testing how well the network could recreate a given input sequence, allowing activation to flow from the provided input forms to meaning and then back again. Ungrammatical sentences were recreated less accurately than grammatical sentences, and the network was thus able to distinguish grammatical from ungrammatical sentences. They lesioned the network by removing 10 percent of the weights in the network. Grammaticality judgments were then elicited from the impaired network for ten different sentence types that Linebarger, Schwartz, and Saffran (1983) used in their study of aphasic grammaticality judgments. The network exhibited impaired performance on exactly the same three sentence types as the aphasic patients.

These simulation results suggest that recurrent networks may be viable models of sentence processing. However, connectionist models of language learning (i.e., Chalmers, 1990; Elman, 1990; McClelland & Kawamoto, 1986; Miyata et al., 1993; Pollack, 1990; Smolensky, 1990; St. John & McClelland, 1990) have recently been attacked for not affording the kind of generalization abilities that would be expected from models of language. Hadley (1994a) correctly pointed out that generalization in much connectionist research has not been viewed in a sophisticated fashion. The testing of generalization is typically done by recording network output given a test set consisting of items not occurring in the original training set, but potentially containing many similar structures and word sequences. Hadley insisted that to demonstrate genuine, "strong" generalization a network must be shown to learn a word in one syntactic position and then generalize to using–processing that word in another, novel syntactic position. He challenged connectionists to adopt a more rigorous training and testing regime in assessing whether networks really generalize successfully in learning syntactically structured material.

Christiansen and Chater (1994) addressed this challenge, providing a formalization of Hadley's original ideas as well as presenting evidence that connectionist models are able to attain strong generalization. In their training corpus (generated by the grammar from Christiansen, 1994), the noun *boy* was prevented from ever occurring in a noun-phrase conjunction (i.e., noun phrases such as *John and boy* and *boy and John* did not occur). During training the SRN had therefore only been presented with singular verbs following *boy*. Nonetheless, the network was able to correctly predict that a plural verb must follow *John and boy* as prescribed by the grammar. In addition, the network was still able to correctly predict a plural verb when a prepositional phrase was attached to *boy*, as in *John and boy from town*, providing even stronger evidence for strong generalization. This suggests that the SRN is able to make nonlocal generalizations based on the structural regularities in the training corpus (see Christiansen & Chater, 1994, for further details). If the SRN relied solely on local information it would not have been able to make correct predictions in either case. More recently, Christiansen (2000) demonstrated that the same SRN also was able to generalize appropriately when presented with completely novel words, such as *zorg*, in a noun-phrase conjunction by predominately activating the plural verbs.[5] In contrast, when the SRN was presented with ungrammatical lexical items in the second noun position, as in *John and near*, it did not activate the plural nouns. Instead, it activated lexical items that were not grammatical given the previous context. The SRN was able to generalize to the use of known words in novel syntactic positions as well as to the use of completely novel words. At the same time, it was also able to distinguish items that were grammatical given previous context from those that were not. Thus, the network demonstrated sophisticated generalization abilities, ignoring local word cooccurrence constraints while appearing to comply with structural information at the constituent level. Additional evidence of strong generalization in connectionist nets are found in Niklasson and van Gelder (1994) (but see Hadley, 1994b, for a rebuttal).

One possible objection to these models of syntax is that connectionist (and other bottom-up statistical) models of language learning will not be able to scale up to solve human language acquisition because of arguments pertaining to the purported poverty of the stimulus (see Seidenberg, 1994, for a discussion). However, there is evidence that some models employing simple statistical analysis may be able to scale up and even attain strong generalization. When Redington, Chater, and Finch (1993) applied a method of distributional statistics (see also Finch & Chater, 1993; Redington, Chater, & Finch, 1998) to a corpus of child-directed speech (the CHILDES corpus collected by MacWhinney & Snow, 1985), they found that the syntactic category of a nonsense word could be derived from a single occurrence of that word in the training corpus. This indicates that strong generalization may be learnable through the kind of bottom-up statistical analysis that connectionist models appear to employ, even on a scale comparable with that of a child learning his or her first language. In this context, it is also important to note that achieving strong generalization is not only a problem for learning-based connectionist models of syntactic processing. As pointed out by Christiansen and Chater (1994), most symbolic models cannot be ascribed strong generalization because in most cases they are provided with the lexical categories of words via syntactic tagging, and hence do not actually *learn* this aspect of language. The question of strong generalization is therefore just as pressing for symbolic approaches as for connectionist approaches to language acquisition. The results outlined here suggest that connectionist models may be closer to solving this problem than their symbolic counterparts.

Overall, connectionist models of syntactic processing are at an early stage of development. Current connectionist models of syntax typically use toy fragments of grammar and small vocabularies, and thus have low input representativeness. Nevertheless, these models have good data contact and a reasonable degree of task veridicality. However, more research is required to decide whether promising initial results can be scaled up to deal with the complexities of real language, or whether a purely connectionist approach is beset by fundamental limitations, so that connectionism can only succeed by providing reimplementations of symbolic methods (see the chapters in Part II of this volume for further discussion).

LANGUAGE PRODUCTION

In connectionist psycholinguistics, as in the psychology of language in general, there is relatively little work on language production. However, some important steps have been taken, most notably by Dell and colleagues. Dell's (1986) spreading activation model of retrieval in sentence production constitutes one of the first connectionist attempts to account for speech production.[6] Although the model was presented as a sentence-production model, only the phonological encoding of words was computationally implemented in terms of an interactive activation model. This lexical network consisted of hierarchically ordered layers of nodes corresponding to the following linguistically motivated units: morphemes (or lexical nodes), syllables, rimes and consonant clusters, phonemes, and features. The individual nodes are connected bidirectionally to each other in a straightforward manner without lateral connections within layers, with the exception of the addition of special null-element nodes and syllabic position coding of nodes that correspond to syllables. For example, the lexical node for the word (morpheme) *spa* is connected to the /spa/ node in the syllable layer. The latter is linked to the consonant cluster /sp/ (onset) and the rime /a/ (nucleus). On the phoneme level, /sp/ is connected to /s/ (which in turn is linked to the features *fricative, alveolar*, and *voiceless*) and /p/ (which is connected to the features *bilabial, voiceless*, and *stop*). The rime /a/ is linked to the vowel /a/ in the phoneme layer (and subsequently is connected to the features *tense, low*, and *back*) and to a node signifying a null coda.

Processing begins with the activation of a lexical node (meant to correspond to the output from higher-level morphological, syntactic, and semantic processing), and activation then gradually spreads downward in the network. Activation also spreads upward via the feedback connections. After a fixed period of time (determined by the speaking rate), the nodes with the highest activations are selected for the onset, vowel, and coda slots. Using this network model, Dell (1986) was able to account for a variety of speech errors, such as substitutions (e.g., *dog → log*), deletions (*dog → og*), and additions (*dog → drog*). Speech errors occur in the model when an incorrect node becomes more active than the correct node (given the activated lexical node) and therefore gets selected instead. Such erroneous activation may be due to the feedback connections activating nodes other than those directly corresponding to the initial word node. Alternatively, other words in the sentence context as well as words activated as a product of internal noise may interfere with the processing of the network. This model also made a number of empirical predictions concerning the retrieval of phonological forms during production, some of which were later confirmed experimentally in Dell (1988).

Dell's (1986) account of speech errors and the phonological encoding of words has had a considerable impact on subsequent models of speech production, both the connectionist (e.g., Harley, 1993) as well as the more symbolic kind (e.g., Levelt, 1989). More recently, Dell, Schwartz, Martin, Saffran, and Gagnon (1997) used an updated version of this model to fit error data from twenty-one aphasics and sixty normal controls. This network has three layers, corresponding to semantic features, words, and phonemes, with the word units connected bidirectionally to the other layers. It maps from semantic features denoting a concept to a choice of word, and then to the phonemes realizing that word. The model distinguishes itself from the interactive activation models, such as TRACE, by incorporating a two-step approach to production. First, activation at the semantic features spreads throughout the network for a fixed time. The most active word unit (typically the best match to the semantic features) is "selected," and its activation boosted. Second, activation again spreads throughout the network for a fixed time, and the most highly activated phonemes are selected, with a phonological frame that specifies the sequential ordering of the phonemes.

Even in normal production, processing sometimes breaks down, leading to semantic errors (*cat → dog*), phonological errors (*cat → hat*), mixed semantic and phonological errors (*cat → rat*), nonword errors (*cat → zat*), and unrelated errors (*cat → fog*). Dell, Schwartz, et al. (1997) propose that normal and aphasic errors reflect the same processes, differing only in degree. Therefore, they set their model parameters by fitting data from controls relating to the five types of errors listed. To simulate aphasia, the model was "damaged" by reducing two global parameters (connection weight and decay rate), leading to more errors. Adjusting these parameters, Dell et al. modeled the five types of errors found for twenty-one aphasics, as well as derived and confirmed predictions about the effect of syntactic categories on phonological errors (*dog → log*), phonological effects on semantic errors (*cat → rat*), naming error patterns after recovery, and errors in word repetition.

Despite their impressive empirical coverage, these spreading activation models nonetheless suffer from a number of shortcomings. As previously mentioned, in interactive activation models the connections between the nodes on the various levels have to be hand coded. This means that no learning is possible. In itself this is not a problem if it assumed that the relevant linguistic knowledge is innate, but the information encoded in Dell's (1986) model is language-specific and could not be innate. There is, however, a more urgent, practical side of this problem. It is very difficult to scale these models up, because hand coding becomes prohibitorily complex as the number of weights in the network increases. This shortcoming is alleviated by a recent recurrent network model presented by Dell, Juliano, and Govindjee (1993). The model learns to form mappings from lexical items to the appropriate sequences of phonological segments. The model consists of an SRN with an additional modification: the current output, as well as the current hidden-unit state, are copied back as additional input to the network. This allowed both past activation states of the hidden-unit layer as well as the output from the previous time step to influence current processing. When given an encoding of, for example, *can* as the lexical input, the network was trained to produce the features of the first phonological segment /k/ on the output layer, then /æ/ followed by /n/, and then finally generate an end-of-word marker (null segment). Trained in this manner, Dell, Juliano, et al. (1993) were able to account for speech error data without having to build syllabic frames and phonological rules into the network, as was the case in Dell (1986; see Dell, Chang, & Griffin, Chapter 7, this volume, for further discussion; but cf. Dell, Burger, & Svec, 1997). It is important that this recent connectionist model suggests that sequential biases and similarity may explain aspects of human phonology that have previously been attributed to separate phonological rules and frames. Furthermore, the model indicates that future speech-production models may have to incorporate learning and distributed representations in order to accommodate the role that the entire vocabulary appears to play in phonological speech errors.

Connectionist models have also been applied to experimental data on sentence production, particularly concerning structural priming. Structural priming arises when the syntactic structure of a previously heard or spoken sentence influences the processing or production of a subsequent sentence. Chang, Griffin, Dell, and Bock (1997) (see also Dell et al., Chapter 7, this volume) present an SRN model of grammatical encoding, suggesting that structural priming may be an instance of implicit learning (i.e., acquiring sequential structure with little or no conscious awareness of doing this; see Cleeremans, Destrebecqz, & Boyer, 1998, for a review). This model can be seen as an extension of the Dell, Juliano, et al. (1993) approach. The input to the model was a "proposition," coded by units for semantic features (e.g., *child*), thematic roles (e.g., *agent*) and action descriptions (e.g., *walking*), and some additional input encoding the internal state of an unimplemented comprehension network. The network outputs a sequence of words expressing the proposition. Structural priming was simulated by allowing learning to occur during testing. This created transient biases in the weights of the network, and these are sufficiently robust to cause the network to favor (i.e., to be primed by) recently encountered syntactic structures.

Chang, Griffin, et al. (1997) fitted data from Bock and Griffin (in press) concerning the priming, across up to ten unrelated sentences, of active and passive constructions as well as prepositional (*The boy gave the guitar to the singer*) and double-object (*The boy gave the singer the guitar*) dative constructions. The model fitted the passive data well, and showed priming from intransitive locatives (*The 747 was landing by the control tower*) to passives (*The 747 was landed by the control tower*). However, it fitted the dative data less well, and showed no priming from transitive locatives (*The wealthy woman drove the Mercedes to the church*) to prepositional datives (*The wealthy woman gave the Mercedes to the church*). Chang, Dell, Bock, and Griffin (2000) provide a better fit to these data with a model combining the production network with an implemented comprehension network, and employing a more "fuzzy" representation of thematic roles.

The connectionist production models make good contact with the data, and have reasonable task veridicality, but suffer from low input representativeness, as they are based on small fragments of natural language. It seems likely that connectionist models will continue to play a central role in future research on language production; scaling up these models to deal with more realistic input is a major challenge for future work.

READING

The psychological processes engaged in reading are extremely complex and varied, ranging from early visual processing of the printed word, to syntactic, semantic, and pragmatic analysis, to integration with general knowledge. Connectionist models have concentrated on simple aspects of reading: (1) recognizing letters and words from printed text, and (2) word "naming" (i.e., mapping visually presented letter strings onto sequences of sounds). We focus on models of these two processes here.

One of the earliest connectionist models was McClelland and Rumelhart's (1981) interactive activation model of visual word recognition (see also Rumelhart & McClelland, 1982). This network has three layers of units standing for visual features of letters, whole letters (in particular positions within the word), and words. The model uses the same principles as TRACE, but without the need for a temporal dimension, as the entire word is presented at once.

Word recognition occurs as follows. A visual stimulus is presented, which activates in a probabilistic fashion visual feature units in the first layer. As the features become activated, they send activation via their excitatory and inhibitory connections to the letter units, which, in turn, send activation to the word units. The words compete via their inhibitory connections, and reinforce their component letters via excitatory feedback to the letter level (there is no word-to-letter inhibition). Thus, an "interactive" process occurs: Bottom-up information from the visual input is combined with the top-down information flow from the word units. This process involves a cascade of overlapping and interacting processes: Letter and word recognition do not occur sequentially, but overlap and are mutually constraining.

This model accounted for a variety of phenomena, mainly concerning context effects on letter perception. For example, it captures the fact that letters presented in the context of a word are recognized more rapidly than letters presented individually, or in random letter strings (Johnston & McClelland, 1973). This is because the activation of the word containing a particular letter provides top-down confirmation of the identity of that letter in addition to the activation provided by the bottom-up feature-level input. Moreover, it has been shown that letters presented in the context of pronounceable nonwords (i.e., pseudowords, such as *mave*, which are consistent with English phonotactics) are recognized more rapidly than letters presented singly (Aderman & Smith, 1971) or in contexts of random letter strings (McClelland & Johnston, 1977). In this case the facilitation is caused by a "conspiracy" of partially activated similar words, which are triggered in the nonword context but not in the random letter string context. These partially active words provide a top-down confirmation of the letter identity, and thus they conspire to enhance recognition. In a similar fashion, the model explains how degraded letters can be disambiguated by their letter context, and how occurring in a word context can facilitate the disambiguation of component letters, even when they are all visually ambiguous. Moreover, the model provides an impressively detailed demonstration of how interactive processing can account for a range of further experimental effects.

The interactive activation model of reading is closely related with the TRACE model of speech perception, and explains effects of linguistic context on letter or phoneme perception in a similar way. If the interactive activation framework is appropriate in both domains, then we should expect that the pattern of data in speech and reading should show striking similarities. In line with this expectation, striking parallels between contextual effects in speech perception and reading continue to be discovered. Recently, for example, Jordan, Thomas, and Scott-Brown (1999) demonstrated a "graphemic restoration effect" that parallels the phonemic restoration effect. If a word is viewed from a long distance with some letters deleted and replaced by "noise" (e.g., a spurious character), the "missing" letters are frequently subjectively "seen," just as people report hearing phonemes that have been replaced by noise in the phoneme restoration effect.

But even if strong parallels between speech perception and reading can be established, this connection can, of course, cut both ways. Proponents of a bottom-up view of speech perception can argue that a bottom-up approach can also deal with contextual effects found in reading. Thus, Massaro (1979) has argued that in the context of reading, just as in speech perception, the bottom-up fuzzy logic model of perception provides a better account of the data. Similarly, Norris (e.g., 1994), also a strong advocate of bottom-up models in speech perception, has developed bottom-up accounts of reading. The debate between bottom-up and interactive accounts remains unresolved, although, as we shall see, bottom-up connectionist accounts have been more popular than interactive accounts in the next aspect of reading that we consider: word naming rather than word recognition.

Recent connectionist models of reading have focused not on word recognition but on word naming, which involves relating written word forms to their pronunciations. The first such model was Sejnowski and Rosenberg's (1987) NETtalk, which learns to read aloud from text. NETtalk is a two-layer feed-forward net, with input units representing a "window" of consecutive letters of text and output units representing the network's suggested pronunciation for the middle letter. The network pronounces a written text by shifting the input window across the text, letter by letter, so that the central letter to be pronounced moves onward a letter at a time. In English orthography there is not, of course, a one-to-one mapping between letters and phonemes. NETtalk relies on a rather ad hoc strategy to deal with this: In clusters of letters realized by a single phoneme (e.g., "th," "sh," "ough"), only one letter is chosen to be mapped onto the speech sound, and the others are not mapped onto any speech sound. NETtalk learns from exposure to text associated with the correct pronunciation using back-propagation (Rumelhart et al., 1986). Its pronunciation is good enough to be largely comprehensible when fed through a speech synthesizer.

Sejnowski and Rosenberg gained some insight into what their network was doing by computing the average hidden-unit activation given each of a total of seventy-nine different letter-to-sound combinations. For example, the activation of the hidden-unit layer was averaged for all the words in which the letter c is pronounced as /k/, another average calculated for words in which c corresponds to /s/, and so on. Next, the relationships among the resulting seventy-nine vectors—each construed as the network's internal representation of a particular letter-to-sound correspondence—were explored via cluster analysis. Interestingly, all the vectors for vowel sounds clustered together, suggesting that the network had learned to treat vowels different from consonants. Moreover, the network had learned a number of subregularities among the letter-to-sound combinations (e.g., evidenced by the close clustering of the labial stops /p/ and /b/ in hidden-unit space).

NETtalk was intended as a demonstration of the power of neural networks, rather than as a psychological model. Seidenberg and McClelland (1989) provided the first detailed psychological model of reading aloud. They also used a feed-forward network with a single hidden layer, but they represented the entire written form of the word as input and the entire phonological form as output. This network implemented one side of a theoretical "triangle" model of reading in which the two other sides were a pathway from orthography to semantics and a pathway from phonology to semantics (these sides are meant to be bidirectional, and, in fact, the implemented network also produced a copy of the input as a second output to attempt to model performance on lexical decision tasks, but we shall ignore this aspect of the model here). Seidenberg and McClelland restricted their attention to 2,897 monosyllabic words of English, rather than attempting to deal with unrestricted text like NETtalk. Inputs and outputs used the highly distributed wickelfeature type of representation that proved so controversial in the context of past-tense models, as discussed earlier.

The net's performance captured a wide range of experimental data (on the reasonable assumption that the net's error can be mapped onto response time in experimental paradigms). For example, frequent words are read more rapidly (with lower error) than rare words (Forster & Chambers, 1973); orthographically regular words are read more rapidly than irregulars and the difference between regulars and irregulars is much greater on rare rather than frequent words (Seidenberg, Waters, Barnes, & Tanenhaus, 1984; Taraban & McClelland, 1987).

As with the past-tense debate, a controversial claim concerning this reading model was that it uses a single route to handle a quasi-regular mapping. This contrasts with the standard view of reading, which assumes that there are two (nonsemantic) routes in reading, a "phonological route," which applies rules of pronunciation, and a "lexical route," which is simply a list of words and their pronunciations. Regular words can be read using either route, but irregulars must be read by using the lexical route and nonwords must use the phonological route (these will not be known by the lexical route). Seidenberg and McClelland (1989) claim to have shown that this dual-route view is not necessarily correct, because their single route can pronounce both irregular words and nonwords. Moreover, they have provided a fully explicit computational model, while previous dual-route theorists had merely sketched the reading system at the level of "boxes and arrows" (though see Coltheart, Curtis, Atkins, & Haller, 1993, and Coltheart & Rastle, 1994, for recent exceptions).

A number of criticisms have been leveled at Seidenberg and McClelland's account. Besner, Twilley, McCann, and Seergobin (1990) argued that the model's nonword reading is actually very poor compared with people (though see Seidenberg & McClelland, 1990). Moreover, Coltheart et al. (1993) argued that better performance at nonword reading can be achieved by symbolic learning methods, using the same word-set as Seidenberg and McClelland.

As in the past-tense debate, the wickelfeature representation has been criticized, leading to alternative representational schemes. For example, Plaut and McClelland (1993) and Plaut, McClelland, Seidenberg, and Patterson (1996) use a localist code that exploits regularities in English orthography and phonology to avoid a completely position-specific representation. Specifically, Plaut et al. segment monosyllable words into onset, vowel, and coda, and orthographic units can stand for groups of letters (e.g., wh, ea, and so on) that can correspond to a single phoneme. Their model learns to read nonwords very well, but it does so by building in a lot of knowledge into the representation, rather than having the network learn this knowledge. One could plausibly assume (cf. Plaut et al.) that some of this knowledge is acquired prior to reading acquisition; that is, children normally know how to pronounce words (i.e., talk) before they start learning to read. This idea was explored by Harm, Altmann, and Seidenberg (1994), who showed that pretraining a network on phonology can help learning the mapping from orthography to phonology, and was further developed by Harm and Seidenberg (1999), to which we will return.

One problem with this representational scheme, however, is that it only works for monosyllabic words. Bullinaria (1997), on the other hand, also obtains very high nonword reading performance for words of any length. He gives up the attempt to provide a single-route model of reading and aims to model the phonological route, using a variant of NETtalk in which orthographic and phonological forms are not prealigned by the designer. Instead of having a single output pattern, the network has many output patterns corresponding to all possible alignments between phonology and orthography. All possibilities are considered, and the one that is nearest to the network's actual output is taken as the correct output, and used to adjust the weights. This approach, like NETtalk, uses an input window that moves gradually over the text, producing one phoneme at a time. Hence, a simple phoneme-specific code can be used; the order of the phonemes is implicit in the order in which the network produces them.

Another limitation of the Seidenberg and McClelland (1989) model is the use of frequency compression during training. Rather than present rare and frequent words equally often to the network, they presented words with a probability proportional to their log frequency of occurrence in English (using Kucera & Francis, 1967). Had they used raw frequency rather than log frequency, the network could have encountered low-frequency items too rarely to learn them at all; this must be counted as a difficulty for this and many other network models, since the human learner must deal with absolute frequencies. Recently, however, Plaut et al. (1996) demonstrated that a feed-forward network can be trained successfully using the actual frequencies of words instead of their log frequency, even to a level of performance similar to that of human subjects on both word and nonword pronunciation.[7]

Connectionist models of reading have been criticized more generally for not modeling effects of specific lexical items (Spieler & Balota, 1997). One defense is that current models are too partial (e.g., containing no letter recognition and phonological output components) to be expected to model word-level effects (Seidenberg & Plaut, 1998). But Plaut (Chapter 8, this volume) takes up the challenge in relation to word-length effects, and trains an SRN to pronounce words phoneme by phoneme. The network can also refixate on the input when unable to pronounce part of a word. The model performs well on words and nonwords, and provides a reasonably good fit with the empirical data on word-length effects (e.g., Rastle & Coltheart, 1998; Weekes, 1997). These encouraging results suggest that the model may provide a first step toward a connectionist account of the temporal aspects of reading. Complementary work by Harm and Seidenberg (1999) using a recurrent network focuses on providing a richer model of phonological knowledge and processing, which is widely viewed as importantly related to reading and reading development (e.g., Bradley & Bryant, 1983; Goswami & Bryant, 1990).

A further difficulty for Seidenberg and McClelland's (1989) model is the apparent double dissociation between phonological and lexical reading in acquired dyslexia: Surface dyslexics (Bub, Cancelliere, & Kertesz, 1985; McCarthy & Warrington, 1986) can read exception words but not nonwords, but phonological dyslexics (Funnell, 1983) can pronounce nonwords but not irregular words. The standard (although not certain) inference from double dissociation to modularity of function suggests that normal nonword and exception-word reading are subserved by distinct systems, leading to a dual-route model (e.g., Morton & Patterson, 1980). Acquired dyslexia can be simulated by damaging Seidenberg and McClelland's network in various ways (e.g., removing connections or units). Although the results of this damage do have neuropsychological interest (Patterson, Seidenberg, & McClelland, 1989), they do not produce this double dissociation. An analogue of surface dyslexia is found (i.e., regulars are preserved), but no analogue of phonological dyslexia is observed. Furthermore, Bullinaria and Chater (1995) have explored a range of rule-exception tasks using feed-forward networks trained by back-propagation, and concluded that while double dissociations between rules and exceptions can occur in single-route models, this appears to occur only in very small-scale networks. In large networks the dissociation in which the rules are damaged but the exceptions are preserved does not occur. It remains possible that a realistic single-route model of reading incorporating factors that have been claimed to be important to connectionist accounts of reading, such as word frequency and phonological consistency effects (cf. Plaut et al., 1996), might give rise to the relevant double dissociation.[8] However, Bullinaria and Chater's results indicate that modeling phonological dyslexia is potentially a major challenge for any single-route connectionist model of reading.

Single- and dual-route theorists argue about whether nonword and exception-word reading is carried out by a single system, but agree that there is an additional "semantic" route, in which pronunciation is retrieved via a semantic code. This pathway is evidenced by deep dyslexics, who make semantic errors in reading aloud, such as reading the word *peach* aloud as "apricot." Interestingly, the behavior of the putative semantic route used by deep dyslexics has itself been modeled using connectionist methods (Hinton & Shallice, 1991; Plaut & Shallice, 1993). Roughly, a back-propagation network is trained to form a highly distributed mapping between words and their meanings (a mapping that is largely, although not completely, arbitrary). If such a network is damaged, then the resulting pattern of errors can involve confusing visually similar or semantically similar words, as well as a surprisingly large number of errors that apparently have both a visual and a semantic component. The profile of errors produced by networks of this kind seems to map, at least in a qualitative way, onto the patterns observed in deep dyslexics. The semantic route used by deep dyslexics is, according to Plaut et al. (1996), also involved in normal reading. In particular, they suggest that a division of labor emerges between the phonological and the semantic pathways during reading acquisition. Roughly, the phonological pathway moves toward a specialization in regular (consistent) orthography-to-phonology mappings at the expense of exception words, which are read by the semantic pathway.

The putative effect of the latter pathway was simulated by Plaut et al. (1996) as extra input to the phoneme units in a feed-forward network trained to map orthography to phonology. The strength of this external input is frequency dependent and gradually increases during learning. As a result, the network comes to rely on this extra input. If eliminated (following a simulated lesion to the semantic pathway), the net loses much of its ability to read exception words, but retains good reading of regular words as well as nonwords. Thus, Plaut et al. provide a more accurate account of surface dyslexia than Patterson et al. (1989). Conversely, selective damage to the phonological pathway (or to phonology itself) should produce a pattern of deficit resembling phonological dyslexia: reasonably good word reading but impaired nonword reading. However, this hypothesis was not tested directly by Plaut et al.

The Plaut et al. (1996) account of surface dyslexia has been challenged by the existence of patients with considerable semantic impairments but who demonstrate a near-normal reading of exception words. Plaut (1997) presents simulations results, suggesting that variations in surface dyslexia may stem from premorbid individual differences in the division of labor between the phonological and semantic pathways. In particular, if the phonological pathway is highly developed prior to lesioning, a pattern of semantic impairment with good exception-word reading can be observed in the model.

Whereas Seidenberg and McClelland (1989) and Plaut et al. (1996) defend the viewpoint that there is just one nonsemantic route in reading, it is also possible for computational models of reading to embody the opposite view, that there are two nonsemantic routes in reading. Coltheart et al. (1993) have implemented a nonlexical route in which the "grapheme–phoneme correspondences" embodying regular English pronunciation is a nonconnectionist, symbolic algorithm. A second lexical pathway is modeled as a connectionist interactive activation network (Coltheart & Rastle, 1994), building on McClelland and Rumelhart's (1981) model of letter and word recognition, described earlier. This implementation of the dual-route view closely follows previous dual-route theoretical proposals (Baron & Strawson, 1976; Coltheart, 1978; Morton & Patterson, 1980). One route is specifically designed to learn grapheme–phoneme correspondences; the other is specifically designed to read whole words.

In Coltheart's models, the characteristics of each of the two routes are built in, rather than emerging in some natural way from the constraints of the learning task. Zorzi, Houghton, and Butterworth (1998a, 1998b; see also Zorzi, 2000) suggest an elegant alternative. They show that the grapheme–phoneme correspondences in English monosyllabic words can be learned by a connectionist network with no hidden units. Input and output are represented in a simple localist code. There is a separate unit for each letter at each location in the word, and the alignment of the letters and phonemes represents letter positions in relation to the onset–rime structure of the word (the onset is the consonant cluster before the vowel, if any, and the rime is the rest of the word) (Zorzi et al., 1998a). This route learns to read regular words and nonwords correctly, but it cannot deal with exception words effectively. Zorzi et al. (1998b) consider a standard feed-forward network that has a "direct" path from orthography to phonology (i.e., there are no hidden units as before), but which also has an "indirect" path, mediated by a single layer of hidden units. Training this network using standard backpropagation (Rumelhart et al., 1986) leads to an automatic decomposition of the reading task into two functionally separate procedures. Whereas the direct pathway learns grapheme–phoneme correspondences, the indirect pathway uses its hidden units to deal with the word-specific information required to handle exception words. The overall reading performance of this very simple model is surprisingly good, and lesions to the direct or indirect routes produce errors broadly in line with the patterns observed in phonological and surface dyslexia.

Finally, a recent connectionist model has provided insights into developmental rather than acquired dyslexia. Harm and Seidenberg (1999) trained a network to read in two stages, embodying the observation that children clearly learn a great deal about the phonology of their natural language before learning to map written material onto that phonology. First, they trained a subnetwork consisting of units representing phonetic features to learn the structure of monosyllabic English words. This was done by training the network to auto-associate patterns representing words via a layer of "clean-up" units: The idea is that, after training, the clean-up units are able to correct any errors or omissions in the phonetic representation of a word (the idea of clean-up units had previously been used by Hinton & Shallice, 1991, and Plaut & Shallice, 1993, in the context of cleaning up semantic representations in models of deep dyslexia). To restore errors in the phonetic representation effectively, the subnetwork has to learn the regularities of English phonology. Then they trained a back-propagation network to map orthography to phonology, where the output units that embodied the phonological representation were still associated with the clean-up units. After both phases of training, the resulting network showed a good level of reading performance and replicated the main findings of previous reading models (Seidenberg & McClelland, 1989; Plaut et al., 1996). Moreover, the model shows the potential significance that phonological knowledge may play in assisting reading development: The model trained in two stages learns more quickly than a model that is given no pretraining on phonology.

Harm and Seidenberg (1999) argue that different kinds of damage to the model give rise to analogues of developmental phonological dyslexia and developmental surface dyslexia. This is surprising, because the network does not have separate phonological and lexical reading routes; instead, it is a single homogeneous network. Specifically, Harm and Seidenberg argue that phonological dyslexia can be modeled by impairing the phonological knowledge learned in the first stage of training; for example, by imposing a "decay" on weights in the trained phonological subnetwork or, more drastically, removing the clean-up units entirely. These kinds of damages explain developmental phonological dyslexia in terms of an underlying difficulty with phonological processing, and hence predict that developmental phonological dyslexics will have difficulties with, for example, phonological awareness tasks, as well as difficulties learning the grapheme–phoneme correspondence rules of English. This prediction appears to be born out in the literature (e.g., Share, 1995). By contrast, Harm and Seidenberg view what is often termed developmental surface dyslexia as no more than a delay in the development of normal reading. If this hypothesis is right, then the pattern of reading performance for children with this disorder should be similar to that of younger normal readers. Thus, for example, developmental surface dyslexics should be impaired in their reading not just of irregular words, but also of regular words, when compared to age-matched controls. Harm and Seidenberg argue that this slowing could arise from a number of factors, including lack of exposure to written materials or an inappropriate "learning rate." A learning rate may be inappropriate if it is either too small, slowing the learning process unnecessarily, or too large, so that the weights jump about excessively rather than converging on a "good" solution. In their simulations, Harm and Seidenberg adopt yet a further approach, slowing learning by using too few hidden units in the back-propagation network mapping orthography to phonology (this approach was previously explored in a preliminary way by Seidenberg & McClelland, 1989). Harm and Seidenberg provide detailed comparisons of the performance of their accounts of both phonological and surface forms of developmental dyslexia with the empirical data. This model therefore stands as a powerful challenge to conventional two-route views of developmental dyslexia (e.g., Castles & Coltheart, 1993; Coltheart et al., 1993). Indeed, Harm and Seidenberg have also shown how a strong double dissociation between reading nonwords and exception words can arise using a single homogeneous network. Although suggestive in relation to similar arguments from neuropsychology, as discussed earlier, it remains to be shown that a similarly crisp pattern of dissociation can be obtained in modeling acquired rather than developmental dyslexia.

Overall, it is clear that the debate between single- and dual-route accounts of nonsemantic reading have not been settled by the growing prevalence of connectionist models. But the advent of connectionist modeling has shifted the debate from typically qualitative discussions of the rival accounts to increasingly sophisticated computational models of the rival positions, which are explicit and produce testable empirical predictions concerning normal reading and the acquired dyslexias. More generally, connectionist models of reading have become central to theory building in the study of reading, and have therefore had a substantial influence on the direction of related experimental and neuropsychological research. With respect to the three criteria for connectionist psycholinguistics, connectionist research on reading has good data contact and reasonable input representativeness. Task veridicality is open to questioning: Children may typically not directly associate written and spoken forms for individual words when learning to read (though Harm and Seidenberg, 1999, partially address this issue). A major challenge for future research is to synthesize the insights gained from detailed models of different aspects of reading into a single model.

PROSPECTS FOR CONNECTIONIST PSYCHOLINGUISTICS

We have seen that controversy surrounds both the past and current significance of connectionist psycholinguistics. Current connectionist models as exemplified in Part I of this volume involve drastic simplifications with respect to real natural language. How can connectionist models be scaled up to provide realistic models of human language processing? Part II provides three different perspectives on how connectionist models may develop.

Seidenberg and MacDonald (Chapter 9, this volume) argue that connectionist models will be able to replace the currently dominant symbolic models of language structure and language processing throughout the cognitive science of language. They suggest that connectionist models exemplify a probabilistic rather than a rigid view of language that requires the foundations of linguistics as well as the cognitive science of language more generally to be radically rethought.

Smolensky (Chapter 10, this volume), by contrast, argues that current connectionist models alone cannot handle the full complexity of linguistic structure and language processing. He suggests that progress requires a match between insights from the generative grammar approach in linguistics and the computational properties of connectionist systems (e.g., constraint satisfaction). He exemplifies this approach with two grammar formalisms inspired by connectionist systems, Harmonic Grammar and Optimality Theory.

Steedman (Chapter 11, this volume) argues that claims that connectionist systems can take over the territory of symbolic views of language, such as syntax or semantics, are premature. He suggests that connectionist and symbolic approaches to language and language processing should be viewed as complementary, but as currently dealing with different aspects of language processing. Nonetheless, Steedman believes that connectionist systems may provide the underlying architecture on which high-level symbolic processing occurs.

Whatever the outcome of these important debates, we note that connectionist psycholinguistics has already had an important influence on the psychology of language. First, connectionist models have raised the level of theoretical debate in many areas by challenging theorists of all viewpoints to provide computationally explicit accounts. This has provided the basis for more informed discussions about processing architecture (e.g., single- versus dual-route mechanisms and interactive versus bottom-up processing). Second, the learning methods used by connectionist models have reinvigorated interest in computational models of language learning (Bates & Elman, 1993). While Chomsky (e.g., 1986) has argued for innate "universal" aspects of language, the vast amount of language-specific information that the child acquires must be learned. Connectionist models may account for how some of this learning occurs. Furthermore, connectionist models provide a test bed for the learnability of linguistic properties previously assumed to be innate. Finally, the dependence of connectionist models on the statistical properties of their input has contributed to the upsurge of interest in statistical factors in language learning and processing (MacWhinney, Leinbach, Taraban, & McDonald, 1989; Redington & Chater, 1998).

Connectionist psycholinguistics has thus already had considerable influence on the psychology of language. But the final extent of this influence depends on the degree to which practical connectionist models can be developed and extended to deal with complex aspects of language processing in a psychologically realistic way. If realistic connectionist models of language processing can be provided, then the possibility of a radical rethinking, not just of the nature of language processing but of the structure of language itself, may be required. It might be that the ultimate description of language resides in the structure of complex networks, and can only be approximated by rules of grammar. Or perhaps connectionist learning methods do not scale up and connectionism can only succeed by reimplementing standard symbolic models. The future of connectionist psycholinguistics is therefore likely to have important implications for the theory of language processing and language structure, either in overturning or reaffirming traditional psychological and linguistic assumptions.

FURTHER READINGS

The suggested readings are grouped according to the general structure of the chapter.

Background

The PDP volumes (McClelland & Rumelhart, 1986, and Rumelhart & McClelland, 1986b) provide a solid introduction to the application of connectionist networks in cognitive models. Smolensky (1988) offers a connectionist alternative to viewing cognition as symbol manipulation, whereas Fodor and Pylyshyn (1988) is a classic critique of connectionism. Elman et al. (1996) details a more recent, broad perspective on connectionism and cognitive development, but see Marcus (1998) for an opposing view. For further discussions, see Seidenberg and MacDonald (Chapter 9, this volume) and Smolensky (Chapter 10, this volume). Finally, McLeod, Plunkett, and Rolls (1998) is a good introduction to the art of conducting connectionist simulations. The book includes simulators for PC and MacIntosh computers as well as exercises with the major network architectures discussed in this chapter.

Speech Processing

The influential TRACE model of speech perception is described in McClelland and Elman (1986). The empirical study of the compensation for coarticulation is found in Elman and McClelland (1988). Gaskell and Marslen-Wilson (Chapter 3, this volume) explore issues related to a connectionist, bottom-up approach to spoken-word recognition. Turning to word segmentation, Cairns et al. (1997) and Christiansen, Allen, et al. (1998) present two models of this area of speech processing.

Morphology

The classic connectionist model of English past-tense acquisition is Rumelhart and McClelland (1986a), with Pinker and Prince (1988) providing the first comprehensive criticism of this model. See Plunkett and Marchman (1993) and Pinker (1991) for recent updates. Over time the debate has also spread to other areas of inflectional morphology, such as the acquisition of English noun plurals (dual mechanism, Marcus, 1995; single mechanism, Plunkett & Joula, Chapter 4, this volume), as well as cross-linguistically to the acquisition of German noun plurals (dual mechanism, Clahsen et al., 1993; single mechanism, Hahn & Nakisa, in press).

Sentence Processing

Elman (1990, 1991) presents an influential connectionist approach to the learning of syntactic regularities, but see Hadley (1994a) for a criticism of this and other connectionist models of syntax. Christiansen and Chater (Chapter 5, this volume) extend this approach to cover complex recursive processing, whereas Tabor and Tanenhaus (Chapter 6, this volume) investigate the effects of semantic role expectations on sentence processing. For a structured connectionist approach to the processing of sentences, see Miikkulainen (1996). Steedman (Chapter 11, this volume) provides a critical perspective on connectionist models of syntax.

Language Production

The classic spreading activation model of speech production and speech errors is Dell (1986). Dell et al. (Chapter 7, this volume) describe three subsequent models: an extension to the original model applied to the modeling of aphasic patient data, a bottom-up alternative to the original model of speech errors, and a model of syntactic priming in sentence production. Other connectionist approaches are found in Harley (1993), among others.

Reading

The early interactive activation model of visual word recognition is found in McClelland and Rumelhart (1981). Seidenberg and McClelland (1989) is the classic single-mechanism, connectionist model of reading. Coltheart et al. (1993) provide a criticism of this model and a symbolic alternative. For the most recent advancement of this discussion, see Plaut et al. (1996), Harm and Seidenberg (1999), and Zorzi et al. (1998b), as well as Plaut (Chapter 8, this volume).

NOTES

This work was partially supported by the Leverhulme Trust and by European Commission Grant RTN-HPRN-CT-99-00065 to Nick Chater.
   1. The term "connectionism," referring to the use of artificial neural networks to model cognition, was coined by Feldman and Ballard (1982).

2. The idea of copying back output as part of the next input was first proposed by Jordan (1986).

3. Wickelfeatures are generated in a similar way to wickelphones. The latter involve decomposing a phoneme strings into consecutive triples. Thus, the phoneme string /kæt/ (*cat*) is decomposed into the /_kæ/, /kæt/, and /æt_/. Notice that the triples are position independent, but that the overall string can be pieced together again from the triples (in general, as Pinker & Prince, 1988, have noted, this piecing together process cannot always be carried out successfully, but in this context it is adequate). Wickelfeatures correspond to triples of phonetic features rather than triples of entire phonemes.

4. In this connection, type frequency refers to the number of different words belonging to a given class, each counted once (e.g., the number of different regular verbs). Token frequency, on the other hand, denotes the number of instances of a particular word (e.g., number of occurrences of the verb *have*). As pointed out by Pinker and Prince (1988), the Rumelhart and McClelland (1986a) model was not able to adequately accommodate the subregularities.

5. In these simulations, novel words corresponded to units that had not been activated during training.

6. A somewhat similar model of speech production was developed independently by Stemberger (1985). This model was inspired by the interactive activation framework of McClelland and Rumelhart (1981), whereas Dell's (1986) work was not.

7. Note that Plaut et al. (1996) used these (actual) frequencies to scale the contribution of error for each word during back-propagation training, rather than to determine the number of word presentations. They also employed a different representational scheme (due to Plaut & McClelland, 1993) than Seidenberg and McClelland (1989).

8. Whereas "regularity" (the focus of the Bullinaria & Chater, 1995, simulations) can be taken as indicating that the pronunciation of a word appears to follow a rule, "consistency" refers to how well a particular word's pronunciation agrees with other similarly spelled words. The magnitude of the latter depends on how many "friends" a word has (i.e., the summed frequency of words with similar spelling patterns and similar pronunciation) compared with how many "enemies" (i.e., the summed frequency of words with similar spelling patterns but different pronunciations) (Jared, McRae, & Seidenberg, 1990).

REFERENCES

Aderman, D., & Smith, E. E. (1971). Expectancy as a determinant of functional units in perceptual cognition. *Cognitive Psychology, 2,* 117–129.

Allen, J., & Seidenberg, M. S. (1999). The emergence of grammaticality in connectionist networks. In B. MacWhinney (Ed.), *The emergence of language* (pp. 115–151). Mahwah, NJ: Lawrence Erlbaum.

Ashby, W. R. (1952). *Design for a brain.* New York: Wiley.

Bach, E., Brown, C., & Marslen-Wilson, W. (1986). Crossed and nested dependencies in German and Dutch: A psycholinguistic study. *Language and Cognitive Processes, 1,* 249–262.

Baron, J., & Strawson, C. (1976). Use of orthographic and word-specific knowledge in reading words aloud. *Journal of Experimental Psychology: Human Perception and Performance, 2,* 386–392.

Bates, E. A., Bretherton, I., & Snyder, L. (1988). *From first word to grammar: Individual differences and dissociable mechanisms*. New York: Cambridge University Press.

Bates, E. A., & Elman, J. L. (1993). Connectionism and the study of change. In M. J. Johnson (Ed.), *Brain development and cognition* (pp. 623–642). Cambridge, MA: Basic Blackwell.

Besner, D., Twilley, L., McCann, R. S., & Seergobin, K. (1990). On the connection between connectionism and data: Are a few words necessary? *Psychological Review, 97*, 432–446.

Bock, J. K., & Griffin. Z. M. (in press). The persistence of structural priming: Transient activation or implicit learning? *Journal of Experimental Psychology: General*.

Boole, G. (1854). *The laws of thought*. London: Macmillan.

Bradley, L., & Bryant, P. E. (1983). Categorising sounds and learning to read—causal connection. *Nature, 301*, 419–421.

Brill, E., Magerman, D., Marcus, M., & Santorini, B. (1990). Deducing linguistic structure from the statistics of large corpora. In *DARPA Speech and Natural Language Workshop*. Hidden Valley, PA: Morgan Kaufmann.

Bruner, J. (1957). On perceptual readiness. *Psychological Review, 65*, 14–21.

Bryson, A. E., & Ho, Y.-C. (1975). *Applied optimal control: Optimization, estimation, and control*. New York: Hemisphere.

Bub, D., Cancelliere, A., & Kertesz, A. (1985). Whole-word and analytic translation of spelling to sound in a non-semantic reader. In K. E. Patterson, J. C. Marshall, & M. Coltheart (Eds.), *Surface dyslexia: Neuropsychological and cognitive studies of phonological reading* (pp. 15–34). London: Lawrence Erlbaum.

Bullinaria, J. A. (1997). Modelling reading, spelling and past tense learning with artificial neural networks. *Brain and Language, 59*, 236–266.

Bullinaria, J. A., & Chater, N. (1995). Connectionist modelling: Implications for neuropsychology. *Language and Cognitive Processes, 10*, 227-264.

Bybee, J. (1995). Regular morphology and the lexicon. *Language and Cognitive Processes, 10*, 425–455.

Bybee, J., & Slobin, D. I. (1982). Rules and schemas in the development and use of the English past tense. *Language, 58*, 265–289.

Cairns, P., Shillcock, R. C., Chater, N., & Levy, J. (1995). Bottom-up connectionist modelling of speech. In J. Levy, D. Bairaktaris, J. A. Bullinaria, & P. Cairns (Eds.), *Connectionist models of memory and language* (pp. 289–310). London: UCL Press.

Cairns, P., Shillcock, R. C., Chater, N., & Levy, J. (1997). Bootstrapping word boundaries: A bottom-up corpus-based approach to speech segmentation. *Cognitive Psychology, 33*, 111–153.

Castles, A., & Coltheart, M. (1993). Varieties of developmental dyslexia. *Cognition, 47*, 149–180.

Chalmers, D. J. (1990). Syntactic transformations on distributed representations. *Connection Science, 2*, 53–62.

Chang, F., Dell, G. S., Bock, J. K., & Griffin, Z. M. (2000). Structural priming as implicit learning: A comparison of models of sentence production. *Journal of Psycholinguistic Research, 29*, 217–229.

Chang, F., Griffin, Z. M., Dell, G. S., & Bock, J. K. (1997). *Modeling structural priming as implicit learning*. Poster presented at the Computational Psycholinguistics Conference, August, University of California, Berkeley, CA.

Charniak, E. (1993). *Statistical language learning*. Cambridge, MA: MIT Press.

Chater, N., & Oaksford, M. (1990). Autonomy, implementation and cognitive architecture: A reply to Fodor and Pylyshyn. *Cognition, 34*, 93–107.

Chomsky, N. (1957). *Syntactic structures*. The Hague: Mouton.

Chomsky, N. (1965). *Aspects of the theory of syntax*. Cambridge, MA: MIT Press.

Chomsky, N. (1986). *Knowledge of language*. New York: Praeger.

Christiansen, M. H. (1994). *Infinite languages, finite minds: Connectionism, learning and linguistic structure*. Unpublished doctoral dissertation, University of Edinburgh.

Christiansen, M. H. (2000). *Intrinsic constraints on the processing of recursive sentence structure*. Manuscript in preparation.

Christiansen, M. H., Allen, J., & Seidenberg, M. S. (1998). Learning to segment speech using multiple cues: A connectionist model. *Language and Cognitive Processes, 13*, 221–268.

Christiansen, M. H., & Chater, N. (1994). Generalization and connectionist language learning. *Mind and Language, 9*, 273–287.

Christiansen, M. H., & Chater, N. (1999). Towards a connectionist model of recursion in human linguistic performance. *Cognitive Science, 23*, 157–205.

Christiansen, M. H., Conway, C. M., & Curtin, S. (2000). A connectionist single-mechanism account of rule-like behavior in infancy. In *Proceedings of the Twenty-Second Annual Conference of the Cognitive Science Society* (pp. 83–88). Mahwah, NJ: Lawrence Erlbaum.

Christiansen, M. H., & MacDonald, M. C. (2000). *Processing of recursive sentence structure: Testing predictions from a connectionist model*. Manuscript in preparation.

Clahsen, H., Rothweiler, M., Woest, A., & Marcus, G. F. (1993). Regular and irregular inflection in the acquisition of German noun plurals. *Cognition, 45*, 225–255.

Cleeremans, A., Destrebecqz, A., & Boyer, M. (1998). Implicit learning: News from the front. *Trends in Cognitive Sciences, 2*, 406–416.

Cole, R. A., & Jakimik, J. (1978). Understanding speech: How words are heard. In G. Underwood (Ed.), *Strategies of information processing*. New York: Academic Press.

Cole, R. A., & Jakimik, J. (1980). A model of speech perception. In R. A. Cole (Ed.), *Perception and production of fluent speech* (pp. 133–164). Hillsdale, NJ: Lawrence Erlbaum.

Coltheart, M. (1978). Lexical access in simple reading tasks. In G. Underwood (Ed.), *Strategies of information processing* (pp. 151–216). London: Academic Press.

Coltheart, M., Curtis, B., Atkins, P., & Haller, M. (1993). Models of reading aloud: Dual-route and parallel-distributed-processing approaches. *Psychological Review, 100*, 589–608.

Coltheart, M., & Rastle, K. (1994). Serial processing in reading aloud: Evidence for dual-route models of reading. *Journal of Experimental Psychology: Human Perception and Performance, 20*, 1197–1211.

Cottrell, G. W., & Plunkett, K. (1991). Learning the past tense in a recurrent network: Acquiring the mapping from meanings to sounds. In *Proceedings of the Thirteenth Annual Conference of the Cognitive Science Society* (pp. 328–333). Hillsdale, NJ: Lawrence Erlbaum.

Crain, S. (1991). Language acquisition in the absence of experience. *Behavioral and Brain Sciences, 14*, 597–650.

Cutler, A., Mehler, J., Norris, D., & Segui, J. (1987) Phoneme identification and the lexicon. *Cognitive Psychology, 19*, 141–177.

Cutler, A., & Norris, D. (1979). Monitoring sentence comprehension. In W. E. Cooper & E.C.T. Walker (Eds.), *Sentence processing: Psycholinguistic studies presented to Merrill Garrett* (pp. 113–134). Hillsdale, NJ: Lawrence Erlbaum.

Daugherty, K., & Hare, M. (1993). What's in a rule? The past tense by some other name might be called a connectionist net. In M. Mozer, P. Smolensky, D. Touretzky, J. Elman, & A. Weigand (Eds.), *Proceedings of the 1993 Connectionist Models Summer School* (pp. 149–156). Hillsdale, NJ: Lawrence Erlbaum.

Daugherty, K., MacDonald, M. C., Petersen, A. S., & Seidenberg, M. S. (1993). Why no mere mortal has ever flown out to center field, but often people say they do. In *Proceedings of the Fifteenth Annual Conference of the Cognitive Science Society* (pp. 383–388). Hillsdale, NJ: Lawrence Erlbaum.

Daugherty, K., & Seidenberg, M. S. (1992). Rules or connections? The past tense revisited. In *Proceedings of the Fourteenth Annual Conference of the Cognitive Science Society* (pp. 259–264). Hillsdale, NJ: Lawrence Erlbaum.

Dell, G. S. (1986). A spreading activation theory of retrieval in language production. *Psychological Review, 93*, 283–321.

Dell, G. S. (1988). The retrieval of phonological forms in production: Tests of predictions from a connectionist model. *Journal of Memory and Language, 27*, 124–142.

Dell, G. S., Burger, L. K., & Svec, W. R. (1997). Language production and serial order: A functional analysis and a model. *Psychological Review, 104*, 123–147.

Dell, G. S., Juliano, C., & Govindjee, A. (1993). Structure and content in language production: A theory of frame constraints in phonological speech errors. *Cognitive Science, 17*, 149–195.

Dell, G. S., Schwartz, M. F., Martin, N., Saffran, E. M., & Gagnon, D. A. (1997). Lexical access in aphasic and nonaphasic speakers. *Psychological Review, 104*, 801–838.

Elman, J. L. (1988). *Finding structure in time* (Tech. Rep. No. CRL-8801). San Diego: University of California, Center for Research in Language.

Elman, J. L. (1990). Finding structure in time. *Cognitive Science, 14*, 179–211.

Elman, J. L. (1991). Distributed representation, simple recurrent networks, and grammatical structure. *Machine Learning, 7*, 195–225.

Elman, J. L. (1993). Learning and development in neural networks: The importance of starting small. *Cognition, 48*, 71–99.

Elman, J. L., Bates, E. A., Johnson, M. H., Karmiloff-Smith, A., Parisi, D., & Plunkett, K. (1996). *Rethinking innateness: A connectionist perspective on development*. Cambridge, MA: MIT Press.

Elman, J. L., & McClelland, J. L. (1988). Cognitive penetration of the mechanisms of perception: Compensation for coarticulation of lexically restored phonemes. *Journal of Memory and Language, 27*, 143–165.

Fanty, M. (1985). *Context-free parsing in connectionist networks* (Tech. Rep. No. TR-174). Rochester, NY: University of Rochester, Department of Computer Science.

Feldman, J. A., & Ballard, D. H. (1982). Connectionist models and their properties. *Cognitive Science, 6,* 205-254.

Finch, S., & Chater, N. (1993). Learning syntactic categories: A statistical approach. In M. Oaksford & G.D.A. Brown (Eds.), *Neurodynamics and psychology* (pp. 295-321). New York: Academic Press.

Fodor, J. A. (1983). *Modularity of mind.* Cambridge, MA: MIT Press.

Fodor, J. A., & Pylyshyn, Z. W. (1988). Connectionism and cognitive architecture: A critical analysis. *Cognition, 28,* 3-71.

Forrester, N., & Plunkett, K. (1994). Learning the Arabic plural: The case for minority mappings in connectionist networks. In *Proceedings of the Sixteenth Annual Conference of the Cognitive Science Society* (pp. 319-324). Hillsdale, NJ: Lawrence Erlbaum.

Forster, K. I., & Chambers, S. (1973). Lexical access and naming time. *Journal of Verbal Learning and Verbal Behavior, 12,* 627-635.

Fox, R. A. (1984). Effect of lexical status on phonetic categorization. *Journal of Experimental Psychology: Human Perception and Performance, 10,* 526-540.

Funnell, E. (1983). Phonological processing in reading: New evidence from acquired dyslexia. *British Journal of Psychology, 74,* 159-180.

Ganong, W. F. (1980). Phonetic categorization in auditory word perception. *Journal of Experimental Psychology: Human Perception and Performance, 6,* 110-115.

Gaskell, M. G., Hare, M., & Marslen-Wilson, W. D. (1995). A connectionist model of phonological representation in speech perception. *Cognitive Science, 19,* 407-439.

Gaskell, M. G., & Marslen-Wilson, W. D. (1997). Integrating form and meaning: A distributed model of speech perception. *Language and Cognitive Processes, 12,* 613-656.

Goswami, U., & Bryant, P. (1990). *Phonological skills and learning to read.* London: Lawrence Erlbaum.

Gow, D. W., & Gordon, P. C. (1995). Lexical and pre-lexical influences on word segmentation: Evidence from priming. *Journal of Experimental Psychology: Human Perception and Performance, 21,* 344-359.

Hadley, R. F. (1994a). Systematicity in connectionist language learning. *Mind and Language, 9,* 247-272.

Hadley, R. F. (1994b). Systematicity revisited: Reply to Christiansen & Chater and Niklasson & van Gelder. *Mind and Language, 9,* 431-444.

Hahn, U., & Nakisa, R. C. (in press). German inflection: Single or dual route? *Cognitive Psychology.*

Hanson, S. J., & Kegl, J. (1987). PARSNIP: A connectionist network that learns natural language grammar from exposure to natural language sentences. In *Proceedings of the Eighth Annual Conference of the Cognitive Science Society* (pp. 106-119). Hillsdale, NJ: Lawrence Erlbaum.

Hare, M., & Elman, J. L. (1995). Learning and morphological change. *Cognition, 56,* 61-98.

Hare, M., Elman, J. L., & Daugherty, K. (1995). Defaultgeneralization in connectionist networks. *Language and Cognitive Processes, 10,* 601-630.

Harley, T. A. (1993). Phonological activation of semantic competitors during lexical access in speech production. *Language and Cognitive Processes, 8,* 291-309.

Harm, M. W., Altmann, L., & Seidenberg, M. S. (1994). Using connectionist networks to examine the role of prior constraints in human learning. In *Proceedings of the Sixteenth Annual Conference of the Cognitive Science Society* (pp. 392–396). Hillsdale, NJ: Lawrence Erlbaum.

Harm, M. W., & Seidenberg, M. S. (1999). Phonology, reading acquisition, and dyslexia: Insights from connectionist models. *Psychological Review, 106*, 491–528.

Hinton, G. E., & Sejnowski, T. J. (1986). Learning and relearning in Boltzmann machines. In J. L. McClelland & D. E. Rumelhart (Eds.), *Parallel distributed processing* (Vol. 1, pp. 282–317). Cambridge, MA: MIT Press.

Hinton, G. E., & Shallice, T. (1991). Lesioning an attractor network: Investigations of acquired dyslexia. *Psychological Review, 98*, 74–95.

Hoeffner, J. (1997). *Are rules a thing of the past? A single mechanism account of English past tense acquisition and processing*. Unpublished doctoral dissertation, Carnegie Mellon University, Pittsburgh.

Howells, T. (1988). VITAL, a connectionist parser. In *Proceedings of the Tenth Annual Conference of the Cognitive Science Society*. Hillsdale, NJ: Lawrence Erlbaum.

Jared, D., McRae, K., & Seidenberg, M. S. (1990). The basis of consistency effect effects in word naming. *Journal of Memory and Language, 29*, 687–715.

Jelinek, F., Lafferty, J. D., & Mercer, R. L. (1990). *Basic methods of probabilistic context-free grammars* (Tech. Rep. RC 16374-72684). Yorktown Heights, NY: IBM.

Johnston, J. C., & McClelland, J. L. (1973). Visual factors in word perception. *Perception and Psychophysics, 14*, 365–370.

Jordan, M. I. (1986). *Serial order: A parallel distributed approach* (Tech. Rep. No. 8604). San Diego: University of California, Institute for Cognitive Science.

Jordan, T. R., Thomas, S. M., & Scott-Brown, K. C. (1999). The illusory-letters phenomenon: An illustration of graphemic restoration in visual word recognition. *Perception, 28*, 1413–1416.

Jusczyk, P. W. (1997). *The discovery of spoken language*. Cambridge, MA: MIT Press.

Kim, J. J., Pinker, S., Prince, A., & Prasada, S. (1991). Why no mere mortal has ever flown out to center field. *Cognitive Science, 15*, 173–218.

Koch, C., & Segev, I. (Eds.). (1989). *Methods in neuronal modeling: From synapses to networks*. Cambridge, MA: MIT Press.

Kučera, H., & Francis, W. (1967). *Computational analysis of present day American English*. Providence, RI: Brown University Press.

Kuczaj, S. A. (1977). The acquisition of regular and irregular past tense forms. *Journal of Verbal Learning and Verbal Behavior, 16*, 589–600.

Kuczaj, S. A. (1978). Children's judgments of grammatical and ungrammatical irregular past tense verbs. *Child Development, 49*, 319–326.

Kwasny, S. C., & Faisal, K. A. (1990). Connectionism and determinism in a syntactic parser. *Connection Science, 2*, 63–82.

Lachter, J., & Bever, T. G. (1988). The relation between linguistic structure and associative theories of language learning: A constructive critique of some connectionist learning models. *Cognition, 28*, 195–247.

Levelt, W.J.M. (1989). *Speaking: From intention to articulation*. Cambridge, MA: MIT Press.

Linebarger, M. C., Schwartz, M. F., & Saffran, E. M. (1983). Sensitivity to grammatical structure in so-called agrammatic aphasics. *Cognition, 13*, 361–392.

MacDonald, M. C., & Christiansen, M. H. (in press). Reassessing working memory: A comment on Just & Carpenter (1992) and Waters & Caplan (1996). *Psychological Review*.

MacWhinney, B., & Leinbach, J. (1991). Implementations are not conceptualizations: Revising the verb learning model. *Cognition, 40*, 121–157.

MacWhinney, B., Leinbach, J., Taraban, R., & McDonald, J. (1989). Language learning: Cues or rules? *Journal of Memory and Language, 28*, 255–277.

MacWhinney, B., & Snow, C. (1985). The Child Language Data Exchange System. *Journal of Child Language, 12*, 271–295.

Mann, V. A., & Repp, B. H. (1980). Influence of vocalic context of perception of the [ʃ]–[s] distinction. *Perception and Psychophysics, 28*, 213–228.

Marcus, G. F. (1995). Children's overregularization of English plurals: A quantitative analysis. *Journal of Child Language, 22*, 447–459.

Marcus, G. F. (1998). Can connectionism save constructivism? *Cognition, 66*, 153–182.

Marcus, G. F., Brinkmann, U., Clahsen, H., Wiese, R., & Pinker, S. (1995). German inflection: The exception that proves the rule. *Cognitive Psychology, 29*, 189–256.

Marcus, G. F., Vijayan, S., Rao, S. B., & Vishton, P. M. (1999). Rule learning by seven-month-old infants. *Science, 283*, 77–80.

Marr, D. (1982). *Vision*. San Francisco: Freeman.

Marslen-Wilson, W. D. (1973). Linguistic structure and speech shadowing at very short latencies. *Nature, 244*, 522–523.

Marslen-Wilson, W. D., & Tyler, L. K. (1975). Processing structure of sentence perception. *Nature, 257*, 784–786.

Marslen-Wilson, W. D., & Warren, P. (1994). Levels of perceptual representation and process in lexical access: Words, phonemes, and features. *Psychological Review, 101*, 653–675.

Massaro, D. W. (1979). Letter information and orthographic context in word perception. *Journal of Experimental Psychology: Human Perception and Performance, 5*, 595–609.

Massaro, D. W. (1981). Sound to representation: An information-processing analysis. In T. Myers, J. Laver, & J. Anderson (Eds.), *The cognitive representation of speech* (pp. 181–193). New York: North Holland.

Massaro, D. W. (1989). Testing between the TRACE model and the fuzzy logic model of speech perception. *Cognitive Psychology, 21*, 398–421.

Massaro, D. W., & Cohen, M. M. (1991). Integration versus interactive activation: The joint influence of stimulus and context in perception. *Cognitive Psychology, 23*, 558–614.

McCarthy, R., & Warrington, E. K. (1986). Phonological reading: Phenomena and paradoxes. *Cortex, 22*, 359–380.

McClelland, J. L. (1991). Stochastic interactive processes and the effects of context on perception. *Cognitive Psychology, 23*, 1–44.

McClelland, J. L., & Elman, J. L. (1986). Interactive processes in speech perception: The TRACE model. In J. L. McClelland & D. E. Rumelhart (Eds.), *Parallel distributed processing: Explorations in the microstructure of cognition*. Vol. 2: *Psychological and biological models* (pp. 58–121). Cambridge, MA: MIT Press.

McClelland, J. L., & Johnston, J. C. (1977). The role of familiar units in the perception of words and non-words. *Perception and Psychophysics, 22,* 249–261.

McClelland, J. L., & Kawamoto, A. H. (1986). Mechanisms of sentence processing. In J. L. McClelland & D. E. Rumelhart (Eds.), *Parallel distributed processing: Explorations in the microstructure of cognition.* Vol. 2: *Psychological and biological models* (pp. 272–325). Cambridge, MA: MIT Press.

McClelland, J. L., & Rumelhart, D. E. (1981). An interactive activation model of context effects in letter perception: Part 1. An account of basic findings. *Psychological Review, 88,* 375–407.

McClelland, J. L., & Rumelhart, D. E. (Eds.) (1986). *Parallel distributed processing: Explorations in the microstructure of cognition.* Vol. 2: *Psychological and biological models.* Cambridge, MA: MIT Press.

McCulloch, W. S., & Pitts, W. (1943). A logical calculus of ideas immanent in nervous activity. *Bulletin of Mathematical Biophysics, 5,* 115–133.

McLeod, P., Plunkett, K., & Rolls, E. T. (1998). *Introduction to connectionist modeling of cognitive processes.* Oxford: Oxford University Press.

McQueen, J. M. (1991). The influence of the lexicon on phonetic categorization: Stimulus quality in word-final ambiguity. *Journal of Experimental Psychology: Human Perception and Performance, 17,* 433–443.

McQueen, J. M., Norris, D. G., & Cutler, A. (in press). Lexical influence in phonetic decision-making: Evidence from subcategorical mismatches. *Journal of Experimental Psychology: Human Perception and Performance.*

McRae, K., Spivey-Knowlton, M. J., & Tanenhaus, M. K. (1998). Modeling the influence of thematic fit (and other constraints) in on-line sentence comprehension. *Journal of Memory and Language, 38,* 282–312.

Miikkulainen, R. (1996). Subsymbolic case-role analysis of sentences with embedded clauses. *Cognitive Science, 20,* 47–73.

Miller, G. A., & Chomsky, N. (1963). Finitary models of language users. In R. D. Luce, R. R. Bush, & E. Galanter (Eds.), *Handbook of mathematical psychology* (Vol. 2, pp. 419–491). New York: Wiley.

Minsky, M. (1954). *Neural nets and the brain-model problem.* Unpublished doctoral dissertation, Princeton University, NJ.

Minsky, M., & Papert, S. (1969). *Perceptrons.* Cambridge, MA: MIT Press.

Miyata, Y., Smolensky, P., & Legendre, G. (1993). Distributed representation and parallel distributed processing of recursive structures. In *Proceedings of the Fifteenth Annual Conference of the Cognitive Science Society* (pp. 759–764). Hillsdale, NJ: Lawrence Erlbaum.

Morton, J., & Patterson, K. E. (1980). A new attempt at an interpretation, or, an attempt at a new interpretation. In M. Coltheart, K. E. Patterson, & J. C. Marshall (Eds.), *Deep dyslexia* (pp. 91–118). London: Routledge.

Neisser, U. (1967). *Cognitive psychology.* New York: Appleton–Century–Crofts.

Newell, A., & Simon, H. A. (1972). *Human problem solving.* Englewood Cliffs, NJ: Prentice-Hall.

Niklasson, L., & van Gelder, T. (1994). On being systematically connectionist. *Mind and Language, 9,* 288–302.

Norris, D. G. (1993). Bottom-up connectionist models of "interaction." In G. Altmann & R. Shillcock (Eds.), *Cognitive models of speech processing: The Second Sperlonga Meeting* (pp. 211–234). Hillsdale, NJ: Lawrence Erlbaum.

Norris, D. G. (1994). A quantitative multiple-levels model of reading aloud. *Journal of Experimental Psychology: Human Perception and Performance, 20,* 1212-1232.

Norris, D. G., McQueen, J. M., & Cutler, A. (in press). Merging information in speech recognition: Feedback is never necessary. *Behavioral and Brain Sciences.*

Patterson, K. E., Seidenberg, M. S., & McClelland, J. L. (1989). Connections and disconnections: Acquired dyslexia in a computational model of reading processes. In R.G.M. Morris (Ed.), *Parallel distributed processing: Implications for psychology and neuroscience* (pp. 131-181). Oxford: Oxford University Press.

Pearlmutter, B. A. (1989). Learning state space trajectories in recurrent neural networks. *Neural Computation, 1,* 263-269.

Pinker, S. (1991). Rules of language. *Science, 253,* 530-535.

Pinker, S. (1994). *The language instinct: How the mind creates language.* New York: William Morrow.

Pinker, S., & Prince, A. (1988). On language and connectionism: Analysis of a parallel distributed processing model of language acquisition. *Cognition, 28,* 73-193.

Pisoni, D. B., & Tash, J. (1974). Reaction times to comparisons within and across phonetic categories. *Perception and Psychophysics, 15,* 285-290.

Pitt, M. A., & McQueen, J. M. (1998). Is compensation for coarticulation mediated by the lexicon? *Journal of Memory and Language, 39,* 347-370.

Pitt, M. A., & Samuel, A. G. (1993). An empirical and meta-analytic evaluation of the phoneme identification task. *Journal of Experimental Psychology: Human Perception and Performance, 19,* 699-725.

Plaut, D. C. (1997). Structure and function in the lexical system: Insights from distributed models of word reading and lexical decision. *Language and Cognitive Processes, 12,* 765-805.

Plaut, D. C., & McClelland, J. L. (1993). Generalization with componential attractors: Word and nonword reading in an attractor network. In *Proceedings of the Fifteenth Annual Conference of the Cognitive Science Society* (pp. 824-829). Hillsdale, NJ: Lawrence Erlbaum.

Plaut, D. C., McClelland, J. L., Seidenberg, M. S., & Patterson, K. E. (1996). Understanding normal and impaired word reading: Computational principles in quasi-regular domains. *Psychological Review, 103,* 56-115.

Plaut, D. C., & Shallice, T. (1993). Deep dyslexia: A case study of connectionist neuropsychology. *Cognitive Neuropsychology, 10,* 377-500.

Plunkett, K., & Marchman, V. (1991). U-shaped learning and frequency effects in a multi-layered perceptron: Implications for child language acquisition. *Cognition, 38,* 43-102.

Plunkett, K., & Marchman, V. (1993). From rote learning to system building: Aquiring verb morphology in children and connectionists. *Cognition, 48,* 21-69.

Pollack, J. B. (1988). Recursive auto-associative memory: Devising compositional distributed representations. In *Proceedings of the Tenth Annual Conference of the Cognitive Science Society* (pp. 33-39). Hillsdale, NJ: Lawrence Erlbaum.

Pollack, J. B. (1990). Recursive distributed representations. *Artificial Intelligence, 46,* 77-105.

Prasada, S., & Pinker, S. (1993). Generalisation of regular and irregular morphological patterns. *Language and Cognitive Processes, 8*, 1–56.

Rastle, K., & Coltheart, M. (1998). Whammies and double whammies: The effect of length on nonword reading. *Psychonomic Bulletin & Review, 5*, 277–282.

Redington, M., & Chater, N. (1998). Connectionist and statistical approaches to language acquisition: A distributional perspective. *Language and Cognitive Processes, 13*, 129–191.

Redington, M., Chater, N., & Finch, S. (1993). Distributional information and the acquisition of linguistic categories: A statistical approach. In *Proceedings of the Fifteenth Annual Conference of the Cognitive Science Society* (pp. 848–853). Hillsdale, NJ: Lawrence Erlbaum.

Redington, M., Chater, N., & Finch, S. (1998). Distributional information: A powerful cue for acquiring syntactic categories. *Cognitive Science, 22*, 425–469.

Reilly, R. G. (1984). A connectionist model of some aspects of anaphor resolution. In *Proceedings of the Tenth International Conference on Computational Linguistics*. Stanford, CA.

Rosenblatt, F. (1962). *Principles of neurodynamics*. New York: Spartan Books.

Rumelhart, D. E., Hinton, G. E., & Williams, R. J. (1986). Learning internal representations by error propagation. In D. E. Rumelhart & J. L. McClelland (Eds.), *Parallel distributed processing: Explorations in the microstructure of cognition*. Vol. 1: *Foundations* (pp. 318–362). Cambridge, MA: MIT Press.

Rumelhart, D. E., & McClelland, J. L. (1982). An interactive activation model of context effects in letter perception: Part 2. The contextual enhancement effects and some tests and enhancements of the model. *Psychological Review, 89*, 60–94.

Rumelhart, D. E., & McClelland, J. L. (1986a). On learning of past tenses of English verbs. In J. L. McClelland & D. E. Rumelhart (Eds.), *Parallel distributed processing: Explorations in the microstructure of cognition*. Vol. 2: *Psychological and biological models* (pp. 216–271). Cambridge, MA: MIT Press.

Rumelhart, D. E., & McClelland, J. L. (Eds.) (1986b). *Parallel distributed processing: Explorations in the microstructure of cognition*. Vol. 1: *Foundations*. Cambridge, MA: MIT Press.

Rumelhart, D. E., & McClelland, J. L. (1987). Learning the past tenses of English verbs: Implicit rules or parallel distributed processing? In B. MacWhinney (Ed.), *Mechanisms of language acquisition* (pp.195–248). Hillsdale, NJ: Lawrence Erlbaum.

Salmela, P., Lehtokangas, M., & Saarinen, J. (1999). Neural network based digit recognition system for voice dialing in noisy environments. *Information Sciences, 121*, 171–199.

Samuel, A. G. (1996). Does lexical information influence the perceptual restoration of phonemes? *Journal of Experimental Psychology: General, 125*, 28–51.

Samuel, A. G. (1997). Lexical activation produces potent phonemic percepts. *Cognitive Psychology, 32*, 97–127.

Seidenberg, M. S. (1992). Connectionism without tears. In S. Davis (Ed.), *Connectionism: Advances in theory and practice* (pp. 84–122). Oxford: Oxford University Press.

Seidenberg, M. S. (1994). Language and connectionism: The developing interface. *Cognition, 50*, 385–401.

Seidenberg, M. S., & McClelland, J. L. (1989). A distributed, developmental model of word recognition and naming. *Psychological Review, 96*, 523–568.

Seidenberg, M. S., & McClelland, J. L. (1990). More words but still no lexicon: Reply to Besner et al. (1990). *Psychological Review, 97*, 447–452.

Seidenberg, M. S., & Plaut, D. C. (1998). Evaluating word-reading models at the item level: Matching the grain of theory and data. *Psychological Science, 9*, 234–237.

Seidenberg, M. S., Waters, G. S., Barnes, M. A., & Tanenhaus, M. K. (1984). When does irregular spelling or pronunciation influence word recognition? *Journal of Verbal Learning and Verbal Behavior, 23*, 383–404.

Sejnowski, T. J. (1986). Open questions about computation in the cerebral cortex. In J. L. McClelland & D. E. Rumelhart (Eds.), *Parallel distributed processing: Explorations in the microstructure of cognition.* Vol. 2: *Psychological and biological models* (pp. 372–389). Cambridge, MA: MIT Press.

Sejnowski, T. J., & Rosenberg, C. R. (1987). Parallel networks that learn to pronounce English text. *Complex Systems, 1*, 145–168.

Selman, B., & Hirst, G. (1985). A rule-based connectionist parsing system. In *Proceedings of the Seventh Annual Conference of the Cognitive Science Society* (pp. 212–221). Hillsdale, NJ: Lawrence Erlbaum.

Share, D. L. (1995). Phonological recoding and self-teaching: *Sine qua non* of reading acquisition. *Cognition, 55*, 151–218.

Small, S. L., Cottrell, G. W., & Shastri, L. (1982). Towards connectionist parsing. In *Proceedings of the National Conference on Artificial Intelligence.* Pittsburgh, PA.

Smolensky, P. (1988). On the proper treatment of connectionism. *Behavioral and Brain Sciences, 11*, 1–23.

Smolensky, P. (1990). Tensor product variable binding and the representation of symbolic structures in connectionist systems. *Artificial Intelligence, 46*, 159–216.

Sopena, J. M. (1991). *ERSP: A distributed connectionist parser that uses embedded sequences to represent structure* (Tech. Rep. No. UB-PB-1-91). Departament de Psicologia Bàsica, Universitat de Barcelona, Spain.

Spieler, D. H., & Balota, D. A. (1997). Bringing computational models of word recognition down to the item level. *Psychological Science, 8*, 411–416.

Stemberger, J. P. (1985). An interactive activation model of language production. In W. W. Ellis (Ed.), *Progress in the psychology of language* (Vol. 1, pp. 143–186). Hillsdale, NJ: Lawrence Erlbaum.

St. John, M. F., & McClelland, J. L. (1990). Learning and applying contextual constraints in sentence comprehension. *Artificial Intelligence, 46*, 217–257.

Stolcke, A. (1991). Syntactic category formation with vector space grammars. In *Proceedings from the Thirteenth Annual Conference of the Cognitive Science Society* (pp. 908–912). Hillsdale, NJ: Lawrence Erlbaum.

Tabor, W., Juliano, C., & Tanenhaus, M. K. (1997). Parsing in a dynamical system: An attractor-based account of the interaction of lexical and structural constraints in sentence processing. *Language and Cognitive Processes, 12*, 211–271.

Taraban, R., & McClelland, J. L. (1987). Conspiracy effects in word recognition. *Journal of Memory and Language, 26*, 608–631.

Turing, A. M. (1936). On computable numbers, with an application to the *Entscheidungsproblem*. *Proceedings of the London Mathematical Society, Series 2, 42*, 230–265.

Waltz, D. L., & Pollack, J. B. (1985). Massively parallel parsing: A strongly interactive model of natural language interpretation. *Cognitive Science, 9*, 51–74.

Weckerly, J., & Elman, J. L. (1992). A PDP approach to processing center-embedded sentences. In *Proceedings of the Fourteenth Annual Conference of the Cognitive Science Society* (pp. 414–419). Hillsdale, NJ: Lawrence Erlbaum.

Weekes, B. S. (1997). Differential effects of number of letters on word and nonword latency. *Quarterly Journal of Experimental Psychology, 50A*, 439–456.

Werbos, P. J. (1974). *Beyond regression: New tools for prediction and analysis in the behavioral sciences*. Unpublished doctoral dissertation, Harvard University, Cambridge, MA.

Wickelgren, W. A. (1969). Context-sensitive coding, associative memory, and serial order in (speech) behavior. *Psychological Review, 76*, 1–15.

Williams, R. J., & Peng, J. (1990). An efficient gradient-based algorithm for on-line training of recurrent network trajectories. *Neural Computation, 2*, 490–501.

Zorzi, M. (2000). Serial processing in reading aloud: No challenge for a parallel model. *Journal of Experimental Psychology: Human Perception and Performance, 26*, 129–136.

Zorzi, M., Houghton, G., & Butterworth, B. (1998a). The development of spelling–sound relationships in a model of phonological reading. *Language and Cognitive Processes, 13*, 337–371.

Zorzi, M., Houghton, G., & Butterworth, B. (1998b). Two routes or one in reading aloud? A connectionist dual-process model. *Journal of Experimental Psychology: Human Perception and Performance, 24*, 1131–1161.

3

Simulating Parallel Activation in Spoken Word Recognition

M. Gareth Gaskell and
William D. Marslen-Wilson

Several recent models of lexical processing assume that cognitive processing can be treated as dynamic settling activity, where activations of nodes in a network represent relevant perceptual and lexical information (Kawamoto, 1993; Masson, 1995; Plaut & Shallice, 1993). In these models there is no single node representing a single lexical item; instead, word "activations" must be assessed with respect to the pattern of activation across all nodes. In visual word recognition, for example, the input to the network would consist of orthographic features representing the visual input, and the task of the network would be to settle into a stable state across phonological, semantic, and orthographic nodes (Masson, 1995).

Learning new mappings in these models corresponds to altering the network weights to form stable attractor states, and various psycholinguistic measures can be compared to the time the network takes to fall into a particular activation state. For models of this type, therefore, the final state of the network is only part of the story. The manner in which processing takes place, the intermediate states, and the time (in processing cycles) taken to reach the target state are central to the account (e.g., Kawamoto, Farrar, & Kello, 1994).

Our research on speech perception is closely allied to this approach to cognitive modeling. For speech perception the focus is even more strongly on the course of processing events, rather than just the end point. This emphasis is forced by the nature of the stimulus. The speech signal is spread across time, transient, highly variable, and lacks reliable cues to word boundaries. This combination of properties makes states of ambiguity normal rather than exceptional, and necessitates a perceptual system capable of continuous reappraisal of the speech signal, based on partial information.

This sequential processing environment leads to the potential parallel activation of multiple lexical candidates as the speech is heard. Explicitly or implicitly, word recognition involves a process of whittling down of potential candidates (the word-initial cohort) as more sensory input is encountered. Where there is insufficient information to reduce this set to one, there is evidence suggesting that some or all of the meanings of the remaining candidates are activated (Marslen-Wilson, 1987; Zwitserlood, 1989).

The connectionist models we have mentioned treat ambiguity by activating a "blend" of the relevant distributed representations (Smolensky, 1986). Because each word representation involves setting an activation level for every representational node, multiple representations cannot be activated without interference. The resulting activation pattern is a weighted average of the relevant constituents, which may bear some similarity to each of those patterns, depending on various factors. The apparently inescapable interference between distributed word representations contrasts with some localist models, where each lexical item is represented by the activation of an independent node (Morton, 1969; Marslen-Wilson & Welsh, 1978). The contrast between local and distributed models of coactivation becomes crucial in the case of speech perception, where states of transient ambiguity form a dominant part of the perceptual process.

This chapter explores the ability of distributed connectionist networks to accommodate parallel activation through blending. We take as a starting point the basic properties of our network model of speech perception—the distributed cohort model (Gaskell & Marslen-Wilson, 1997b)—and describe simulations that quantify the model's predictions with respect to parallel activation. To allow precise exploration of many variables, these simulations dispense with connectionist networks and use idealized statistical analyses based on randomly generated or corpus-derived vector populations. These analyses evaluate the effects of parameters like sparseness on the capacity to activate distributed representations in parallel. They then explore the effects of employing more realistic representations, which encode phonological and semantic similarities between words.

The analyses show that standard distributed network models of cognitive processes are generally poor at supporting the parallel activation of multiple word representations. However, later simulations show that the degree of coactivation depends critically on the organization of the representational space, such that dimensions in phonological space are substantially more suitable for accommodating multiple cohort competitors than semantic dimensions. The final analyses simulate experiments specifically designed to test the predictions of the distributed cohort model. The simulations successfully model the behavioral disparity between good coactivation of phonological representations and poor coactivation of semantic representations during the perception of a word.

A DISTRIBUTED MODEL OF SPEECH PERCEPTION

Our research builds on other models of speech perception and word recognition, such as Cohort (Marslen-Wilson & Welsh, 1978; Marslen-Wilson, 1987), TRACE (McClelland & Elman, 1986), and SHORTLIST (Norris, 1994). These are essentially localist, logogen-type models (Morton, 1969), in which the goodness of fit between each word candidate and the incoming speech is represented by a separate activation value. Gaskell and Marslen-Wilson (1997b) examined the effects of implementing lexical access in a distributed system in which lexical phonological information is an output of the system along with semantic information. We trained a simple recurrent network (Elman, 1991) to map from a stream of phonetic features onto distributed representations encompassing the meaning and phonological form of words (see Figure 3.1). Such a model can be thought of as localist at a featural level if consistent meanings are assigned to the individual node values making up the word representation. Alternatively, the lexical representations may be context sensitive "all the way down" (Clark, 1993), with no fixed meanings attached to node values. Either way, the critical issue is that the model contains no equivalent of the word nodes found in localist models such as TRACE or SHORTLIST, and so is distributed at the word level.

Lexical access in this model is interpreted as a trajectory through a high-dimensional space, with the position at any time defined by the activations of the output nodes (the activation of each node corresponds to a position along a separate dimension in the space). Lexical items are represented by relatively stable points and can be thought of as the desired endpoints for the trajectory. As speech information enters the network, the activation of matching words is reflected by constructing a blend of their representations. When a word onset is presented, the network outputs a blend of the representations of all words matching that onset. As more speech comes in, this blend is refined to represent the reduced set of words that still match the speech. This refinement continues until just one word matches the input. At this point (the uniqueness point [UP]) the network can isolate the full distributed representation of the remaining word.

A number of points about this method of modeling speech perception are worth noting. Other models have taken a more serial and hierarchical approach to the representation of different types of information. For example, TRACE (McClelland & Elman, 1986) employs an initial featural level of representation that feeds into a phoneme level followed by a localist word

Figure 3.1
The Gaskell and Marslen-Wilson (1997b) Distributed Connectionist Model of Speech Perception

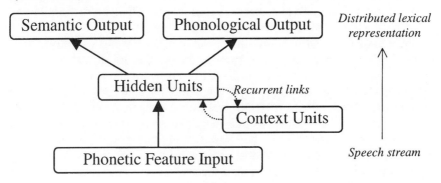

level, which, in a fuller model, would presumably map onto one or more levels incorporating lexical information such as word meaning (see Christiansen & Chater, Chapter 2, this volume, for further discussion). The distributed cohort model maintains a less hierarchical structure, in which a representation of speech is mapped directly onto lexical representations of form and meaning without undergoing a preliminary stage of categorial labelling as phonemes or similar units.[1]

An advantage of this approach is that it preserves subphonemic detail throughout lexical access rather than integrating information into larger sublexical units (Andruski, Blumstein, & Burton, 1994). This property allowed us to simulate data from lexical and phonetic decision experiments (Marslen-Wilson and Warren, 1994), which specifically addressed the nature of the input to lexical analysis and argued that featural information was not integrated prelexically to form phonemic labels.

The location of phonological nodes alongside semantic nodes also allows lexical representations of phonological information to be abstract and dissociated from the acoustics of speech while retaining the sensitivity of the semantic mapping to fine-grained information. This makes the system intolerant of even minor random deviations in the form of words while accommodating major phonological changes, provided they occur as the result of regular variation in connected speech. This view of lexical phonology is supported by experiments on the perception of phonological changes caused by assimilation of place of articulation in English (Gaskell & Marslen-Wilson, 1996, 1998). We have shown previously, using network simulations, that the perceptual system develops elements of both representational abstraction and contextual sensitivity through exposure to normal variability in the surface form of speech (Gaskell, Hare, & Marslen-Wilson, 1995).

A final aspect of the current model is its probabilistic nature. Recent experimental and computational research has demonstrated the value of statistical and distributional information in both the development of language abilities and the adult system (Brent & Cartwright, 1996; Cairns, Shillcock, Chater, & Levy, 1997; Saffran, Aslin, & Newport, 1996). The use of a simple recurrent network allows the model to pick up statistical information during training and to reflect conditional probabilities during states of ambiguity (for example, before a word's UP). The network learns to bias its output during states of ambiguity toward more frequent word candidates (Gaskell & Marslen-Wilson,1997b), reflecting the greater number of training instances involving those words. Indeed, both interactive activation and recurrent network models can be classed as imperfect ways of implementing a purer probabilistic model that bases word "activations" on conditional probabilities derived from previous experience.

BLENDING AND PARALLEL ACTIVATION

The remainder of this chapter focuses on one prominent aspect of the model: its ability to simulate parallel activation during word recognition. The strongest evidence for parallel activation comes from priming studies using ambiguous speech stimuli (Marslen-Wilson, 1987; Zwitserlood, 1989). Zwitserlood showed that a spoken word fragment (e.g., /kæpt/ spliced out of the word *captain*) would facilitate timed lexical decisions to visually presented words associated with two potential continuations (e.g., *ship* related to *captain, guard* related to *captive*). It seems aspects of both words' meanings are accessed while speech remains ambiguous and that these facilitate related target words. When faced with transient ambiguity, the perceptual system does not wait until speech is uniquely identifiable before accessing lexical semantic information. Other experiments have showed similar priming patterns under a variety of conditions (Marslen-Wilson, 1990; Zwitserlood & Schriefers, 1995).

Localist models easily accommodate this property. These models use the activation metaphor to indicate the status of the recognition process. The degree of match between each word and the incoming speech is reflected in the word's activation value. Localist models can therefore accommodate parallel activation simply by increasing the activation of the relevant word nodes. This means that coactivation can occur without cost in terms of reduced activation, because of the independence of word representations. Regardless of the number of lexical matches to a speech fragment, the nodes representing each lexical item can be independently fully activated (e.g., Marslen-Wilson & Welsh, 1978). However, this property is not obligatory in localist models. TRACE (McClelland & Elman, 1986) and SHORTLIST (Norris, 1994) use inhibitory links between word nodes to implement direct competition between word candidates. Nonetheless, all localist models offer a simple mechanism for representing the coactivation of word representations during lexical access. Indeed, given the importance of parallel activation in speech perception, it is unsurprising that localist activation-based models dominate current theorizing.

In the distributed cohort model, activations are encoded implicitly in the similarity between the network output and each word's distributed representation. In terms of the multidimensional state space through which the network output plots a trajectory, the activation of any word's lexical representation depends on the proximity of that representation to the output of the network. If the output of the network is near to a point representing some word, then that word is said to be activated.

Our simulations investigate this correspondence between distance in the distributed model and localist activations. There are clear differences between the systems; localist models can potentially coactivate multiple word representations simultaneously without cost, whereas distributed systems in general cannot (i.e., the output of the network cannot be identical to two different distributed word representations).[2] We explore how properties of the representational space, like sparseness, affect the capacity of a distributed system to support coactivation. The aim is to determine whether distributed models provide a plausible alternative to localist models, and to generate a set of predictions from the distributed cohort model, that can then be tested experimentally.

MONTE CARLO SIMULATIONS

Our discussion of the distributed cohort model stated explicitly and precisely how it operates in circumstances of ambiguity, when there is insufficient information in the speech signal to isolate a single matching candidate. The network outputs a blend of the distributed representations of the relevant words. This blend is weighted according to the frequency of the matching candidates. To pursue the *captain–captive* example, if the speech input is /kΘπτI/ and *captain* occurred twice as often as *captive* in the network's training corpus, then twice as many weight adjustments will have biased the network toward the lexical representation of *captain* than *captive*.

Because the network's behavior can be characterized at this abstract level, actually running network simulations to address parallel activation would only add noise. Instead, we use techniques similar to signal-detection analyses (Green & Swets, 1966) to investigate parallel activation based on Monte Carlo simulations with randomly generated vectors. We generate two vector sets with prespecified properties. These represent a "snapshot" of the recognition process at some point during the perception of a word. One, the "cohort" set, represents the matching word candidates for some speech input, with each vector being a hypothetical distributed representation of a single matching word. The second, "mismatch" set represents all words mismatching the current input. Word recognition can be thought of in terms of setting up a large cohort set based on little or no speech information and then gradually transferring word representations from the cohort to the mis match set as more speech is processed. When enough of the speech waveform is available to uniquely identify a word, the cohort set contains one word representation (the identified word) and the mismatch set contains all other lexical items.

Given these two sets, we can then calculate a blend vector—the arithmetic mean of all cohort vectors (weighted according to frequency). This is the idealized output of the network model given the current state of ambiguity. Thus, if the network has learned that its current input could be any of the words in the cohort set, it will produce a blend of all the cohort vectors. We can then examine this blend and ask how well it represents those cohort words. For example, is it more similar to the cohort than to the mismatch set? To address this question we look at the distributed equivalent of localist activation: distance in lexical space. We can calculate the distance (using an appropriate metric, such as root-mean squared [RMS] distance) between the blend and each vector in the cohort and mismatch sets. In localist logogentype models an effective model will activate all cohort words above the mismatch words. In the distributed model an effective blend vector should be nearer the vectors in the cohort set than the vectors in the mismatch set. In signal-detection terms the issue is whether the cohort and mismatch sets are separable along the dimension of distance from the lexical blend. We can therefore measure the system's effectiveness by examining the degree of separation between different cohort and mismatch populations.

Cohort Size

The first simulation illustrates this procedure by demonstrating the effect of cohort size on coactivation through blending. In later simulations we will examine the influence of realistic clustering of words in lexical space. However, in this simulation the "lexical representation" of each word was simply a randomly chosen 200-component binary vector, with each component having a 50-percent chance of being set to 1 or 0. The size of the cohort set was varied to simulate different stages of word recognition, when different numbers of lexical items match the speech input. We chose cohort sets consisting of one, two, four, eight, sixteen, thirty-two, and sixty-four items to illustrate the behavior of the model. To control for the differing extent of random variation between cohort sets of different sizes, the results were based in each case on sixty-four values (i.e., for the sets of size one, sixty-four analyses were carried out and the results averaged; for the set of size sixty-four, only one analysis was carried out). In each analysis a blend vector was calculated by taking the mean over all cohort vectors (in this simulation, without frequency weighting). The RMS distance from this blend vector was then calculated for all cohort vectors.

It is important to relate the distance of these lexical blends from cohort representations to the overall population of distances. An effective blend representation of the cohort set should not only be near the cohort vectors; it should also be relatively far from the mismatch vectors. We also examined the distances between each blend and a set of vectors representing mismatching words in the network's mental lexicon. These were 3,000 vectors generated randomly using the same procedure as for the cohort vectors. The data are plotted with decreasing cohort set size along the x-axis, illustrating the reduction of the cohort set during the perception of a spoken word (see Figure 3.2).

When there are many cohort patterns the signal and noise are merged and the blends are uninformative. At word onset, when the speech signal is highly ambiguous, the model predicts that it will be impossible to decide on the basis of proximity which of the words the blend is intended to represent. However, when the cohort set size is reduced, lexical blends become much closer to their constituent cohort vectors and further from the mismatch vectors. For example, when the blend is based on two cohort patterns the

Figure 3.2
The Effect of Varying Cohort Set Size on the Distance between the Cohort Blend and the Cohort and Mismatch Populations

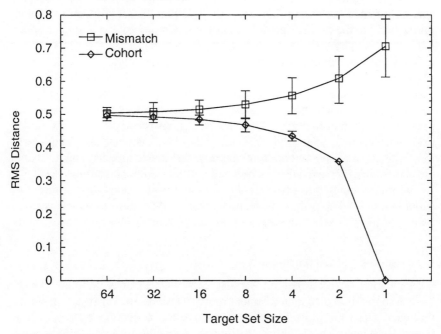

For each population, the mean, maximum, and minimum distances are marked, with cohort set size plotted on a reversed log scale.

RMS distance between these patterns and the blend is 0.36, comfortably closer than the nearest mismatch word.

Clearly, modeling parallel activation in this way imposes a limit on the number of words that can be informatively activated in parallel. If too many distributed patterns are blended together they interfere strongly and there is a good chance of some spurious pattern falling closer to the blend than some cohort patterns. This behavior is a basic statistical property of sampling: The greater the sample size, the better the estimate of population mean. For our purposes the population mean is the least informative blend state, because it is likely to be equally close to vectors representing cohort and mismatch set members. Hinton and Shallice (1991) show that a blend of two vectors in this type of system is as close to those vectors as any other vector (if not closer). For blends of more words this does not hold: It becomes possible (and even probable) that other vectors will fall closer to the blend than some cohort vectors.

This result confirms that a distributed system cannot match the ability of localist models to represent the activation of multiple word candidates early in the processing of a speech stimulus. When representations are localist, these candidates can be simultaneously activated without any danger of confusing the active candidates with the inactive ones. The situation for distributed models is more complicated. The simulation does not imply that distributed networks will fail to resolve widespread ambiguity, but it shows that the activations of lexical nodes may not fully dissociate words that currently match the speech input from words that do not. In localist terms, this is like having a noisy model that early on in processing activates some noncohort members more than some cohort members.

In conclusion, parallel activation of fully distributed representations is possible, but only to a limited degree. This places restrictions on the kinds of experimental results that a distributed model could accommodate. Existing research showing coactivation of lexical representations does not tell us whether parallel activation of multiple lexical representations is complete or only partial (Marslen-Wilson, 1987, 1990; Zwitserlood, 1989; Zwitserlood & Schriefers, 1995). This is an important question, because distributed models cannot accommodate complete coactivation of competing lexical representations.

The initial simulation provides a basic picture of coactivation in the distributed model. The following sections explore the extent to which various lexical properties affect the capacity of the system to support coactivation.

Sparseness and Dimensionality

Many models (e.g., Hinton & Shallice, 1991; Plaut & Shallice, 1993) have assumed that distributed lexical representations are "sparse," meaning that each word's representation will involve the activation of only a few nodes. This factor seems bound to affect the capacity for coactivation—after all, the localist position, which is ideally suited to parallel activation, occupies one end of the sparseness continuum. The representations examined so far, in which 50 percent of all components were randomly set to 1, lie at the other end of this continuum.

We examined the effect of varying sparseness for cohort and mismatch sets consisting of fifty vectors each. These vectors were generated randomly, with a fixed probability of any component being set to 1 within any simulation. However, this probability varied across simulations from 1 percent to 50 percent in units of 1 percent. A second independent variable was the dimensionality of the space (i.e., the number of components in the vectors), which was set to 100, 200, 400, 800, or 1,600. For each combination of sparseness and dimensionality, cohort and mismatch sets were generated and their distances from the blend vector calculated. The separability of the two distributions is summarized using the t-statistic. A high t-value indicates that the blend vector is generally closer to the cohort vectors than to the mismatch vectors. However, even a very high t-value does not imply that the two distributions are fully separate, since their tails may still overlap to some extent.[3] Results are plotted for both RMS and cosine distances (see Figure 3.3). The cosine measure was included because it was expected to be more sensitive than RMS distance for the sparse measures.

The overall effect of increasing dimensionality is clear and unsurprising. The higher dimensional spaces provide a better basis for separating cohort and mismatch sets using either distance measure. In order to discriminate between cohort words (the "active" words) and the mismatch set (all other words in the mental lexicon), the cohort members must be nearer the blend in the lexical space than the mismatch words. If there are few dimensions then the lexical space will be relatively crowded and there is a good chance of at least one mismatch item being sufficiently close to a lexical blend to cause interference. As the number of dimensions rises, this likelihood diminishes and the capability of the lexical system to accommodate multiple representations increases.

The effect of sparseness and its interaction with dimensionality is more complex. Looking first at the results using RMS distance, there is a strong effect of sparseness on the separability of the cohort and mismatch sets. The distributed representation of multiple lexical items deteriorates as sparseness increases (toward the left of the graph). For very sparse representations the separability of the sets becomes so low that the two sets are indistinguishable, in that the t-value is not significantly higher than would be expected by chance. Localist representations are excluded because the t-value for such a system without noise is infinite. Even allowing for some noise, there is a big difference between the results for a localist system and a sparse system in terms of representational capacity.

The results for the same simulation using the cosine metric are in certain respects quite different. For low dimensionalities the effect of sparseness is

Figure 3.3
The Effect of Sparseness and Dimensionality on the Separability of Target and Competitor Populations Using Either RMS Distance (left-hand graph) or Cosine Distance (right-hand graph)

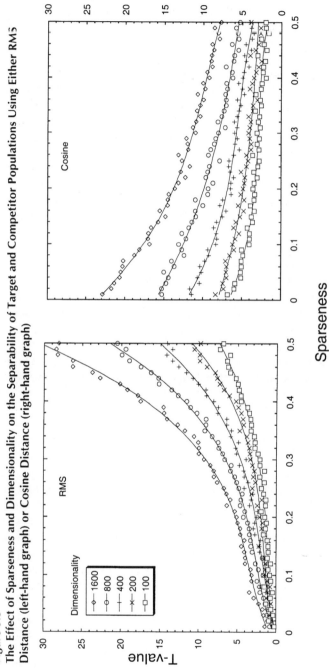

In all cases, the t-statistic for the target and competitor distances from the blend vector is the dependent variable. The curves are the cubic best-fit lines for each level of dimensionality.

small, with sparser representations producing more separable cohort and mismatch sets. However, for high-dimensional spaces the advantage of sparse representations is clear, with t-values close to the peaks reached using the least sparse representations and RMS distance.

The pattern of results using RMS distance can be explained using an extension of the dimensionality argument. Generally, increasing sparseness in a distributed representation deepens the problem of coactivation, despite the fact that the sparser representations seem more similar to a localist representation. Sparse representations are problematic because they place a restriction on the positions in lexical space that words can occupy. This is like reducing dimensionality, which also reduces the capacity of the system. However, the very extreme of sparseness—the localist system—is crucially different. It restricts the lexical space but also guarantees that each word is orthogonal to and equidistant from every other word. This compartmentalizes the space, meaning that a blend of any number of words will always be closer to those words than to all others.

To see why the cosine measure works better for sparse representations, we need to look in more detail at how the distances are calculated. In a sparse system, word representations consist of a few 1s and many 0s. The blend vector will therefore consist of some 0s and some near-0 components (the result of averaging a few 1s and lots of 0s). The advantage of cohort vectors over mismatch representations is that the components set to 1 in a cohort vector are guaranteed to be non-0 in the blend vector, whereas the corresponding components in a mismatch vector will be non-0 in some cases and 0 in others. This advantage is greater in the cosine measure, because it doesn't matter that the value of the blend component is far less than the value of the cohort component in these cases; only the angle of the two vectors is calculated. This advantage is small when calculating RMS (or any other Minkowski) distance because a small non-0 value is only slightly closer to the target value than 0, and the small advantage is obscured by noise.

But what do these mathematical diversions tell us about the focus of our research, the coactivation of word representations in a distributed system? Increasing the dimensionality of the representational space clearly reduces the problems of coactivation, but it is difficult to determine where the human system lies along this continuum. It may be best to think of dimensionality as a measure of richness or degrees of freedom in lexical representations. Each way of distinguishing between two words adds an extra dimension to the representation and more obliquely increases the capacity of the system to coactivate multiple lexical entries.

Perhaps then the solution is to ensure that lexical representations are rich. However, there may be quite separate constraints operating that restrict the dimensionality of these representations. Landauer and Dumais (1997) proposed a method for determining the optimal dimensionality of distributed word representations. They examined the extent to which dimensionality reduction of matrices based on word cooccurrence statistics affected the similarity structure of the resulting word representations. They found a peak in performance at roughly 300 dimensions, with fewer or more dimensions merely serving to obscure the similarity structure of many words. If their characterization of word learning is more generally applicable, this would impose a relatively low upper limit on coactivation, at least at a semantic level.

Turning to the evaluation of sparseness, we find that sparser representations are better served by the cosine measure, whereas less sparse representations are better served by the RMS measure. It is unclear which of these is most relevant to the mechanics of activation in distributed systems. RMS distance is more obviously comparable to the process of changing node activations, because the actual deviation on each node is considered in the calculation of distance, whereas only the angle between two vectors is relevant to the cosine measure.

Leaving these differences aside, the system that performed best in terms of ease of separation of cohort and mismatch sets was in fact the least sparse system, which gave a t-value of over 28 for the largest space, using RMS distance. This argues against any attempt to improve the ability of a distributed system to coactivate words by making representations sparser or near-localist. Any reduction in the overlap between word representations comes at a cost of increased interference between coactive representations.

ENCODING STRUCTURE IN LEXICAL SPACE

Semantic Structure

So far we have assumed a random distribution of word representations in lexical space. However, many researchers assume that distributed mental representations support some kind of similarity structure or "semantic metric" (Clark, 1993), such that items with similar "meanings" have similar representations. The distributed cohort model assumes that lexical representations reflect similarities and differences between words in terms of phonology and word meaning. Each provides structure, which shapes the lexical space and may affect the blending of representations as speech is perceived.

First, we will address the effects of semantic structure on coactivation of distributed representations. Many connectionist models have built semantic structure into representations by selecting a set of simple features that words can be rated on (e.g., *does X have legs?*), resulting in a binary vector for each word. However, the choice of features, whether hand picked by the experimenter (Plaut & Shallice, 1993) or selected by a panel of subjects (McRae, de Sa, & Seidenberg, 1997), is largely arbitrary, and makes it difficult to assess how well they reflect true lexical organization. A rapidly growing body of research has focused on the proposal that semantic similarity can be captured using cooccurrence statistics drawn from large language corpora (Burgess & Lund, 1997; Landauer & Dumais, 1997). This relies on the assumption that words with similar meanings will occur in similar contexts, and has the advantage of automatically generating large sets of distributed representations, which are proving to correlate well with experimental psycholinguistic data on semantic representation.

For these reasons, we analyzed the effects of semantic organization on coactivation using an automatically generated set of cooccurrence vectors taken from Lund, Burgess, and Atchley (1995). There were 2,779 word representations, with components ranging in value from 0 to 645. Each value signified the number of times the represented word occurred in the context of another specified word in their corpus. The 200 dimensions accounting for the most variation were selected, with distances in this space normalized for comparison with the binary spaces. On the assumption that cohort members are semantically unrelated (i.e., excluding morphological relatives and words like *glisten* and *glimmer* that have common semantic features), the cohort word representations were selected randomly from this set, with all other vectors representing mismatching words. The control condition used a random space of 200 binary dimensions, with each component having a 50-percent chance of being set to 1. As in the initial simulation, we varied the size of the cohort set between one and sixty-four, with all other vectors used for the mismatch set. However, in this simulation we defined the separability of the cohort and mismatch sets as the difference between the mean cohort distance and the minimum mismatch distance from the blend. This gives a simple measure of the representational effectiveness of the blend, and unlike t-values is informative when the cohort set size is small. A high separability value implies that the two populations are separable on the basis of distance from the blend vector and indicates that the system is adequately representing the cohort patterns in parallel. A separability value of zero or less indicates that the two populations are intermixed and that the system is working less well.

We expected the structured representations to differ from the random controls in two ways. First, we assumed they would reflect semantic similarities between words. Second, the dimensions were more continuous compared to the binary vectors examined so far. To tease apart these two factors, a third analysis used a binary form of the cooccurrence vectors, in which each component was set to either 1 or 0 depending on whether it was above or below the mean value across all words.[4]

Figure 3.4 displays the effects of coactivation as the size of the cohort set is reduced. Both forms of structured vectors suffer more from coactivation than the random vectors. The zero crossing for the random vectors is at roughly sixteen patterns, whereas for the binary structured vectors it is under four, and for the continuous structured system it is below two. Thus, for the latter system there is a fair chance of a blend of even two vectors falling closer to some other word than to the constituents of the blend.

Figure 3.4
Effect of Semantic Clustering on Separability for Three Models of Semantic Representation

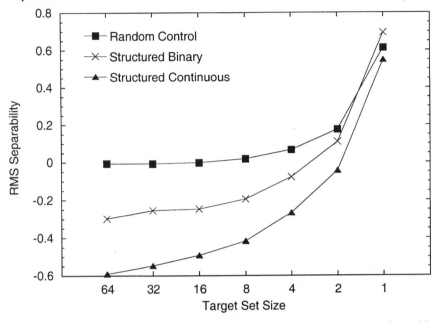

The separability scores for the continuous space are normalized to facilitate comparison with the other distances.

The more realistic space creates problems distinguishing signal from noise because groups of words form tight clusters in the space. Representations of food words, for example, may be similar to each other but very different from all other representations. When one of these is blended with the representation of an unrelated word there is a good chance that another word in the cluster will be as close or closer to the blend than the cohort member. In terms of using proximity to separate cohort and mismatch populations, semantic clustering causes problems. However, in some cases the important question is not whether cohort and mismatch populations are discriminable. Instead, one might ask whether there is any useful semantic information encoded in the blend. This is the case in semantic priming, where the target activation is compared to a single (usually representative) member of the mismatch set. We return to this issue in the final simulation.

The nonbinary form of the structured representation fares even worse, because there are no restrictions on the positions that word representations can occupy in the space. In particular, words may occupy positions near the middle of the space, which is where the blends, being arithmetic means, tend to sit. The partitioning of the binary spaces into blend states near the center and single word representations at the "corners" of the space (cf. Anderson & Mozer, 1981; Plaut, 1997) can be useful, because it provides a simple, explicit metric for determining the state of the recognition process without having an external decision mechanism requiring information about which states in the space correspond to words.

Phonological Structure

The previous simulation indicated that adding realistic clustering generally worsens the problem of activating distributed representations simultaneously. However, there is one case where realistic clustering lessens this problem. For speech perception, this is the case where lexical dimensions reflect similarities in the phonological form of words, as in the distributed cohort model (see Figure 3.1). This is because the phonological representations of words that must be activated in parallel (i.e., cohort members) are guaranteed to be more similar to each other than to unrelated words. Along the dimensions that encode the similarities, the blend will match the cohort representations exactly but will mismatch other words. This gives the cohort set a head start in terms of overall distance to the blend in lexical space, and decreases the chances of noncohort members falling close to the blend vector.

This leads to strong predictions about the effects of coactivation in different subsections of lexical space. We assume that during the course of hearing a spoken word a blend of the matching lexical representations is built up and continuously modified based on the uptake of new information. This blending process will take place across both semantic and phonological nodes, with coactivation on phonological nodes generally more coherent than on semantic nodes (because of the phonological similarities between the coactivated words).

These effects of coactivation in different areas of lexical space can be teased apart by examining the facilitation of different types of target words in cross-modal priming experiments. We assume that priming in a distributed model of lexical processing depends on the similarity between the relevant words' representations (cf. Burgess & Lund, 1997; Masson, 1995; Plaut, 1995). A prime word will facilitate recognition of a target word to the extent that its lexical representation is more similar to the target representation than an unrelated baseline. In effect, the prime representation enjoys a proximity advantage over the control representation. In repetition priming, the target lexical representation is related to the prime representation in all dimensions, so recognition of the target can take advantage of overlap on both semantic and phonological nodes (for a prime stimulus consisting of a word fragment, the coherence on phonological nodes will be particularly useful in the recognition of the target word). In contrast, semantic priming relies on overlap on the semantic nodes alone, so any coherence built up on the phonological nodes is unable to facilitate responses.

Experimental Data

We will demonstrate the effects of coherence on coactivation in phonological and semantic lexical space by simulating a set of experiments designed specifically to test the predictions of our model and developed in parallel with the modeling work. The experiments (see Gaskell & Marslen-Wilson, 1997a, 1999, for a fuller description) were a development of previous research on parallel activation, using cross-modal priming to measure the activation level of lexical items as the speech signal is heard (Zwitserlood & Schriefers, 1995). We used bisyllabic auditory prime words, which were presented either complete (e.g., *captain*, pronounced /kæptɪn/) or in two splice conditions. At Splice 1 (see Table 3.1) the final vowel and consonant(s) were removed (e.g., /kæpt/), and at Splice 2 just final consonant(s) was spliced out (e.g., /kæptɪ/). These fragmented primes were intended to generate different levels of competition or ambiguity in the perceptual system, reflecting the different numbers and frequencies of words that transiently match the speech input during the course of spoken word recognition. Competitor environment was also manipulated by choosing prime words with varying sizes of cohort sets and varying uniqueness points. These are referred to in Table 3.1 as the Early UP and Late UP conditions. In the Early UP conditions the prime words became uniquely discriminable from other cohort members by Splice 2. In the Late UP conditions the primes became unique at the ends of the words.

These manipulations of prime fragment length and competitor environment were intended to create sets of word fragments that varied widely in the number and frequency of the matching lexical items. To more formally assess the degree of ambiguity, we calculated a conditional probability value for each prime stimulus. This was the CELEX database frequency (Baayen, Piepenbrock, & van Rijn, 1993) of the complete prime word, divided by the summed frequencies of all morphologically unrelated words matching the stimulus in terms of phonemic representation. The result is an estimate of the probability of the given prime stimulus turning out to be the complete prime rather than some other member of the same cohort. A value of 1 on this scale implies that the prime stimulus unambiguously matches a single lexical item, whereas a value close to 0 implies either many cohort competitors or a few high-frequency competitors. Table 3.1 includes the mean probability estimates for each prime condition.

To measure the effects of these variations in competitor environment at different splice points, a related visual target was presented immediately at prime offset. Activation of the lexical representation of the complete prime word was assessed by measuring the speed of response to the target compared to the response time to the same target when preceded by an unrelated control prime. The standard assumption here is that the degree to which recognition of the target is speeded by the related prime (compared to the

Table 3.1
Priming Experiments: Design, Stimuli, and Results (conditional probability measures are given for each prime condition, followed by the mean priming effects [control-test] for the repetition priming and semantic priming experiments)

	Early UP			Late UP		
	Splice1	Splice2	Complete	Splice1	Splice2	Complete
Test Prime	"garm"	"garme"	"garment"	"capt"	"captai"	"captain"
Control Prime	"chis"	"chise"	"chisel"	"mount"	"mountai"	"mountain"
Conditional Probability	0.75	0.95	1.00	0.24	0.44	1.00
Repetition Priming (ms)	35**	78**	92**	36**	47**	64**
Semantic Priming (ms)	12(*)	28*	22**	3	10(*)	15*

Note: The priming values are marked according to their statistical significance based on the least significant F-ratio of the items and participants analyses.

** $p < .01$; * $p < .05$; (*) $p < .1$.

control condition) reflects the degree to which the prime's lexical representation has been activated. Crucially, the experiments used two types of prime–target relationships, as described later.

According to our model, the response of the perceptual system to these prime stimuli is to generate a frequency-weighted lexical blend made up of the distributed representations of the phonological form and meanings of all matching words. We predicted that because of the greater coherence between the cohort members' phonological representations, coactivation would operate more effectively on the phonological nodes than the semantic nodes. We tested this across experiments by using two types of visual targets expected to be sensitive to overlap of different types of lexical information. In the repetition priming experiment the target was the orthographic form of the complete prime word (e.g., CAPTAIN). We assumed this target would access the same modality-independent lexical representation as the complete prime, so that the preactivation of the full target lexical entry (semantic and phonological) by the prime would facilitate responses to the target. Where the prime was fragmented, the facilitation would depend on how similar the resultant lexical blend was to the target representation, both phonologically and semantically. The fact that phonological information was shared between prime and target in this case meant that the effects of increasing competition (or ambiguity) on priming should be weak, because of the coherence of the coactive words' phonological representations.

In the semantic priming experiments the target was related to the prime in meaning, but not in form (e.g., *captain*–COMMANDER).[5] In this case the state of the lexical blend in terms of the phonological representation generated should not affect target recognition, since it is unrelated to the prime word in terms of form. Instead, the only basis for priming is semantic, which we have argued does not provide a sound basis for parallel activation of many cohort members. We expected that the effects of competition on priming in this experiment would be severe, because highly ambiguous prime tokens would create an uninformative blend at the semantic level, which would fail to facilitate target recognition.

To summarize, the experiments aimed to examine coactivation and blending of lexical representations across the whole distributed vector (using repetition priming) and across the semantic vector alone (using semantic priming). Facilitation in the semantic priming experiments (the response-time advantage when the target is preceded by the related prime as opposed to the unrelated control) should be weaker and more prone to competition effects than in the repetition priming experiment.

The results of the three experiments were analyzed in two ways. First, analyses of variance were carried out based on the factors of competitor environment (Early–Late Uniqueness) and prime fragment length (Splice 1, Splice 2, Complete; see Table 3.1 for condition means). For the repetition priming experiment the facilitatory effect of the related primes was robust for all combinations of UP and prime fragment length, but the amount of priming in each case was affected by both prime fragment length and competitor environment. Longer primes with fewer competitors produced the largest priming effects. Facilitatory effects in the semantic priming analyses were far smaller, and were marginal or nonsignificant for the conditions containing the most ambiguous primes (the late separation stimuli at the first two splice points and the early separation stimuli at the first splice point). Competition effects were evident in the significant effect of competitor environment on priming.

The second form of analysis examined the overall linear correlations in each experiment between the degree of ambiguity associated with each individual test prime and the amount of facilitation found (see Figure 3.5). We will focus on these analyses, as they are more closely comparable to the simulations reported here.

Comparing the linear plots for each experiment, the most obvious result is that repetition priming effects were much larger than semantic priming effects. This is predicted by almost any model of lexical access, and is relatively unimportant. The critical issue is the effect of ambiguity or competition on the basic priming effect. Does increasing the ambiguity of the stimulus gradually eliminate priming, or does some residual priming remain? To examine this question we looked at the y-axis crossovers. Here we found a significant dissociation between the two types of priming. In the semantic experiments, facilitation dropped to zero as the conditional prob-

Figure 3.5
Summary of the Gaskell and Marslen-Wilson (1999) Results

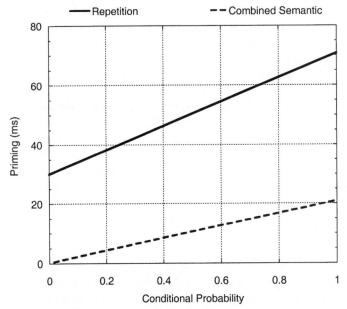

The lines plot the correlation between the conditional probability attached to each prime stimulus and the amount of facilitation (unrelated RT minus related RT) for repetition (solid line) and semantic (dashed line) priming. The plot of the semantic priming data combines the results from two experiments.

ability dropped to zero. Using the combined semantic priming data, there was a significant correlation between conditional probability and facilitation and no significant constant factor in the regression equation for these variables. It seems that semantic priming directly reflects conditional probabilities. The degree to which any prime-facilitated recognition of a semantically related word was proportional to the probability of the stimulus actually being that prime word, based only on the speech information contained in the fragment.

The competition effect for the repetition stimuli was different. As before, there was a significant correlation between conditional probability and facilitation, but there was also a significant constant in the regression equation. This is evidence of weaker competition, in that the facilitation did not drop to zero with conditional probability. In states of strong competition or high ambiguity (toward the left side of the graph) there was nonetheless some facilitation of the target word. We argue that this support comes from the coherence of the cohort members' phonological representations, which provides a basis for their coactivation, facilitating the activation of the target word.

Simulation

The pattern of experimental results broadly agrees with the predictions of the distributed cohort model. Here we model these findings in detail, using blending rather than connectionist simulations to provide a clearer analysis of the fit between theory and data. The procedure for this simulation is slightly different from the preceding ones. Previously we have used large sets of "mismatch" vectors as our baseline for examining the effectiveness of coactivation. Here we simulate the experimental situation, where a related prime is compared to a control prime in the extent to which it facilitates recognition of a single target word. For this reason we compared a single target to two blends, representing the lexical activation caused by hearing either the related prime or the unrelated control. If the related prime blend is closer to the target position than the unrelated control, priming should occur (cf. Plaut, 1995; Burgess & Lund, 1997). To perform this simulation accurately we need plausible semantic and phonological representations of all words relevant to the experiment (i.e., forty-two test primes, forty-two control primes, and forty-two semantic targets, as well as 697 cohort competitors of the primes, selected from CELEX to match the phonemic representation of at least one fragmented test prime).

Word meaning was again represented by vectors taken from corpus analyses of cooccurrence data, this time extracted from the British National Corpus of speech (Levy, Bullinaria, & Patel, 1997).[6] The vectors were generated from two large cooccurrence matrices, created by calculating the proportion of times the words of interest occurred in the context of the 4,100 most frequent words in the corpus. For one matrix, cooccurrences were counted using a window of two words to the left of the target word. For the second matrix, cooccurrences were counted in a window of two words to the right of the target word. The fifty-five columns that accounted for the greatest variation between the rows representing the experimental stimuli were chosen, resulting in a fifty-five-component vector for each word. The values of the components were all between 0 and 1 and were generally close to 0.

Capturing the phonology of the stimuli required a representation that encoded similarities between words of widely varying length. The representation we chose consisted simply of a component for each phoneme in the English language, with the value of each component for any particular word being the number of occurrences of the associated phoneme in that word. An additional component encoded the number of syllable boundaries within the word, bringing the total number of components to fifty-five, matching the dimensionality of the semantic representation. The representation of the word *connectionist* (/kʌnɛkʃʌnɪst/) using this system would have values of 3 on the syllable boundary node (four syllables, so three boundaries), 2 on the /k/, /n/, and /ʌ/ nodes, 1 on the /ɛ/, /ʃ/, /ɪ/, /s/, and /t/ nodes, and 0 elsewhere. This simple representation is not optimal, because it does not capture order information and so cannot distinguish between pairs like *cat* and *act*. Nonetheless, as a rough measure of similarity between words of varying length it works well.

To check the suitability of the semantic vectors, we calculated the mean RMS distances from the target representation to the related and unrelated prime representations. Within each triplet the target representation was generally closer to the related than the unrelated prime representation (this was the case for seventy-five out of eighty-four triplets). The differences were small, but nonetheless significant (mean distance from related prime = .010, mean distance from unrelated prime = .019; difference = .009; $t = 9.5, p < .001$). Thus, the cooccurrence vectors correctly predict that semantic priming should occur, based on a lexical proximity model of priming. The experimental data by comparison are noisier: Of the eighty-four mean response-time difference scores, only fifty-seven had positive facilitation values.[7]

We then conducted two blending simulations, one using only the semantic vectors (semantic priming) and one using the combined semantic and phonological vectors (repetition priming). Our assumption was that semantic priming would depend only on the activation of the semantic nodes, because both test and control primes are phonologically unrelated to the target. On the other hand, repetition priming can make use of overlap of the full lexical representations on both semantic and phonological nodes. In each simulation, three vectors were constructed for each related prime word. One was simply the relevant part of the vector for that word (the full vector for repetition priming or the semantic part only for semantic priming). This vector represented the idealized output of the network after presentation of the complete prime word. The other two vectors were blends, representing the state of the network at earlier points, when less of the speech had been presented and the identity of the prime word was ambiguous. These were frequency-weighted blends of all the word representations that matched the particular fragments used in the experiment. For example, if the prime stimulus was /wɪkɪ/—a fragment of *wicket* that also matches *wicked*—the blend would be the mean of the two vectors for *wicked* and *wicket*, weighted according to relative frequency. This vector corresponds to the expected output of the model at the point where the second /ɪ/ of /wɪkɪ/ is presented as input.

The vectors for the control words were calculated using exactly the same procedure, but with vectors that were unrelated to the target word. We then calculated the distances between all prime vectors and the target vector. For the repetition priming simulation the target vector was the full vector representing the prime word (e.g., the vector for *captain*), whereas for the semantic priming simulation it was the vector representing only the meaning of the semantically related target word (e.g., the vector for *commander*). The difference between the test and control prime distances yielded a proximity advantage for each related test item. These results are summarized in Figure 3.6 in terms of the correlation between this distance and the frequency-weighted competition measure for each item.

Looking first at the results for the full semantic and phonological space (see Figure 3.6, left-hand graph), we find both a significant correlation ($r = .87$, $p < .001$) and a significant constant in the regression analysis ($t = 19.3$, $p < .001$). The proximity advantage is linearly related to the conditional probability, but does not diminish to zero as ambiguity increases. Instead, there is a residual advantage, due to the coherence between the phonological representations of the target word and its higher-frequency competitors. This pattern of results is similar to the repetition priming results from our experiments.

When the same simulation was carried out using semantic vectors alone, and with semantically related target words (see Figure 3.6, right-hand graph), we again found a positive correlation between the conditional probability of the prime stimulus and the simulated priming effect ($r = .34$; $p < .001$). Related prime fragments that were less ambiguous showed a greater proximity advantage to the target. The simulation also shows that the proximity advantage diminishes to zero as the conditional probability drops to zero (in a regression analysis, the constant factor was not significant; $t = .82, p = .41$). This again replicates the experimental findings.

Because the correlation in the semantic priming was weaker, there is a possibility that the greater level of noise in this simulation was obscuring the presence of a constant factor in the regression analysis. This was one of the reasons for running multiple semantic priming experiments behaviorally. To test this theoretically, nine replications of the semantic priming simulation were carried out, with the same set of semantic vectors but a random assignation of vectors to control primes (i.e., the representations of the test primes were unchanged, but the control representations were randomly chosen each time). The analysis of the average results across the ten simulations showed a strengthened correlation ($r = .55, p < .001$), but still not a hint of a residual constant in the regression analysis ($t = 1.1, p = 0.27$).[8]

We have assumed that repetition priming is based on full overlap between prime and target along all dimensions. However, a further simulation showed that much the same pattern of results emerges if repetition priming only makes use of overlap along lexical phonological dimensions. Again, there was a significant correlation and a significant constant in the regression analysis.

One further point is worth noting about these data. A potential discrepancy between experimental results and the simulation involves the comparison of absolute distance between experiments. The proximity differences in the repetition simulation are a full order of magnitude greater than the differences in the semantic simulation. This is largely because the semantic vectors contain very small numbers. The actual values of the components are probabilities of cooccurrence, and so are often 0 and seldom higher than

Figure 3.6
Correlation between the Conditional Probability Associated with Each Stimulus and Proximity Advantage for the Repetition (left-hand graph) and Semantic (right-hand graph) Priming Simulations

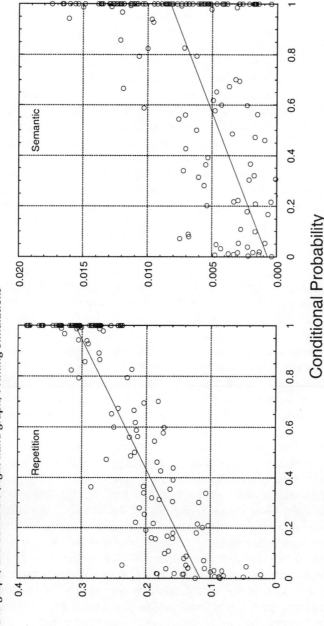

The circles mark individual data points and the lines illustrate the linear best fit. In order to focus on the best-fit lines, the y-axis limits are chosen to exclude a small proportion of the data points (mostly from the bottom of the semantic priming graph).

0.01, meaning that the word representations were all near the origin in the representational space. In contrast, the components of the phonemic vectors had a greater proportion of 1s, with occasionally 2s or 3s. We could easily scale up the semantic vectors or change the dimensionality to reduce the difference between these spaces, but this would simply be a post hoc data-fitting exercise.

A more valid comparison looks at percentage priming: What proportion of the control–target distance does the proximity advantage comprise? If we examine the best-fit lines in this way, we find at least a rough correspondence. The percentage proximity advantage for the semantic simulation rises from 5 to 45 percent as the conditional probability goes from 0 to 1. Along the same continuum, the repetition simulation rises from 40 to 100 percent. Therefore, the maximum semantic priming is about 1.1 times the minimum repetition priming (0.7 in the experiments) and about half the maximum repetition priming (0.3 in the experiments). However, the fact that the prime–target relationship was varied between experiments with different subjects makes it difficult to get a good comparison of priming magnitudes.

To summarize, we have demonstrated the importance of phonological coherence in the distributed model. This provides a sound basis for coactivation of cohort members, allowing partial activation of many different words on the phonological nodes. The differences between coactivation for semantically distributed and phonologically organized representations allow us to simulate the priming results of Gaskell and Marslen-Wilson (1999) in some detail and provide an insight into the reduced competition effect found using repetition priming.

The qualitative correspondence between the model and the experimental data supports the proposal that overlap along distributed lexical dimensions provides a basis for modeling priming (cf. Burgess & Lund, 1997; Lund, Burgess, & Atchley, 1995). In both repetition and semantic priming, overlap between prime and target along the relevant dimensions can explain the pattern of priming. This is unlike the standard model of priming, particularly in the case of repetition priming, where the prime is assumed to preactivate a localist representation of the target word. However, we should stress that these results do not rule out the localist representation of word nodes. One possibility is that a localist word level exists below the semantic level, with semantic priming dependent on activations at a semantic level and repetition priming dependent on activations at the word level. Such a model would still need to explain the weakness of competition effects in repetition priming, but a suitable combination of activation-, inhibition-, and resting-level parameters could possibly be found. An alternative is that the localist word level resides below the distributed semantic and phonological level that we are proposing, but does not take part in semantic or repetition priming. This would shift the focus of competition effects from a localist word level to the domain of lexical content.

DISCUSSION

This chapter has addressed a critical test case, not only for our model of speech perception, but for distributed models of language processing in general. Ambiguity is present in many areas of cognition, but speech perception involves a particularly protracted state of ambiguity, when many different words are transiently compatible with the sensory evidence. We have looked at how distributed systems cope with this widespread ambiguity, and at the consequences in terms of activation of lexical information.

There is quite a strict limit on the number of distributed patterns that can be usefully represented by a single blend. In general, more than a handful of representations results in a noisy blend, for which simple distance in lexical space does not properly distinguish the components of the blend (the word-initial cohort) from their competitors. This means that distributed networks do not simply reimplement localist, activation-based systems such as the Cohort (Marslen-Wilson, 1987) or logogen (Morton, 1969) models.

Various structural factors affect the capacity for representation of multiple lexical items. It correlates positively with the dimensionality or degrees of freedom in the lexical space, implying that the capacity for coactivation of lexical representations will be somewhat greater if a high-dimensional space is used. However, this positive effect of increasing dimensionality may have to be balanced against the potential for high-dimensional spaces to become noisy in their representation of similarity (Landauer & Dumais, 1997). The sparseness of lexical representations has a more complex effect, but even quite sparse representations do not increase the capacity to accommodate multiple distributed representations, despite their surface similarity to localist representations.

To us, the most interesting result of our simulations is the finding that the organization of lexical representations in the multidimensional space has powerful effects on the capacity of the system for coactivation. With no external constraints on the organization of the space, linearly independent distributed patterns can be chosen that behave as a localist system (Smolensky, 1986). However, if the structure of the space is required to reflect similarities and differences between words in terms of what we know about them, then this luxury cannot be afforded. Instead, the degree of coherence between the distributed representations becomes all-important. Competition in this type of model is interpreted in terms of activation of lexical content, rather than interaction between abstract word identifiers.

We have characterized speech perception as a mapping onto distributed semantic and phonological representations, although other forms of knowledge may also be activated. What is important in terms of coactivation is the degree of regularity involved in the mapping from the speech wave onto lexical knowledge. The mapping onto meaning is usually arbitrary, so words that are required to be activated in parallel will have incompatible semantic

representations, causing strong competition between the distributed semantic representations. On the other hand, lexical phonology has a far more
regular relationship with the surface form of speech, providing coherence
between the phonological representations of cohort members and supporting a weaker form of competition on the phonological nodes. These novel
predictions receive detailed support from cross-modal priming experiments
(Gaskell & Marslen-Wilson, 1997a, 1999), showing the predicted dissociation between effects of competitor environment on repetition and semantic
priming.

FURTHER READINGS

The classic interactive activation model of spoken word recognition is
TRACE (McClelland & Elman, 1986). The SHORTLIST model (Norris,
1994; see also Norris, McQueen, Cutler, & Butterfield, 1997) incorporates
a lexical competition network similar to TRACE, but uses only bottom-up
processing. Our distributed model is described more fully in Gaskell &
Marslen-Wilson (1997b).

In terms of the experimental data we have addressed, Zwitserlood (1989)
provides some of the clearest evidence for parallel activation during speech
perception in her cross-modal priming study, and the priming studies we simulated are reported in detail in Gaskell and Marslen-Wilson (1997a, 1999).

The semantic representations employed in this research were derived from
corpus analyses. For an introduction to the use of corpus analyses to derive
useful multidimensional representations, see Landauer and Dumais (1997)
or Burgess and Lund (1997). These are examples of a broader statistical
approach to psycholinguistic modeling also developed by many other researchers (e.g., Cairns et al., 1997), and to some extent derived from the
work of Elman (e.g., Elman, 1990).

NOTES

Part of the research was carried out while the authors were at Birkbeck College,
London (supported by a U.K. MRC grant awarded to William Marslen-Wilson and
Lorraine Tyler), and part while the first author was at the Cognition and Brain
Sciences Unit in Cambridge. This article is based in part on a paper presented at the
Eighteenth Annual Cognitive Science Society Conference in San Diego, California.

We thank Curt Burgess, Kevin Lund, Joe Levy, and John Bullinaria for providing
corpus-based vectors, and members of the Centre for Speech and Language for
valuable discussion and comments. Thanks are due also to Morten Christiansen,
Nick Chater, and two anonymous reviewers for their comments.

1. The use of phonological features as input in the current implementation of the
model reflects the demands of computational tractability, rather than a theoretical
claim about the format in which speech input is input to the lexical system.

2. Note that distributed representations can behave exactly like localist ones in combination, as long as they are unbounded and linearly independent (Smolensky, 1986). Thus, a network may be able to develop distributed representations that are ideally suited for the purposes of parallel activation. However, the case we consider here is one in which distributed representations are constrained by other factors (such as encoding semantic and phonological similarity) and will generally not be linearly independent.

3. In a small number of cases (for some of the 800- and 1,600-dimensional spaces with high sparseness values and using the RMS measure) the cohort and mismatch set distances did not overlap. However, this state of affairs would be unlikely if the mismatch set was of a more realistic size (e.g., 50,000 rather than 50 words).

4. This method of binarizing the vectors is not particularly sensitive to the similarity structure of the representations. Less clumsy techniques exist (Clouse & Cottrell, 1996), but these also increase the dimensionality of the space, introducing a confounding factor.

5. Two semantic priming experiments were conducted, varying the delay between the offset of the prime and the onset of the target. An associative priming experiment was also carried out for Gaskell & Marslen-Wilson (1999), finding a similar pattern of priming. Here we report the combined results of the two semantic priming experiments.

6. The corpus analyses were carried out by John Bullinaria and Joe Levy. We thank them for making their results available to us.

7. Levy et al. (1997) used our semantic priming experiments as one of their yardsticks for a systematic analysis of various parameters involved in corpus analyses, such as window size and type. They found that a range of different windows provided similar degrees of priming, but that certain distance measures were more effective than others (Hellinger distance was the most effective). However, to maintain compatibility with earlier simulations, we continue to use RMS distance here.

8. For each individual simulation there was a significant correlation between proximity advantage and condition probability (ranging from 0.28 to 0.39). For one of the nine replications the constant factor in the regression analysis reached significance at the 5-percent level ($t = 2.07, p = .039$), while the remaining t-values were less than one. One out of ten tests reaching the 5-percent significance level is much as one would expect by chance.

REFERENCES

Anderson, J. A., & Mozer, M. C. (1981). Categorization and selective neurons. In G. Hinton & J. Anderson (Eds.), *Parallel models of associative memory* (pp. 213–236). Hillsdale, NJ: Lawrence Erlbaum.

Andruski, J. E., Blumstein, S. E., & Burton, M. (1994). The effect of subphonetic differences on lexical access. *Cognition, 52*, 163–187.

Baayen, R. H., Piepenbrock, R., & van Rijn, H. (1993). *The CELEX lexical database [CD-ROM]*. Philadelphia: Linguistic Data Consortium, University of Pennsylvania.

Brent, M. R., & Cartwright, T. A. (1996). Distributional regularity and phonotactic constraints are useful for segmentation. *Cognition, 61*, 93–125.

Burgess, C., & Lund, K. (1997). Modelling parsing constraints with high-dimensional context space. *Language and Cognitive Processes, 12*, 177–210.

Cairns, P., Shillcock, R. C., Chater, N., & Levy, J. (1997). Bootstrapping word boundaries: A bottom-up corpus-based approach to speech segmentation. *Cognitive Psychology, 33*, 111–153.

Clark, A. (1993). *Associative engines: Connectionism, context and representational change*. Cambridge, MA: MIT Press.

Clouse, D. S., & Cottrell, G. W. (1996). Discrete multi-dimensional scaling. In *Proceedings of the Eighteenth Annual Conference of the Cognitive Science Society* (pp. 284–289). Mahwah, NJ: Lawrence Erlbaum.

Elman, J. L. (1990). Finding structure in time. *Cognitive Science, 14*, 179–211.

Elman, J. L. (1991). Distributed representations, simple recurrent networks, and grammatical structure. *Machine Learning, 7*, 195–225.

Gaskell, M. G., Hare, M., & Marslen-Wilson, W. D. (1995). A connectionist model of phonological representation in speech perception. *Cognitive Science, 19*, 407–439.

Gaskell, M. G., & Marslen-Wilson, W. D. (1996). Phonological variation and inference in lexical access. *Journal of Experimental Psychology: Human Perception and Performance, 22*, 144–158.

Gaskell, M. G., & Marslen-Wilson, W. D. (1997a). Discriminating local and distributed models of competition in spoken word recognition. *Proceedings of the Nineteenth Annual Conference of the Cognitive Science Society* (pp. 247–252). Mahwah, NJ: Lawrence Erlbaum.

Gaskell, M. G., & Marslen-Wilson, W. D. (1997b). Integrating form and meaning: A distributed model of speech perception. *Language and Cognitive Processes, 12*, 613–656.

Gaskell, M. G., & Marslen-Wilson, W. D. (1998). Mechanisms of phonological inference in speech perception. *Journal of Experimental Psychology: Human Perception and Performance, 24*, 380–396.

Gaskell, M. G., & Marslen-Wilson, W. D. (1999). *Representation and competition in the processing of spoken words*. Manuscript submitted for publication.

Green, D. M., & Swets, J. A. (1966). *Signal detection theory and psychophysics*. New York: Wiley.

Hinton, G. E., & Shallice, T. (1991). Lesioning an attractor network: Investigations of acquired dyslexia. *Psychological Review, 98*, 74–95.

Kawamoto, A. H. (1993). Nonlinear dynamics in the resolution of lexical ambiguity: A parallel distributed processing account. *Journal of Memory and Language, 32*, 474–516.

Kawamoto, A. H., Farrar, W. T., & Kello, C. (1994). When two meanings are better than one: Modeling the ambiguity advantage using a recurrent distributed network. *Journal of Experimental Psychology: Human Perception and Performance, 20*, 1233–1247.

Landauer, T. K., & Dumais, S. T. (1997). A solution to Plato's problem: The latent semantic analysis theory of acquisition, induction, and representation of knowledge. *Psychological Review, 104*, 211–240.

Levy, J. P., Bullinaria, J. A., & Patel, M. (1997, July). *The evaluation of the use of co-occurrence statistics*. Paper presented at the First International Conference on Computational Psycholinguistics, University of California at Berkeley.

Lund, K., Burgess, C., & Atchley, R. A. (1995). Semantic and associative priming in high-dimensional semantic space. *Proceedings of the Seventeenth Annual Conference of the Cognitive Science Society* (pp. 660–665). Mahwah, NJ: Lawrence Erlbaum.

Marslen-Wilson, W. D. (1987). Functional parallelism in spoken word recognition. *Cognition, 25,* 71–102.

Marslen-Wilson, W. D. (1990). Activation, competition, and frequency in lexical access. In G.T.M. Altmann (Ed.), *Cognitive models of speech processing: Psycholinguistic and computational perspectives* (pp. 148–172). Cambridge, MA: MIT Press.

Marslen-Wilson, W. D., & Warren, P. (1994). Levels of representation and process in lexical access: Words, phonemes, and features. *Psychological Review, 101,* 653–675.

Marslen-Wilson, W. D., & Welsh, A. (1978). Processing interactions and lexical access during word recognition in continuous speech. *Cognitive Psychology, 10,* 29–63.

Masson, M.E.J. (1995). A distributed memory model of semantic priming. *Journal of Experimental Psychology: Learning, Memory and Cognition, 21,* 3–23.

McClelland, J. L., & Elman, J. L. (1986). The TRACE model of speech perception. *Cognitive Psychology, 18,* 1–86.

McRae, K., de Sa, V., & Seidenberg, M. (1997). On the nature and scope of featural representations of word meaning. *Journal of Experimental Psychology: General, 126,* 99–130.

Morton, J. (1969). The interaction of information in word recognition. *Psychological Review, 76,* 165–178.

Norris, D. G. (1994). Shortlist: A connectionist model of continuous speech recognition. *Cognition, 52,* 189–234.

Norris, D. G., McQueen, J. M., Cutler, A., & Butterfield, S. (1997). The possible-word constraint in the segmentation of continuous speech. *Cognitive Psychology, 34,* 191–243.

Plaut, D. C. (1995). Semantic and associative priming in a distributed attractor network. *Proceedings of the Seventeenth Annual Conference of the Cognitive Science Society* (pp. 37–42). Mahwah, NJ: Lawrence Erlbaum.

Plaut, D. C. (1997). Structure and function in the lexical system: Insights from distributed models of word reading and lexical decision. *Language and Cognitive Processes, 12,* 765–805.

Plaut, D. C., & Shallice, T. (1993). Deep dyslexia: A case study of connectionist neuropsychology. *Cognitive Neuropsychology, 10,* 377–500.

Saffran, J. R., Aslin, R. N., & Newport, E. L. (1996). Statistical learning by 8-month old infants. *Science, 274,* 1926–1928.

Smolensky, P. (1986). Neural and conceptual interpretation of PDP models. In D. E. Rumelhart & J. L. McClelland (Eds.), *Parallel distributed processing: Explorations in the microstructure of cognition.* Vol. 2. *Psychological and biological models* (pp. 390–431). Cambridge, MA: MIT Press.

Zwitserlood, P. (1989). The locus of the effects of sentential-semantic context in spoken-word processing. *Cognition, 32,* 25–64.

Zwitserlood, P., & Schriefers, H. (1995). Effects of sensory information and processing time in spoken-word recognition. *Language and Cognitive Processes, 10,* 121–136.

4

A Connectionist Model of English Past-Tense and Plural Morphology

Kim Plunkett and Patrick Juola

The acquisition of past tense in English has long been studied as a general touchstone for the development of morphology and productive linguistic rules in children. The general pattern of past-tense formation for English is well understood; the overwhelming majority of English verbs have a simple past-tense form that can be described as the addition of one of three variants of the *-ed* suffix to a base stem. A significant minority, particularly of relatively common verbs, take a so-called "irregular" form, which may or may not be systematically related to the stem form or to the forms of other words. The developmental course is also well understood; children typically begin by correctly producing a small number of both regular and irregular forms, then produce characteristically "overregularized" forms for a small but significant fraction of their verb forms. They then appear to relearn the correct form, producing the classic U-shaped developmental profile (Berko, 1958; Ervin, 1964; Kuczaj, 1977; Marcus et al., 1992).

Interpretations and models of this phenomenon vary; Marcus et al. (1992) have suggested (see also Pinker & Prince, 1988, 1991; Marcus, Brinkmann, Clahsen, Wiese, & Pinker, 1995) that the emergence of the overregularized forms is indicative of the development of "a mental operation implementing the *-ed*-suffixation rule posited by grammarians" (p. 8). According to this theory, there are two routes to produce a past tense, either by reproduction of a memorized (irregular) form or by applying a general rule to any word form not recognized as being one of the forms in memory. Other researchers (Daugherty & Seidenberg, 1992; Rumelhart & McClelland, 1986; Plunkett & Marchman, 1991; MacWhinney & Leinbach, 1991) have argued instead that a single connectionist network is capable of producing appropriate patterns of behavior, and thus that a single associative route suffices to explain the evidence (see Christiansen & Chater, Chapter 2, this volume).

English noun plurals share many of the same characteristics as verb past tenses. There is a similar general rule describing most forms and a small, semiregular group of common exceptions. Brown (1973), Marcus (1995), and Marchman, Plunkett, and Goodman (1997) have described broadly similar time courses for the acquisition of plural nouns, including the U-shaped curve, and approximately similar overall rates of overregularization. Similarly, many of the same phonotactic features (such as voicing assimilation and/or epenthesis) are relevant to the acquisition of both noun and verb morphology. There are some crucial differences, however. The number of irregular noun types is nearly an order of magnitude smaller (about 20 irregular nouns versus about 150 irregular verbs), but they are individually more frequent. Nouns themselves are more frequent in running text, when measured in terms of either token or type frequency. Nouns are also less complex in the (irregular) inflections that they undergo. For example, all noun plurals share their onsets with the singular form (unlike the present–past pair *go–went*), and most irregular nouns involve a simple change in voicing of the final consonant from /f/ to /v/ (as in *thief–thieves*). By contrast, verbs participate in a wider variety of irregular paradigms and the corpora include some verbs that appear to bear no relationship to their inflected forms. There also are some subtle developmental psycholinguistic differences. For example, noun plurals are typically learned more quickly than verb past tenses (Brown, 1973; Marchman et al., 1997). Similarly, overregularization of noun plurals is likely to be observed earlier and more frequently in development than overregularization of past-tense forms (Marcus, 1995; Marchman et al., 1997).

These similarities and differences suggest that modeling the interactions between the acquisition of noun and verb morphology may also reveal important insights into the nature of the mechanisms underlying the cognitive architecture of these two inflectional processes. For instance, is it necessary to posit separate inflectional routes for regular nouns and regular verbs? Do irregular nouns and verbs inhabit the same associative memory system? How can the functional separation between irregular and regular forms be best explained?

A related question concerns the nature of the processing involved when the verb form itself is derived from a noun stem (as in denominal verbs). Kim, Pinker, Prince, and Prasada (1991) argue that denominal verbs are treated differently from identically sounding verb tokens in the inflectional process, suggesting that word meaning can be an important factor in inflection. On the other hand, evidence from slips of the tongue (Fromkin, 1973; Garrett, 1980) suggests that the process of inflection can occur independently of the intended sentence meaning (e.g., Fromkin's *days* /deIj + z/ *of the week* becomes *weeks* /wijk + s/ *of the day*, accommodating to the new location for the plural inflection). Garrett has even demonstrated a case where the irregularization process is automatic and the (incorrect) word token takes an irregular inflected form in place of a regular token (*I'd know one if I heard it* becoming *I'd hear one if I knew it*), suggesting that accommodation and irregularization are automatic and independent of meaning. This argues for a functional separation between the syntactic process of inflection and the semantic process of the meaning incorporated by the inflectional process, which occasionally separates, as in the errors already shown.

One obvious weakness of the dual-route model is its inability to generalize to multiple paradigms cleanly. A word may be irregular (and thus a memorized exception) with respect to one syntactic form but not others: *go* takes an irregular past tense, but its plural is the regular *goes* instead of **wents*. Some nouns derive their inflected denominal forms from the singular (e.g., *knife, to knife, knifed*), while others from the plural (e.g., *half, to halve, halved*). These variations cannot be explained without resorting to further rules and a detailed (and complex) theory of the timing of rule application. Similarly, dual-route models assume system-general rules to account for the processes of voicing assimilation and epenthesis in inflected forms. However, dual-route accounts offer no motivation as to why these rules should be identical for nouns and verbs. The single-route model has the potential to provide a natural explanation, in that noun and verb inflections are accommodated within the same system.

Here we present a single-system, feed-forward, connectionist model to compare the acquisition of noun and verb inflection head to head. To this end, we have constructed a model that simultaneously acquires noun plurals and verb past tenses. We use this model to determine the patterns of mastery (and errors) produced by a network that only has access to phonological representations of stems and their inflected forms, their type, and their token frequencies. We demonstrate that the patterns of performance in the network are comparable with acquisition data for young children.

In particular, the network exhibits a general advantage in acquiring noun morphology before verb morphology. Nevertheless, both regular and irregular nouns and verbs exhibit an early stage of error-free performance before overregularization errors occur. Although the onset of overregularization errors is earlier for nouns than verbs, errors in both categories are shown to be driven by critical-mass effects (Marchman & Bates, 1994; Plunkett & Marchman, 1993). The network model also predicts a developmental shift in the relative ease of learning irregular nouns and verbs. Early in development irregular nouns show an advantage, but this advantage shifts as training proceeds.

We also examine the network model's behavior on denominal verbs and deverbal nouns. Both categories show a strong tendency to be regularized by the network. In order to deal with denominal verbs that are homophonic with irregular verbs, we introduce a supplementary set of simulations in which the phonology-to-phonology network is augmented with semantic inputs, thereby offering the network the opportunity to inflect phonologically identical forms in different ways. Previous work has demonstrated that neural networks can be trained to produce homophonic phonological outputs given distinct semantic inputs (MacWhinney & Leinbach, 1991; Cottrell & Plunkett, 1994; Hare & Elman, 1995). Again, under these conditions the augmented network shows a strong tendency to regularize denominal verbs. These findings capture patterns of behavior reported elsewhere in the literature (Kim et al., 1991). Finally, we discuss the implications of these simulations for characterizing the cognitive machinery underlying past-tense and plural morphology.

METHOD

Modeling Assumptions

We model the acquisition of inflectional morphology as the process of converting a representation of the stem of a word (in this work, more specifically, a phonological representation of the sound of the uninflected form of a word) to a representation of the sound of an appropriately inflected form, such as a past tense or a plural. Our focus is on the time course of development for acquisition, using the standard metaphor that increasing training epochs corresponds roughly to the increasing age and experience of the child. The system is presented with input–output pairs (stems and their inflected forms) and is allowed to operate on its internal weight states to reduce the difference between the actual output (of the current weights) and the desired output.

In this system, the child's processing is viewed as a "hypothesis generator" that runs concurrently with the normal tasks of production and comprehension and can be functionally described as the child's attempt to systematize the preexisting representations of inflectional sets (such as stem–singular–plural or stem–present tense–past tense). We assume that the child already has some form of a mental lexicon, including (at a minimum) a representation of the phonology of a word, plus some concept of syntax and semantics describing the word's pattern of use. The child is continually taking in word tokens and comparing the words actually heard (e.g., *went*) to the tokens that the child's hypothesis generator would have expected to produce as inflected forms of a given stem; when they differ, this provides evidence to the child that the hypotheses are wrong and should be modified. The hypothesis generator comes into its own when the child produces words, as the generator describes the current best guess (to the child) of how words ought to be inflected, especially in the case of nonce words, for which the child has no semantics, little syntax, and no lexical entry.

Our model therefore hinges on some sort of a priori notion of "stem" available to the child (which is stable across different words), and a mental lexicon, which we assume also includes aspects of syntax and semantics that are not part of this modeling work. We assume further that the child is comfortable with different inflectional paradigms, and has the ability to analyze the sounds–phonemes of the language of interest correctly. We do not model the very earliest stages of language acquisition before these abilities are stably available to a child. Similarly, this work does not deal with the difficulties of correct analysis (determining whether or not a word is being used as a noun or a verb), or the difficulties of semantic acquisition.

Network Configuration

The connectionist simulations use a multilayer perceptron network employing back-propagation of error (Rumelhart, Hinton, & Williams, 1986). For every input pattern presented to the system during training, the system calculates its current best guess of the relevant output pattern, which is then compared to the actual desired output pattern. Error is allocated to the output and hidden units proportionally with the RMS error and then weight changes are propagated backward through the connecting layers. The simulation was built using the PlaNet simulator (Miyata, 1991), using 130 units for the input layer, 160 units for the output layer, and 200 units as the hidden layer. The system was trained with a learning rate (η) of 0.1 and no momentum ($\alpha = 0$). Weights were initially randomized in the range ± 0.5. Training was performed via a pattern-update schedule, where each pattern was presented individually to the network (in random order) and training performed on each pattern.

Training Corpus and Representation

The training data for the simulations were taken from the CELEX corpus (Baayan, Piepenbrock, & van Rijn, 1993); we extracted from this database all words that were monosyllabic, contained no "foreign" sounds in their pronunciation according to the Moby pronunciator database (Ward, 1997), and for which we had evidence that they could be used as nouns or verbs. This yielded a total corpus of 2,626 stems, which encompassed 3,226 total inflected word types (2,280 nouns and 946 verbs). Of these word types, 26 were irregular nouns and 122 were irregular verbs. For these words, we took the corresponding token frequencies (of the stems) from the Brown corpus (Kučera & Francis, 1967) as a rough measure of token frequencies in running speech. These token frequencies were also heavily dominated by nouns; for the 17,129 tokens in the training set, 13,045 were noun tokens (204 of them irregular), and 4,084 were verb tokens (997 of them irregular).

These numbers, although accurate, may justly be regarded with a certain degree of suspicion with regard to their appropriateness as a measure of a child's input, as the Brown corpus (from which the frequency data derives) is a sample not of children's (or child-directed) spontaneous speech, but of written, edited, adult-to-adult communication, such as novels, magazines, and newspapers. On the other hand, measuring only child-directed or child-initiated speech could also be misleading, as most children certainly listen to adult conversation (and even edited adult speech, e.g., on television). In the absence of accurate frequency counts of individual nouns and verbs for children, we have opted to use published frequency data. Further refinement of this work would employ frequency counts taken from computerized databases such as CHILDES (MacWhinney, 1991).

The training corpus was prepared by converting the Moby symbolic pronunciation (Ward, 1997) into a large binary vector using a modification of the PGPfone alphabet representation (Juola & Zimmermann, 1996), summarized in Table 4.1. Each phoneme was represented as a cluster of sixteen binary phonetic features, including aspects such as place, manner, and height of articulation, as described in Figure 4.1. Each word was divided into onset–nucleus–coda constituents and right-justified within a CCCVVCCC template (e.g., the word *cat* [/kAt/] would be represented by the training pattern ##k#A##t, and the word *ox* [/Aks/] by ####A#ks, where # represents an absent sound). To this 128-bit pattern, two additional bits were appended representing the syntactic form to be inflected into either the past tense (of a verb) or the plural (of a noun). The desired outputs were a similar encoding of the phonology of the inflected form, including an optional epenthetic vowel and final consonant. For instance, *cat* becomes *cats* (/kAts/), represented by ##k#A##t#s.

The token frequencies of words were individually tabulated as nouns and verbs, then the function $\log_2 (freq^2 + 1)$ was applied to these frequencies to flatten the distribution between the high- and low-frequency forms. This manipulation ensured the network would have sufficient opportunity to learn low-frequency irregular forms. The final variance was between one and twenty-one tokens–inflected type, meaning that the most frequent words appeared just over twenty times as often as the least. We also carried out a separate series of simulations in which a reduced frequency compression scheme was employed (a frequency variation of approximately 400 to 1 instead of 20 to 1). We report on the effect of this frequency compression manipulation later.

Simulations were run under two training schedules: mass training and incremental training. In mass training, all the stems and inflected forms are available to the network throughout the training process. In incremental training, training starts out with a small number of high-frequency words. The training set is then gradually expanded to include words of decreasing frequency until the entire corpus is absorbed. These two training schedules

Table 4.1
Binary Encoding Based on Moby Pronunciator

Phoneme code	rough pronunciation	binary vector
&	"a" in "dab"	0001001111000111
(	"a" in "air"	0010001011000111
@	"a" in "ado"	0010001111000011
A	"a" in "far"	0000001111000001
a	first half of "i" in "ice"	0001001111000001
b	"b" in "nab"	1110001000111111
C	"ch" in "ouch"	1110000000000011
D	"th" in "the"	1110001001001111
d	"d" in "pod"	1110001000000111
E	"e" in "red"	0010001111000111
e	first half of "a" in "day"	0011001111000111
f	"f" in "elf"	1110000001011111
g	"g" in "fig"	1110001000000001
h	"h" in "had"	1110000011000001
I	"i" in "hid"	0110001111000111
i	"e" in "see"	0111001111000111
J	"g" in "vegetable"	1110001000000011
j	"y" in "you"	0110001011000000
k	"c" in "act"	1110000000000001
l	"l" in "ail"	1110011011000111
m	"m" in "aim"	1110101000111111
N	"ng" in "bang"	1110101000000001
n	"n" in "and"	1110101000000111
O	"o" in "dog"	0010001111000001
o	first half of "o" in "boat"	0011001111000001
p	"p" in "imp"	1110000000111111
R	"u" in "burn"	0010001011000011
r	"r" in "ire"	1110001011000111
S	"sh" in "she"	1110000001000011
s	"s" in "sip"	1110000001000111
T	"th" in "bath"	1110000001001111
t	"t" in "tap"	1110000000000111
U	"oo" in "book"	0110001111000001
u	"oo" in "too"	0111001111000001
v	"v" in "average"	1110001001011111
w	"w" in "win"	0110001011000001
Z	"s" in "vision"	1110001001000011
z	"z" in "zoo"	1110001001000111
#	silence/vacant	0000000000000000

Figure 4.1
Composition of Binary Vector Representation

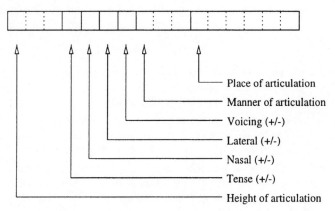

Place of articulation
Manner of articulation
Voicing (+/-)
Lateral (+/-)
Nasal (+/-)
Tense (+/-)
Height of articulation

Tenseness, nasality, laterality, and voicing are binary features, coded as either on or off; height, manner, and place are multivalued features and coded with a thermometer coding using a right-justified string of 1s.

are intended to capture the distinction between input (mass training) to the child and uptake (incremental training) by the child (Plunkett & Marchman, 1993). Incremental training is also designed to reflect the finding that highly frequent word forms are acquired early by children (Barrett, Harris, & Chasin, 1991; Huttenlocher, Haight, Bryk, Seltzer, & Lyons, 1991; Morrison, Chappell, & Ellis, 1997).

Analysis Techniques

All simulations were performed with five different random starting seeds to assess the consistency of the findings. Unless otherwise stated, all results reflect the mean over these five simulations. At the end of every epoch (which may contain over 17,000 individual pattern trials), the system was evaluated to determine what, and how much, had been learned. Every output pattern was examined to determine the nearest legal phoneme (using the RMS distance) in each template position and then compared with the "correct" sequence. It should be noted that this is not the only possible way of identifying phonemes; an alternative method, in which individual output units were thresholded to the closer of 0 or 1 was also used in some analyses, but did not appear to produce markedly different results; these analyses have thus been omitted for brevity and clarity.

Each output (type) from the network was analyzed as belonging to one of the following categories:

Correct. The network produced an inflected form identical to the training output for that form (*cat–cats*).

Regularized. The network produced an inflected form for a novel stem that was consonant with the "rules" for inflection (n.b., this is only applicable to novel forms such as nonce words or denominalized forms) (*wug–wugs*, pronounced /wugz/).

Overregularized. The network produced an inflected form for an irregular training item that was partially consonant with the rules as given (n.b., this is only applicable to irregular forms) (*take–taked* or *take–tooked*).

Irregularized. The network produced an inflected form similar to a known irregular form (n.b., this is applicable to both regular and irregular forms, as illustrated) (*think–thunk* [similar to *sink–sunk*] or *sight–sit* [similar to *light–lit*]).

Blend. The network produced an inflected form that shows evidence of partial irregularization as well as partial regularization (n.b., this is only applicable to regular forms, as otherwise these would be categorized as overregularized) (*towtewed* [similar to *throw–threw* + *-ed*]).

Wrongly Suffixed. The network affixed an incorrect suffix to an otherwise correctly inflected onset, nucleus, and coda (*cat–catZ*).

No Change. The network (incorrectly) reproduced the input stem exactly at the output (*dish–dish*).

Other. The network produced a form not otherwise classifiable.

The careful definition of these categories is important for comparative purposes, as a certain amount of ambiguity persists in the literature. For example, Marcus et al. (1992) include inflected versions of past-tense forms (e.g., *camed*) as overregularizations, while Plunkett and Marchman (1993) exclude them. However, this variation in definition makes direct numerical comparisons between various findings difficult. In this analysis we have classified *camed* as partially (and incorrectly) regularized, and hence as an overregularization error.

An important feature of the feed-forward networks employed in these simulations is that they are deterministic, in the sense that the same inputs (phonemes and syntax cues) will always produce the same outputs for a given weight set. Children, on the other hand, will sometimes switch forms within a single conversational turn (Kuczaj, 1977; Marcus et al., 1992). This makes direct numerical comparison of overregularization rate somewhat problematic. We chose therefore to calculate error rates twice, on the basis of types and tokens. For example, overregularization rates on the basis of tokens are given by the formula

$$100\% \left[1 - \frac{\text{overregularized tokens}}{(\text{overregularized tokens + correctly inflected tokens})} \right]$$

It should be kept in mind, however, that since errors are more likely to occur on low-frequency words, a typewise assessment will yield a higher error rate than a tokenwise assessment. Furthermore, there is considerable variation in error rates across children (see Marcus et al., 1992). We prefer to focus on the general profile of inflectional development rather than predict the profile for the individual child, for whom, after all, we lack the relevant vocabulary and frequency data.

We tested generalization performance in a variety of ways. First, we compiled a corpus of cross-paradigmatic inflections; words (like *year*) attested only in one syntactic category (in this case, as a noun). These words were presented to the network to be inflected in the other category as a simulation of 1,497 denominal verbs (to receive past tense) and 212 deverbal nouns (to be pluralized).[1] Furthermore, we collected 1,541 "novel" forms, encompassing every noncapitalized (eliminating proper names, acronyms, etc.) monosyllable in the Moby corpus that did not duplicate, in spelling or pronunciation, an existing stem. We categorized the inflectional processes applied to these novel forms by the network. Finally, we examined the network's capacity to select the correct suffix by targeting different portions of the stem for presentation to the network. This provided an evaluation of the extent to which the network had abstracted a general representation of voicing assimilation and epenthesis.

SIMULATION 1

Our first simulation involved presenting the entire training corpus to the network at each epoch (in random order) and updating the weights after each presentation. Our goal in this simulation was to establish a baseline performance for the corpus properties, as opposed to the properties of the training schedule. We do not suppose that the child attempts to learn the inflections of all monosyllabic nouns and verbs simultaneously. Nevertheless, network performance under these training conditions provides a rough estimate of the relative ease of acquisition of the different inflectional types.

Results

Figure 4.2 shows that a single unified network is capable of learning both noun plural and verb past-tense morphology; in fact, performance on the regular types is near perfect after the first full epoch of training. Performance on irregular types lags significantly; performance after 200 epochs of training yielded 80 percent of irregular noun types and 95 percent of irregular verb types that were correctly inflected.

Discussion

After only a single epoch of training (which, recall, incorporated nearly 20,000 individual pattern trials), the system had mastered most of the basic "rules" for regular inflection of nouns. The dominant factor in both time

Figure 4.2
Percentage of Types Correct by Training Epoch (mass training)

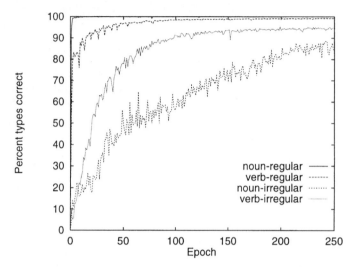

course and eventual performance level for this sort of mass training is the sheer volume of a particular category that appears in the training set. The most common category, regular nouns, was learned near perfectly and almost instantly relative to the other categories. On the other hand, irregular verbs are more common, both in terms of types and tokens (there are 997 irregular verb tokens [122 types] in the training set, compared with only 204 irregular noun tokens [26 types]), and this is apparently enough to offset the fact that the category "irregular verb" appears to cover more widely varying and difficult inflectional paradigms than the category of irregular nouns. Another way of measuring this effect is by noting that irregular nouns constitute only 1.56 percent of the noun tokens and 1.14 percent of the noun types, while 24.4 percent and 12.90 percent of the verb tokens and types, respectively, are irregular.

In this simulation, individual token frequency does not play a decisive role; irregular forms are learned slowly and poorly, despite the fact that the individual tokens are among the most common in the entire training corpus. Specifically, we note a distinct absence of common, high-frequency forms such as *man–men* or *give–gave* being learned quickly relative to less frequent regular forms (such as *walk–walked*).

SIMULATION 2

An important consideration in the simulation of U-shaped learning curves is the initial acquisition of the correct forms for some irregular forms. Because the learning of a connectionist system is strongly influenced by the frequency of training patterns, rare forms are generally only learned well when they are made especially salient to such systems. The statistical dominance of regular forms tends to make these more influential unless irregular forms are somehow made more salient. In particular, the initial error-free period of irregular production can be problematic for connectionist systems (and does not, for instance, appear in Simulation 1).

The salience of the early acquired irregulars can be achieved by a manipulation of the training schedule to enforce learning of a small, usually irregular-rich set of training samples that is then enlarged to a more representative final set. This manipulation can be justified in terms of children's vocabulary development; although the words that children hear may be relatively constant, the words that children understand, and thus attend to, are a constantly increasing set that (presumably) starts with the more common words. We assume, then, that common words are more salient and develop an expanding corpus from more common to less common words. We thus followed standard practice (Elman, 1993; Plunkett & Marchman, 1993, 1996; Jackson & Cottrell, 1997) in our second simulation by beginning with a small (and irregular-rich) training set and gradually increasing the size of the training set at regular intervals.

The initial training set consisted of the twenty most frequent forms (comprising 375 tokens). Of these twenty forms, twelve were regular nouns, two were irregular nouns, five were irregular verbs, and one was a regular verb. The system was trained for 5 epochs, then the training set was increased by 5 percent (of current types) at every fifth epoch in decreasing token frequency order until the complete training corpus was presented at epoch 575 (115 incremental stages). Again, the system was run five times with different random seeds and the mean results are presented in identical format.

Results

In analysis of incremental training, it is important to keep in mind the difference between performance on words already presented to (and known by) the network and words that will eventually be part of the training corpus but have not yet been added. Accordingly, two graphs (Figures 4.3 and 4.4) are presented, displaying the mean number of types correctly inflected as a function of the total corpus and as a function of the corpus thus far seen.

As training progresses, the network learns to correctly inflect the entire training corpus. Furthermore, we note the classic U-shaped curve in Figure 4.4. As in Simulation 1, we see that performance on regular nouns eventually dominates regular verbs as well as irregulars of all sorts, and that irregular nouns are the most difficult overall. Regular nouns are also learned more quickly than regular verbs (Figure 4.3). However, Figure 4.3 clearly demonstrates an initial period during which the networks' performance on irregular forms is superior to their performance on regular forms.

Figure 4.3
Percentage of Types Correct by Training Increment (incremental training)

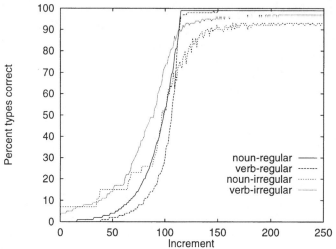

Note that incremental training reaches full vocabulary by increment 115. Training beyond this point corresponds to the mass-training regime.

Final levels of performance in the two training regimes are remarkably consistent; the only substantial difference is a marginally lower rate for irregular noun types in the second (incremental) experiment. However, the developmental course of the two experiments is radically different; the incremental network is able to master the noun and verb inflections irrespective of regularity until approximately the ninetieth training increment, at which point performance drops dramatically. This can be compared with Figure 4.5, in which the overregularization rate on nouns similarly grows explosively at the ninetieth increment, indicating a qualitative shift in representation despite a relatively continuous growth rate in vocabulary size. By the end of training, performance on noun plurals and verb past-tense forms (types) is 99.9 percent and 99.2 percent, respectively.

Role of Frequency Compression

These exact performance figures, of course, are to some extent influenced by the composition of the training set. Varying, for instance, the amount of frequency compression–flattening will produce different performance levels. In particular, a less extreme flattening may cause infrequent forms (and paradigms) to be ignored in the sea of frequent forms. Common wisdom, which holds that irregulars are frequent and regulars are not, is not entirely correct in this assessment; for example, the pairs *goose–geese, sheaf–*

Figure 4.4
Percentage of Known Types Correct by Increment

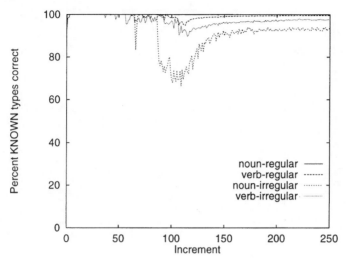

sheaves, and *flee–fled* are irregular, but have very low frequencies. The most common single category and paradigm is, by far, the regular noun.

To examine these effects, we ran additional simulations using a compression scheme of $\log_2 (\text{freq}^2 + 1)^2$ (instead of $\log_2 [\text{freq}^2 + 1]$), resulting in the most frequent type appearing about 400 times as often as the least (instead of 20 times as often). Under this scheme the percentage of regular noun tokens is vastly increased, which is reflected in training. Using a similar incremental training regime, we found that regular nouns are still learned well (97.7% of types correctly inflected), but all other forms were significantly lost. Irregular nouns performed at only 76 percent, irregular verbs at 50 percent, and regular verbs at only 43 percent. Furthermore, most of the errors were miscategorization errors: The less frequent verb morphology was lost in an attempt to pluralize everything. This further confirms that salient but rare forms are difficult for a network to learn. These results also lend further credence to the view, originally suggested by Plunkett and Marchman (1991), that it is important to distinguish the input to the child from the uptake by the child. Raw frequency comparisons are unlikely to provide an accurate assessment of the relative saliency of individual word forms for the child. Here we have assumed that a high-frequency compression captures the relative saliency of different word forms. Of course, a fuller account of the acquisition of inflectional morphology in children would need to take account of other factors, such as the word's meaning, in determining the saliency of a particular form.

Figure 4.5
Noun and Verb Overregularization Rate

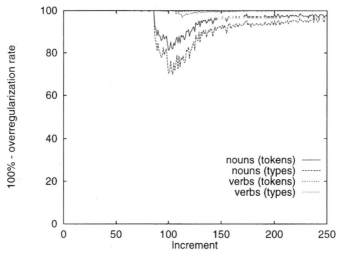

(1 – overregularization rate) as a function of training increment (incremental training), until increment 116, at which the full corpus is reached and increment becomes synonymous with epoch.

Error Analysis

Overregularization

The most widely studied measure of the acquisition of inflectional morphology is overregularization rate. In accordance with other work (Marcus et al., 1992; Plunkett & Marchman, 1993, 1996), we define overregularization rate as

$$100\% \left[1 - \frac{\text{overregularized tokens (types)}}{\text{overregularized tokens (types)} + \text{correctly inflected tokens (types)}} \right]$$

The curves for both noun and verb types and tokens are presented in Figure 4.5. Every "increment" of the graph represents five complete passes through the corpus thus far, which includes from twenty (early training) to several thousand (late training) types. The maximum corpus size is achieved at increment 115, so increments 116 to 250 show the results of additional training on the complete corpus. Note that these curves do not represent the averages of five simulations. They are taken from an individual simulation. Average rates are reported later.

The network produces the characteristic developmental profile of a period of highly accurate production of a small, irregular-rich set of words, followed by a characteristic loss of accuracy on (some) irregulars as the system's experiential vocabulary increases and is more and more dominated by regular words. Performance then returns to near-perfect levels.

The mean overregularization rate of the network for noun types was 11.50 percent $\pm$ 8.44 percent and 0.67 percent $\pm$ 1.25 percent for verb types. These averages were obtained by calculating means from the point of first observed overregularization. It is worth noting that the network starts to overregularize nouns consistently earlier and continues to overregularize nouns marginally longer than it overregularizes verbs.

Studies of the time course and error rate of noun inflections in children are unfortunately rather rare; the best known is probably Marchman et al. (1997) and their response to the claims of Marcus (1995) about relative rates of overregularization of nouns and verbs. The Marchman et al. study is limited, in that they focused on the development of only five nouns and sixteen verbs, compared to the nearly 170 irregular forms modeled here. Nonetheless, they report an average overregularization rate of 16 percent for nouns and 10 percent for verbs. Marcus reports comparable rates of overregularization for both nouns and verbs of less than 10 percent. These results are broadly similar to those found in the network. Furthermore, Marchman et al. found that overregularizations of nouns happened both earlier and more frequently than those of verbs, again in line with the behavior of the network (and the predictions of Marcus).

Categorial Error Analysis

Tables 4.2 and 4.3 present an analysis of the mean number of overall error types. The first 60 incremental stages are omitted as being near perfect. The tables' extension past increment 115 represents additional training (five epochs per increment) with the final and complete vocabulary set. This tabular format was chosen because of the difficulties in establishing reasonable baseline corpus comparisons, as well as the fact that the nature of network errors changes over time. As a general comparison, however, the mean overregularization rate for noun types (of all samples) was 7.46 percent, while all other categories had a less than 0.01 percent error rate; for verb types, the mean overregularization rate was 0.45 percent, which is of the same order of magnitude as suffixation errors (0.12%), no-change errors (0.18%), and unanalyzable errors (0.39%), reflecting a wider variety of error categories (all other verb categories were below 0.01% of types).

Marcus et al. (1992) state that children make irregularization errors significantly less frequently (i.e., an order of magnitude less) than overregularization errors. It is worth noting, then, that even using the broadest possible definition of "irregularization" (including what we have here categorized as "blend") at the worst possible time for the network (at 110 increments), we calculate an irregularization rate of only 0.67 percent for verb types (and

Table 4.2
Mean Number of Noun Type Errors of Each Category under Study (incremental training)

	Overreg	Blend	Irreg	Suffix	N. C.	Other	Irregs	Regs
60	0.0	0.0	0.0	0.0	0.0	0.0	4	177
65	0.0	0.0	0.0	0.0	0.0	.6	5	220
70	0.0	0.0	0.0	0.0	0.0	0.0	6	278
75	0.0	0.0	0.0	0.0	0.0	0.0	6	351
80	0.0	0.0	0.0	0.0	0.0	0.0	7	453
85	0.0	0.0	0.0	0.0	0.0	0.0	7	579
90	1.4	0.0	0.0	0.0	.8	.4	10	750
95	3.6	.2	0.0	0.0	0.0	.2	15	944
100	6.2	0.0	0.0	0.0	0.0	0.0	20	1198
105	6.2	.2	0.0	0.0	0.0	2.4	23	1495
110	6.6	.4	0.0	0.0	0.0	.4	25	1827
115	7.0	1.2	0.0	0.0	0.0	2.2	26	2254
120	6.2	.6	0.0	0.0	.4	1.4	26	2254
125	5.2	.6	0.0	0.0	.2	1.4	26	2254
130	4.4	.6	0.0	0.0	.2	1.0	26	2254
135	2.8	.6	0.0	0.0	0.0	1.0	26	2254
140	2.4	.6	0.0	0.0	0.0	1.0	26	2254
145	2.6	.6	0.0	0.0	0.0	1.2	26	2254
150	2.6	.4	0.0	0.0	0.0	1.0	26	2254
155	2.8	.4	0.0	0.0	.2	1.0	26	2254
160	2.2	.2	0.0	0.0	0.0	1.0	26	2254
165	2.2	.2	0.0	0.0	0.0	1.0	26	2254
170	2.0	.2	0.0	0.0	.2	1.0	26	2254
175	1.8	.2	0.0	0.0	0.0	1.2	26	2254
180	1.8	.4	0.0	.2	.0	1.2	26	2254
185	1.8	.2	0.0	0.0	0.0	1.2	26	2254
190	1.8	.2	0.0	0.0	0.0	.8	26	2254
195	1.8	.2	0.0	.2	.0	.8	26	2254
200	1.6	.2	0.0	.4	.2	.4	26	2254
205	1.8	.2	0.0	0.0	0.0	.4	26	2254
210	1.6	.2	0.0	.4	.2	.4	26	2254
215	1.4	.2	0.0	0.0	.4	.4	26	2254
220	1.4	.2	0.0	0.0	.4	.4	26	2254
225	1.6	.2	0.0	.2	.2	.4	26	2254
230	1.6	.2	0.0	0.0	.2	.2	26	2254
240	1.4	.2	0.0	0.0	.2	.4	26	2254
250	1.2	.2	0.0	0.0	.4	.4	26	2254

significantly less for noun types), compared with the much higher overregularization rate of 3.68 percent for irregular verbs.

A significant finding is that the most frequent irregular words were remarkably resistent to overregularization; no word with a token frequency of greater than 243 (fifteen in our training set) was ever overregularized. Thus, moderately common words like *keep, tell,* and *let* (as well as extremely common forms like *see* and *man*) were immune to overregularization, while only marginally less common words like *wife, child,* and *hold* were overregularized upon occasion.

Phonological conditioning of errors was also apparent on the verb forms. Although few in number throughout training, no-change errors were more likely to occur on stems that end with an alveolar consonant. Furthermore,

Table 4.3
Mean Number of Verb Type Errors of Each Category under Study
(incremental training)

Overreg	Blend	Irreg	Suffix	N. C.	Other	Irregs	Regs
0.0	0.0	0.0	0.0	0.0	.6	22	28
0.0	0.0	0.0	0.0	1.0	0.0	29	38
0.0	0.0	0.0	0.0	.6	.8	37	49
.8	0.0	0.0	1.0	.2	1.0	45	68
0.0	0.0	0.0	1.0	0.0	2.2	51	86
0.0	0.0	0.0	0.0	.4	1.4	60	113
0.0	0.0	0.0	.8	0.0	.4	65	139
1.0	0.0	.2	.2	.2	2.4	81	188
1.2	1.2	0.0	1.0	0.0	3.2	92	255
1.2	.4	.4	1.6	.6	5.0	101	377
4.2	2.6	2.0	4.0	3.6	12.6	114	578
5.2	3.8	2.4	5.0	4.6	14.6	122	824
2.8	3.0	1.6	3.8	3.2	9.4	122	824
2.4	1.8	2.0	1.6	3.0	6.4	122	824
1.6	2.2	1.2	1.6	2.8	6.4	122	824
.8	2.0	1.6	1.4	2.8	4.8	122	824
.6	1.8	1.2	1.4	2.4	4.4	122	824
.6	1.2	1.0	.2	2.2	6.2	122	824
1.0	.8	1.0	.6	2.4	3.6	122	824
.6	.8	1.0	.2	2.4	3.0	122	824
.2	1.0	1.0	.2	2.8	2.8	122	824
.2	1.0	1.4	0.0	2.4	2.0	122	824
.2	.8	1.0	.2	2.4	2.4	122	824
.6	.8	1.2	.2	2.4	1.6	122	824
.2	.8	1.2	.2	2.4	1.6	122	824
0.0	1.0	1.0	.2	2.6	1.8	122	824
0.0	.6	1.2	.2	2.2	2.0	122	824
0.0	.4	1.0	.2	2.0	1.6	122	824
.2	.4	.8	0.0	2.2	2.4	122	824
0.0	.2	1.2	0.0	2.0	1.4	122	824
.2	.4	1.0	1.0	1.8	1.2	122	824
.2	.2	1.2	.6	1.6	1.4	122	824
0.0	.2	1.0	0.0	1.6	1.0	122	824
.2	.6	1.0	0.0	1.2	1.2	122	824
0.0	.2	1.0	0.0	1.6	1.0	122	824
0.0	.2	1.0	0.0	1.6	1.0	122	824
.2	.2	1.0	.2	1.4	1.0	122	824

no-change verbs (like *hit–hit*) were less likely to be overregularized than other irregular verbs. Of the 122 irregular verb types, 27 (22.13%) are no-change verbs. Of the 18 types that are ever attested as being overregularized, 2 (11.11%) are no-change verbs. No-change verbs are thus overregularized at half the expected rate.

Generalization

We also tested the model on its ability to generalize to novel forms as training progresses, the so-called wug test. This involves evaluating the extent to which the network produces the correct inflection on a novel stem, which in this context means the form consonant with the rule-based description. For this test, we used 1,541 monosyllables taken from the Moby pronunciator that were not part of the Kučera-Francis (1967) data. The developmental course of generalization to novel stems is depicted in Figure 4.6. For purposes of comparison, we also include the profile of generalization to novel forms under the mass-training schedule used in Simulation 1.

Figure 4.6 shows that the network is able to generalize the correct suffix to novel nouns and verbs. By the end of training over 90 percent of all novel nouns are inflected with the correct suffix, as are over 80 percent of all novel verbs. Second, the final level of generalization of the network is independent of the training regime adopted (mass versus incremental), indicating that generalization is determined more by the training corpus than by the training method.

Generalization also shows a pronounced developmental profile for the incremental training regime. During early training the network is unable to add an appropriate suffix to a novel form. As the training vocabulary expands, the generalization performance increases exponentially until it asymptotes at the levels indicated. However, the developmental profile of generalization differs for nouns and verbs. The network regularizes novel verbs considerably later than novel nouns.

We also analyzed the likelihood of appending a suffix to a novel verb contingent upon its form. In English, most irregular verbs that take "null suffixes" have stems that end in alveolar stop consonants (/d/ or /t/), such as *light–lit*, *hit–hit*, and *sit–sat*. Pairs ending in velar consonants (*dig–dug*, *stick–stuck*) are rarer, and pairs ending in dental fricatives are rarer still; in

Figure 4.6
Regularization of Nonce Words by Epoch or Increment across Training Regimes

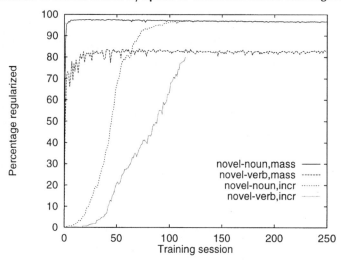

the training corpus we used, only one stem–inflection pair (*tooth–teeth*) ended in a dental fricative, and that, of course, is a noun inflection and not a verb. We examined the percentage of nonce verbal forms that were inflected regularly (i.e., correctly suffized) against those that were inflected without a suffix. Table 4.4 shows the distribution of null suffixes over selected stem endings.

Table 4.4 indicates that a higher percentage of novel verbs ending in alveolar stops (such as /t/) receive null suffixes than those ending in dental fricatives. In particular, four times as many nonce forms ending in dental fricatives were regularized as were null inflected, while this ratio was nearly reversed for nonce forms ending in alveolar stops.

Critical-Mass Effects

The profiles of development in the incremental training schedule suggest that there is a close relationship between levels of generalization and performance, on the one hand, and the number of words in the training set, on the other. For example, the profiles of development depicted in Figure 4.6 suggest that a critical mass of nouns and verbs is required in the training set before high levels of generalization are achieved. Similarly, the sudden onset of overregularization errors depicted in Figure 4.5 indicate a mass-action effect at work. These findings are consistent with earlier work (Plunkett & Marchman, 1993; Marchman & Bates, 1994). However, in the current simulations there is substantial delay between sudden increases in the various performance measures for nouns and verbs. The critical-mass hypothesis predicts that these delays are directly related to the number of nouns and verbs in the corpus at different points in training.

Figure 4.7 shows the relationship between the average number of novel forms regularized and the number of types of a given syntactic category present in the training set at each point.

Figure 4.7 (in conjunction with Figure 4.6) provides support for this critical-mass hypothesis. This graph plots the regularization rate for novel forms against the number of types of the same category in the current training increment. The curves for nouns and verbs in Figure 4.7 are nearly identical, showing that a similar process of mass action is operating for both

Table 4.4
Distribution of Null Suffixes over Selected Novel Verb-Stem Endings

Category	% regularized	% "null" inflected	ratio (R/N)
Verb, alveolar stop (d/t)	12.7 (%)	39.9 (%)	0.318
Verb, velar stop (g/k)	43.1	30.1	1.332
Verb, labial stop (b/p)	38.4	20.9	1.837
Verb, dental fric. (D/T)	45.5	9.52	4.779

Figure 4.7
Evidence for Critical-Mass Effect; Regularization Rate against Type Rate Scatter Plot

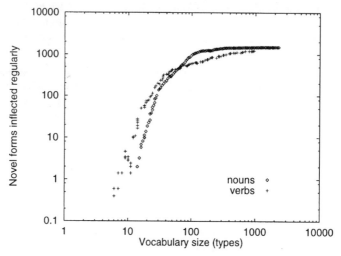

syntactic types. Both curves show a rapid increase in regularization rate, beginning to saturate at about 100 types of the appropriate syntactic category. The developmental delay between nouns and verbs shown in Figure 4.6 reflects the composition of the input vocabulary at different stages in training. The small advantage of nouns over verbs in Figure 4.7 reflects the relative homogeneity of noun inflections compared to verbs (recall that there are many more irregular verbs than irregular nouns).

Assimilation Effects

One of the more prominent aspects of noun and verb inflection, studied jointly, is that the voicing of the final phoneme of the stem is critical in determining the correct inflection for either a plural or past tense. Both inflectional types involve perseverative assimilation, in which a feature of a prior sound persists and attaches itself to another sound. In the human vocal tract this assimilation can be explained by the observation that changing voicing requires time and energy and can thus be lost in fast, fluent speech, resulting in the stem-final voicing feature causally affecting the voicing of the suffix.

The argument and architecture presented by Pinker and Prince (1988) attempts to capture this in a separate voicing module that is "downstream" from the stem-affixation module and examines (and projects) the voicing appropriately. Pinker and Prince argue that the Rumelhart and McClelland (1986) model is unable to capture the redundancy of morphophonological and phonological processes that apply across paradigms. They discuss at some length the virtue of rule systems, and argue that the main contribution of the rule approach is not (as they claim Rumelhart and McClelland suggest) to account for U-shaped phenomena. Rather, it is the ability of rules to factor out common processes that cut across different domains. Voicing assimilation and epenthesis are two rules they give as examples, applying not only to the past tense, but also to third-person singular, noun plurals, the possessive, contractions, and so on. This analysis penetrates to the heart of what generative linguists like about rule systems: the notion that a handful of rules may recur, interact, and generate a fair amount of apparent complexity. There is enormous combinatoric power in rule systems. Pinker and Prince criticized the Rumelhart and McClelland model for implying that processes like epenthesis and voicing assimilation are idiosyncratic phenomena peculiar to the past-tense paradigm. They claim, strongly, that there is no way for this information to be shared across different corners of the grammar. We argue that the modular decomposition demanded by Pinker and Prince is not necessary and that our network is capable of capturing such regularity within a single system.

The causal structure of a neural network is somewhat different from the physics of a vocal tract; as each unit is independent and unordered (within a layer), there is by construction no causal link between independent output units. There is, however, an associative link between independent outputs, and a possible causal link between the voicing feature of the final consonant of the input stem and the voicing feature of the final consonant of the (output) suffix.

To investigate this possibility, "don't care" inputs (units with output activations of 0.5) were used to construct a 128-bit "neutral" stem. Each feature–bit in the final phoneme was set, then reset, and presented to the five incrementally trained networks at their final weight states to inflect as a noun, a verb, and a "don't care" inflection. All other bits in the final phoneme remained at "don't care," so the test vector consisted of only one meaningful bit. The differences between output activations with the feature set and unset were evaluated as a measure of the significance of that feature. If a strong causal link existed between input voicing and output voicing, then toggling the voicing bit in the input should produce an output with a strongly varying voicing.

No evidence for this level of learned voicing assimilation, however, was found. In point of fact, no single feature change produced a substantive change in the output representations of the final consonant. Major effects of some features were found on the production (or lack thereof) of an epenthetic vowel: The features by which an epenthetic schwa differs from an empty slot were strongly affected by some features (such as nasality or labialism) that strongly predicted the absence of such an epenthetic vowel.

This finding should not, however, be interpreted as demonstrating that these feed-forward networks—or neural networks in general—cannot acquire "principles" such as voicing assimilation.[2] The evidence from the generalization tests clearly indicates that these networks have mastered voicing assimilation at the level of the entire, pronounceable word. We thus conclude not that voicing assimilation is impossible for such networks, but that voicing assimilation (and possibly other properties) can be described in a subsymbolic way as a property of the representation of an entire word.

To investigate this possibility further, we tested network performance on novel stems presented with "don't care" syntactic units. Despite the absence of meaningful inflection instructions, the networks still usually produced meaningful and recognizable attempts at inflection. Unexpectedly, despite the tremendous dominance of both noun types and noun tokens, novel stems were inflected as nouns and verbs with nearly equal frequency. Finally, and most important for a study of inflectional assimilation, the number of voicing errors was tremendously small; of 7,705 novel stem trials (1,541 novel stems times five different "subjects"), only 927 were inflected to produce a suffix-final consonant with different voicing than the stem-final consonant, and of those 927 "errors," 216 were examples of the /t/–/@d/ pair (as in *swat–swatted*), which is, of course, correct in context. We thus observe a maximum of 9.2 percent voicing errors, even in the absence of syntactic information, clear evidence that these networks can successfully generalize to produce principles such as cross-inflectional voicing assimilation.

Denominal and Deverbal Forms

Recent work by Kim et al. (1991) and Kim, Marcus, Pinker, Hollander, and Coppola (1994) has demonstrated that speakers do not rely exclusively on phonological information to determine the manner in which verb forms are inflected. For example, a noun stem that is identical to the stem of an irregular verb will nevertheless be regularized when used as a denominal verb. Unfortunately, it is not possible in the present simulations to model this process, since the network, by design, only has access to phonological information. Nevertheless, it is possible to evaluate the extent to which the network regularizes noun stems and verb stems when they are inflected outside of their trained categories. Therefore, we analyzed the performance of the network on cross-categorial (denominal and deverbal) forms by presenting the network with all of the unicategorial forms in the wrong category. This gave us a set of 1,497 denominal verbs and 212 deverbal nouns to be inflected in the new category. Figure 4.8 indicates the percentage of regularized types as a function of training epoch. Again, for comparison, we also plot the same measure for the mass-training schedule reported in Simulation 1.

By the end of training over 80 percent of denominal verbs and over 90 percent of deverbal nouns were regularized. These results indicate that the network clearly has the ability to produce cross-categorial (denominal or

Figure 4.8
Network Performance on Cross-Paradigmatic Inflections

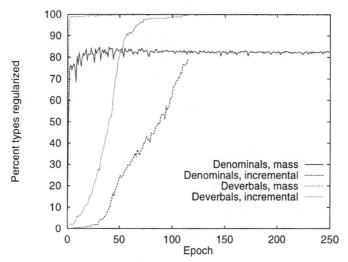

deverbal) inflections despite having no direct (training) evidence about their status as cross-categorial stems. Note also that the regularization profiles for cross-paradigmatic inflections (Figure 4.8) and generalization to novel stems (Figure 4.6) are almost identical. The cross-paradigmatic inflections are treated as though they are novel forms. In other words, information about the derivational history of these unicategorial stems is not a causal factor in determining their high level of regularization.

A slight modification of the network permits a more direct comparison of the Kim et al. (1991, 1994) results. We enlarged the input layer of the network moderately, adding to each input type a random set of fifty bits as a form of random pseudosemantics. These semantics were chosen by simply setting (or not) each bit independently with a 50-percent probability. The network was then trained to associate the appropriate inflected form with the stem, the syntactic category, and the semantics appropriate to that form. This constitutes training the network to inflect various forms in the context of a representation of their conventional meanings.

We then tested the performance of the system (after 115 increments) in producing inflected forms of irregular stems associated with new and previously unseen semantics, reflecting a stem used in an atypical or novel context, such as with a completely new denominalized form. These new semantics, which can formally be regarded (in this model) as high-level noise, will of course distort the outputs in a way similar to lesioning. We expect, therefore, a certain level of degraded performance and simple errors. The important question is whether the analyzable forms produced reflect the original irregular inflection, or are regularized in keeping with human practice on novel meanings and form.

The data from Kim et al. (1991) suggest that most of these stems should be regularized; we find that with fifty units of pseudosemantics, eleven (of twenty-six) noun stems are regularized, compared with only three with the "correct" irregular inflection. Similarly, of 122 verb stems, we find 32 stems regularized and only 7 irregularized. In either case, the number of regularized forms exceeds the number of irregular forms by about 4:1, a clear demonstration of the ability of the network to produce regularized forms when presented with novel uses and meanings. Varying the number of semantic units shows that as the number of such units increases, and the importance of semantics to the overall representation of the word form correspondingly increases, the number of stems regularized also increases. These results suggest that humanlike levels of denominal regularization can be obtained by using an appropriate number of semantics units.

DISCUSSION

The simulations reported here track the developmental trajectory of a neural network trained on a realistic corpus of English nouns (2,280 types) and verbs (946 types). Indeed, the model incorporated all the monosyllabic nouns and verbs from the Brown corpus.[3]

The performance of the networks mimics that of children and adults in a number of important respects. First, all simulations (mass and incremental) are able to learn the training corpus to near perfection. Recall that by the end of training, performance on noun plurals and verb past-tense forms is 99.9 percent and 99.2 percent, respectively. Second, the profile of over-regularization errors for both nouns and verbs in the network mimics the well-documented U-shaped profile of development in children. For verb past-tense forms, this result replicates and extends the findings reported for models trained on smaller vocabularies (Plunkett & Marchman, 1993, 1996). However, this is the first demonstration in which a neural network model has simulated the well-known U-shaped development for noun plurals, in particular producing an initial phase of error-free performance. This finding shows that Marcus's (1995) criticism of the original Rumelhart and McClelland (1986) model is unwarranted: "Because irregular noun plurals are so rare, there is unlikely to ever be a stage in which irregular plurals dominate regular plurals; hence the Rumelhart & McClelland model would probably overregularize even its earliest plurals" (Marcus, 1995, p. 450). Our model not only produces initial error-free performance on noun plurals but does so in the context of initial error-free performance on verb past-tense forms.

The onset of overregularization errors on nouns tends to occur earlier than overregularization errors on verbs in the network. This result is consistent with the data reported in Marchman et al. (1997). The data for the four children analyzed in Marcus (1995) are heterogenous in this respect: Adam overregularizes nouns before he overregularizes verbs, Eve and Sarah show the reverse pattern, and Abe starts overregularizing nouns and verbs around the same time.[4] However, both studies demonstrate that the rate of over-regularization for nouns is greater than that for verbs. This is also true of the simulation, as can be seen in Figure 4.5. Children make few overregu-larization errors on forms with a high token frequency (Marcus et al., 1992). Again, this is true of the current set of simulations, replicating the results of earlier work with smaller verb vocabularies and demonstrating that the frequency effect scales up to larger vocabularies and extends to noun morphology.

The model also mimics children's early acquisition of regular noun plu-rals relative to regular past-tense forms reported in previous empirical in-vestigations (Brown, 1973; Marchman et al., 1997). This result is apparent from the network's performance on the training data (see Figure 4.3) and its ability to generalize to novel forms (see Figure 4.6). We do not suppose that the earlier acquisition of regular noun plurals in the network provides a complete explanation of why regular past-tense forms should be acquired later in children. Presumably, conceptual, semantic, and grammatical fac-tors also have a role to play in this acquisition story. However, our results indicate that phonological and frequency factors (the only sources of infor-mation available to the network) may contribute much to the variance in the acquisition rate for these two grammatical forms in young children.

Regular nouns are always easier to learn than regular verbs for the net-work. However, this pattern does not hold for irregular nouns and verbs. During the earliest stage of training, irregular nouns have the advantage over irregular verbs. As training proceeds, performance on irregular verbs consistently exceeds that of irregular nouns (see Figures 4.2, 4.3, and 4.4). We know of no detailed empirical investigation that charts the acquisition of irregular noun plurals relative to irregular verb past tenses in young chil-dren. Brown (1973) indicates the early acquisition of some irregular plural forms. The prediction of the model that the class of irregular past-tense forms subsequently becomes easier to acquire than the class of irregular plurals (despite the former being more numerous) must await further inves-tigation. From the point of view of network learning, this regularity by word-category interaction is unsurprising; regular nouns, the most frequent type of inflection, were learned fastest and most accurately, while the net-work had the most difficulty with irregular nouns, the rarest category. The critical-mass analysis also shows that the number of nouns and verbs in the training set is the factor determining generalization to novel forms (Figure 4.7). The networks show high levels of generalization (appending the appropriate suffix ending) to novel stems only when they have learned around 100 forms from the relevant category (nouns or verbs). Marchman and Bates (1994) report parallel findings for young children.

Errors in the simulations show evidence of phonological conditioning. Networks make a small number of no-change errors on verbs throughout training (Table 4.3). These are more likely to occur on stems that end with an alveolar consonant (Table 4.4) (e.g., *tread* → *tread* and *rend* → *rend*. This pattern of response is consonant with that reported for children by Bybee and Slobin (1982). Networks are less likely to make overregularization errors on no-change irregular verbs. In fact, the rate of overregularization of other irregular verbs is double that of the no-change subclass. This result parallels the finding of Marcus et al. (1992) that children's no-change past-tense forms are resistant to overregularization. The networks make very few no-change errors on nouns (Table 4.2). We know of no empirical reports on no-change errors for nouns in children. As can be seen from Table 4.3, irregularization is the least frequent error type produced on nouns and verbs. After overregularization errors, the most common error type is no change, then blend. No-change errors are the predominant verb error type during the later phases of training. A similar rank ordering of error types is observed for nouns, though the absolute level of errors is less than that observed for verbs. Again, the pattern of errors on verbs is consonant with that reported for past-tense errors in children (Kuczaj, 1977; Marcus et al., 1992). Lack of empirical data prevents us from evaluating the rank ordering of error types for nouns.

Performance on denominal verbs and deverbal nouns indicates that cross-categorial generalization is not difficult for networks of this type. The network has no difficulty learning to inflect two phonologically identical forms in quite different ways when they are taken from different syntactic classes. In particular, a stem that behaves as an irregular noun plural can behave as a regular verb past-tense form within this system (or vice versa). For example, the irregular noun plural *men* is treated as a regular verb in its past-tense form, *manned*. These networks cannot (by design) add a regular verb inflection to a noun stem that is identical to the stem of an irregular verb (it only has access to phonological information). However, the tendency of these networks to regularize across categories suggests that the provision of other information such as meaning and/or distributional properties might well result in the regularization of noun stems that are phonologically identical with an irregular verb when used as a verb. This was confirmed in a set of supplementary simulations in which pseudosemantic vectors were used to distinguish novel usage of irregular verbs from their routine usage. Well-formed phonological outputs to irregular stems were predominantly regularized. Similar results held for deverbals that were identical in phonology (but not semantics) to irregular nouns.

Finally, the capacity of these networks to choose the correct inflectional allomorph to attach to a novel stem demonstrates that processes controlling voicing assimilation can be observed in these networks. This result is obtained even in the absence of syntactic information. Clearly, the network exploits information about stem-final voicing even as it attempts at the same time to determine whether an input should be inflected as a regular or irregular form.

CONCLUSION

The dual-route model of inflectional morphology, as proposed by Pinker and Prince (1988), has the advantages of being easy to understand and to decompose, and has an easily described and tested generalization performance. Unfortunately, like many symbolic descriptions of human mental processing, the simple and clean solution to a small problem (verb past tenses) becomes significantly less simple and clean when scaled up (Is yet another route required for noun plurals?), and can result in needless complexity. Furthermore, the many similarities between these two processes of noun and verb inflection argue for a closer coupling than is required by the dual-route model. The complex requirements of the similarities and differences in processing argue for an equally complex and unparsimonious modular decomposition of thought, seeded through with questions about module ordering, data flow, and so forth.

We have presented a single-route or, more accurately, single-process model based on a connectionist associative network that is capable of inflecting verb stems to produce their past-tense forms or noun stems to produce their plurals. It handles both regular and irregular verbs with reasonable accuracy, despite having a much larger vocabulary than many related projects (e.g., Daugherty and Seidenberg, 1992; Plunkett and Marchman, 1991, 1993). Furthermore, it produces linguistically plausible generalizations, capturing important aspects such as performance on nonce words, the generalization of voicing assimilation even in the absence of syntactic information, and regularized inflection of cross-categorial processes such as denominal verbs or deverbal nouns. It is important that the model mimics well-established facts about children's acquisition of noun and plural morphology, as well as offering several novel empirical predictions.

This system thus demonstrates that a single route to inflectional morphology is capable of producing the generalization and productivity levels necessary for a psycholinguistically meaningful model of noun and verb inflection, even on a very limited set of information (excluding semantics entirely, for example), and provides a baseline performance describing what can be done in this limited domain, and to which new performance can be compared as representations and information improve.

FURTHER READINGS

Rumelhart and McClelland (1986) offered the first connectionist account of the acquisition of the English past tense. This model was criticized at length by Pinker and Prince (1988), though subsequent reformulations of the original model (MacWhinney & Leinbach, 1991; Plunkett & Marchman, 1991, 1993) have shown that many of these criticisms can be answered while maintaining a similar information-processing architecture. Further improvements in the performance of the model have been achieved by implementing an attentional device that picks out specific verbs for further training depending on the current level of error for that verb (Jackson & Cottrell, 1997). Recently, focus has shifted to other languages in which the default inflection is represented by a minority of forms in the language (e.g., the German and Arabic plural systems). Marcus et al. (1995) argue that these linguistic systems pose a challenge for connectionist models of inflection. Attempts to answer this challenge can be found in Hare, Elman, and Daugherty (1995), Nakisa and Hahn (1996), Plunkett and Nakisa (1997), and Nakisa, Plunkett, and Hahn (2000).

NOTES

This work was supported by a research project grant from the Economic and Social Reasearch Council to Kim Plunkett. We thank Jeff Elman, Mary Hare, and two anonymous reviewers for comments on earlier drafts of this manuscript.

1. An additional set of simulations dealing with the case of denominal verbs that are homophonic with extant irregular verbs is described in a later section.

2. It is worth noting that assimilative and epenthetic processes have already been demonstrated in other types of network architectures, such as recurrent networks. See Hare (1990), Gasser and Lee (1992), and Cottrell and Plunkett (1994) for examples of recurrent networks that deal with assimilative processes within single inflectional paradigms. However, our aim is to evaluate whether these processes can be shared across inflectional paradigms when there are only associative connections rather than causal links between consecutive output sounds.

3. MacWhinney and Leinbach (1991) describe a simulation incorporating an even larger corpus of verbs and a wider range of inflections. However, their paper does not provide a detailed analysis of the developmental trajectory of the network's performance. In particular, they provide no account of early U-shaped learning.

4. Onsets of verb overregularization for these four children are taken from Marcus et al. (1992).

REFERENCES

Baayan, R. H., Piepenbrock, R., & van Rijn, H. (1993). *The CELEX lexical database [CD-ROM]*. Philadelphia: Linguistic Data Consortium, University of Pennsylvania.

Barrett, M., Harris, M., & Chasin, J. (1991). Early lexical development and maternal speech: A comparison of children's initial and subsequent uses of words. *Journal of Child Language, 18*, 21–40.

Berko, J. (1958). The child's learning of English morphology. *Word, 14*, 150–177.

Brown, R. (1973). *A first language: The early stages*. Cambridge, MA: Harvard University Press.

Bybee, J., & Slobin, D. (1982). Rules and schemes in the development and use of the English past tense. *Language, 58*, 265–289.

Cottrell, G. W., & Plunkett, K. (1994). Acquiring the mapping from meaning to sound. *Connection Science, 6*, 379–412.

Daugherty, K., & Seidenberg, M. S. (1992). Rules or connections? The past tense revisited. In *Proceedings of the Fourteenth Annual Conference of the Cognitive Science Society* (pp. 259–264). Hillsdale, NJ: Kawrebce Erlbaum.

Elman, J. L. (1993). Learning and development in neural networks: The importance of starting small. *Cognition, 48*, 71–99.

Ervin, S. M. (1964). Imitation and structural change in children's language. In E. H. Lenneberg (Ed.), *New directions in the study of language*. Cambridge, MA: MIT Press.

Fromkin, V. A. (Ed.). (1973). *Speech errors in linguistic evidence*. The Hague: Mouton.

Garrett, M. F. (1980). The limits of accommodation: Arguments for independent processing levels in sentence production. In V. A. Fromkin (Ed.), *Errors in linguistic performance: Slips of the tongue, ear, pen, hand* (pp. 263–271). New York: Academic Press.

Gasser, M., & Lee, C. D. (1992). Networks that learn about phonological feature persistence. In N. Sharkey (Ed.), *Connectionist natural language processing* (pp. 349–362). Oxford: Intellect.

Hare, M. (1990). The role of similarity in Hungarian vowel harmony: A connectionist account. *Connection Science, 2*, 123–150.

Hare, M., & Elman, J. L. (1995). Learning and morphological change. *Cognition, 56*, 61–98.

Hare, M., Elman, J. L., & Daugherty, K. (1995). Default generalisation in connectionist networks. *Language and Cognitive Processes, 10*, 601–630.

Huttenlocher, J., Haight, W., Bryk, A., Seltzer, M., & Lyons, T. (1991). Early vocabulary growth: Relation to language input and gender. *Developmental Psychology, 27*, 236–248.

Jackson, D., & Cottrell, G. W. (1997). Attention and U-shaped learning in the acquisition of the past tense. In *Proceedings of the Nineteenth Annual Conference of the Cognitive Science Society* (pp. 325–330). Mahwah, NJ: Lawrence Erlbaum.

Juola, P., & Zimmermann, P. (1996). Whole-word phonetic distances and the PGPfone alphabet. In *Proceedings of the International Conference on Spoken Language Processing (ICSLP-96)*. Philadelphia, Pennsylvania.

Kim, J. J., Marcus, G. F., Pinker, S., Hollander, M., & Coppola, M. (1994). Sensitivity of children's inflection to grammatical structure. *Journal of Child Language, 21*, 173–210.

Kim, J. J., Pinker, S., Prince, A., & Prasada, S. (1991). Why no mere mortal has ever flown out to center field. *Cognitive Science, 15*, 173–218.

Kuczaj, S. A. (1977). The acquisition of regular and irregular past tense forms. *Journal of Verbal Learning and Verbal Behavior, 16*, 589–600.

Kučera, H., & Francis, W. N. (1967). *Computational analysis of present-day American English*. Providence, RI: Brown University Press.

MacWhinney, B. (1991). *The CHILDES project: Tools for analyzing talk.* Hillsdale, NJ: Lawrence Erlbaum.

MacWhinney, B., & Leinbach, J. (1991). Implementations are not conceptualisations: Revising the verb learning model. *Cognition, 40,* 121–157.

Marchman, V., & Bates, E. (1994). Continuity in lexical and morphological development: A test of the critical mass hypothesis. *Journal of Child Language, 21,* 331–336.

Marchman, V., Plunkett, K., & Goodman, J. (1997). Overregularization in English plural and past tense inflectional morphology. *Journal of Child Language, 24,* 767–779.

Marcus, G. F. (1995). Children's overregularization of English plurals: A quantitative analysis. *Journal of Child Language, 22,* 447–459.

Marcus, G. F., Brinkmann, U., Clahsen, H., Wiese, R., & Pinker, S. (1995). German inflection: The exception that proves the rule. *Cognitive Psychology, 29,* 189–256.

Marcus, G. F., Pinker, S., Ullman, M., Hollander, J., Rosen, T., & Xu, F. (1992). Overregularization in language acquisition. *Monographs of the Society for Research in Child Development, 57* [Serial no. 228].

Miyata, Y. (1991). *A user's guide to PlaNet version 5.6: A tool for constructing, running, and looking into a PDP network.*

Morrison, C., Chappell, T., & Ellis, A. (1997). Age of acquisition norms for a large set of object names and their relation to adult estimates and other variables. *Quarterly Journal of Experimental Psychology: Section A—Human Experimental Psychology, 50,* 528–559.

Nakisa, R. C., & Hahn, U. (1996). Where defaults don't help: The case of the German plural system. In *Proceedings of the Eighteenth Annual Conference of the Cognitive Science Society* (pp. 177–182). Hillsdale, NJ: Lawrence Erlbaum.

Nakisa, R. C., Plunkett, K., & Hahn, U. (2000). A cross-linguistic comparison of single and dual-route models of inflectional morphology. In P. Broeder & J. Murre (Eds.), *Models of language acquisition.* Oxford: Oxford University Press.

Pinker, S., & Prince, A. (1988). On language and connectionism: Analysis of a parallel distributed processing model of language acquisition. *Cognition, 28,* 73–193.

Pinker, S., & Prince, A. (1991). Regular and irregular morphology and the psychological status of rules of grammar. In L. Sutton (Ed.), *Proceedings of the Seventeenth Annual Meeting of the Berkeley Linguistics Society.* Berkeley, CA: Berkeley Linguistics Society.

Plunkett, K., & Marchman, V. (1991). U-shaped learning and frequency effects in a multi-layered perceptron: Implications for child language acquisition. *Cognition, 38,* 43–102.

Plunkett, K., & Marchman, V. (1993). From rote learning to system building: Acquiring verb morphology in children and connectionist nets. *Cognition, 48,* 21–69.

Plunkett, K., & Marchman, V. (1996). Learning from a connectionist model of the English past tense. *Cognition, 61,* 299–308.

Plunkett, K., & Nakisa, R. (1997). A connectionist model of the Arabic plural system. *Language and Cognitive Processes, 12*, 807–836.
Rumelhart, D. E., Hinton, G. E., & Williams, R. J. (1986). Learning internal representations by error propagation. In D. E. Rumelhart & J. L. McClelland (Eds.), *Parallel distributed processing: Explorations in the microstructure of cognition.* Vol. 1: *Foundations* (pp. 318–362). Cambridge, MA: MIT Press.
Rumelhart, D. E., & McClelland, J. L. (1986). On learning the past tenses of English verbs. In J. L. McClelland & D. E. Rumelhart (Eds.), *Parallel distributed processing: Explorations in the microstructure of cognition.* Vol. 2: *Psychological and biological models* (pp. 216–271). Cambridge, MA: MIT Press.
Ward, G. (1997). *Moby pronunciator.* Arcata, California. Available at <http://www.dcs.shef.ac.uk/research/ilash/Moby/index.html>.

5

Finite Models of Infinite Language: A Connectionist Approach to Recursion

Morten H. Christiansen and Nick Chater

In linguistics and psycholinguistics it is standard to assume that natural language involves rare but important recursive constructions. This assumption originates with Chomsky's (1957, 1959, 1965) arguments that the grammars for natural languages exhibit potentially unlimited recursion. Chomsky assumed that if the grammar allows a recursive construction it can apply arbitrarily many times. Thus, if (1) is sanctioned with one level of recursion, then the grammar must sanction arbitrarily many levels of recursion, generating, for example, (2) and (3).

(1) *The mouse that the cat bit ran away.*

(2) *The mouse that the cat that the dog chased bit ran away.*

(3) *The mouse that the cat that the dog that the man frightened chased bit ran away.*

But people can only deal easily with relatively simple recursive structures (e.g., Bach, Brown, & Marslen-Wilson, 1986). Sentences like (2) and (3) are extremely difficult to process.

Note that the idea that natural language is recursive requires broadening the notion of which sentences are in the language to include sentences like (2) and (3). To resolve the difference between language so construed and the language that people produce and comprehend, Chomsky (e.g., 1965) distinguished between linguistic *competence* and human *performance*. Competence refers to a speaker–hearer's knowledge of the language, as studied by linguistics. In contrast, psycholinguists study performance—that is, how linguistic knowledge is used in language processing, and how nonlinguistic factors interfere with using that knowledge. Such "performance factors" are invoked to explain why some sentences, while consistent with linguistic competence, will not be said or understood.

The claim that language allows unbounded recursion has two key implications. First, processing unbounded recursive structures requires unlimited memory; this rules out finite-state models of language processing. Second, unbounded recursion was said to require innate knowledge, because the child's language input contains so few recursive constructions. These implications struck at the heart of the then-dominant approaches to language. Both structural linguistics and behaviorist psychology (e.g., Skinner, 1957) lacked the generative mechanisms to explain unbounded recursive structures. And the problem of learning recursion undermined both the learning mechanisms described by the behaviorists and the corpus-based methodology of structural linguistics. More important, for current cognitive science, both problems appear to apply to connectionist models of language. Connectionist networks consist of finite sets of processing units, and therefore appear to constitute a finite-state model of language, just as behaviorism assumed; connectionist models learn by a kind of associative learning algorithm, more elaborate than but similar in spirit to that postulated by behaviorism. Furthermore, connectionist models attempt to learn the structure of the language from finite corpora, echoing the corpus-based methodology of structural linguistics. Thus, it seems that Chomsky's arguments from the 1950s and 1960s may rule out, or at least limit the scope of, current connectionist models of language processing.

One defense of finite-state models of language processing to which the connectionist might turn is that connectionist models should be performance models, capturing the limited recursion people can process, rather than the unbounded recursion of linguistic competence (e.g., Christiansen, 1992), as the examples illustrate. Perhaps, then, finite-state models can model actual human language processing successfully.

This defense elicits a more sophisticated form of the original argument: What is important about generative grammar is not that it allows arbitrarily complex strings, but that it gives simple rules capturing *regularities* in language. An adequate model of language processing must somehow embody grammatical knowledge that can capture these regularities. In symbolic computational linguistics, this is done by representing grammatical information and processing operations as symbolic rules. While these rules could, in principle, apply to sentences of arbitrary length and complexity, in practice they are bounded by the finiteness of the underlying hardware. Thus, a symbolic model of language processing, such as CC-READER (Just & Carpenter, 1992), embodies the competence–performance distinction in this way: Its grammatical competence consists of a set of recursive production rules that are applied to produce state changes in a working memory. Limitations on the working memory's capacity explain performance limitations without making changes to the competence part of the model. Thus, a finite processor like CC-READER captures underlying recursive structures. Unless connectionist networks can perform the same trick, they cannot be complete models of natural language processing.

From the perspective of cognitive modeling, therefore, the unbounded recursive structure of natural language is not axiomatic. Nor need the suggestion that a speaker–hearer's knowledge of the language captures such infinite recursive structure be taken for granted. Rather, the view that "unspeakable" sentences that accord with recursive rules form a part of the knowledge of language is an assumption of the standard view of language pioneered by Chomsky and now dominant in linguistics and much of psycholinguistics. The challenge for a connectionist model is to account for those aspects of human comprehension–production performance that suggest the standard recursive picture. If connectionist models can do this without making the assumption that the language processor really implements recursion, or that arbitrarily complex recursive structures really are sentences of the language, then they may present a viable, and radical, alternative to the standard "generative" view of language and language processing.

Therefore, in assessing the connectionist simulations that we will report, which focus on natural language recursion, we need not require that connectionist systems be able to handle recursion in full generality. Instead, the benchmark for performance of connectionist systems will be set by human abilities to handle recursive structures. Specifically, the challenge for connectionist researchers is to capture the recursive regularities of natural language, while allowing that arbitrarily complex sentences cannot be handled. This requires handling recursion at a comparable level to human performance, and learning from exposure and generalizing to novel recursive constructions. Meeting this challenge involves providing a new account of people's limited ability to handle natural language recursion, without assuming an internally represented grammar that allows unbounded recursion (i.e., without invoking the competence–performance distinction).[1]

Here, we consider natural language recursion in a highly simplified form. We train connectionist networks on small artificial languages that exhibit the different types of recursion in natural language. This directly addresses Chomsky's (1957) arguments that recursion in natural language in principle rules out associative and finite-state models of language processing. Considering recursion in a pure form permits us to address the in-principle viability of connectionist networks in handling recursion, just as simple artificial languages have been used to assess the feasibility of symbolic parameter-setting approaches to language acquisition (Gibson & Wexler, 1994; Niyogi & Berwick, 1996).

The structure of this chapter is as follows. We begin by distinguishing varieties of recursion in natural language. We then summarize past connectionist research on natural language recursion. Next, we introduce three artificial languages, based on Chomsky's (1957) three kinds of recursion, and describe the performance of connectionist networks trained on these languages. These results suggest that the networks handle recursion to a degree comparable with humans. We close with conclusions on the prospects of connectionist models of language processing.

VARIETIES OF RECURSION

Chomsky (1957) introduced the notion of a recursive generative grammar. Early generative grammars were assumed to consist of phrase structure rules and transformational rules (which we shall not consider). Phrase structure rules have the form $A \rightarrow BC$, meaning that the symbol A can be replaced by the concatenation of B and C. A phrase structure rule is recursive if a symbol X is replaced by a string of symbols that includes X itself (e.g., $A \rightarrow BA$). Recursion can also arise through applying recursive sets of rules, none of which need individually be recursive. When such rules are used successively to expand a particular symbol, the original symbol may eventually be derived. A language-construction modeled using recursion rules is a recursive construction; a language has recursive structure if it contains such constructions.

Modern generative grammar employs many formalisms, some distantly related to phrase-structure rules. Nevertheless, corresponding notions of recursion within those formalisms can be defined. We shall not consider such complexities here, but use phrase-structure grammar throughout.

Several kinds of recursion are relevant to natural language. First, there are those generating languages that could equally well be generated nonrecursively, by iteration. For example, the rules for right-branching recursion shown in Table 5.1 can generate the right-branching sentences (4) through (6):

(4) *John loves Mary.*

(5) *John loves Mary who likes Jim.*

(6) *John loves Mary who likes Jim who dislikes Martha.*

But these structures can be produced or recognized by a finite-state machine using iteration. The recursive structures of interest to Chomsky, and of interest here, are those where recursion is indispensable.

Chomsky (1957) invented three artificial languages generated by recursive rules from a vocabulary consisting only of a's and b's. These languages cannot be generated or parsed by a finite-state machine. The first

Table 5.1
A Recursive Set of Rules for Right-Branching Relative Clauses

S → NP VP
NP → N (comp S)
VP → V (NP)

Key: S = sentence; NP = noun phrase; VP = verb phrase; N = noun; comp = complementizer; V = verb; constituents in parentheses are optional.

language, which we call *counting recursion*, was inspired by sentence constructions like *if S₁, then S₂* and *either S₁ or S₂*. These can, Chomsky assumed, be nested arbitrarily, as in (7) through (9):

(7) *if S₁ then S₂.*
(8) *if if S₁ then S₂ then S₃.*
(9) *if if if S₁ then S₂ then S₃ then S₄.*

The corresponding artificial language has the form $a^n b^n$, and includes the following strings:

(10) *ab, aabb, aaabbb, aaaabbbb, aaaaabbbbb, . . .*

Unbounded counting recursion cannot be parsed by any finite device processing from left to right, because the number of *a*s must be stored, and this can be unboundedly large and hence can exceed the memory capacity of any finite machine.

The second artificial language was modeled on the center-embedded constructions in many natural languages. For example, in sentences (1) through (3) the dependencies between the subject nouns and their respective verbs are center-embedded, so that the first noun is matched with the last verb, the second noun with the second to last verb, and so on. The artificial language captures these dependency relations by containing sentences that consists of a string *X* of *a*s and *b*s followed by a "mirror image" of *X* (with the words in the reverse order), as illustrated by (11):

(11) *aa, bb, abba, baab, aaaa, bbbb, aabbaa, abbbba, . . .*

Chomsky (1957) used the existence of center-embedding to argue that natural language must be at least context-free, and beyond the scope of any finite machine.

The final artificial language resembles a less common pattern in natural language, cross-dependency, which is found in Swiss-German and in Dutch, as in (12) through (14) (from Bach et al., 1986):[2]

(12) *De lerares heeft de knikkers opgeruimd.*
    Literal: The teacher has the marbles collected up.
    Gloss: *The teacher collected up the marbles.*

(13) *Jantje heeft de lerares de knikkers helpen opruimen.*
    Literal: Jantje has the teacher the marbles help collect up.
    Gloss: *Jantje helped the teacher collect up the marbles.*

(14) *Aad heeft Jantje de lerares de knikkers laten helpen opruimen.*
    Literal: Aad has Jantje the teacher the marbles let help collect up.
    Gloss: *Aad let Jantje help the teacher collect up the marbles.*

Here, the dependencies between nouns and verbs are crossed such that the first noun matches the first verb, the second noun matches the second verb, and so on. This is captured in the artificial language by having all sentences consist of a string X followed by an identical copy of X, as in (15):

(15) *aa, bb, abab, baba, aaaa, bbbb, aabaab, abbabb, . . .*

The fact that cross-dependencies cannot be handled using a context-free phrase-structure grammar has meant that this kind of construction, although rare even in languages in which it occurs, has assumed considerable importance in linguistics.[3] Whatever the linguistic status of complex recursive constructions, they are difficult to process compared to right-branching structures. Structures analogous to counting recursion have not been studied in psycholinguistics, but sentences such as (16), with just one level of recursion, are plainly difficult (see Reich, 1969):

(16) *If if the cat is in, then the dog cannot come in then the cat and dog dislike each other.*

The processing of center-embeddings has been studied extensively, showing that English sentences with more than one center-embedding (e.g., sentences [2] and [3]) are read with the same intonation as a list of random words [Miller, 1962]), that they are hard to memorize (Foss & Cairns, 1970; Miller & Isard, 1964), and that they are judged to be ungrammatical (Marks, 1968). Using sentences with semantic bias or giving people training can improve performance on such structures to a limited extent (Blaubergs & Braine, 1974; Stolz, 1967). Cross-dependencies have received less empirical attention, but present similar processing difficulties to center-embeddings (Bach et al., 1986; Dickey & Vonk, 1997).

CONNECTIONISM AND RECURSION

Connectionist models of recursive processing fall into three broad classes. Some early models of syntax dealt with recursion by "hard-wiring" symbolic structures directly into the network (e.g., Fanty, 1986; Small, Cottrell, & Shastri, 1982). Another class of models attempted to learn a grammar from "tagged" input sentences (e.g., Chalmers, 1990; Hanson & Kegl, 1987; Niklasson & van Gelder, 1994; Pollack, 1988, 1990; Stolcke, 1991). Here, we concentrate on a third class of models that attempts the much harder task of learning syntactic structure from strings of words (see Christiansen & Chater, Chapter 2, this volume, for further discussion of connectionist sentence-processing models). Much of this work has been carried out using the simple recurrent network (SRN) (Elman, 1990) architecture. The SRN involves a crucial modification to a standard ·feed-forward network—a so-called context layer—allowing past internal states to influence subsequent states (see Figure 5.1). This provides the SRN with a memory for past input, and therefore an ability to process input sequences, such as those generated by finite-state grammars (e.g., Cleeremans, Servan-Schreiber, & McClelland, 1989; Giles et al., 1992; Giles & Omlin, 1993; Servan-Schreiber, Cleeremans, & McClelland, 1991).

Previous efforts at modeling complex recursion fall into two categories: simulations using language-like grammar fragments and simulations relating to formal language theory. In the first category, networks are trained on relatively simple artificial languages, patterned on English. For example, Elman (1991, 1993) trained SRNs on sentences generated by a small context-free grammar incorporating center-embedding and one kind of right-branching recursion. Within the same framework, Christiansen (1994, 2000) trained SRNs on a recursive artificial language incorporating four kinds of right-branching structures, a left-branching structure, and center-embedding or cross-dependency. Both found that network performance degradation on complex recursive structures mimicked human behavior (see Christiansen & Chater, Chapter 2, this volume, for further discussion of SRNs as models of language processing). These results suggest that SRNs can capture the quasi-recursive structure of actual spoken language. One of the contributions of this chapter is to show that the SRN's general pattern of performance is relatively invariant over variations in network parameters and training corpus. Thus, we claim, the humanlike pattern of performance arises from *intrinsic* constraints of the SRN architecture.

While work in the first category has been suggestive but relatively unsystematic, work in the second category has involved detailed investigations of small artificial tasks, typically using very small networks. For example,

Figure 5.1
The Basic Architecture of a Simple Recurrent Network

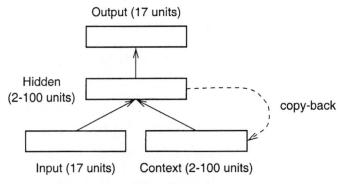

The rectangles correspond to layers of units. Arrows with solid lines denote trainable weights, whereas the arrow with the dashed line denotes the copy-back connections.

Wiles and Elman (1995) made a detailed study of counting recursion with recurrent networks with 2 hidden units and found a network that generalized to inputs far longer than those used in training.[4] Batali (1994) used the same language, but employed 10HU SRNs and showed that networks could reach good levels of performance when selected by a process of "simulated evolution" and then trained using conventional methods. Based on a mathematical analysis, Steijvers and Grünwald (1996) hard-wired a second-order 2HU recurrent network (Giles et al., 1992) to process the context-sensitive counting language $b(a)^k b(a)^k$ . . . for values of k between 1 and 120. An interesting question, which we will address, is whether performance changes with more than two vocabulary items; for example, if the network must learn to assign items to different lexical categories ("noun" and "verb") as well as paying attention to dependencies between these categories. This question is important with respect to the relevance of these results for natural language processing.

No detailed studies have previously been conducted with center-embedding or cross-dependency constructions. The studies presented here comprehensively compare all three types of recursion discussed in Chomsky (1957), with simple right-branching recursion as a baseline. Using these abstract languages allows recursion to be studied in a "pure" form, without interference from other factors. Despite the idealized nature of these languages, the SRN's performance qualitatively conforms to human performance on similar natural language structures.

A novel aspect of these studies is comparison with performance benchmarks from statistical linguistics. The benchmark method is based on n-grams; that is, strings of n consecutive words. It is trained on the same input as the networks, and records the frequency of each n-gram. It predicts new words from the relative frequencies of the *n*-grams that are consistent with the previous $n - 1$ words. The prediction is a vector of relative frequencies for each possible successor item, scaled to sum to 1 so that they can be interpreted as probabilities, and are comparable with the output vectors of the networks. We will compare network performance with the predictions of bigram and trigram models.[5] These simple models can provide insight into the sequential information the networks pick up, and make a link with statistical linguistics (e.g., Charniak, 1993).

THREE BENCHMARK TESTS CONCERNING RECURSION

We constructed three languages to provide input to the network. Each language has two recursive structures: one of the three complex recursive constructions and the right-branching construction as a baseline. Vocabulary items were divided into "nouns" and "verbs," incorporating both singular or plural forms. An end of sentence marker (EOS) completes each sentence.

i. Counting Recursion

aabb   *NNVV*

For counting recursion, we treat Chomsky's symbols *a* and *b* as the categories of noun and verb, respectively, and ignore singular–plural agreement.

ii. Center-Embedding Recursion

a b b a $S_N P_N P_V S_V$ *the boy girls like runs*

In center-embedding recursion, we map *a* and *b* onto the categories of singular and plural words (whether nouns or verbs). Nouns and verbs agree for number, as in center-embedded constructions in natural language.

iii. Cross-Dependency Recursion

a b a b $S_N P_N S_V P_V$ *the boy girls runs like*

In cross-dependency recursion, we map *a* and *b* onto the categories of singular and plural words. Nouns and verbs agree for number, as in cross-dependency constructions.

iv. Right-Branching Recursion

$a\ a\ b\ b$ $P_N\ P_V\ S_N\ S_V$ *girls like the boy that runs*

For right-branching recursion, we map a and b onto the categories of singular and plural words. Nouns and verbs agree, as in right-branching constructions.

Thus, the counting-recursive language consisted of both counting-recursive constructions (i) interleaved with right-branching recursive constructions (iv), the center-embedding recursive language of center-embedded recursive constructions (ii) interleaved with right-branching recursive constructions (iv), and the cross-dependency recursive language of cross-dependency recursive constructions (iii) interleaved with right-branching recursive constructions (iv).

How can we assess how well a network has learned these languages? By analogy with standard linguistic methodology, we could train the net to make "grammaticality judgments," that is, to distinguish legal and nonlegal sentences. But this chapter focuses on performance on recursive structures, rather than metalinguistic judgments (which are often assumed to relate to linguistic competence).[6] Therefore, we use a task that directly addressed how the network processes sentences, rather than requiring it to make metalinguistic judgments. Elman (1990) suggested such an approach, which has become standard in SRN studies of natural language processing. The network is trained to predict the next item in a sequence, given previous context. That is, the SRN gets an input word at time t and then predicts the word at $t + 1$. In most contexts in real natural language, as in these simulations, prediction will not be perfect. But while it is not possible to be certain what item will come next, it is possible to predict successfully which items are possible continuations and which are not, according to the regularities in the corpus. To the extent that the network can predict successfully, then, it is learning the regularities underlying the language.

SIMULATION RESULTS

We trained SRNs on the three languages, using a sixteen-word vocabulary with four singular nouns, four singular verbs, four plural nouns, and four plural verbs.[7] All nets had 17 input and output units (see Figure 5.1), where units correspond to words or the EOS marker. The hidden layer contained between 2 and 100 units. Except where noted, training corpora consisted of 5,000 variable-length sentences, and test corpora of 500 novel sentences, generated in the same way. The training and test corpora did not overlap. Each corpus was concatenated into a single long string and presented to the network word by word. Both training and test corpora comprised 50 percent complex recursive constructions interleaved with 50 percent right-branching constructions. The distribution of depth of embedding is shown in Table 5.2. The mean sentence length in training and test corpora was 4.7 words (SD. 1.3).

Since the input consists of a single concatenated string of words, the network has to discover that the input consists of sentences, that is, nouns followed by verbs (ordered by the constraints of the language being learned) and delineated by EOS markers. Consider an SRN trained on the center-embedding language and presented with the two sentences, $n_1 v_5 \# N_3 n_8 v_2 V_4 \#$.[8] First, the network gets n_1 as input and is expected to produce v_5 as output. The weights are then adjusted depending on the discrepancy between the actual and desired output and the desired output using back-propagation (Rumelhart, Hinton, & Williams, 1986). Next, the SRN receives v_5 as input and should produce as output the end-of-sentence marker #. At the next time step # is provided as input and N_3 is the target output, followed by the input–output pairs: N_3–n_8, n_8–v_2, v_2–V_4, and V_4–#. Training continues in this manner for the whole training corpus.

Test corpora were then presented to the SRNs and output recorded, with learning turned off. As noted, in any interesting languagelike task the next item is not deterministically specified by the previous items. In the example given, at the start of the second sentence the grammar for the center-embedding language permits both noun categories, n and N, to begin a sentence. If the SRN has acquired the relevant aspects of the grammar that generated the training sentences, then it should activate all word tokens in both n and N following an EOS marker. Specifically, the network's optimal output is the conditional probability distribution over possible next items. We can therefore measure amount of learning by comparing the network's output with an estimate of the true conditional probabilities (this gives a less noisy measure than comparing against actual next items). This overall performance measure is used next. Later, we introduce a measure of grammatical prediction error to evaluate performance in more detail.

Table 5.2
The Distribution of Embedding Depths in Training and Test Corpora

Recursion Type	Embedding Depth			
	0	1	2	3
Complex	15%	27.5%	7%	.5%
Right-Branching	15%	27.5%	7%	.5%
Total	30%	55%	14%	1%

Note: The precise statistics of the individual corpora varied slightly from this ideal distribution.

Overall Performance

As noted, our overall performance measure compared network outputs with estimates of the true conditional probabilities given prior context, which, following Elman (1991), can be estimated from the training corpus. However, such estimates cannot assess performance on novel test sentences, because a naïve empirical estimate of the probability of any novel sentence is zero, as it has never previously occurred. One solution to this problem is to estimate the conditional probabilities based on the prior occurrence of lexical categories—for example, *NVnvnvNV#*—rather than individual words. Thus, with c_i denoting the category of the ith word in the sentence, we have the following relation:[9]

$$P(c_p | c_1, c_2, \ldots, c_{p-1}) \simeq \frac{Freq(c_1, c_2, \ldots, c_{p-1}, c_p)}{Freq(c_1, c_2, \ldots, c_{p-1})} \tag{5.1}$$

where the probability of getting some member of a given lexical category as the pth item, c_p, in a sentence is conditional on the previous $p-1$ lexical categories. Note that for the purpose of performance assessment, singular and plural nouns are assigned to separate lexical categories throughout this chapter, as are singular and plural verbs.

Given that the choices of lexical item for each category are independent, and that each word in the category is equally frequent, the probability of encountering a word w_n, which is a member of a category c_p, is inversely proportional to the number of items, C_p, in that category.[10] So, overall,

$$P(w_n | c_1, c_2, \ldots, c_{p-1}) \simeq \frac{Freq(c_1, c_2, \ldots, c_{p-1}, c_p)}{Freq(c_1, c_2, \ldots, c_{p-1}) \, C_p} \tag{5.2}$$

If the network is performing optimally, the output vector should exactly match these probabilities. We measure network performance by the summed squared difference between the network outputs and the conditional probabilities, defining squared error as follows:

$$\text{Squared Error} = \sum_{j \in W} (out_j - P(w_n = j))^2 \tag{5.3}$$

where W is the set of words in the language (including the end of sentence marker) and there is an output unit of the network corresponding to each word. The index j runs through each possible next word, and compares the network output to the conditional probability of that word. Finally, we obtain an overall measure of network performance by calculating the mean squared error (MSE) across the whole test corpus. MSE will be used as a global measure of the performance of both networks and n-gram models.

Intrinsic Constraints on SRN Performance

Earlier simulations concerning the three languages (Christiansen, 1994) showed that performance degrades as embedding depth increases. As mentioned earlier, SRN simulations in which center-embeddings were included in small grammar fragments have the same outcome (Christiansen, 1994, 2000; Elman, 1991, 1993; Weckerly & Elman, 1992), and this is also true for cross-dependencies (Christiansen, 1994, 2000). But does this humanlike pattern arise intrinsically from the SRN architecture, or is it an artifact of the number of HUs used in typical simulations?

To address this objection, SRNs with 2, 5, 10, 15, 25, 50, and 100 HUs were trained on the three artificial languages. Across all simulations, the learning rate was 0.1, no momentum was used, and the initial weights were randomized to values in the interval [−0.25, 0.25]. Although the results presented here were replicated across different initial weight randomizations, we focus on a typical set of simulations for the ease of exposition. Networks of the same size were given the same initial random weights to facilitate comparisons across the three languages.

Figure 5.2 shows performance averaged across epochs for different size nets tested on corpora consisting entirely of either complex recursive structures (left panels) or right-branching recursive structures (right panels). All test sentences were novel and varied in length (following the distribution in Table 5.2). The MSE values were calculated as the average of the MSEs sampled at every second epoch (from epoch 0 to epoch 100). The MSE for bigram and trigram models are included (black bars) for comparison.

The SRNs performed well. On counting recursion, nets with 15 HUs or more obtained low MSE on complex recursive structures (top left panel). Performance on right-branching structures (top right panel) was similar across different numbers of HUs. For both types of recursion, the nets outperformed the bigram and trigram models. For the center-embedding language, nets with at least 10 HUs achieved essentially the same level of performance on complex recursive structures (middle left panel), whereas nets with 5 HUs or more performed similarly on the right-branching structures (middle right panel). Again, the SRNs generally outperformed bigram and trigram models. Nets with 15 HUs or more trained on the cross-dependency language all reached the same level of performance on complex recursive structures (bottom left panel). As with counting recursion, performance was quite uniform on right-branching recursive constructions (bottom right panel) for all numbers of HUs, and the SRNs again outperformed bigram and trigram models. These results suggest that the objection does not apply to

Figure 5.2
Performance Averaged across Epochs for Different Size Nets

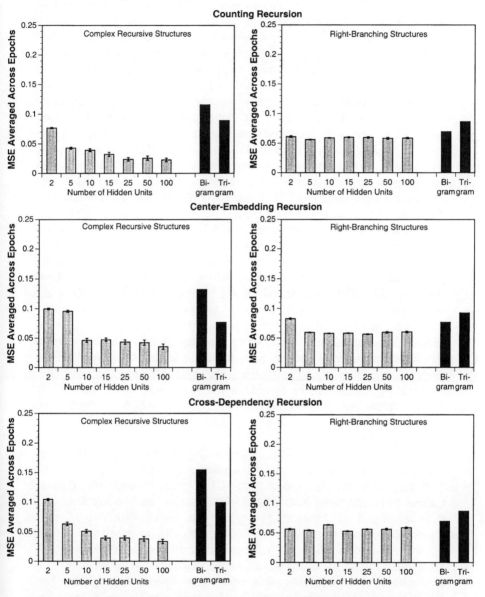

The performances are averaged across epochs on complex recursive constructions (left panels) and right-branching constructions (right panels) of nets of different sizes, as well as the bigram and trigram models trained on the counting-recursion language (top panels), the center-embedding recursion language (middle panels), and the cross-dependency recursion language (bottom panels). Error bars indicate the standard error of the mean.

the SRN. Above 10 to 15 HUs, the number of HUs seems not to affect performance.

Comparing across the three languages, the SRN found the counting-recursion language the easiest and found cross-dependencies easier than center-embeddings. This is important, because people also appear to be better at dealing with cross-dependency constructions than equivalent center-embedding constructions. This is surprising for linguistic theory, in which cross-dependencies are typically viewed as more complex than center-embeddings, because, as noted, they cannot be captured by phrase-structure rules. Interestingly, the bigram and trigram models showed the opposite effect, with better performance on center-embeddings than cross-dependencies. Finally, the SRNs with at least 10 HUs had a lower MSE on complex recursive structures than on right-branching structures. This could be because the complex recursive constructions essentially become deterministic (with respect to length) once the first verb is encountered, but this is not generally true for right-branching constructions.

These results show that the number of HUs, when sufficiently large, does not substantially influence performance on these test corpora. Yet perhaps the number of HUs may matter when processing the doubly embedded complex recursive structures that are beyond the limits of human performance. To assess this, Christiansen and Chater (1999) retested the SRNs (trained on complex and right-branching constructions of varying length) on corpora containing just novel doubly embedded structures. Their results showed a similar performance uniformity to that in Figure 5.2. These simulations also demonstrated that once an SRN has a sufficient size (5 to 10 HUs) it outperforms both n-gram models on doubly embedded constructions. Thus, above a sufficient number of hidden units, the size of the hidden layer seems irrelevant to performance on novel doubly embedded complex constructions drawn from the three languages. Two further objections may be raised, however.

First, perhaps the limitations on processing complex recursion is due to the interleaving of right-branching structures during training. To investigate this objection, SRNs with 2, 5, 10, 15, 25, 50 and 100 HUs were trained (with the same learning parameters as before) on versions of the three languages only containing complex recursive constructions of varying length. The results were almost identical to those in the left panels of Figure 5.2, with a very similar performance uniformity across the different HU sizes (above 5 to 10 units) for all three languages. Also as before, this performance uniformity was evident for corpora consisting entirely of doubly embedded complex constructions. Moreover, similar results were found for SRNs of different HU sizes trained on a smaller, five-word vocabulary. These additional simulations show that the interleaving of the right-branching constructions does not significantly alter performance on complex recursive constructions.

Second, perhaps processing limitations result from an inefficient learning algorithm. An alternative training regime for recurrent networks, back-propagation through time (BPTT), appears preferable on theoretical grounds, and is superior to SRN training in various artificial tasks (see Chater & Conkey, 1992). But choice of learning algorithm does not appear to be crucial here. Christiansen (1994) compared the SRN and BPTT learning algorithms on versions of the three languages only containing complex recursive constructions of varying length (and the same embedding depth distribution as in Table 5.2). In one series of simulations, SRNs and BPTT training (unfolded seven steps back in time) with 5, 10, and 25 HUs were trained using a five-word vocabulary. There was no difference across the three languages between SRN and BPTT training. Further simulations replicated these results for nets with 20 HUs and a seventeen-word vocabulary. Thus, there is currently no evidence that the human-level processing limitations that are exhibited in these simulations are artifacts of using an inefficient learning algorithm.

Performance at Different Depths of Embedding

We have seen that the overall SRN performance roughly matches human performance on recursive structures. We now consider performance at different levels of embedding. Human data suggest that performance should degrade rapidly as embedding depth increases for complex recursive structures, but that it should degrade only slightly for right-branching constructions.

Earlier we used empirical conditional probabilities based on lexical categories to assess SRN performance (Equations 5.2 and 5.3). However, this measure is not useful for assessing performance on novel constructions that either go beyond the depth of embedding found in the training corpus or deviate, as ungrammatical forms do, from the grammatical structures encountered during training. For comparisons with human performance we therefore use a different measure: grammatical prediction error (GPE).

When evaluating how the SRN has learned the grammar underlying the training corpus, it is not only important to determine whether the words the net predicts are grammatical, but also that the net predicts all the possible grammatical continuations. GPE indicates how a network is obeying the training grammar in making its predictions, taking hits, false alarms, correct rejections, and misses into account. Hits and false alarms are calculated as the accumulated activations of the set of units, G, that are grammatical and the set of ungrammatical activated units, U, respectively:

$$\text{hits} = \sum_{i \in G} u_i \tag{5.4}$$

$$\text{false alarms} = \sum_{i \in U} u_i \tag{5.5}$$

Traditional sensitivity measures, such as *d'* (Signal-Detection Theory; Green & Swets, 1966) or α (Choice Theory; Luce, 1959), assume that misses can be calculated as the difference between total number of relevant observations and hits. But in terms of network activation, "total number of relevant observations" has no clear interpretation.[11] Consequently, we need an alternative means of quantifying misses; that is, to determine an activation-based penalty for not activating all grammatical units and/or not allocating sufficient activation to these units. With respect to GPE, the calculation of misses involves the notion of a target activation, t_i, computed as a proportion of the total activation (hits and false alarms) determined by the lexical frequency, f_i, of the word that unit i designates and weighted by the sum of the lexical frequencies, f_j, of all the grammatical units:

$$t_i = \frac{(\text{hits} + \text{misses})f_i}{\sum_{j \in G} f_j} \quad (5.6)$$

The missing activation for each unit can be determined as the positive discrepancy, m_i, between the target activation, t_i, and actual activation, u_i, for a grammatical unit:

$$m_i = \begin{cases} 0 & \text{if } t_i - u_i \leq 0 \\ t_i - u_i & \text{otherwise} \end{cases} \quad (5.7)$$

Finally, the total activation for misses is the sum over missing activation values:

$$\text{misses} = \sum_{i \in G} m_i \quad (5.8)$$

The GPE for predicting a particular word given previous sentential context is thus measured by

$$\text{GPE} = 1 - \frac{\text{hits}}{\text{hits} + \text{false alarms} + \text{misses}} \quad (5.9)$$

GPE measures how much of the activation for a given item accords with the grammar (hits) in proportion to the total amount of activation (hits and false alarms) and the penalty for not activating grammatical items sufficiently (misses). Although not a term in Equation 5.9, correct rejections are taken into account by assuming that they correspond to zero activation for units that are ungrammatical given previous context.

GPEs range from 0 to 1, providing a stringent measure of performance. To obtain a perfect GPE of 0 the SRN must predict all and only the next items prescribed by the grammar, scaled by the lexical frequencies of the legal items. Notice that to obtain a low GPE the network must make the correct subject noun–verb agreement predictions (Christiansen & Chater, 1999). The GPE value for an individual word reflects the difficulty that the SRN experienced for that word, given the previous sentential context. Previous studies (Christiansen, 2000; MacDonald & Christiansen, in press) have found that individual-word GPE for an SRN can be mapped qualitatively onto experimental data on word reading times, with low GPE reflecting short reading times. Average GPE across a sentence measures the difficulty that the SRN experienced across the sentence as a whole. This measure maps onto sentence grammaticality ratings, with low average GPEs indicating high-rated "goodness" (Christiansen & MacDonald, 2000).

Embedding Depth Performance

We now use GPE to measure SRN performance on different depths of embedding. Given that number of HUs seems relatively unimportant, we focus just on 15HU nets in the following. Inspection of MSE values across epochs revealed that performance on complex recursive constructions asymptotes after 35 to 40 training epochs. From the MSEs recorded for epochs 2 through 100, we chose the number of epochs at which the 15HU nets had the lowest MSE. The best level of performance was found after 54 epochs for counting recursion, 66 epochs for center-embedding, and 92 epochs for cross-dependency. The results reported use SRNs trained for these numbers of epochs.

Figure 5.3 plots average GPE on complex and right-branching recursive structures against embedding depth for 15HU nets, bigram models, and trigram models (trained on complex and right-branching constructions of varying length). Each data point represents the mean GPE on ten novel sentences. For the SRN trained on counting recursion, there was little difference between performance on complex and right-branching recursive constructions, and performance only deteriorated slightly with increasing embedding depth. In contrast, the n-gram models (and especially the trigram model) performed better on right-branching structures than complex recursive structures. Both n-gram models showed a sharper decrease in performance across depth of recursion than the SRN. The SRN trained on center-embeddings also outperformed the n-gram models, although it also had greater difficulty with complex recursion than with right-branching structures. Interestingly, SRN performance on right-branching recursive structures decreased slightly with depth of recursion. This contrasts with many symbolic models in which unlimited right-branching recursion poses no processing problems (e.g., Church, 1982; Gibson, 1998; Marcus, 1980; Stabler, 1994). However, the performance deterioration of the SRN appears in line with human data (see later). A comparison between the n-gram models' performance on center-embedding shows that whereas both exhibited a similar

Figure 5.3
Average GPE Scores on Complex and Right-Branching Recursive Structures

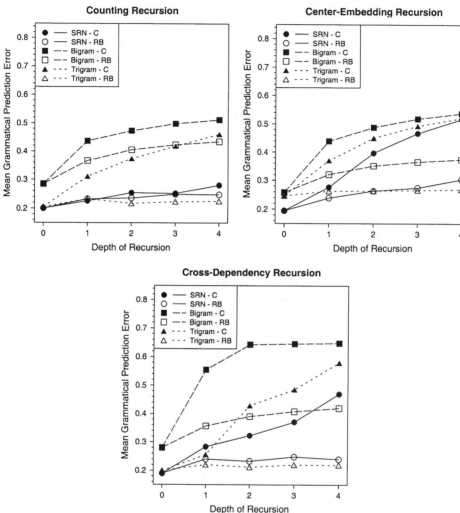

The mean grammatical prediction error on complex (C) and right-branching (RB) recursive constructions as a function of embedding depth (0–4). Results are shown for the SRN as well as the bigram and trigram models trained on the counting-recursion language (top left panel), the center-embedding recursion language (top right panel), and the cross-dependency recursion language (bottom panel).

pattern of deteriorating with increasing depth on the complex recursive constructions, the trigram models performed considerably better on the right-branching constructions than the bigram model. As with the MSE results already presented, SRN performance on cross-dependencies was better than on center-embeddings. Although the SRN, as before, obtained lower GPEs on right-branching constructions compared with complex recursive structures, the increase in GPE across embedding depth on the latter was considerably less for the cross-dependency net than for its center-embedding counterpart. Bigrams performed poorly on the cross-dependency language, both on right-branching and complex recursion. Trigrams performed substantially better, slightly outperforming the SRN on right-branching structures, though still lagging behind the SRN on complex recursion. Finally, note that recursive depth 4 was not seen in training. Yet there was no abrupt breakdown in performance for any of the three languages at this point, for both SRNs and n-gram models. This suggests that these models are able to generalize to at least one extra level of recursion beyond what they have been exposed to during training (and this despite only 1% of the training items being of depth 3).

Overall, the differential SRN performance on complex recursion and right-branching constructions for center-embeddings and cross-dependencies fit well with human data.[12]

Training Exclusively on Doubly Embedded Complex Constructions

An alternative objection to the idea of intrinsic constraints being the source of SRN limitations is that these limitations might stem from the statistics of the training corpora. For example, perhaps the fact that just 7 percent of sentences involved doubly embedded complex recursive structures explains the poor SRN performance with these structures. Perhaps adding more doubly embedded constructions would allow the SRN to process these constructions without difficulty.

We therefore trained 15HU SRNs on versions of the three languages consisting exclusively of doubly embedded complex recursion without interleaving right-branching constructions. Using the same number of words as before, best performance was found for the counting recursion depth 2 trained SRN (D2-SRN) after forty-eight epochs, after sixty epochs for the center-embedding D2-SRN, and after ninety-eight epochs for the cross-dependency D2-SRN. When tested on the test corpora containing only novel doubly embedded sentences, the average MSE found for the counting recursion network was 0.045 (versus 0.080 for the previous 15HU SRN), 0.066 for the center-embedding net (versus 0.092 for the previous 15HU SRN), and 0.073 for the cross-dependency net (versus 0.079 for the previous 15HU SRN). Interestingly, although there were significant differences between the MSE scores for the SRNs and D2-SRNs trained on the counting recursion ($t[98] = 3.13, p < .003$) and center-embeddings ($t[98] = 3.04, p < .004$), the difference between the two nets was not significant for cross-dependencies ($t[98] = .97, p > .3$). The performance of the D2-SRNs thus appear to be somewhat better than the performance of the SRNs trained on the corpora of varying length—at least for the counting and center-embedding recursion languages. However, D2-SRNs are only slightly better than their counterparts trained on sentences of varying length.

Figure 5.4 plots GPE against word position across doubly embedded complex recursive constructions from the three languages, averaged over ten novel sentences. On counting-recursion sentences (top panel), both SRN and D2-SRN performed well, with a slight advantage for the D2-SRN on the last verb. Both networks obtained lower levels of GPE than the bigrams and trigrams, which were relatively inaccurate, especially for the last two verbs. On center-embeddings (middle panel), the two SRNs showed a gradual pattern of performance degradation across the sentence, with the D2-SRN achieving somewhat better performance, especially on the last verb. Bigrams and trigrams performed similarly, and again performed poorly on the two final verbs. When processing doubly embedded cross-dependency sentences (bottom panel), SRN performance resembled that found for counting recursion. The GPE for both SRNs increased gradually, and close to each other, until the first verb. Then the SRN GPE for the second verb dropped, whereas the D2-SRN GPE continued to grow. At the third verb the GPE for the D2-SRN dropped, whereas the SRN GPE increased.

Although this pattern of SRN GPEs may seem puzzling, it appears to fit recent results concerning the processing of similar cross-dependency constructions in Dutch. Using a phrase-by-phrase self-paced reading task with stimuli adapted from Bach et al. (1986), Dickey and Vonk (1997) found a significant jump in reading times between the second and third verb, preceded by a (nonsignificant) decrease in reading times between the first and second verb. When the GPEs for individual words are mapped onto reading times, the GPE pattern of the SRN, but not the D2-SRN, provides a reasonable approximation of the pattern of reading times found by Dickey and Vonk.

Returning to Figure 5.4, the trigram model—although not performing as well as the SRN—displayed a similar general pattern, whereas the bigram model performed very poorly. Overall, Figure 5.4 reveals that despite being trained exclusively on doubly embedded complex recursive constructions and despite not having to acquire the regularities underlying the right-branching structures, the D2-SRN only performed slightly better on doubly embedded complex recursive constructions than the SRN trained on both complex and right-branching recursive constructions of varying length. This suggests that SRN performance does not merely reflect the statistics of the training corpus, but also reflects intrinsic architectural constraints.

It is also interesting to note that the SRNs are not merely learning subsequences of the training corpus by rote. They substantially outperformed the n-gram models. This is particularly important because the material that we have used in these studies is the most favorable possible for n-gram models, since there is no intervening material at a given level of recursion. In natural language, of course, there is generally a considerable amount of material between changes of depth of recursion, which causes problems for n-gram models because they concentrate on short-range dependencies. While n-gram models do not generalize well to more linguistically natural examples of recursion, SRN models, by contrast, do show good performance on such

Figure 5.4
GPE against Word Position

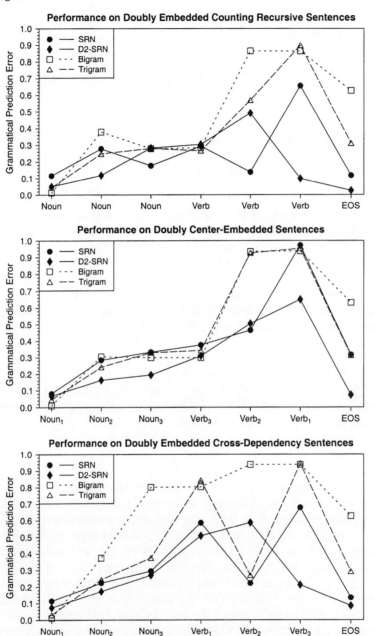

Grammatical prediction error for each word in doubly embedded sentences for the net trained on constructions of varying length (SRN), the net trained exclusively on doubly embedded constructions (D2-SRN), and the bigram and trigram models. Results are shown for counting recursion (top panel), center-embedding recursion (middle panel), and cross-dependency recursion (bottom panel). Subscripts indicate subject noun–verb agreement patterns.

material. We have found (Christiansen, 1994, 2000; Christiansen & Chater, 1994) that the addition of intervening nonrecursive linguistic structure does not significantly alter the pattern of results found with the artificial lan guages reported here. Thus, SRNs are not merely learning bigrams and trigrams, but acquiring richer grammatical regularities that allow them to exhibit behaviors qualitatively similar to humans. We now consider the match with human data in more detail.

Fitting Human Data

Center-Embedding versus Cross-Dependency

As we have noted, Bach et al. (1986) found that cross-dependencies in Dutch were comparatively easier to process than center-embeddings in German. They had native Dutch speakers listen to sentences in Dutch involving varying depths of recursion in the form of cross-dependency constructions and corresponding right-branching paraphrases with the same meaning. Native German speakers were tested using similar materials in German, but with the cross-dependency constructions replaced by center-embedded constructions. Because of differing intuitions among German informants concerning whether the final verb should be an infinitive or a past participle, two versions of the German materials were used. After each sentence, subjects rated its comprehensibility on a 9-point scale (1 = easy, 9 = difficult). Subjects were also asked comprehension questions after two-thirds of the sentences. In order to remove effects of processing difficulty due to length, Bach et al. subtracted the ratings for the right-branching paraphrase sentences from the matched complex recursive test sentences. The same procedure was applied to the error scores from the comprehension questions. The resulting difference should thus reflect the difficulty caused by complex recursion.

Figure 5.5 (left panel) shows the difference in mean test–paraphrase ratings for singly and doubly embedded cross-dependency sentences in Dutch and German. We focus on the past-participle German results because these were consistent across both the rating and comprehension tasks and were comparable with the Dutch data. Mean GPE across a sentence reflects how difficult the sentence was to process for the SRN. Hence, we can map GPE onto the human sentence-rating data, which are thought to reflect the difficulty that subjects experience when processing a given sentence. We used the mean GPEs from Figure 5.3 for the SRNs trained on center-embeddings and cross-dependencies to model the Bach et al. (1986) results. For recursive depths 1 and 2, mean GPEs for the right-branching constructions were subtracted from the average GPEs for the complex recursive constructions, and the differences were plotted in Figure 5.5 (right panel).[13] The net trained on cross-dependencies maps onto the Dutch data and the net trained on center-embedding maps onto the German (past-participle) data. At a single

Figure 5.5
Mean Test–Paraphrase Ratings

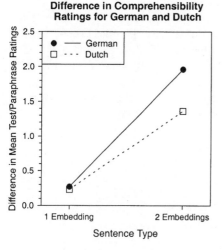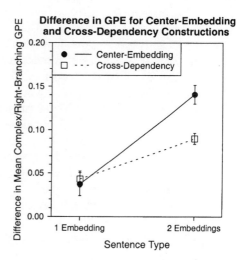

Human performance (from Bach et al., 1986) on singly and doubly center-embedded German (past-participle) sentences compared with singly and doubly embedded cross-dependency sentences in Dutch (left panel), and SRN performance on the same kinds of constructions (right panel). Error bars indicate the standard error of the mean.

level of embedding, Bach et al. found no difference between Dutch and German, and this holds in the SRN data ($t[18] = .36, p > .7$). However, at two levels of embedding Bach et al. found that Dutch cross-dependency stimuli were rated significantly better than their German counterparts. The SRN data also show a significant difference between depth 2 center-embeddings and cross-dependencies ($t[18] = 4.08, p < .01$). Thus, SRN performance mirrors the human data quite closely.

Grammatical versus Ungrammatical Double Center-Embeddings

The study of English sentences with multiple center-embeddings is an important source of information about the limits of human sentence processing (e.g., Blaubergs & Braine, 1974; Foss & Cairns, 1970; Marks, 1968; Miller, 1962; Miller & Isard, 1964; Stolz, 1967). A particularly interesting recent finding (Gibson and Thomas, 1999) using an off-line rating task suggests that some ungrammatical sentences involving doubly center-embedded object-relative clauses may be perceived as grammatical.

(17) *The apartment that the maid who the service had sent over was cleaning every week was well decorated.*

(18) **The apartment that the maid who the service had sent over was well decorated.*

In particular, they found that when the middle verb phrase (VP) was removed (18), the result was rated no worse than the grammatical version (17).

Turning to the SRN, in the artificial center-embedding language, (17) corresponds to **NNNVVV**, whereas (18) corresponds to **NNNVV**. Does the output activation following **NNNVV** fit the Gibson and Thomas (1999) data? Figure 5.6 shows mean activation across ten novel sentences and grouped into the four lexical categories and EOS marker. In contrast to the results of Gibson and Thomas, the network demonstrated a significant preference for the ungrammatical 2VP construction over the grammatical 3VP construction, predicting that (17) should be rated worse than (18).

Gibson and Thomas (1999) employed an off-line task, which might explain why (17) was rated worse than (18). Christiansen and MacDonald (2000) conducted an on-line self-paced word-by-word (center presentation) grammaticality judgment task using Gibson and Thomas's stimuli. At each point in a sentence subjects judged whether what they had read was a grammatical sentence or not. Following each sentence (whether accepted or rejected), subjects rated the sentences on a 7-point scale (1 = good, 7 = bad). Christiansen and MacDonald found that the grammatical 3VP construction was again rated significantly worse than the ungrammatical 2VP construction.

One potential problem with this experiment is that the 2VP and 3VP stimuli were different lengths, introducing a possible confound. The Gibson and Thomas (1999) stimuli also incorporated semantic biases (e.g., *apartment–decorated, maid–cleaning, service–sent over* in [17]), which may make

Figure 5.6
The Mean Output Activation for the Four Lexical Categories and the EOS Marker Given the Context NNNVV

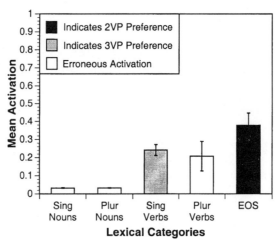

Error bars indicate the standard error of the mean.

the 2VP stimuli seem spuriously plausible. Christiansen and MacDonald (2000) therefore replicated their first experiment using stimuli controlled for length and without noun–verb biases, such as (19) and (20):

(19) *The chef who the waiter who the busboy offended appreciated admired the musicians.*

(20) **The chef who the waiter who the busboy offended frequently admired the musicians.*

Figure 5.7 shows the rating from the second experiment in comparison with SRN mean GPEs. As before, Christiansen and MacDonald (2000) found that grammatical 3VP constructions were rated as significantly worse than the ungrammatical 2VP constructions. The SRN data fitted this pattern, with significantly higher GPEs in 3VP constructions compared with 2VP constructions ($t[18] = 2.34$, $p < .04$).

Right-Branching Subject Relative Constructions

Traditional symbolic models suggest that right-branching recursion should not cause processing problems. In contrast, we have seen that the SRN shows some decrement with increasing recursion depth. This issue has re-

Figure 5.7
Comparing Human and SRN Center-Embedding Data

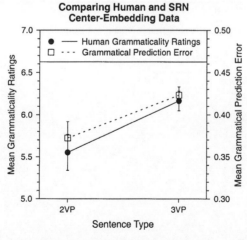

Human ratings (from Christiansen & MacDonald, 2000) for 2VP and 3VP center-embedded English sentences (left ordinate axis) compared with the mean grammatical prediction error produced by the SRN for the same kinds of constructions (right ordinate axis). Error bars indicate the standard error of the mean.

ceived little empirical attention. However, right-branching constructions are often control items in studies of center-embedding, and some relevant information can be gleaned from some of these studies. For example, Bach et al. (1986) report comprehensibility ratings for their right-branching paraphrase items. Figure 5.8 shows the comprehensibility ratings for the German past-participle paraphrase sentences as a function of recursion depth, and mean SRN GPEs for right-branching constructions (from Figure 5.3) for the center-embedding language. Both the human and SRN data show the same pattern of increasing processing difficulty with increasing recursion depth.

A similar fit with human data is found by comparing the human comprehension errors as a function of recursion depth reported in Blaubergs and Braine (1974) with mean GPE for the same depths of recursion (again for the SRN trained on the center-embedding language). Christiansen and MacDonald (2000) present on-line rating data concerning right-branching prepositional-phrase (PP) modifications of nouns in which the depth of recursion varied from 0 to 2 by modifying a noun by either one PP (21), two PPs (22), or three PPs (23):

(21) *The nurse with the vase says that the [flowers by the window] resemble roses.*

(22) *The nurse says that the [flowers in the vase by the window] resemble roses.*

(23) *The blooming [flowers in the vase on the table by the window] resemble roses.*

Figure 5.8
Comparing Human and SRN Right-Branching Data

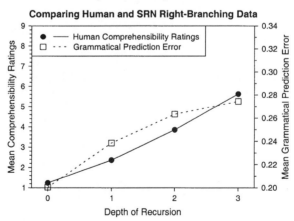

Human comprehensibility ratings (left ordinate axis) from Bach et al. (1996; German past-participle paraphrases) compared with the average grammatical prediction error for right-branching constructions produced by the SRN trained on the center-embedding language (right ordinate axis), both plotted as a function of recursion depth.

The stimuli were controlled for length and propositional and syntactic complexity. The results showed that subjects rated sentences with recursion of depth 2 (23) worse than sentences with recursion depth 1 (22), which, in turn, were rated worse than sentences with no recursion (21). Although these results do not concern subject-relative constructions, they suggest that processing right-branching recursive constructions is affected by recursion depth, although the effect of increasing depth is less severe than in complex recursive constructions. It is important that this dovetails with the SRN predictions (Christiansen, 1994, 2000; Christiansen & MacDonald, 2000), though not with symbolic models of language processing (e.g., Church, 1982; Gibson, 1998; Marcus, 1980; Stabler, 1994).

Counting Recursion

Finally, we briefly discuss the relationship between counting recursion and natural language. We contend that, despite Chomsky (1957), such structures may not exist in natural language. Indeed, the kind of structures that Chomsky had in mind (e.g., nested *if–then* structures) seem closer to center-embedded constructions than to counting-recursive structures. Consider the earlier-mentioned depth 1 example (16), repeated here as (24):

(24) *If$_1$ if$_2$ the cat is in, then$_2$ the dog cannot come in then$_1$ the cat and dog dislike each other.*

As the subscripts indicate, the *if–then* pairs are nested in a center-embedding order. This structural ordering becomes even more evident when we mix *if–then* pairs with *either–or* pairs (as suggested by Chomsky, 1957, p. 22):

(25) *If$_1$ either$_2$ the cat dislikes the dog, or$_2$ the dog dislikes the cat then$_1$ the dog cannot come in.*

(26) *If$_1$ either$_2$ the cat dislikes the dog, then$_1$ the dog dislikes the cat or$_2$ the dog cannot come in.*

The center-embedding ordering seems necessary in (25) because if we reverse the order of *or* and *then*, then we get the obscure sentence in (26). Thus, we predict that human behavior on nested *if–then* structures should follow the same breakdown pattern as for nested center-embedded constructions (perhaps with a slightly better overall performance).

Probing the Internal Representations

We now consider the basis of SRN performance by analyzing the HU representations with which the SRNs store information about previous linguistic material. We focus on the doubly embedded constructions, which represent the limits of performance for both people and the SRN. Moreover, we focus on what information the SRN's HUs maintain about the number agreement of the three nouns encountered in doubly embedded constructions (recording the HUs' activations immediately after the three nouns have been presented).

We first provide an intuitive motivation for our approach. Suppose that we aim to assess how much information the HUs maintain about the number agreement of the last noun in a sentence; that is, the noun that the net has just seen. If the information is maintained well, then the HU representations of input sequences that end with a singular noun (and thus belong to the lexical category combinations nn–**n**, nN–**n**, Nn–**n**, and NN–**n**) will be well-separated in HU space from the representations of the input sequences ending in a plural noun (i.e., NN–**N**, Nn–**N**, nN–**N**, and nn–**N**). Thus, it should be possible to split the HU representations *along* the plural–singular noun-category boundary such that inputs ending in plural nouns are separated from inputs ending in singular nouns. It is important to contrast this with a situation in which the HU representations instead retain information about the agreement number of individual nouns. In this case we should be able to split the HU representations *across* the plural–singular noun-category boundary such that input sequences ending with particular nouns, say, N_1, n_1, N_2, or n_2 (i.e., nn–$\{N_1, n_1, N_2, n_2\}$, nN–$\{N_1, n_1, N_2, n_2\}$, Nn–$\{N_1, n_1, N_2, n_2\}$, and NN–$\{N_1, n_1, N_2, n_2\}$) are separated from inputs ending with remaining nouns N_3, n_3, N_4, or n_4 (i.e., nn–$\{N_3, n_3, N_4, n_4\}$, nN–$\{N_3, n_3, N_4, n_4\}$, Nn–$\{N_3, n_3, N_4, n_4\}$, and NN–$\{N_3, n_3, N_4, n_4\}$).[14] Note that the separation along lexical categories is a special case of across-category separation in which inputs ending with the particular (singular) nouns n_1, n_2, n_3, or n_4 are separated from input sequences ending with the remaining (plural) nouns N_1, N_2, N_3, or N_4. Only by comparing the separation along and across the lexical categories of singular–plural nouns can we assess whether the HU representations merely maintain agreement information about individual nouns or whether more abstract knowledge has been encoded pertaining to the categories of singular and plural nouns. In both cases, information is maintained relevant to the prediction of correctly agreeing verbs, but only in the latter case are such predictions based on a generalization from the occurrences of individual nouns to their respective categories of singular and plural nouns.

We can measure the degree of separation by attempting to split the HU representations generated from the 512 (i.e., $8 \times 8 \times 8$) possible sequences of three nouns into two equal groups. We attempt to make this split using a plane in HU space; the degree to which two groups can be separated either along or across lexical categories therefore provides a measure of what information the network maintains about the number agreement of the last noun. A standard statistical test for the separability of two groups of items is discriminant analysis (Cliff, 1987; see Bullinaria, 1994; Wiles & Bloesch, 1992; Wiles & Ollila, 1993, for earlier applications to connectionist networks).

The left panel of Figure 5.9 illustrates a separation along lexical categories with a perfect differentiation of the two groups, corresponding to a 100-
percent correct vector classification. The same procedure can be used to
assess the amount of information that the HUs maintain concerning the
number agreement of the nouns in second and first positions. We split the
same HU activations generated from the 512 possible input sequences into
groups both along and across lexical categories. The separation of the HU
vectors along the lexical categories according to the number of the second
noun in the center panel of Figure 5.9 is also perfect. However, as illustrated by the right panel of Figure 5.9, the separation of the HU activations
along the lexical categories according to the first encountered noun is less
good, with 75 percent of the vectors correctly classified, because **N**–Nn is
incorrectly classified with the singulars and **n**–nN with the plurals.

We recorded HU activations for the 512 possible noun combinations for
complex and right-branching recursive constructions of depth 2 (ignoring
the interleaving verbs in the right-branching structures). Table 5.3 lists the
percentage of correctly classified HU activations for each combination. Classification scores were found for these combinations both before and after
training, and both for separation along and across singular–plural noun categories. Scores were averaged over different initial weight configurations
and collapsed across the SRNs trained on the three languages (there were no
significant differences between individual scores). The results from the separations across singular–plural noun categories show that prior to any training the SRN retained a considerable amount of information about the
agreement number of individual nouns in the last and middle positions.
Only for the first encountered noun was performance essentially at chance
(i.e., close to the performance achieved through a random assignment of
the vectors into two groups). The SRN had, not surprisingly, no knowledge

Figure 5.9
Schematic Illustration of Hidden-Unit State Space

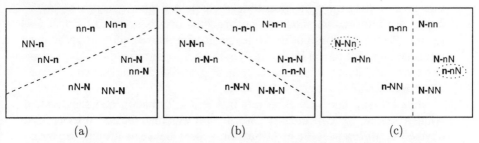

(a)   (b)   (c)

Each of the noun combinations denotes a cluster of hidden-unit vectors recorded for a particular set of agreement patterns (with **N** corresponding to plural nouns and **n** to singular
nouns). The straight dashed lines represent three linear separations of this hidden unit space
according to the number of the last seen noun (left panel), the second noun (center panel),
and the first encountered noun (with incorrectly classified clusters encircled) (right panel).

Table 5.3
Percentage of Cases Correctly Classified Given Discriminant Analyses of Network Hidden-Unit Representations

Noun Position	Recursion Type			
	Separation Along Singular/Plural Noun Categories		Separation Across Singular/Plural Noun Categories	
	Complex	Right-Branching	Complex	Right-Branching
	Before Training			
First	62.60	52.80	57.62	52.02
Middle	97.92	94.23	89.06	91.80
Last	100.00	100.00	100.00	100.00
Random	56.48	56.19	55.80	55.98
	After Training			
First	96.91	73.34	65.88	64.06
Middle	92.03	98.99	70.83	80.93
Last	99.94	100.00	97.99	97.66
Random	55.99	55.63	54.93	56.11

Note: Noun position denotes the left-to-right placement of the noun being tested, with Random indicating a random assignment of the vectors into two groups.

of lexical categories of singular and plural nouns before training, as indicated by the lack of difference between the classification scores along and across noun categories. The good classification performance of the untrained nets on the middle noun in the right-branching constructions is, however, somewhat surprising, because this noun position is two words (a verb and a noun) away from the last noun. In terms of absolute position from the point where the HU activations were recorded, the middle noun in right-branching constructions (e.g., $N_1 V_3 - N_3 - V_2 n_4$) corresponds to the first noun in complex recursive constructions (e.g., $N_1 - N_3 n_4$). Whereas untrained classification performance for this position was near chance on complex recursion, it was near perfect on right-branching recursion. This suggests that in the latter case information about the verb, which occurs between the last and the middle nouns, does not interfere much with the retention of agreement information about the middle noun. Thus, prior to learning the SRN appears to have an architectural bias that facilitates processing right-branching structures over complex recursive structures.

After training the SRN HUs retained less information about individual nouns. Instead, lexical category information was maintained, as evidenced by the big differences in classification scores between groups separated along and across singular–plural noun categories. Whereas classification scores along the two noun categories increased considerably as a result of training, the scores for classifications made according to groups separated across the categories of singular and plural nouns actually decreased, especially for the middle noun position. The SRN appears to have learned about the importance of the lexical categories of singular and plural nouns for the purpose of successful performance on the prediction task, but at the cost of losing information about individual nouns in the middle position.

The results of the discriminant analyses suggest that the SRN is well-suited for learning sequential dependencies. The feedback between the context layer and the hidden layer allows the net to retain information relevant to appropriate distinctions between previously encountered plural and singular items, even prior to learning. Of course, a net has to learn to take advantage of this initial separation of the HU activations to produce the correct output, which is a nontrivial task. Prior to learning, the output of an SRN consists of random activation patterns. Thus, it must discover the lexical categories and learn to apply agreement information in the right order to make correct predictions for center-embeddings and cross-dependencies.

On a methodological level, these results suggest that analyses of the untrained networks should be used as baselines for analyses of HU representations in trained networks. This may provide insight into which aspects of network performance are due to architectural biases and which arise from learning. A network always has some bias with respect to a particular task, and this bias depends on several factors, such as overall network configuration, choice of activation function, choice of input–output representations, initial weight setting, and so forth. As evidenced by our discriminant analyses, even prior to learning, HU representations may display some structural differentiation, emerging as the combined product of this bias (also cf. Kolen, 1994) and the statistics of the input–output relations in the test material. However, all too often HU analyses—such as cluster analyses, multidimensional scaling analyses, and principal component analyses—are conducted without any baseline analysis of untrained networks.

GENERAL DISCUSSION

We have shown that SRNs can learn to process recursive structures with similar performance limitations regarding depth of recursion as in human language processing. The SRNs' limitations appear relatively insensitive to the size of the network and the frequency of deeply recursive structures in the training input. The qualitative pattern of SRN results match human performance on natural language constructions with these structures. The SRNs trained on center-embedding and cross-dependency constructions performed well on singly embedded sentences, although, as for people, performance was by no means perfect (Bach et al., 1986; Blaubergs & Braine, 1974; King & Just, 1991). Of particular interest is the pattern of performance degradation on sentences involving center-embeddings and cross-dependencies of depth 2, and its close match with the pattern of human performance.

These encouraging results suggest a reevaluation of Chomsky's (1957, 1959) arguments that the existence of recursive structures in language rules out finite-state and associative models of language processing. These arguments have been taken to indicate that connectionist networks cannot in principle account for human language processing. But we have shown that this in-principle argument is not correct. Connectionist networks can learn to handle recursion with a comparable level of performance to people. Our simulations are, of course, small scale, and do not show that this approach generalizes to model the acquisition of the full complexity of natural language. But this limitation applies equally well to symbolic approaches to language acquisition (e.g., Anderson, 1983), including parameter-setting models (e.g., Gibson & Wexler, 1994; Niyogi & Berwick, 1996) and other models that assume an innate universal grammar (e.g., Berwick & Weinberg, 1984).

Turning to linguistic issues, the better SRN performance on cross-dependencies over center-embeddings may reflect the fact that the problem of learning limited versions of context-free and context-sensitive languages may be very different from the problem of learning the full, infinite versions of these languages (compare Vogel, Hahn, & Branigan, 1996). Within the framework of Gibson's (1998) Syntactic Prediction Locality Theory, center-embedded constructions (of depth 2 or less) are harder to process than their cross-dependency counterparts because center-embedding requires holding information in memory over a longer stretch of intervening items. Although a similar explanation is helpful in understanding the difference in SRN performance on the two types of complex recursive constructions, this cannot be the full explanation. First, this analysis incorrectly suggests that singly embedded cross-dependency structures should be easier than comparable center-embedded constructions. As illustrated by Figure 5.5, this is not true of the SRN predictions, nor in the human data from Bach et al. (1986). Second, the analysis predicts a flat or slightly rising pattern of GPE across the verbs in a sentence with two cross-dependencies. In contrast, the GPE pattern for the cross-dependency sentences (Figure 5.4) fits the reading-time data from Dickey and Vonk (1997) because of a *drop* in the GPEs for the second verb. Overall, the current results suggest that we should be wary of drawing strong conclusions for language processing, in networks and perhaps also in people, from arguments concerning idealized infinite cases.

A related point concerns the architectural requirements for learning languages involving, respectively, context-free and context-sensitive structures. In our simulations the very same network learned the three different artificial languages to a degree similar to human performance. To our knowledge, no symbolic model has been shown to be able to learn these three kinds of recursive structures given identical initial conditions. For example, Berwick and Weinberg's (1984) symbolic model of language acquisition has a built-in stack and would therefore not be able to process cross-dependencies. Of course, if one builds a context-sensitive parser, then it can also by definition parse context-free strings. However, the processing models that are able to account for the Bach et al. (1986) data (Gibson, 1998; Joshi, 1990; Rambow & Joshi, 1994) do not incorporate theories of learning that can explain how the ability to process center-embedding and cross-dependency could be acquired.

In this chapter we have presented results showing a close qualitative similarity between breakdowns in human and SRN processing when faced with complex recursion. This was achieved without assuming that the language processor has access to a competence grammar that allows unbounded recursion, subject to performance constraints. Instead, the SRN account suggests that the recursive constructions that people actually say and hear may be explained by a system with no representation of unbounded grammatical competence, and performance limitations arise from intrinsic constraints on processing. If this hypothesis is correct, then the standard distinction between competence and performance, which is at the center of contemporary linguistics, may need to be rethought.

FURTHER READINGS

Most of the early connectionist models of recursion were essentially simple reimplementations of symbolic parsers (e.g., Fanty, 1986; Small, Cottrell, & Shastri, 1982). The first more comprehensive model of this kind was McClelland and Kawamoto's (1986) neural network model of case-role assignment. Many of the subsequent models of sentence processing and recursion have sought to provide alternatives to the symbolic-processing models. One approach has been to learn recursive structure from "tagged" input sentences. Among these, Pollack's (1988, 1990) recursive auto-associative memory network has inspired several subsequent modeling efforts (e.g., Chalmers, 1990; Niklasson & van Gelder, 1994; see also Steedman, Chapter 11, this volume). Another approach is to construct a modular system of networks, each of which is trained to acquire different aspects of syntactic processing. Miikkulainen's (1996) three-network system provides a good example of this approach. But the most popular connectionist approach to recursion and syntactic processing builds on Elman's (1990, 1991, 1993) simple recurrent network model.

Recently, efforts have been made to model reading-time data from recursive sentence-processing experiments. The work by Christiansen (2000; Christiansen & Chater, 1999; MacDonald & Christiansen, in press) is perhaps the best example of this line of research. Turning to syntactic processing more generally, Tabor, Juliano, and Tanenhaus (1997) provide a dynamical sentence-processing model (see also Tabor & Tanenhaus, Chapter 6, this volume). The most influential nonconnectionist model of sentence-processing results is Gibson's (1998) Syntactic Prediction Locality Theory model. A slightly older nonconnectionist model is the CC-READER model by Just and Carpenter (1992).

For discussions of the future prospects of connectionist models of syntax (and recursion), see Seidenberg and MacDonald (Chapter 9, this volume) and Steedman (Chapter 11, this volume).

NOTES

This chapter is in large part based on Christiansen and Chater (1999). We would like to thank Joe Allen, Jim Hoeffner, Mark Seidenberg, and Paul Smolensky for discussions and comments on the work presented here.

1. We leave aside generalization, which we discuss elsewhere (Christiansen, 1994, 2000; Christiansen & Chater, 1994).

2. Cross-dependency has also been alleged to be present in "respectively" constructions in English, such as *Anita$_1$ and the girls$_2$ walks$_1$ and skip$_2$, respectively*. Church (1982) questions the acceptability of these constructions with two cross-dependencies, and even one, as in this example, seems bizarre.

3. Pullum and Gazdar (1982) have argued, controversially, that natural language is, nonetheless, context-free (see Gazdar & Pullum, 1985; Shieber, 1985).

4. Their nets were trained using back-propagation through time (Rumelhart et al., 1986).

5. Intuition may suggest that higher-order *n*-gram models should outperform simple bigram and trigram models because they can encode more extended regularities. However, results using text corpora have shown that higher-order *n*-grams provide for poor predictions due to distributional "undersampling": Many higher-order *n*-grams only have one or very few instances, or do not occur at all in a given corpus (Gale & Church, 1990; Redington, Chater, & Finch, 1998).

6. The relation between grammaticality judgments and processing mechanisms is controversial (see Christiansen, 1994; Schütze, 1996).

7. These simulations used the *Tlearn* simulator available from the Center for Research on Language, University of California, San Diego.

8. We adopt the convention that **n** and **N** correspond to categories of nouns and **v** and **V** to categories of verbs, with capitalization indicating plural agreement. The EOS marker is denoted by #. Individual word tokens are denoted by adding a subscript (e.g., N_3).

9. We use bold for random variables.

10. These assumptions are, of course, very unrealistic given the skewed distribution of word frequencies in natural language, but are nonetheless used for simplicity.

11. Note that "total network activation" is not a possible interpretation, because the difference between the total activation and hit activation (see Equation 5.4) corresponds to the false-alarm activation (see Equation 5.5).

12. Could GPE hide a failure to make correct agreement predictions for singly center-embedded sentences, such as *The man$_1$ the boys$_2$ chase$_2$ likes$_1$ cheese*? If so, one would expect high agreement error for the two verb predictions in the singly center-embedded (complex depth 1) constructions in Figure 5.3. Agreement error can be calculated as the percentage of verb activation allocated to verbs that do not agree in number with their respective nouns. The agreement error for the first and

second verbs was 1 percent and 16.85 percent, respectively. This level of agreement error is comparable with human performance (Larkin and Burns, 1977).

13. The human data presented here and later involve three different scales of measurement (i.e., differences in mean test–paraphrase comprehensibility ratings, mean grammaticality ratings from 1 to 7, and mean comprehensibility ratings from 1 to 9). It was therefore necessary to adjust the scales for the comparisons with the mean GPEs accordingly.

14. Curly brackets indicate that any of the nouns may occur in this position, creating the following combinations: $nn\text{-}N_1$, $nn\text{-}n_1$, $nn\text{-}N_2$, and $nn\text{-}n_2$.

REFERENCES

Anderson, J. R. (1983). *The architecture of cognition*. Cambridge, MA: Harvard University Press.

Bach, E., Brown, C., & Marslen-Wilson, W. (1986). Crossed and nested dependencies in German and Dutch: A psycholinguistic study. *Language and Cognitive Processes, 1*, 249–262.

Batali, J. (1994). Artificial evolution of syntactic aptitude. In *Proceedings of the Sixteenth Annual Conference of the Cognitive Science Society* (pp. 27–32). Hillsdale, NJ: Lawrence Erlbaum.

Berwick, R. C., & Weinberg, A. S. (1984). *The grammatical basis of linguistic performance: Language use and acquisition*. Cambridge, MA: MIT Press.

Blaubergs, M. S., & Braine, M.D.S. (1974). Short-term memory limitations on decoding self-embedded sentences. *Journal of Experimental Psychology, 102*, 745–748.

Bullinaria, J. A. (1994). Internal representations of a connectionist model of reading aloud. In *Proceedings of the Sixteenth Annual Conference of the Cognitive Science Society* (pp. 84–89). Hillsdale, NJ: Lawrence Erlbaum.

Chalmers, D. J. (1990). Syntactic transformations on distributed representations. *Connection Science, 2*, 53–62.

Charniak, E. (1993). *Statistical language learning*. Cambridge, MA: MIT Press.

Chater, N., & Conkey, P. (1992). Finding linguistic structure with recurrent neural networks. In *Proceedings of the Fourteenth Annual Conference of the Cognitive Science Society* (pp. 402–407). Hillsdale, NJ: Lawrence Erlbaum.

Chomsky, N. (1957). *Syntactic structures*. The Hague: Mouton.

Chomsky, N. (1959). Review of Skinner (1957). *Language, 35*, 26–58.

Chomsky, N. (1965). *Aspects of the theory of syntax*. Cambridge, MA: MIT Press.

Christiansen, M. H. (1992). The (non)necessity of recursion in natural language processing. In *Proceedings of the Fourteenth Annual Conference of the Cognitive Science Society* (pp. 665–670). Hillsdale, NJ: Lawrence Erlbaum.

Christiansen, M. H. (1994). *Infinite languages, finite minds: Connectionism, learning and linguistic structure*. Unpublished doctoral dissertation, University of Edinburgh.

Christiansen, M. H. (2000). *Intrinsic constraints on the processing of recursive sentence structure*. Manuscript in preparation.

Christiansen, M. H., & Chater, N. (1994). Generalization and connectionist language learning. *Mind and Language, 9*, 273–287.

Christiansen, M. H., & Chater, N. (1999). Toward a connectionist model of recursion in human linguistic performance. *Cognitive Science, 23*, 157–205.

Christiansen, M. H., & MacDonald, M. C. (2000). *Processing of recursive sentence structure: Testing predictions from a connectionist model.* Manuscript in preparation.

Church, K. (1982). *On memory limitations in natural language processing.* Bloomington: Indiana University Linguistics Club.

Cleeremans, A., Servan-Schreiber, D., & McClelland, J. L. (1989). Finite state automata and simple recurrent networks. *Neural Computation, 1,* 372–381.

Cliff, N. (1987). *Analyzing multivariate data.* Orlando, FL: Harcourt Brace Jovanovich.

Dickey, M. W., & Vonk, W. (1997, 20–22 March). Center-embedded structures in Dutch: An on-line study. Poster presented at the Tenth Annual CUNY Conference on Human Sentence Processing. Santa Monica, California.

Elman, J. L. (1990). Finding structure in time. *Cognitive Science, 14,* 179–211.

Elman, J. L. (1991). Distributed representation, simple recurrent networks, and grammatical structure. *Machine Learning, 7,* 195–225.

Elman, J. L. (1993). Learning and development in neural networks: The importance of starting small. *Cognition, 48,* 71–99.

Fanty, M. (1986). Context-free parsing with connectionist networks. In J. S. Denker (Ed.), *Neural networks for computing* (AIP conference proceedings 151) (pp. 140–145). New York: American Institute of Physics.

Foss, D. J., & Cairns, H. S. (1970). Some effects of memory limitations upon sentence comprehension and recall. *Journal of Verbal Learning and Verbal Behavior, 9,* 541–547.

Gale, W., & Church, K. (1990). Poor estimates of context are worse than none. In *Proceedings of the June 1990 DARPA Speech and Natural Language Workshop.* Hidden Valley, Pennsylvania.

Gazdar, G., & Pullum, G. K. (1985). *Computationally relevant properties of natural languages and their grammars* (Tech. Rep. No. CSLI-85-24). Palo Alto, CA: Stanford University, Center for the Study of Language and Information.

Gibson, E. (1998). Linguistic complexity: Locality of syntactic dependencies. *Cognition, 68,* 1–76.

Gibson, E., & Thomas, J. (1999). Memory limitations and structural forgetting: The perception of complex ungrammatical sentences as grammatical. *Language and Cognitive Processes, 14,* 225–248.

Gibson, E., & Wexler, K. (1994). Triggers. *Linguistic Inquiry, 25,* 407–454.

Giles, C., & Omlin, C. (1993). Extraction, insertion and refinement of symbolic rules in dynamically driven recurrent neural networks. *Connection Science, 5,* 307–337.

Giles, C., Miller, C., Chen, D., Chen, H., Sun, G., & Lee, Y. (1992). Learning and extracting finite state automata with second-order recurrent neural networks. *Neural Computation, 4,* 393–405.

Green, D. M., & Swets, J. A. (1966). *Signal detection theory and psychophysics.* New York: Wiley.

Hanson, S. J., & Kegl, J. (1987). PARSNIP: A connectionist network that learns natural language grammar from exposure to natural language sentences. In *Proceedings of the Eighth Annual Conference of the Cognitive Science Society* (pp. 106–119). Hillsdale, NJ: Lawrence Erlbaum.

Joshi, A. K. (1990). Processing crossed and nested dependencies: An automaton perspective on the psycholinguistic results. *Language and Cognitive Processes, 5,* 1–27.

Just, M. A., & Carpenter, P. A. (1992). A capacity theory of comprehension: Individual differences in working memory. *Psychological Review, 99*, 122–149.

King, J., & Just, M. A. (1991). Individual differences in syntactic processing: The role of working memory. *Journal of Memory and Language, 30*, 580–602.

Kolen, J. F. (1994). The origin of clusters in recurrent neural network state space. In *Proceedings of the Sixteenth Annual Conference of the Cognitive Science Society* (pp. 508–513). Hillsdale, NJ: Lawrence Erlbaum.

Larkin, W., & Burns, D. (1977). Sentence comprehension and memory for embedded structure. *Memory & Cognition, 5*, 17–22.

Luce, D. (1959). *Individual choice behavior*. New York: Wiley.

MacDonald, M. C., & Christiansen, M. H. (in press). Reassessing working memory: A comment on Just & Carpenter (1992) and Waters & Caplan (1996). *Psychological Review*.

Marcus, M. (1980). *A theory of syntactic recognition for natural language*. Cambridge, MA: MIT Press.

Marks, L. E. (1968). Scaling of grammaticalness of self-embedded English sentences. *Journal of Verbal Learning and Verbal Behavior, 7*, 965–967.

McClelland, J. L., & Kawamoto, A. H. (1986). Mechanisms of sentence processing. In J. L. McClelland & D. E. Rumelhart (Eds.), *Parallel distributed processing: Explorations in the microstructure of cognition*. Vol. 2: *Psychological and biological models* (pp. 272–325). Cambridge, MA: MIT Press.

Miikkulainen, R. (1996). Subsymbolic case-role analysis of sentences with embedded clauses. *Cognitive Science, 20*, 47–73.

Miller, G. A. (1962). Some psychological studies of grammar. *American Psychologist, 17*, 748–762.

Miller, G. A., & Isard, S. (1964). Free recall of self-embedded English sentences. *Information and Control, 7*, 292–303.

Niklasson, L., & van Gelder, T. (1994). On being systematically connectionist. *Mind and Language, 9*, 288–302.

Niyogi, P., & Berwick, R. C. (1996). A language learning model for finite parameter spaces. *Cognition, 61*, 161–193.

Pollack, J. B. (1988). Recursive auto-associative memory: Devising compositional distributed representations. In *Proceedings of the Tenth Annual Conference of the Cognitive Science Society* (pp. 33–39). Hillsdale, NJ: Lawrence Erlbaum.

Pollack, J. B. (1990). Recursive distributed representations. *Artificial Intelligence, 46*, 77–105.

Pullum, G. K., & Gazdar, G. (1982). Natural languages and context-free languages. *Linguistics and Philosophy, 4*, 471–504.

Rambow, O., & Joshi, A. K. (1994). A processing model for free word-order languages. In C. Clifton, L. Frazier, & K. Rayner (Eds.), *Perspectives on sentence processing* (pp. 267–301). Hillsdale, NJ: Lawrence Erlbaum.

Redington, M., Chater, N., & Finch, S. (1998). Distributional information: A powerful cue for acquiring syntactic categories. *Cognitive Science, 22*, 425–469.

Reich, P. (1969). The finiteness of natural language. *Language, 45*, 831–843.

Rumelhart, D. E., Hinton, G. E., & Williams, R. J. (1986). Learning internal representations by error propagation. In J. L. McClelland & D. E. Rumelhart (Eds.), *Parallel distributed processing: Explorations in the microstructure of cognition*. Vol. 1: *Foundations* (pp. 318–362). Cambridge, MA: MIT Press.

Schütze, C. T. (1996). *The empirical base of linguistics: Grammaticality judgments and linguistic methodology*. Chicago: University of Chicago Press.

Servan-Schreiber, D., Cleeremans, A., & McClelland, J. L. (1991). Graded state machines: The representation of temporal contingencies in simple recurrent networks. *Machine Learning, 7*, 161–193.

Shieber, S. (1985). Evidence against the context-freeness of natural language. *Linguistics and Philosophy, 8*, 333–343.

Skinner, B. F. (1957). *Verbal Behavior*. New York: Appleton–Century–Crofts.

Small, S. L., Cottrell, G. W., & Shastri, L. (1982). Towards connectionist parsing. In *Proceedings of the National Conference on Artificial Intelligence*. Pittsburgh, Pennsylvania.

Stabler, E. P. (1994). The finite connectivity of linguistic structure. In C. Clifton, L. Frazier, & K. Rayner (Eds.), *Perspectives on sentence processing* (pp. 303–336). Hillsdale, NJ: Lawrence Erlbaum.

Steijvers, M., & Grünwald, P. (1996). A recurrent network that performs a context-sensitive prediction task. In *Proceedings of the Eighteenth Annual Conference of the Cognitive Science Society* (pp. 335–339). Mahwah, NJ: Lawrence Erlbaum.

Stolcke, A. (1991). Syntactic category formation with vector space grammars. In *Proceedings of the Thirteenth Annual Conference of the Cognitive Science Society* (pp. 908–912). Hillsdale, NJ: Lawrence Erlbaum.

Stolz, W. S. (1967). A study of the ability to decode grammatically novel sentences. *Journal of Verbal Learning and Verbal Behavior, 6*, 867–873.

Tabor, W., Juliano, C., & Tanenhaus, M. K. (1997). Parsing in a dynamical system: An attractor-based account of the interaction of lexical and structural constraints in sentence processing. *Language and Cognitive Processes, 12*, 211–271.

Vogel, C., Hahn, U., & Branigan, H. (1996). Cross-serial dependencies are not hard to process. In *Proceedings of COLING-96, the 16th International Conference on Computational Linguistics* (pp. 157–162). Copenhagen.

Weckerly, J., & Elman, J. (1992). A PDP approach to processing center-embedded sentences. In *Proceedings of the Fourteenth Annual Conference of the Cognitive Science Society* (pp. 414–419). Hillsdale, NJ: Lawrence Erlbaum.

Wiles, J., & Bloesch, A. (1992). Operators and curried functions: Training and analysis of simple recurrent networks. In J. E. Moody, S. J. Hanson, & R. P. Lippmann (Eds.), *Advances in Neural Information Processing Systems 4*. San Mateo, CA: Morgan-Kaufmann.

Wiles, J., & Elman, J. (1995). Learning to count without a counter: A case study of dynamics and activation landscapes in recurrent networks. In *Proceedings of the Seventeenth Annual Conference of the Cognitive Science Society* (pp. 482–487). Hillsdale, NJ: Lawrence Erlbaum.

Wiles, J., & Ollila, M. (1993). Intersecting regions: The key to combinatorial structure in hidden unit space. In S. J. Hanson, J. D. Cowan, & C. L. Giles (Eds.), *Advances in Neural Information Processing Systems 5* (pp. 27–33). San Mateo, CA: Morgan-Kaufmann.

6

Dynamical Systems for Sentence Processing

Whitney Tabor and Michael K. Tanenhaus

THE DYNAMICS OF SENTENCE PROCESSING

The syntactic constraints of a language strongly determine the interpretation that a reader or listener arrives at for a sentence. Thus, the human language comprehension system must develop and evaluate hypotheses as to how to map the linguistic input into appropriate syntactic units. Temporary ambiguity is the central problem faced by the system. Because the linguistic input is typically consistent with multiple syntactic possibilities, the processing system must determine the set of possible syntactic hypotheses, maintain some or all of these in memory, and update them as new input arrives.

Behavioral evidence from a rapidly expanding literature on how people read temporarily ambiguous sentences provides an empirical benchmark for evaluating theories of syntactic processing (see Tanenhaus & Trueswell, 1995). Evidence from intuitions and from empirical studies of processing difficulty—typically studies using reading-time measures with temporarily ambiguous sentences—have clearly established that readers have strong preferences for some structures over others. When subsequent input becomes inconsistent with the preferred structure, the result is processing difficulty for the reader.

Sentence (1), taken from Bever (1970), is a classic example of such a "garden-path" sentence:

(1) *The horse raced past the barn fell.*

The reader assumes that the first six words of the sentence form a main clause in the active voice with *raced* being a past-tense main verb, and *the horse* playing the role of "agent" of the racing event. This hypothesis is disconfirmed by the word *fell*, however, resulting in long reading times and confusion. Many readers are unable to arrive at the "grammatical" analysis in which *fell* is the main verb, and *the horse (which was) raced past the barn* as its subject.

Within traditional symbolic systems, syntactic hypotheses are typically computed by a parser, a set of procedures that maps the input onto partial syntactic structures that are consistent with the syntactic constraints of the language. These constraints are described by a grammar consisting of a set of rules and/or constraints defined over syntactic categories, such as Noun and Noun Phrase (NP). The procedures that comprise the parser build structures using the knowledge base defined by the grammar.

A variety of structural hypotheses have been proposed to account for why some structures are preferred over others in an initial stage of structure building. These hypotheses are typically couched in terms of the complexity of structure building operations, and/or memory demands (see Frazier & Clifton, 1996; Gibson, 1998, for recent reviews). In such two-stage models, a second set of procedures is involved in recovering from misanalysis when the preferred structure selected in the initial parse is rejected.

However, recent research has highlighted a number of phenomena that are problematic for this view. A growing body of evidence indicates that syntactic processing is simultaneously affected by semantic, syntactic and discourse-based information (for reviews, see MacDonald, Pearlmutter, & Seidenberg, 1994; Tanenhaus & Trueswell, 1995). Moreover, processing is sensitive to differences among individual lexical items within syntactic categories. Thus, sentences like (2) are much easier to process than sentences like (1), even though the sequence of standard lexical categories ("Det Noun Verb[ed form] Preposition etc.") is identical across the two examples.

(2) *The salmon released in the ocean died.*

In addition, the speed with which readers process the words of sentences like (1) and (2) is correlated with graded properties of the linguistic input that are not easily reduced to purely structural factors. For example, the degree to which readers have difficulty at the second verb in these sentences is negatively correlated with the degree to which the first verb tends to occur, in large natural language corpora, as a past participle (MacDonald et al., 1994; Trueswell, 1996).

Phenomena like these have led a number of researchers to propose constraint-based frameworks in which multiple sources of constraint provide probabilistic evidence in support of the most likely syntactic alternatives. Ambiguity resolution is viewed as a constraint-satisfaction process, involving competition among incompatible alternatives. As a sentence unfolds, the alternatives are evaluated using evidence provided by the current input as well as the preceding context (Cottrell & Small, 1983, 1984; Cottrell, 1985; Waltz & Pollack, 1985; St. John & McClelland, 1990; MacDonald et al., 1994; Spivey-Knowlton, 1996). Processing difficulty occurs when input is encountered that is inconsistent with the previously biased alternative.

Connectionist (or neural network) models are one variety of constraint-based models. Typically, their properties as learning devices play a central role in their use as models. In particular, it is often suggested that the systematic properties of language that motivate the positing of specialized structures in a symbolic paradigm will arise as "emergent properties" under connectionist learning. The interest of this claim is not merely that it provides an explicit proposal about the grammar-induction part of the theory. It also suggests that the emergent counterparts of symbolic mechanisms will be different from them in important ways.

We endorse all these claims here, but note that much previous connectionist modeling of syntactic structures has been inexplicit about what these emergent structures are and how, exactly, they differ from their symbolic counterparts. This chapter and Tabor, Juliano, and Tanenhaus (1997) argue that a connectionist, learning-based system can be explicit about emergent properties by using the constructs of dynamical-systems theory.

Dynamical-systems theory is the theory of systems that are described in terms of how they change. Formally, this description has the form of a differential equation or an iterated map. Commonly studied examples of real dynamical systems are swinging pendulums, orbiting planets, circulating fluids, and so forth. Certain constructs are useful in analyzing such systems: trajectories, fixed points (or stable states), attractors, basins, saddlepoints (see Abraham & Shaw, 1984; Strogatz, 1994, for introductions). Along with Cornell Juliano, we first explored the idea that such constructs might be useful in clarifying the principles underlying connectionist sentence processing (Tabor et al., 1997). There, we focused on the way the dynamical approach allows us to handle class frequency effects and the interaction of formal similarity with structural constraints. This chapter continues this line of investigation by focusing on how the dynamical approach handles early effects of thematic role biases, often put forth as evidence for constraint-based modeling, without losing track of the structural constraints.

Our work is similar to other recent connectionist approaches to parsing in that we train a variant of a simple recurrent network (SRN) using the prediction task developed by Elman (1991). The input to the model is a sequence of words generated by a finite-state or context-free grammar. The model forms representations of parse states in its hidden unit space. It places words that are likely to be followed by similar constructions near one another in the hidden-unit space (Elman, 1990, 1991; Christiansen, 1994; Tabor, 1994). In symbolic parameter-setting models of grammar learning (e.g., Lightfoot, 1991) syntactic structures are listed fully formed in a mental warehouse of possibilities prior to learning. By contrast, in network models like ours, syntactic structure is built up by the network as it learns to process the input. The result is a correspondingly greater influence of the learning process on the final performance of the system (Christiansen, 1994; Christiansen & Chater, 1999; MacDonald & Christiansen, in press).

While prior learning connectionist models have revealed the important role that experience (or training) plays in adult sentence processing, they lack an explicit analog of reading times. Instead, they typically map output activations onto reading times with a formula (Christiansen & Chater, 1999; MacDonald & Christiansen, in press). Moreover, the representations developed by these and many connectionist models are hard to interpret in terms that reveal the structural principles underlying the models' empirical successes.

To address these shortcomings, we add a dynamical processor to the SRN. This processor transforms the sometimes ambivalent representations produced by the network into unique parse hypotheses, requiring varying amounts of time to do so. The model's processing time is taken as an analog of human reading time. The dynamical component operates on the set of states visited by the network when it is processing a large random sample of text, and it uses a gravitational mechanism to group these into distinct classes, thus providing useful structural information about the SRN's representation. We refer to the resulting model, which we first explored in Tabor et al. (1997), as the Visitation Set Gravitation model.

The remainder of this chapter is organized into three sections. In the next section we define the VSG model and motivate it by describing related modeling work. Then we show how the model can incorporate a kind of "semantic constraint" (the thematic role biases of nouns) into the resolution process. An appealing characteristic of the model is that it appears to make the intuitively appropriate distinction between syntactically and semantically incongruous sentences. The final section presents conclusions.

THE VSG MODEL AND RELATED DYNAMICAL MODELS

The VSG Model

The VSG model has two components: a network similar to an SRN (Elman 1990, 1991) and a gravitation module. Elman (1991) describes a procedure for training a particular connectionist network, the SRN, to predict distributional information about a corpus of words. Each word in the corpus is assigned a unique *indexical bit vector* (a vector with one element equal to 1 and all others equal to 0). These vectors are presented on the input layer of the network in the order in which the corresponding words occur in the corpus. The network is trained on the task of predicting on the output layer which word is coming next for each input.

Elman (1991) uses a three-layer feed-forward network with a "context layer" feeding into the hidden layer at each time step. The context layer contains a copy of the hidden-unit activations on the previous time step. The network is trained using the back-propagation algorithm (e.g., Rumelhart, Hinton, & Williams, 1986). This feed-forward network with a context layer has the same relaxation dynamics as a three-layer network with complete interconnection among its hidden units (on the assumption that each unit is updated exactly once each time a word is presented, with the input and context units updated first, then the hidden units, and then the output units). Elman's training procedure is an approximation of the back-propagation through time (BPTT) algorithm (Rumelhart et al., 1986), in which the error propagation through the recurrent connections in the hidden units is cut off after it has been propagated back through just one hidden-layer time step. (Thus, input-to-hidden weights only receive an error signal from the current-time hidden units.)[1]

In the simulations discussed in this chapter we used the same recurrent architecture as Elman (1991) did for the relaxation dynamics, but carried error propagation through two hidden-layer time steps while still adjusting input-to-hidden weights only on the basis of the current time step (see Figure 6.1). The extra time step makes learning the longer-distance dependencies that occur in language tasks a little bit easier. Our network had thirty-seven input units, ten hidden units, and thirty-seven output units. The hidden units at all time steps had fixed sigmoid activation functions [$y_i = 1/(1 + e^{-net_i})$, where net_i is the net input to unit i]. The output units as a group had normalized exponential (or softmax) activation functions ($y_i = e^{net_i}/\sum_{j \in Outputs} e^{net_j}$). The output error for input p was thus defined for "1-of-n" classification by Equation 6.1:

$$E_p = \log \prod_{j \in Outputs} y_j^{t_j} \qquad (6.1)$$

where y_j is the activation of unit j for input p, and t_j is the target for unit j on that input (Rumelhart, Durbin, Golden, & Chauvin, 1995) and back-propagated through the unfolded network.[2] Weights were adjusted after every input presentation. The network was trained on the output of a simple grammar approximating those features of English syntax that appear to be relevant to the phenomenon we model. The phenomenon, the grammar, and the training specifics are described in detail later.

The second component of the VSG model, the gravitation module, operates on the hidden-layer representations of the trained recurrent network. Elman's (1991) work and our earlier work (Tabor, Juliano, & Tanenhaus,

Figure 6.1
Three-Layer Network with Recurrent Connections in the Hidden Layer (implemented as partial unfolding across time)

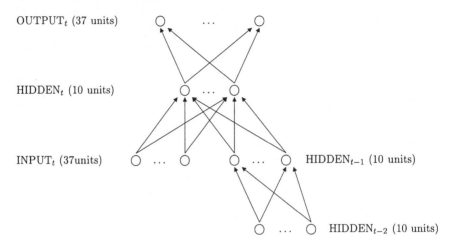

1996) suggest that words in context with similar distributional characteristics are placed near one another in the hidden-unit space by an SRN. A consequence is that if we sample the hidden-unit activations of the trained network over a wide range of constructions from the training language, we may find a set of clusters of points, where points in the same cluster correspond to grammatically equivalent states of the generating language.

The VSG's gravitation module is a clustering mechanism that finds such equivalence classes of states. It operates as follows. Once the network is trained, we present it with a large random sample of sentences generated by the grammar and record all the hidden-unit states visited (that is to say, the *visitation set*) during the processing of this sample. We treat each of these points as a fixed mass of unit magnitude in the ten-dimensional hidden-unit space. We then test the processing of a particular word-in-context by treating the hidden-unit location of that word-in-context as a test mass (also of unit magnitude) that is free to move under the gravitational influence of all the fixed masses. Typically, the test mass will be near the center of mass of some dense cluster and will gravitate into that cluster. We model processing time as the time required to gravitate into the cluster. One can think of the fixed masses as representing typical previous experiences with the language. Thus, the gravitational mechanism implements the idea that in responding to a new instance of a word-in-context the processor analogizes that word-in-context to its previous experiences and gravitates to a cluster corresponding to the most similar previous experience. The points in the centers of the clusters where the system is stable are called *attractors*.[3] The set of all starting points from which the system gravitates into a particular attractor is called its *basin*. In the case we study, under an appropriate parameterization of the gravitational system the system's basin structure defines a partition of the set of words-in-context into equivalence classes. These classes correspond to states of the grammar (Crutchfield, 1994; Hopcroft & Ullman, 1979) that generated the training data.

The change in position of the test mass is defined by Equation (6.2):

$$\frac{\Delta \vec{x}}{\Delta t} = v \sum_{i=1}^{N} \frac{\vec{x}_i - \vec{x}}{r_i^p} \tag{6.2}$$

where x is the position of the test mass, N indexes the fixed masses, x_i is the position of the i'th fixed mass, r_i is the Euclidean distance between x_i and x at time t, and p is a gravitational strength parameter that determines the pulling power of each test mass. This equation is an approximation of Newton's Law of Universal Gravitation when (1) the test mass has zero velocity at infinite distance from the fixed masses, (2) $p = 2$, and (3) v is the Universal Gravitation Constant.

Equation 6.2 implies that every point in the visitation set is a singular point (i.e., a point where the velocity goes to infinity). To avoid infinite velocities, which make the structure of the system hard to detect, we introduce a threshold r_{min} and set $r = r_{min}$ whenever r becomes smaller than r_{min}. This makes the trajectories less prone to wild jumps. The parameters, N, v, r_{min}, Δt, and p are all free parameters of the model. The first four are primarily relevant to making the performance of the model easy to interpret.[4] The last (p, or gravitational strength), is undesirably unconstrained; we set it to a value that makes the attractor basins correspond to distinct parse states as defined by the training grammar. The fact that such a value for p has existed in nearly all the cases we have tried so far indicates that the model is quite restrictive, for varying p over all possible values defines a relatively small set of basin structures. Moreover, the choice of p is closely tied to the constraints on learning and so there may be a way to bind it less stipulatively (see the next subsection for discussion). Under these assumptions, the test mass will typically speed up as it approaches a fixed point (or chaotic attractor) near the center of mass of a cluster, overshoot the attractor (because it is unlikely that the mass will land exactly on a fixed point for positive Δt), and then head back toward the center of mass for another "flyby." Our algorithm for determining gravitation times thus computes the number of steps it takes the test mass to reverse direction for the first time (where a direction reversal is a turn of more than 90 degrees in one step).

In sum, the VSG model is trained like an SRN. It generates predictions of reading times as follows:

1. Feed a sentence one word at a time to the trained network using SRN relaxation dynamics.

2. For each word of the sentence, use the gravitation module to determine a gravitation time.

3. Compare gravitation time profiles (e.g., across words in a sentence) to reading time profiles.

Note that the gravitation module operates completely independently of the recurrent network: The outcome of the relaxation dynamics does not affect the network's processing of the subsequent word.

Previous Related Models

In order to motivate the model we have just described, we review previous related models. Several of the models we discuss are connectionist models. It is worth noting that most connectionist models are dynamical systems of the standard sort: Their operation can be described by a differential equation for which the state change is a continuous function of the parameters (or weights) of the network. In fact, one can distinguish two important dynamical regimes within the connectionist framework: learning dynamics and relaxation dynamics. Learning dynamics involve slow adjustment of connection weights in an attempt to find a minimum of a cost function. Relaxation dynamics involve rapid adjustment of activation values in order to compute an output. The VSG model clarifies the relationship between these two types of dynamical regimes by showing how there are relaxation dynamics (albeit in a nonconnectionist system) that reveal structural properties of the learning dynamical system for one type of network (the SRN).

Earlier connectionist processing models (e.g., McClelland & Rumelhart, 1981; Cottrell & Small, 1983, 1984; Cottrell, 1985; Waltz & Pollack, 1985) usually examined the relaxation dynamics of hand-designed models. Nodes represented concepts that are naturally interpretable by human beings (e.g., the word *throw*, the concept TOSS), and all node properties were explicitly designed by the researchers; no learning was involved. These models had many of the properties that we make use of here. For example, competition between simultaneously valid parses increased processing time. Second, the magnitudes of real-valued weights were adjusted to reflect contrasts in frequency and thus gave rise to biases in favor of more frequently encountered interpretations (e.g., Cottrell & Small, 1984). Third, sometimes "spurious" attractive states arose that corresponded to no interpretation (e.g., Cottrell & Small, 1984). In some earlier models these spurious states were considered a liability because some parsable sentences got stuck in them. Later we show that certain spurious states are an asset, in that they provide a plausible model of what happens when one attempts to parse an ungrammatical string (cf. Plaut, McClelland, Seidenberg, & Patterson, 1996). Fourth, syntactic and semantic information were used simultaneously to constrain the parse (e.g., Cottrell & Small, 1983; Cottrell, 1985).

The development of the back-propagation algorithm for learning (Rumelhart et al., 1986) and its promotion as a useful tool in psychological modeling (Rumelhart & McClelland, 1986) led to a new class of connectionist parsing models. This algorithm made it possible to set weights and hidden-node interpretations in a systematic way, without requiring as many subjective guesses as were needed in hand-designed models. Currently, the most successful learning connectionist models of sentence processing are Elman's (1990, 1991) SRN and its variants (e.g., St. John & McClelland, 1990).[5] Elman's model can approximate the word-to-word transition likelihoods associated with a simple text corpus, thus embodying information relevant to the syntax and semantics of the language of the corpus to the degree that these are reflected in distributional properties.

While the learning dynamics of Elman's (1990, 1991) model are complex and interesting, the relaxation dynamics are uniform and uninformative. Since each node is updated exactly once after a word is presented, the network's processing time is identical from word to word and cannot plausibly be interpreted as a model of human processing time. Several researchers (Christiansen & Chater, 1999; MacDonald & Christiansen, in press) have shown that a well-chosen definition of SRN output error can be mapped onto processing times. A desirable next step is to model word-to-word processing explicitly in the relaxation dynamics. Such explicitness is one goal of the VSG approach.

Moreover, as in many connectionist simulations, the principles governing the Elman (1990, 1991) model's specific predictions are not usually easy to surmise: The trained network's model of its environment is a complexly shaped manifold in a high-dimensional space. Although one-dimensional quantities like error measures and cost functions can give insight into local properties of this manifold, they do not tell us much about its structure. A useful addition would be some summarizing category information indicating which pieces of the manifold are important and what role they play in organizing the linguistic task. Thus, a second aim of the VSG approach is to use dynamical-systems theory to reveal this summarizing category information by approximating certain basins, attractors, saddle points, and so on that are implicit in the SRN's learning dynamics. For example, as noted, the attractors of the VSG model map onto distinct parse states of the language learned by the network.

Although the VSG model is inelegant in that it is a hybrid of two distinct dynamical systems, we view it is a useful stepping stone to a more mathematically streamlined and more neurally plausible model. In particular, the dynamics of the gravitation module are roughly paralleled by the dynamics of recurrent connectionist networks that settle to fixed points after each word presentation. In current work we are exploring the use of the recurrent back-propagation (RBP) algorithm (Almeida, 1987; Pineda, 1995) to train such networks on sentence-processing tasks. In these models the learning process drives the formation of attractor basins, so the free parameter p is eliminated and the categorization system stems from independently motivated constraints such as the number of hidden units and the nature of the activation function. However, the task of learning complex syntax in an RBP network is harder. Thus, an advantage of the VSG model is that it permits us to use the currently more syntactically capable SRN to explore the effectiveness of dynamical constructs. If the predictions are borne out, then the motivation for solving the learning challenges facing RBP becomes greater.

The attractor basins defined by the VSG model are primarily valuable for the insight they provide into the representations learned by an SRN. One may reasonably wonder, though, if they have any motivation independent of the problem of predicting reading times. In fact, there is an independent functional motivation for having attractor basins: When we interpret language, we make, and probably need to make, discrete choices. Waltz and Pollack (1985, p. 52) note that although we can comprehend the multiple meanings of wholly ambiguous sentences (e.g., *Trust shrinks; Respect remains; Exercise smarts*), we seem to flip-flop between them rather than simultaneously understanding both. Moreover, it is clearly important to be able to conclude that in a sentence like *Jack believed Josh was lying, Josh* is not an object of the matrix clause but a subject of the embedded clause, even though processing evidence suggests that we temporarily entertain the former hypothesis. It has not previously been evident how to map the real-valued states of an SRN onto such discrete interpretations. The VSG model provides a principled method of mapping from the SRN state vectors to discrete parse states that may be useful in distinguishing meanings.

We noted earlier that constraint-satisfaction models have been proposed as an alternative to two-stage models of sentence processing (Frazier & Clifton, 1996). The VSG model also performs computations in two distinct stages: the recurrent-network computation and the gravitation computation. But there are important differences between the VSG model and traditional two-stage models. In the VSG model there is no early stage during which some information is systematically ignored. Rather, all information is present from the beginning of each word's settling process. Moreover, the second stage does not involve deconstructing and rebuilding parse trees, but rather migrating in a continuous space. Finally, systematic biases in favor of one structure over another stem mainly from greater experience with the preferred structure, not from an avoid-complexity strategy (see MacDonald & Christiansen, in press).

Previous VSG Results

In our earlier work (Tabor et al., 1997) we showed that the VSG model predicts word-by-word reading times in a set of cases that are challenging for other theories. We summarize the results here in order to situate our further exploration of the model.

In one simulation we considered lexical category ambiguities involving the word *that*, which exhibit an interesting mix of contingent frequency effects (Juliano & Tanenhaus, 1993; Tabor et al., 1997). The following sentences illustrate that *that* can be either a determiner (3 and 5) or a complementizer (4 and 6). The number of the noun disambiguates *that* as either a determiner (singular) or a complementizer (plural).

(3) *That marmot whistles.*

(4) *That marmots whistle is surprising.*

(5) *A girl thinks that marmot whistles.*

(6) *A girl thinks that marmots whistle.*

The results of Juliano and Tanenhaus (1993) indicate that processing times in these four sentences are predicted by the hypothesis that readers slow down when they encounter words that violate their expectations about typical usage, as determined from a corpus analysis. In particular, *that* is more frequent as a determiner than as a complementizer sentence-initially, but it is more frequent as a complementizer than as a determiner postverbally. Thus, (3) is easier than (4), while (5) is harder than (6) at the words following *that*. These results are consistent with a host of experimental results that suggest reading times are correlated with the unexpectedness of continuations (see Jurafsky, 1996, for review). In Tabor et al. (1997) we showed that such effects fall out of the VSG model because of the denser visitation clusters associated with more-frequent continuations. Denser clusters give rise to stronger gravitational pull and hence more rapid gravitation.

On the other hand, the correlation between unexpectedness and reading times is not perfect. It seems to be skewed by the category structure of the grammar. For example, Juliano and Tanenhaus (1993) found that after strictly transitive verbs like *visited*, the word *that* and a following adjective (7) was read more slowly than the word *those* and a following adjective (8).

(7) *The writer visited* that old *cemetery.*

(8) *The writer visited* those old *cemeteries.*

Such a result cannot be attributed to the frequency of *that* versus *those* after transitive verbs, because the frequencies are essentially the same (at least in the Penn Treebank). The VSG model predicts the effect at the determiner as a case of attractor competition. The word *that* following a transitive verb bears a distributional resemblance to *that* following a sentence-complement verb. Therefore, the position assigned by the recurrent net to *that* following a transitive verb is intermediate in the gravitation field between the attractor for *that* following a sentence-complement verb and the attractor for unambiguous determiners following transitive verbs. By contrast, since *those* is not ambiguous, *those* following a transitive verb starts very close to the appropriate attractor. Since *that* starts farther away from the attractor and its gravitation is slowed by the presence of a nearby attractor, it is processed more slowly than *those* in the relevant examples.[6] Tabor et al. (1997) showed how a similar effect predicts the observed higher reading times at *the* after a pure sentence complement verb like *insisted* than at *the* after a transitive verb like *visited* (Juliano & Tanenhaus, 1993).

These two cases illustrate two advantageous properties of the VSG model: (1) It is consistent with the pervasive evidence showing that reading time is inversely correlated with class frequency, and (2) it diverges appropriately from the frequency-based predictions in cases where class similarity effects distort these. The VSG model predicts the latter, smoothing effects by letting similarities between categories distort the internal structure of the attractor basins associated with the categories. It is possible that a similar prediction can be made by a model that computes expectations based on a probabilistic grammar (e.g., Jurafsky, 1996). However, it appears that some kind of as-yet-unspecified statistical smoothing (Charniak, 1993) across grammatical classes is required (Tabor et al., 1997). It is also possible that a model that treats reading time as a kind of output error in an SRN (e.g., Christiansen & Chater, 1999; MacDonald & Christiansen, in press) would also predict divergences from frequency-based predictions due to class similarity, since position contrasts in the hidden-unit space tend to map to position contrasts in the output space. But as we have noted, such one-dimensional measures do not encode information about direction of displacement, so it is hard to tell in such models if similarity is indeed the source of the error.

CASE STUDY: THEMATIC EXPECTATION

The simulations just described only examined pure syntactic contrasts in the sense that the complement requirements of the verbs and the agreement requirements of the determiners were categorical. It is of some interest, then, to investigate how the VSG model performs in a case where the contrast is not categorical in this way. Such cases arise in association with what are generally thought of as "semantic" distinctions. A good example is thematic role assignment. Almost any noun can fill any role, but if a noun that is unsuitable for a given role is forced to play that role, the result is a sentence that sounds "semantically strange" or "incongruous":

(9) # *The customer was served by the jukebox.*
(10) # *The car accused the pedestrian of cheating.*

Semantically strange sentences seem to violate our expectations about what is likely to happen in the world, but they do not violate our expectations about what can happen in the language in the same way that ungrammatical sentences do. Linguistic theories generally posit two distinct mechanisms for handling semantic and syntactic incongruity. Semantic violation is thought to be detected on the basis of world knowledge, whereas syntactic incongruity results from violating rules of grammar. This set of assumptions is very useful in that it has allowed us to recognize the effectiveness of abstract syntactic mechanisms at organizing linguistic information. Moreover, there is psychophysiological data from studies using event-related potentials suggesting that the two kinds of violations result in qualitatively different patterns of brain responses (Garnsey, 1993; Osterhout & Holcomb, 1993; Hagoort, Brown, & Groothusen, 1993; Ainsworth-Darnell, Shulman, & Boland, 1998).

The distinction between syntactic and semantic incongruity is especially interesting from the perspective of connectionist models. Both semantic and syntactic constraints affect the distributional structure of words in the language. This raises the possibility that a connectionist device trained on distributional information could model both classes of constraints. We show that this hypothesis is supported by the VSG model in the following sense: The gravitational mechanism, defined by the representation developed by a connectionist network, exhibits what might best be called a *graded qualitative distinction* between semantic and syntactic incongruity.

The claim that semantic information can be learned by a model that only interacts with corpus data is surprising. Clearly, a model without an extralinguistic world cannot simulate the relationship between language and the extralinguistic world, and thus cannot be a full semantic model, in one common sense of the term. However, we may ask if such a model provides the right "hooks" for interfacing with the world. In this case, corpus-based models may have something useful to contribute. Corpuses contain a good deal of information beyond what the syntax of a language provides. Indeed, Burgess and Lund (1997), Landauer and Dumais (1997), and others have shown that much information that is standardly termed "semantic" can be extracted from a corpus by evaluating cooccurrence statistics. Much of this information is about which words tend to be used in combination with which other words, given that they can be so used. The usual strategy in linguistic modeling is to note that such information reflects properties of the world that can be learned independently of language—indeed, some of it is the kind of knowledge that animals and prelinguistic children seem to have—and to try to simplify the job of the language theory by assuming that it does not incorporate such knowledge. But this may be misguided: Since the information about tendencies of usage is available in the speech we hear, it is possible that the "language mechanism" is actually shaped by this usage as well as by abstract grammatical constraints. In fact, a theory that posits such a "world-molded" language mechanism may be better suited to providing a full model of the language–world relationship than one that assumes strict independence, because it has the structures needed for interfacing. On the other hand, there is a potential problem with trying to let the language mechanism encode too much detail about the world: The theory may become too complex or unduly unrestrictive.[7] The dynamical-systems framework is a way around the latter pitfall: The details of subtle differences in the semantic biases of words are encoded in small differences in position in the metric representation space, but the basin configuration of the system as a whole provides an organizing category structure that is computationally simple.

To explore these issues in a specific case, we examined the role of thematic fit in syntactic ambiguity resolution, focusing on the results of McRae, Spivey-Knowlton, and Tanenhaus (1998).

The Phenomenon

McRae et al. (1998) examined the way the thematic properties of a subject and verb influenced readers' biases in favor of a reduced-relative versus a main-clause reading in sentences like (11) and (12).

(11) *The cop / arrested by / the detective / was guilty / of taking / bribes.*

(12) *The crook / arrested by / the detective / was guilty / of taking / bribes.*

McRae et al. (1998) performed an off-line rating task in which subjects were asked to answer questions such as, *How common is it for a cop to arrest someone?* by providing a number on a scale of 1 to 7 (where 1 corresponds to very uncommon and 7 to very common). On this basis, they grouped *cop* and similarly rated nouns together as "Good Agents" and they grouped *crook* and similarly rated nouns together as "Good Patients." They then studied self-paced reading times in regions like those shown in (11) and (12). A summary of their results is graphed in Figure 6.2. The graph plots a "reduction effect," measured in milliseconds versus sentence region. The reduction effect is the difference between the reading time of sentences like (11) and (12) and the corresponding unreduced cases in which *who was* was inserted before the first verb.

Three properties of the data are worth highlighting. First, there is an immediate effect of thematic bias: In the verb + *by* region, the Good Patients give rise to higher reading times than the Good Agents. Second, reading times are longer where there is a conflict between the biases of the preceding context and the biases of the current word; for example, at the (agentive) verb after a Good Patient subject, and at the NP following a Good Agent subject and verb. Third, reading times show an "inertia" effect. Even when the linguistic input provides information that could, in principle, be used to strongly reject a previously entertained parse (e.g., the word *by* after the verb), the processor seems to shift only gradually over to the new hypothesis.

Figure 6.2
Crossed and Smoothed Latencies in the Main Clause–Reduced Relative Ambiguity
(after McRae et al., 1998)

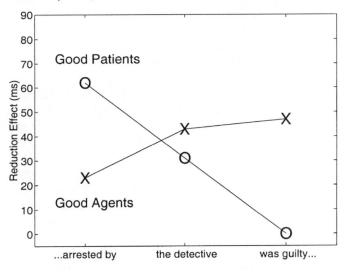

The X sentences began with Good Agents; the O sentences began with Good Patients.

McRae et al. (1998) showed that the reading-time profiles can be plausibly interpreted as stemming from competition between two alternative syntactic hypotheses: Hypothesis X, the first verb (e.g., *arrested*) is the main verb of the sentence, or Hypothesis Y, it is a verb in a reduced relative clause. For Good Patients there is competition between these two hypotheses beginning at the first verb, which resolves quickly when supporting evidence for the reduced relatives comes from the *by*-phrase. For Good Agents there is a strong initial bias for the main clause, with competition beginning when disconfirming information is encountered in the *by*-phrase.

McRae et al. (1998) formalized the competition account by using Spivey-Knowlton's (1996) normalized recurrence algorithm, in which multiple constraints provided support for two competing structures: main clause and reduced relative. The strength of the constraints was determined by norms and corpus analysis. The weights were set to model fragment-completion data using the same materials. The same weights were then used successfully to predict on-line reading times. In the simulation described next we extend this result by showing how the weights can be set via connectionist learning on corpus data resembling the significant distributional properties of the McRae et al. materials. The resulting model then predicts the three phenomena already highlighted: immediate semantic influences, competition-induced slowdowns, and inertia.

Thematic Expectation Simulation

The Training Grammar

The simulation grammar is shown in Table 6.1. This grammar generates a relatively simple, symmetrical set of strings that share a number of properties with the English sentences of interest. The quoted labels in the grammar and in the following discussion (e.g., "Good Agt," "Good Pat") make this analogy explicit for the sake of giving the reader some familiar labels to use as placeholders. Although the analogy is rough, and we do not intend that the model map precisely onto human behavior, it is designed to make the central conceptual issues transparent. Such transparency is critical, we believe, for getting past the typical opaqueness of connectionist models.

The grammar in Table 6.1 is designed so that the first word of each sentence can be classified as belonging to one of two classes, X or Y, which give rise to different expectations about which words are likely to occur next. X and Y correspond to "Good Agent" and "Good Patient," respectively. The dominance of agentive constructions in English is reflected in the fact that sentences starting with Xs outnumber sentences starting with Ys by a ratio of 2 : 1. Also, as in English, there are initial Xs and initial Ys of a range of different frequencies. The second word of each sentence is of the type labeled V. It corresponds conceptually to the English verbs in McRae et al.'s (1998) study in the following way: Both Xs and Ys are followed by the same set of Vs, but, depending on which first word and V occurred, there is a bias as to how the sentence will end. Sentences that begin with X words and are followed by V words with letter labels alphabetically close to "a" tend to end with the most common members of the X2 and X3 categories (ignoring, for a moment, the words with 1 in their labels). Sentences that begin with Y and are followed by Vs with letter labels alphabetically close to "f" tend to end with the most common members of the Y2 and Y3 categories. In fact, the members of the categories X2 and Y2 are the same, as are the members of the categories X3 and Y3, but if the generating category is X2 or X3, then there is a bias toward words with labels alphabetically close to "a," and if the generating category is Y2 or Y3, there is a bias toward words with labels alphabetically close to "f." The word "p" is an end-of-sentence marker, or "period."

The nonabsolute biases of the V, 1, and 2 words mirror the fact that in natural language many words can be constituents of many constructions and thus do not provide a categorical signal, independent of their context, as to which parse hypothesis is correct; but many of these same words have statistical tendencies that can be used to compute a bias toward one construction or another in a given context (Rohde & Plaut, 1999). In the model, the local ambiguity of the words turns out to be essential to the prediction of inertia effects: It forces the network to use its context representation to

Table 6.1
Training Grammar for the Thematic Bias Simulation

0.67 S → X VX VPX p ("MC")

0.33 S → Y VY VPY p ("RR")

0.67 X → xa ("Good Agt")	0.02 Y → ya ("Good Pat")
0.17 X → xb ("Good Agt")	0.03 Y → yb ("Good Pat")
0.07 X → xc ("Good Agt")	0.04 Y → yc ("Good Pat")
0.04 X → xd ("Good Agt")	0.07 Y → yd ("Good Pat")
0.03 X → xe ("Good Agt")	0.17 Y → ye ("Good Pat")
0.02 X → xf ("Good Agt")	0.67 Y → yf ("Good Pat")
0.67 VX → va ("MC Bias Verb")	0.02 VY → va ("RR Bias Verb")
0.17 VX → vb ("MC Bias Verb")	0.03 VY → vb ("RR Bias Verb")
0.07 VX → vc ("MC Bias Verb")	0.04 VY → vc ("RR Bias Verb")
0.04 VX → vd ("MC Bias Verb")	0.07 VY → vd ("RR Bias Verb")
0.03 VX → ve ("MC Bias Verb")	0.17 VY → ve ("RR Bias Verb")
0.02 VX → vf ("MC Bias Verb")	0.67 VY → vf ("RR Bias Verb")
0.67 VPX → 1a X2 X3 ("MC")	0.02 VPY → 1a X2 X3 ("MC")
0.17 VPX → 1b X2 X3 ("MC")	0.03 VPY → 1b X2 X3 ("MC")
0.07 VPX → 1c X2 X3 ("MC")	0.04 VPY → 1c X2 X3 ("MC")
0.04 VPX → 1d Y2 Y3 ("RR")	0.07 VPY → 1d Y2 Y3 ("RR")
0.03 VPX → 1e Y2 Y3 ("RR")	0.17 VPY → 1e Y2 Y3 ("RR")
0.02 VPX → 1f Y2 Y3 ("RR")	0.67 VPY → 1f Y2 Y3 ("RR")
0.67 X2 → 2a ("MC")	0.02 Y2 → 2a ("RR")
0.17 X2 → 2b ("MC")	0.03 Y2 → 2b ("RR")
0.07 X2 → 2c ("MC")	0.04 Y2 → 2c ("RR")
0.04 X2 → 2d ("MC")	0.07 Y2 → 2d ("RR")
0.03 X2 → 2e ("MC")	0.17 Y2 → 2e ("RR")
0.02 X2 → 2f ("MC")	0.67 Y2 → 2f ("RR")
0.67 X3 → 3a ("MC")	0.02 Y3 → 3a ("RR")
0.17 X3 → 3b ("MC")	0.03 Y3 → 3b ("RR")
0.07 X3 → 3c ("MC")	0.04 Y3 → 3c ("RR")
0.04 X3 → 3d ("MC")	0.07 Y3 → 3d ("RR")
0.03 X3 → 3e ("MC")	0.17 Y3 → 3e ("RR")
0.02 X3 → 3f ("MC")	0.67 Y3 → 3f ("RR")

Note: MC = Main Clause; RR = Reduced Relative. The quoted labels specify the analogy with English.

compute expectations. As a result, the network tends to retain the parse bias it had at earlier stages, only relinquishing it gradually.

There are, however, some words in natural languages, the "closed-class" or "function" words, that provide fairly unambiguous cues as to which parse hypothesis is correct. The word *by* is one such word in the McRae et al. (1998) materials. Here, the members of the 1 category provide this kind of categorical constraining information. "1a" through "1c" are only compatible with an X2 X3 ending, while "1d" through "1f" are only compatible with a Y2 Y3 ending. Note that both X and Y initial words can be followed by both kinds of endings, but there is a bias for X initial words to be followed by X2 X3 endings and for Y initial words to be followed by Y2 Y3 endings. Following McRae et al.'s investigation, we will examine a case in which these tendencies are violated.

Training the Network

The grammar was used to generate data for training the network described earlier. Before training began, the weights and biases of the network were assigned uniformly distributed random values in the interval [−0.5, 0.5]. The network's learning rate was set at 0.05. Momentum was not used. The grammar defines ten states (states are distinct if they induce different distributions over the set of all possible future sequences; Crutchfield, 1994; cf. Hopcroft & Ullman, 1979). The network was trained until it was distinguishing and reasonably approximating the transition likelihoods of all ten states. The grammar sanctions 15,552 (12×6^4) grammatical strings. Each juncture between words in a string is associated with a probability distribution over next-words that can be computed from the grammar. We compared the network's output for each juncture to the grammar-generated distribution for that juncture and asked if the distance between these two distributions was less than one-half the minimum distance between any two grammar-determined distributions.[8] We stopped training when a hand-picked sample of such comparisons yielded positive outcomes, and then evaluated this comparison for the whole language to find that the comparison yielded a positive outcome for 94 percent of the 93,312 ($15,552 \times 6$) junctures between words. At this point the network had been trained on 50,000 word presentations. We reinitialized the weights and retrained the network five times for the same number of word presentations. We determined by inspection that the visitation set had nearly identical (ten-cluster) structure in three out of the six cases, and similar structure in all cases. The results reported are based on the first case.

The Gravitation Mechanism

After some experimentation, we set the gravitation module parameters to $n = 2000$, $r_{min} = .01$, $\mu = .0002$, and $p = 2.7$. With these settings the dynamical processor had an attractor corresponding to each state associated with the training grammar. There were two attractors associated with initial words, V words, 1 words, and 2 words. The two attractors correspond to the X ("Main Clause") reading and the Y ("Reduced Relative") readings, respectively, in the sense that sentences that had a high likelihood of finishing with letter labels alphabetically near "a" were consistently drawn into the X attractor and those with a high likelihood of finishing with labels near "f" were consistently drawn into the Y attractor. There was one attractor for the 3 position and one for the end-of-sentence marker, "p."

Reading-Time Results

In analogy with McRae et al.'s (1998) study of reduced relatives after Good Agents and Good Patients, we compared the reading times on a Y ("Reduced Relative") continuation for sentences beginning, respectively, with X ("Main Clause bias") words and Y ("Reduced Relative bias") words. Because our grammar did not include the option of disambiguating the V ("Verb") word syntactically prior to its occurrence (as in English *The cop who was arrested* . . .), we were not able to use such disambiguated cases as a baseline. However, in the simulation we only had a few relevant cases to measure and there was not much noise, so the effect of contrasting initial word biases was evident without such baselining.

A sample result is shown in Figure 6.3. The dotted line shows gravitation times for the string "yd vc 1d 2d 3d p" (*crook arrested by detective escaped*), and the solid line shows times for "xc vc 1d 2d 3d p" (*cop arrested by detective escaped*). The pattern shows the central properties of the human reading-time data: (1) immediate effects of new information, even though the information is merely semantically biasing (at the V word, for example, there is an effect of the bias of the immediately preceding N word), (2) cross-

Figure 6.3
Gravitation Times for the Thematic Bias Simulation

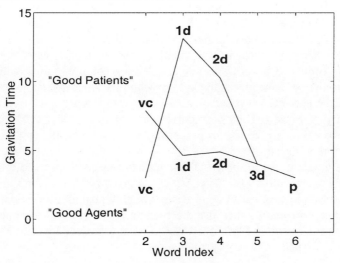

over of the magnitudes of the reading times during the course of the sentence (first the Y or RR-bias sentence shows a spike in reading time, then the X or MC-bias sentence shows one), and (3) inertia in the parse choice (each spike has a tail that dwindles over the course of several following words).

These results suggest that the VSG model can reproduce a number of significant features of human reading-time patterns when trained on distributional information reflecting certain thematic role-induced biases. The next subsection analyzes the model's predictions.

Induction of Competition Effects

The fact that the gravitation times of the VSG model show a similar pattern to the human data is encouraging. Examining the representations and the processing dynamics of the VSG model reveals that the VSG model is predicting the human data by implementing a competition mechanism very much like Spivey-Knowlton's (1996) normalized recurrence algorithm.

Figure 6.4 provides a global view of the visitation set for the simulation. This image was obtained by performing principal component analysis (PCA) on the set of 2,000 hidden-unit locations used in the gravitational model. PCA (Jolliffe, 1986) is a way of choosing coordinate axes that are maximally aligned with the variance across a set of points in a space.[9] It is used here simply as a way of viewing the visitation set, and plays no role in the predictions made by the model.

The visitation set is grouped into major regions corresponding to the six major categories of the grammar (initial word, V word, 1 word, 2 word, 3 word, and final word ["p"]).[10] Two of these categories overlap in the two-dimensional reduced image (V and 2), but they do not overlap in the ten-dimensional space. Several of the major regions seem to have two distinct clusters within them in Figure 6.4. These correspond to the two parse hypotheses, X ("Main Clause") and Y ("Reduced Relative").

To see this more clearly, it is helpful to zero in on one of the major clusters. Figure 6.5 shows a new PCA view of the points where the connectionist network places the system when its input layer is receiving a V word (the new PCA is based on all and only the V word points). Here, we can clearly see the two clusters corresponding to the X and Y readings. These two clusters give rise to two attractors that are at the centers of the circles in the diagram.[11]

Three trajectories are shown. These trajectories correspond to three sentences that start "xc vc . . . ," "yc vc . . . ," and "yf vf . . . ," respectively. The "xc vc . . ." and "yf vf . . ." cases, roughly analogous to *cop arrested* and *evidence examined*, are the the beginnings of normal sentences that typically give rise to X ("Main Clause") and Y ("Reduced Relative") interpretations, respectively. Since their classification status is quite clearcut,

Figure 6.4
Global View of the Visitation Set for the Thematic Bias Simulation

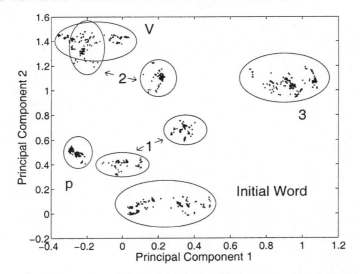

the processor lands close to the appropriate attractor when the V word is presented and gravitation takes only two time steps.[12] By contrast, the sentence that starts with "yc vc" (analogous to *crook arrested*) has conflicting information in it. The first word indicates that the processor should favor the Y attractor, but the second word ("vc") is predominantly associated with an X continuation. As a result, the processor lands in an intermediate position when the second word is presented. It gravitates to the X attractor, but the gravitation takes a long while (eight time steps).

In Figure 6.6 we show a close-up of the 1 region of the visitation set. Here we can observe one-word continuations of the sentences shown in Figure 6.5. The case of central interest is "xc vc 1d." We can think of this case as analogous to a partial sentence like *cop arrested by* . . . which starts off with a Good Agent and is followed by an agentive verb, but continues with a *by*-phrase that strongly signals the unexpected Reduced Relative interpretation. In such cases, people showed latencies at the agentive noun phrase in the *by*-phrase that were quite high compared to a control case with a Good Patient subject (e.g., *crook arrested by detective* . . .). While the model processes "xc vc" with ease, the subsequent "1d" lands it in an intermediate position and thus gives rise to a very long gravitation time (thirteen time steps). The corresponding control case, "yc vc 1d," (*crook arrested by* . . .) produces a nonminimal trajectory at "1d" as well, but the starting point is initially much closer to the Y attractor and the gravitation time is correspondingly shorter (five time steps). Thus, these two strings, when compared at their V words and 1 words, produce the crossing latency-

Figure 6.5
Three Trajectories in the V Region

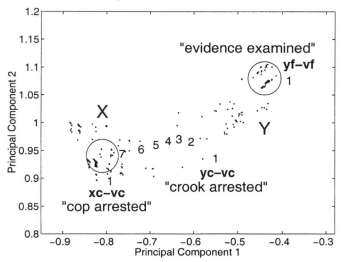

The label "yc-vc" identifies the starting point of the trajectory that ensued when "vc" had been presented on the input layer after "yc." The numbers 1, 2, 3, and so on proceeding from this label indicate the trajectory itself. The other labels have similar interpretations.

values pattern that distinguishes McRae et al.'s (1998) data. It is true that the simulation shows the crossing pattern more immediately in response to the disambiguating information than the human subjects appear to (i.e., at the first disambiguating word), but as we noted, this may be due to the weakness of the parafoveal *by* signal; it may also reflect the more complex ambiguity of natural language *by* that we have noted.

For comparison, Figure 6.6 also shows a case of gravitation to the X attractor in the 1 region: the partial sentence "yf-vf-1a" (presumably comparable to something like, *The evidence examined him . . .*). In this case, the first two words strongly favor a Y ("Reduced Relative") continuation, while the third word requires an X ("Main Clause") continuation. The result is a nonminimal reading time at "1a" but not the superelevated reading time of the focus case, "xc-vc-1d." This intermediate reading time makes sense because high-frequency bias-revising information ("1a") is more effective at overcoming the contextual bias than the relatively low-frequency bias-revising information ("1d") of the focus case.

These examples indicate that the VSG model mirrors the two-attractor account of McRae et al. (1998) in the details of its dynamics. The behavior patterns illustrated are robust in the sense that they recur whenever the same sentences are presented with different preceding contexts, and they persist if we choose appropriately biased cases that are distributionally similar. The

Figure 6.6
Three Trajectories in the 1 Region

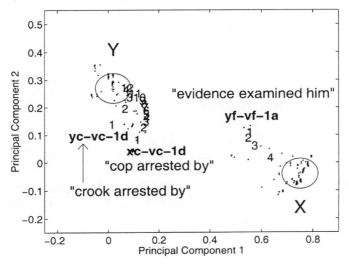

See Figure 6.5 for explanation of labels.

pattern becomes distorted if we make one or another bias especially strong, or change the directions of some of the biases. Nevertheless, the cases we have focused on here seem most closely analogous to the human-subject cases we are using as a standard. Thus, it appears that given the constraint that the gravitation mechanism needs to form a distinct attractor basin for every syntactically distinct context, the VSG model succeeds in deriving the hypothesized competition mechanism from the distributional properties of its training corpus.

Emergence of a Syntax–Semantics Distinction

We now show that the gravitational component of the VSG model in-duces a distinction between types of violations that lines up in a plausible way with the distinction between syntactic and semantic violations as judged by human beings. The essence of the induced contrast is that grammatical process-ing (including the processing of semantically strange sentences) involves gravi-tation directly into an attractor, while ungrammatical processing involves gravitation first into a saddle point (a fixed point that attracts trajectories from one region of the state space and repels them into another), and only later into an attractor. Often, the saddle point delays convergence so long that we can say the processor fails to find an interpretation in "reasonable time."

In order to illustrate this point, we extend the analogy between natural language and our artificial Thematic Bias Grammar. The category sequence of the training grammar is very strict in the sense that none of the five sequential categories is ever omitted and the elements always follow one another in the same order. Thus, skipping or repeating categories produces something analogous to a natural language grammaticality violation. We now describe a simulation in which we compared the VSG model's response to analogs of semantic violation with its response to analogs of syntactic violations.

Figure 6.7 shows two sample trajectories, one corresponding to a semantic violation and one corresponding to a syntactic violation. The semantic violation is one of the cases depicted in Figure 6.6. It occurs at the word "1d" in the sentence "xc vc 1d 2d 3d p" (analogous to *cop arrested by detective left* . . .). As we noted, the bias of the first two words toward X continuations is contradicted by the bias of the third word toward Y continuations, so the processor slows down substantially at this word (thirteen time steps). Nevertheless, the string is grammatical in the sense that its category sequence is sanctioned by the grammar.

The syntactic violation in Figure 6.7 occurs at the word "p" in the string, "xb va 1a p" (analogous to *cop arrested the* . . .). This string is ungrammatical because it ends after the third word, skipping the 2 and 3 categories. The VSG model's response in this case is substantially different from its response in the previous case. The starting point of the trajectory (labeled "1a-p") is remote from all of the clusters that are associated with normal sentence processing. Moreover, the trajectory stretches for a long way across empty space and gets pulled into what looks like an attractor midway between the X1 region and the X2 region. After thirty time steps it still has not gravitated into one of the clusters associated with normal processing. The apparent attractor is a saddle point. If gravitation proceeds for a much longer time, the trajectory will eventually reach an attractor, but it is clearly waylayed in a significant way compared to the trajectory of the semantic violation.

Figure 6.7 provides a suggestion that the VSG model is treating grammatical violations differently from semantic ones: Semantic violations involve direct gravitation into an attractor; syntactic violations involve parse-blocking delay by a saddle point. To probe the legitimacy of this idea more thoroughly, we studied the model's response to a sample of twenty semantic violations and twenty syntactic violations. These examples were constructed by hand in an effort to test a range of types of conditions.

The model's response to syntactic anomaly turned out to have a fairly characteristic pattern, although the results were not as simple as the single test case described suggests. Whenever a word of the wrong category occurred at a particular point in a string, the starting point of the trajectory tended to be a compromise between the contextually appropriate attractor and the attractor associated with the anomalous word. The result was that the syntactic anomalies nearly always placed the processor in a "no man's land," far from any of the attractors. In every case the trajectory was in the

Figure 6.7
Trajectories for a Semantic Anomaly (labeled "vc-1d") and a Syntactic Anomaly (labeled "1a-p")

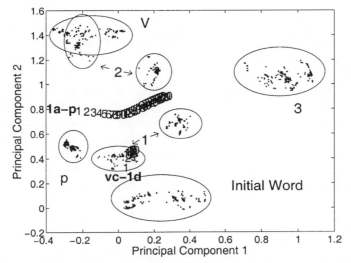

The semantic anomaly occurs at the word "1d" in the sentence "xc-vc-1d-2d-3d-p." The syntactic anomaly occurs at the word "p" in the string "xb-va-1a-p."

basin of the contextually appropriate attractor. In some cases the trajectory was drawn into a saddle point close to the contextually appropriate attractor. The "1a-p" trajectory in Figure 6.7 is a case like this: The contextually appropriate attractor is the X2 attractor (east of label 2 in Figure 6.7). In other cases the trajectory went quickly into the contextually appropriate attractor despite the anomaly. An example is the word "ye" after "yf" in the sentence "yf *ye* vf 1f 2e 3f p," which resulted in gravitation into the YV region in three timesteps. In this latter kind of case the word following the anomalous word often produced a trajectory that was still trapped behind a saddle point at the thirtieth time step. In this sense the model sometimes showed delayed sensitivity to an anomaly.[13] We do not at this point know why the long reaction times were sometimes coincident with the anomalous word and sometimes delayed by a word or two, but we note that this behavior may be consistent with human behavior and bears further exploration. Because of the sometimes delayed response to the anomaly, we assessed the outcome of the twenty-sentence trials by examining the trajectory for the anomalous word and the word following it and tabulating results for whichever of these trajectories was longer. We applied this method to both the semantically anomalous sentences and the syntactically anomalous strings. Figure 6.8 plots the velocity profiles of these maximally anomalous trajectories for the two sets of examples. The velocity between two successive points $\vec{x}_i$ and $\vec{x}_j$ on a trajectory is taken to be the distance between $\vec{x}_i$ and $\vec{x}_j$ (since each step takes unit time). The figure makes the contrast between the two sets apparent, and a t-test shows a clear difference in the mean maximal gravitation times ($p < .0001$, 19 d.f.).

Figure 6.8 suggests thinking of the difference between grammatical and ungrammatical strings as a graded qualitative difference. At one extreme are the parses that involve short, direct trajectories into an attractor and thus result in very short processing times. At the other extreme are trajectories that land on what is called the *stable manifold* of a saddle point. The stable manifold contains those points that happen to be at the balance point between the competing attractors and from which the system gravitates into the saddle point itself, never reaching an attractor. These two kinds of behaviors are qualitatively distinct: In the first case the processor arrives at a representation associated with an interpretation; in the second case it never arrives at such an interpretation. However, almost all real examples are a mixture of these two types: Even the most stoutly grammatical examples show very slight influence of deflection by saddle points; the most atrocious grammatical anomalies are very unlikely to land on a stable manifold of a saddle point, and thus will eventually gravitate into an attractor. But despite the gradedness of the difference, there is a clear clustering of strings into two classes: grammatical and ungrammatical.

This framework provides a useful new conceptualization of the notion of grammaticality. The framework makes several kinds of testable predictions: (1) People should show gradations of reading times on grammatical and ungrammatical sentences even when they are happy to make binary judgments about them, (2) lexical or other contextual biasing can downgrade a semantic anomaly into an ungrammaticality and vice versa, and (3) there can be variation in the location of anomalous latencies with respect to syntactic violations. These predictions differentiate the VSG model from all models that make an absolute distinction between grammatical and ungrammatical sentences, as well as form models like the SRN, which treat all contrasts on a grey scale.

CONCLUSIONS

This chapter has described an application of the VSG model, which was first described in Tabor et al. (1997), to sentence-comprehension phenomena involving graded differences in lexical information. We focused on the results of McRae et al. (1998), showing, in particular, that the VSG model correctly predicts (1) immediate sensitivity to graded lexical biases, (2) a general association between elevated reading times and conflict between the parse biases of the previous context and the current word, and (3) inertia effects; that is, the tendency for the processor to resolve a conflict between parse biases gradually, over the course of reading several words, even if the words provide strongly constraining information. The inertia effect is important because it provides new evidence distinguishing the VSG model

Figure 6.8
Velocity Profiles for Twenty Semantically and Twenty Syntactically Anomalous Transitions

Semantically anomalous transitions.

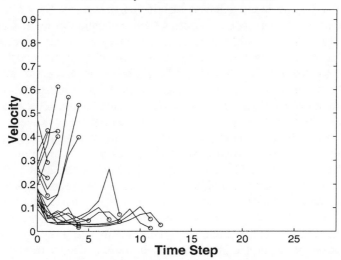

Syntactically anomalous transitions.

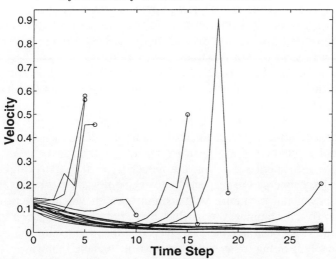

The profile is pictured for either the word at which the anomaly occurred or the word following this word, whichever had a longer gravitation time.

from closely related models that posit a systematic correlation between the unexpectedness of a word class and its reading time (Jurafsky, 1996). Tabor et al. described a related phenomenon, smoothing, in which class-similarity effects cause reading times to diverge from expectation-based predictions.

The main theoretical insight of the chapter, building on Tabor et al. (1997), is that dynamical-systems theory provides a useful set of tools for understanding the representational properties of high-dimensional learning models like Elman's (1991) SRN. We noted, in particular, that the VSG model can be tuned so its attractor basins identify clusters in the SRN's representation space that correspond to states of the generating process. Clustering seems to be an important step in mapping from the continuous representations of learning models to the discrete representations of linguistic models, which are good for research insight and good for discrete assignment of interpretations. The current results suggest that the VSG model provides an improvement over hierarchical clustering methods of discretizing connectionst representations (e.g., Elman, 1990; Pollack, 1990; Servan-Schreiber, Cleeremans, & McClelland, 1991), for these provide no obvious way of picking out a linguistically or statistically relevant subset of a cluster hierarchy.

Finally, we identified a new case in which a construct of dynamical-systems theory is useful in modeling the contrast between semantic violation and syntactic violation, a phenomenon in sentence processing. We found that the processing of grammatical strings (meaning those that could be generated by the training grammar) tended to involve gravitation directly into an attractor, while the processing of ungrammatical strings usually led to gravitation into a saddle point, which greatly delayed arrival at an attractor. This result provides a way of mapping the entirely relativistic representation of an SRN (it rules out no string) onto the intuitively observable contrast between semantic and syntactic violation. It also makes contact with empirical work showing contrasts in brain activity for the two kinds of processing (e.g., Ainsworth-Darnell et al., 1998).

The VSG model has several shortcomings. First, the link between the SRN and the gravitation mechanism is weak, in that we invoke an external constraint (the requirement that attractor basins line up with parse states) to set the parameter p. If varying the parameter p over all possible values could produce arbitrary attractor-basin configurations, then the dynamical component would contribute no structural insight at all in virtue of the machine-state correspondences. But the model is, in fact, fairly tightly constrained: Experimentation suggests that varying p leads to a relatively small range of basin configurations, with a simple case in which there is only one basin ($p = 0$) and a limiting case in which every point in the visitation set has its own basin. This constrainedness suggests that the architectural assumptions of the model are doing some explanatory work. As noted, however, it would be desirable if the value of p could be determined independently of a grammatical oracle. Our current work is investigating this possibility.

Second, we have only analyzed VSG behavior on a very simple formal language. We feel it is useful to do this at first in order to build a foundation. It is desirable, however, to study more realistic cases. For example, one could incorporate a number of specific correlations between subjects and verbs, like the fact that *cop* is a good subject for *arrest* and *employee* is a good object for *hired*, rather than a binary contrast between two biases (Good Agent versus Good Patient). To this end, it is also important to address the question of how to represent phrase-structural relationships as well as simple contrasts between states in a finite-state language. Wiles and Elman (1995), Rodriguez, Wiles, and Elman (1999), and Tabor (1998) provide some insight into this problem by looking at how SRNs and related devices can represent context-free grammars. Here, a central question is, How should the learning mechanism generalize from its finite training experience to an infinite-state language?

Third, as an anonymous reviewer emphasized, the quicker processing of semantic violations than grammatical violations in the current simulation is not surprising, given that the model is likely to have seen most semantic violations in training. A first step toward demonstrating that the model exhibits some generalization ability would be to filter small random samples of the 15,552 possible sentences from the training data, and then test these examples to see if they behave like grammatical strings. Clearly, however, real semantic anomaly is not randomly distributed across grammatically legitimate combinations: It is associated with the juxtaposition of particular word classes. Thus, to make a more interesting test we need to design a grammar in which certain classes of words never directly cooccur although they have a strong higher-order correlation (e.g., *dogs* may never be said to *meow* or *purr*, but they *eat, run, play, sleep*, etc., things that *meow*-ing and *purr*-ing individuals commonly do). The question is whether the gravitation mechanism will be able to appropriately group clusters of clusters into the same attractor basin in such a case.

These challenges are nontrivial, but it is encouraging to note that they are expected consequences of asking the challenging question that motivates the VSG model: How can one get, in a principled way, from the relativistic perspective of a learning model (where we prefer not to assume that anything is impossible) to an absolutist perspective that supports categorical choice making. It is not obvious that there is any universally right way of taking this step. Nevertheless, simpler architectural assumptions seem desirable. Dynamical-systems theory typically starts with a very simple assumption in the form of a class of equations. Many interesting structures emerge. Perhaps these structures are a kind of scaffolding via which emergentist cognitivists can hoist themselves out of the sea of relativism.

FURTHER READINGS

The PDP volumes (McClelland & Rumelhart, 1986, and Rumelhart & McClelland, 1986) provide an excellent introduction to the use of connectionist networks as cognitive models. For a nice visual introduction to dynamical-systems theory, see the five volumes of Abraham and Shaw (1984).

Strogatz (1994) is an enjoyable textbook: It blends theory with colorful examples. Perko (1991) is more rigorous and trenchant. On dynamical systems in cognition, see Port and van Gelder (1995). For good overviews of recurrent connectionist networks, see Williams and Zipser (1995) and Pearlmutter (1995). For a helpful explication of recurrent back-propagation networks in particular, see Haykin (1994). There has been a steady stream of work on connectionist symbol processing: Jagota, Plate, Shastri, and Sun (1999) give a rundown. Tiño and Dorffner (1998) and Tabor (1998) are recent developments on the question of representation. Elman (1995) motivates the dynamical-systems approach to modeling natural language, summarizing the main insights of the two influential papers (Elman 1990, 1991) on the simple recurrent network. Frazier (1987) is a helpful tutorial on two-stage (or garden-path) models of sentence processing. Von Gompel, Pickering, and Traxler (1999) provide evidence that many current models of sentence processing, including current dynamical-systems models, are missing an important probabilistic element. Gibson (1998) provides substantial evidence for effects of memory load, also an important challenge for dynamical and connectionist models (though see Christiansen & Chater, 1999, for helpful insights). For a tour de force on the use of dynamical-connectionist models for word recognition, see Kawamoto (1993).

NOTES

Thanks to Nick Chater, Morten Christiansen, Garrison Cottrell, William Turkel, Michael Spivey-Knowlton, and Gary Dell for helpful comments. Whitney Tabor was supported by NIH Grant 5 T32 MH19389. Michael K. Tanenhaus was supported by NIH Grant HD 27206. We would also like to give special thanks to Cornell Juliano, whose involvement with the predecessor of this chapter helped to steer us in the direction of our recent results.

1. See Williams and Peng (1990) for a discussion of other approximations to BPTT.

2. Thus, the hidden-to-output weights were adjusted according to

$$\Delta w_{ji} \propto y_i \delta_j = y_i (t_j - y_j)$$

while the input-to-hidden and hidden-to-hidden weights were adjusted according to

$$\Delta w_{ji} \propto y_i \delta_j = y_i f'(net_j) \sum_k w_{kj} \delta_k$$

where w_{ji} is the weight from unit i to unit j, k ranges over units that unit j sends activation to, and $f'(net_j) = y_j (1 - y_j)$ is the derivative of the fixed sigmoid activation function (and input-to-hidden weights were adjusted only on the basis of the current inputs).

3. In fact, although some gravitational systems thus defined have fixed points near the centers of clusters, many appear to have chaotic attractors (see Strogatz,

1994). These chaotic attractors behave approximately like fixed points. Since we are only interested in approximations in the models anyway, we treat such attractors as if they are fixed points.

4. *N* must be large enough to make the cluster structure of the visitation set discernible; *v* controls the rate of gravitation but does not affect relative rates of gravitation, so it can be scaled for implementational convenience. Without loss of generality, then, we assume $t = 1$.

5. See also Selman and Hirst (1985) for a systematic method of setting weights in a Boltzmann Machine parser without learning.

6. Gibson and Tunstall (personal communication) argue that all frequency effects in processing are either semantic (and hence outside of grammar) or lexical. In fact, they provide evidence that the contrast between *that* and *those* after transitive verbs is due to the lexical preference of *that* for being a complementizer independent of syntactic context. They invoke a third, memory-based constraint system (Gibson, 1998) to handle the sentence-initial contrast between determiner *that* and complementizer *that*. The VSG model may well treat the effects after transitive verbs as essentially lexical (further simulation studies are needed). But even if the effect is lexical and expectations are semantic, the point still stands that some principled mechanism for mediating between local biases and contextually derived expectations is needed. The VSG account is appealing in this regard because it handles all of these phenomena with one formalism instead of three and specifies a mediating mechanism: the semipliable hidden-unit manifold of the neural network (see Tabor, 1995).

7. See Newmeyer (1986) for an articulation of the viewpoint that the theory of generative semantics foundered on such a shoal.

8. For this grammar, the minimum distance between grammar-determined distributions is 0.9410. This is, for example, the distance between the distribution associated with the partial string "xa . . ." and the distribution associated with the partial string "ya. . . ."

9. In the case at hand the original hidden-unit space had ten dimensions. The first two principal components captured 56 percent of the variance.

10. To make Figure 6.4 interpretable, we have circled and labeled the regions corresponding to distinct classes based on our knowledge of the grammar and of which words correspond to which points.

11. The circles were drawn as follows: An estimation of the location of the attractor was computed by averaging the second- and third-to-last positions of the trajectory for several trajectories and a circle of fixed radius was drawn with this point as its center. Recall that the trajectory is considered at an end when it makes a turn of more than 90 degrees on one step. This happens immediately after it has passed by the attractor. Therefore, the attractor is usually located somewhere between the second- and third-to-last positions, so their average provides a reasonable estimate of its location. The circle radii have no explanatory significance; they are just a method of identifying the attractor location without obscuring the view by putting a label right on it.

12. The first step of each trajectory is marked by 1; the second step brings the trajectory into the attractor and is not shown in order to make the diagram easier to read.

13. Note that all the anomalous sentences ended with sequences of words consistent with the anomalous word. This fact, in combination with the strong contextual dominance exhibited by the model makes it unsurprising that the word after an

anomalous word was often associated with a long gravitation time: The model was still sticking to its original parse bias at this point. By the time three words had passed, however, the model typically shifted its hypothesis to the new perspective. These effects are thus a more extreme version of the inertia effects that we saw in conjunction with semantic anomalies.

REFERENCES

Abraham, R. H., & Shaw, C. D. (1984). *Dynamics: The geometry of behavior* (Books 0–4). Santa Cruz, CA: Aerial Press.

Ainsworth-Darnell, K., Shulman, H., & Boland, J. E. (1998). Dissociating brain responses to syntactic and semantic anomalies: Evidence from event-related potentials. *Journal of Memory and Language, 38*, 112–130.

Almeida, L. B. (1987). A learning rule for asynchronous perceptrons with feedback in a combinatorial environment. In M. Caudil & C. Butler (Eds.), *Proceedings of the IEEE First Annual International Conference on Neural Networks* (pp. 609–618). San Diego, CA: IEEE.

Bever, T. (1970). The cognitive basis for linguistic structures. In J. R. Hayes (Ed.), *Cognition and the development of language* (pp. 279–362). New York: Wiley.

Burgess, C., & Lund, K. (1997). Modeling parsing constraints with a high-dimensional context space. *Language and Cognitive Processes, 12*, 177–210.

Charniak, E. (1993). *Statistical language learning*. Cambridge, MA: MIT Press.

Christiansen, M. H. (1994). *Infinite languages, finite minds: Connectionism, learning and linguistic structure*. Unpublished doctoral dissertation, University of Edinburgh.

Christiansen, M. H., & Chater, N. (1999). Toward a connectionist model of recursion in human linguistic performance. *Cognitive Science, 23*, 157–205.

Cottrell, G. W. (1985). *A connectionist approach to word sense disambiguation* (Tech Rep. No. 154). Rochester, NY: University of Rochester, Dept. of Computer Science.

Cottrell, G. W., & Small, S. (1983). A connectionist scheme for modeling word sense disambiguation. *Cognition and Brain Theory, 6*, 89–120.

Cottrell, G. W., & Small, S. (1984). Viewing parsing as word sense discrimination: A connectionist approach. In B. Bara & G. Guida (Eds.), *Computational models of natural language processing* (pp. 91–119). Amsterdam: North Holland.

Crutchfield, J. P. (1994). The calculi of emergence: Computation, dynamics, and induction. *Physica D, 75*, 11–54.

Elman, J. L. (1990). Finding structure in time. *Cognitive Science, 14*, 179–211.

Elman, J. L. (1991). Distributed representations, simple recurrent networks, and grammatical structure. *Machine Learning, 7*, 195–225.

Elman, J. L. (1995). Language as a dynamical system. In R. Port & T, van Gelder (Eds.), *Mind as motion: Explorations in the dynamics of cognition*. Cambridge, MA: MIT Press.

Frazier, L. (1987). Sentence processing: A tutorial review. In M. Coltheart (Ed.), *Attention and Performance 12: The psychology of reading* (pp. 559–586). Hillsdale, NJ: Lawrence Erlbaum.

Frazier, L., & Clifton, J. C. (1996). *Construal*. Cambridge, MA: MIT Press.

Garnsey, S. M. (1993). Event-related brain potentials in the study of language: An introduction. *Language and Cognitive Processes, 8*, 337–356.

Gibson, E. (1998). Linguistic complexity: Locality of syntactic dependencies. *Cognition, 68*, 1–76.

Hagoort, P., Brown, C., & Groothusen, J. (1993). The syntactic positive shift (SPS) as an ERP measure of syntactic processing. *Language and Cognitive Processes, 8*, 439–483.

Haykin, S. S. (1994). *Neural networks: A comprehensive foundation*. New York: MacMillan.

Hopcroft, J. E., & Ullman, J. D. (1979). *Introduction to automata theory, languages, and computation*. Menlo Park, CA: Addison-Wesley.

Jagota, A., Plate, T., Shastri, L., & Sun, R. (1999). Connectionist symbol processing: Dead or alive? *Neural Computing Surveys* [on-line], 1–40. Available at < http://www.icsi.berkeley.edu/ jagota/NCS > .

Jolliffe, I. T. (1986). *Principal component analysis*. New York: Springer-Verlag.

Juliano, C., & Tanenhaus, M. (1993). Contingent frequency effects in syntactic ambiguity resolution. In *Proceedings of the Fifteenth Annual Conference of the Cognitive Science Society* (pp. 593–598). Hillsdale, NJ: Lawrence Erlbaum.

Jurafsky, D. (1996). A probabilistic model of lexical and syntactic access and disambiguation. *Cognitive Science, 20*, 137–194.

Kawamoto, A. H. (1993). Nonlinear dynamics in the resolution of lexical ambiguity: A parallel distributed processing account. *Journal of Memory and Language, 32*, 474–516.

Landauer, T. K., & Dumais, S. T. (1997). A solution to Plato's problem: The latent semantic analysis theory of acquisition, induction, and representation of knowledge. *Psychological Review, 104*, 211–240.

Lightfoot, D. (1991). *How to set paramters: Arguments from language change*. Cambridge, MA: MIT Press.

MacDonald, M. A., Pearlmutter, N. J., & Seidenberg, M. S. (1994). The lexical nature of syntactic ambiguity resolution. *Psychological Review, 101*, 676–703.

MacDonald, M. C., & Christiansen, M. H. (in press). Individual differences without working memory: A reply to Just & Carpenter (1993) and Waters & Caplan (1996). *Psychological Review*.

McClelland, J. L., & Rumelhart, D. E. (1981). An interactive activation model of context effects in letter perception, Part 1. *Psychological Review, 88*, 375–402.

McClelland, J. L., & Rumelhart, D. E. (Eds.). (1986). *Parallel distributed processing: Explorations in the microstructure of cognition*. Vol. 2: *Psychological and biological models*. Cambridge, MA: MIT Press.

McElree, B., & Griffith, T. (1995). Syntactic and thematic processing in sentence comprehension: Evidence for a temporal dissociation. *Journal of Experimental Psychology: Language, Memory, and Cognition, 21*, 134–157.

McRae, K., Spivey-Knowlton, M. J., & Tanenhaus, M. K. (1998). Modeling the influence of thematic fit (and other constraints) in on-line sentence comprehension, *Journal of Memory and Language, 38*, 283–312.

Newmeyer, F. (1986). *Linguistic theory in America*. Orlando, FL: Academic Press.

Osterhout, L., & Holcomb, P. J. (1993). Event-related potentials and syntactic anomaly: Evidence for anomaly detection during the perception of continuous speech. *Language and Cognitive Processes, 8*, 413–437.

Pearlmutter, B. A. (1995). Gradient calculations for dynamic recurrent neural networks: A survey. *IEEE Transactions on Neural Networks, 6*, 1212–1228.

Perko, L. (1991). *Differential equations and dynamical systems*. New York: Springer-Verlag.

Pineda, F. J. (1995). Recurrent backpropagation networks. In Y. Chauvin & D. E. Rumelhart (Eds.), *Backpropagation: Theory, architectures, and applications* (pp. 99–136). Hillsdale, NJ: Lawrence Erlbaum.

Plaut, D. C., McClelland, J. L., Seidenberg, M. S., & Patterson, K. E. (1996). Understanding normal and impaired word reading: Computational principles in quasi-regular domains. *Psychological Review, 103*, 56–115.

Pollack, J. B. (1990). Recursive distributed representations. *Artificial Intelligence, 46*, 77–105.

Port, R. F., & van Gelder, T. (Eds.). (1995). *Mind as motion: Explorations in the Dynamics of Cognition*. Cambridge, MA: MIT Press.

Rodriguez, P., Wiles, J., & Elman, J. L. (1999). A recurrent neural network that learns to count. *Connection Science, 11*, 5–40.

Rohde, D., & Plaut, D. C. (1999). Language acquisition in the absence of explicit negative evidence: How important is starting small? *Cognition, 72,* 67–109.

Rumelhart, D. E., Durbin, R., Golden, R., & Chauvin, Y. (1995). Backpropagation: The basic theory. In Y. Chauvin & D. E. Rumelhart (Eds.), *Backpropagation: Theory, architectures, and applications*. Hillsdale, NJ: Lawrence Erlbaum.

Rumelhart, D. E., Hinton, G. E., & Williams, R. J. (1986). Learning internal representations by error propagation. In D. E. Rumelhart & J. L. McClelland (Eds.), *Parallel distributed processing: Explorations in the microstructure of cognition*. Vol. 2: *Psychological and biological models* (pp. 318–362). Cambridge, MA: MIT Press.

Rumelhart, D. E., & McClelland, J. L. (Eds.). (1986). *Parallel distributed processing: Explorations in the microstructure of cognition*. Vol. 1: *Foundations*. Cambridge, MA: MIT Press.

Selman, B., & Hirst, G. (1985). A rule-based connectionist parsing system. In *Proceedings of the Seventh Annual Conference of the Cognitive Science Society* (pp. 212–221). Hillsdale, NJ: Lawrence Erlbaum.

Servan-Schreiber, D., Cleeremans, A., & McClelland, J. L. (1991). Graded state machines: The representation of temporal contingencies in simple recurrent networks. *Machine Learning, 7*, 161–193.

Spivey-Knowlton, M. J. (1996). *Integration of visual and linguistic information: Human data and model simulations*. Unpublished doctoral dissertation, University of Rochester.

St. John, M. F., & McClelland, J. L. (1990). Learning and applying contextual constraints in sentence comprehension. *Artificial Intelligence, 46*, 217–257.

Strogatz, S. (1994). *Nonlinear dynamics and chaos*. Reading, MA: Addison-Wesley.

Tabor, W. (1994). *Syntactic innovation: A connectionist model*. Unpublished doctoral dissertation, Stanford University.

Tabor, W. (1995). Lexical change as nonlinear interpolation. In *Proceedings of the Seventeenth Annual Conference of the Cognitive Science Society*. Hillsdale, NJ: Lawrence Erlbaum.

Tabor, W. (1998). *Dynamical automata* (Tech. Report No. TR98-1694). Ithaca, NY: Cornell University, Computer Science Department. Available at < http://cs-tr.cs.cornell.edu/ > .

Tabor, W., Juliano, C., & Tanenhaus, M. K. (1996). A dynamical system for language processing. In *Proceedings of the Eighteenth Annual Conference of the Cognitive Science Society* (pp. 690–695). Hillsdale, NJ: Lawrence Erlbaum.

Tabor, W., Juliano, C., & Tanenhaus, M. K. (1997). Parsing in a dynamical system: An attractor-based account of the interaction of lexical and structural constraints in sentence processing. *Language and Cognitive Processes, 12*, 211–271.

Tanenhaus, M. K., & Trueswell, J. C. (1995). Sentence comprehension. In J. Miller & P. Eimas (Eds.), *Handbook of perception and cognition* (Vol. 11, pp. 217–262). San Diego: Academic Press.

Tiňo, P., & Dorffner, G. (1998). Constructing finite-context sources from fractal representations of symbolic sequences (Tech. Rep. No. TR-98-18). Austria: Austrian Research Institute for Artificial Intelligence.

Trueswell, J. C. (1996). The role of lexical frequency in syntactic ambiguity resolution. *Journal of Memory and Language, 35*, 566–585.

von Gompel, R., Pickering, M., & Traxler, M. (1999). Making and revising syntactic analyses: Evidence against current constraint-based and two-stage models. Manuscript submitted for publication.

Waltz, D. L., & Pollack, J. B. (1985). Massively parallel parsing: A strongly interactive model of natural language interpretation. *Cognitive Science, 9*, 51–74.

Weckerley, J., & Elman, J. L. (1992). A PDP approach to processing center-embedded sentences. In *Proceedings of the Fourteenth Annual Conference of the Cognitive Science Society* (pp. 414–419). Hillsdale, NJ: Lawrence Erlbaum.

Wiles, J., & Elman, J. L. (1995). Landscapes in recurrent networks. In *Proceedings of the Seventeenth Annual Conference of the Cognitive Science Society* (pp. 482–487). Hillsdale, NJ: Lawrence Erlbaum.

Williams, R. J., & Peng, J. (1990). An efficient gradient-based algorithm for on-line training of recurrent network trajectories. *Neural Computation, 2*, 490–501.

Williams, R. J., & Zipser, D. (1995). Gradient-based learning algorithms for recurrent networks. In Y. Chauvin & D. E. Rumelhart (Eds.), *Backpropagation: Theory, architectures, and applications* (pp. 99–136). Hillsdale, NJ: Lawrence Erlbaum.

7

Connectionist Models of Language Production: Lexical Access and Grammatical Encoding

Gary S. Dell, Franklin Chang,
and Zenzi M. Griffin

Psycholinguistic research into language production—the process of translating thoughts into speech—has long been associated with connectionist models. Spreading-activation models of lexical access in production represent some of the earliest applications of connectionist ideas to psycholinguistic data (e.g., Dell & Reich, 1977; Harley, 1984; MacKay, 1982; Stemberger, 1985). These models combined representations from linguistics with interactive activation principles and sought to explain speech errors, particularly errors resulting from multiple causes or processing levels. For example, *Lizst's second Hungarian RESTAURANT* instead of *rhapsody* involves mistakenly using a word that is associatively, syntactically, and phonologically related to the intended word. Activation that spreads interactively among processing levels seems to be a natural way to account for these kinds of slips.

Since the early speech-error models of lexical access, connectionist models of production have progressed on three fronts. First, the empirical basis of the models has been extended. They now have been applied to error data from aphasic patients, children, and older adults (e.g., Berg & Schade, 1992; Burke, MacKay, Worthley, & Wade, 1991; Dell, Schwartz, Martin, Saffran, & Gagnon, 1997; Stemberger, 1989) and to response-time data from experimental paradigms (e.g., Cutting & Ferreira, 1999; Griffin & Bock, 1998; Levelt, Roelofs, & Meyer, 1999; Roelofs, 1996, 1997; Schriefers,

Meyer, & Levelt, 1990). Second, models have begun to address grammatical encoding, the selection and ordering of words in sentences. The third area of progress has concerned connectionist architectures. Whereas all of the early models were hand-wired networks with local representations, some recent production models make use of distributed representations acquired from learning algorithms. In addition, recent architectures allow for the production of true sequences (Eikmeyer & Schade, 1991; Jordan, 1986; Gupta, 1996; Hartley & Houghton, 1996; Houghton, 1990; MacKay, 1987).

In this chapter we examine some connectionist models of production. Our aim is not to review the field, but rather to concentrate on our own recent efforts in two areas, lexical access and grammatical encoding. Lexical access and grammatical encoding are aspects of production that can be located in what has been called the "formulation component" (Levelt, 1989). This component takes a *message*, a nonverbal representation of the utterance, and turns it into linguistic form. Words are accessed and ordered (grammatical encoding) and their sounds are retrieved and organized for articulation (phonological encoding). Thus, the formulation component is distinguished from a prior component responsible for message formation and a subsequent one that executes articulatory movements. Specifically, we will present three models. The first model deals with the access of single words and concentrates on explaining the errors of aphasic patients. The second focuses on the phonological encoding and links error phenomena to the characteristics of the vocabulary and the sequential nature of words. The third model addresses structural priming effects in grammatical encoding (e.g., Bock, 1986b).

In our discussion of language production, two issues will be in focus: serial order and linguistic structure. First, consider serial order. The creation of a temporal sequence is the essence of production. Yet the canonical connectionist architectures, such as feed-forward multilayered networks, cannot create true temporal sequences. Rather, these architectures generate a single output activation pattern for a particular input in parallel. Of course, one can finesse this problem by organizing output units into separate banks for each position in the sequence. But that is not how production proceeds. Sentences are, for the most part, constructed piecemeal from beginning to end. The words that are initially retrieved tend to be placed early in the sentence and these initial placements constrain subsequent lexical and structural decisions (Bock, 1982, 1986a, 1987b; Ferreira, 1996, 1997; Kempen & Hoenkamp, 1987; Levelt, 1989). This property of production, incrementality, demands a model with sequential output and where previous output interacts with the message to guide subsequent output. Even within a word, temporal sequence is important. Not only are the sounds of words articulated in sequence, but they also seem to be retrieved that way from the lexicon (Meyer, 1991; Wheeldon & Levelt, 1995). The sequential retrieval of sounds is likely responsible for several phenomena, such as the vulnerability of word-initial sounds to speech errors (Gupta & Dell, 1999), and, consequently, any model dealing with such phenomena must be sequential.

Furthermore, any production model must get the details of linguistic structure right. Especially here, there is reason to expect production to differ from comprehension. In comprehension, structural features, such as grammatical affixes or function words, are simply cues that are often indirectly related to meaning. In fact, as the comprehensibility of telegraphic speech shows, some structural cues are largely unnecessary for understanding. Consequently, relatively less emphasis on structural cues is required in the process of mapping from spoken or written language to meaning. Production models, in contrast, must make linguistic structure a priority. As pointed out by Garrett (1975) and Bock (1990), structural details such as subject–verb agreement affixes must be produced regardless of whether they code for key aspects of the message. Structural features are even preserved when speakers err. For example, one might say, *I appled a pack*, instead of *I packed an apple*. Notice that the error preserves the phrase structure of the sentence, keeping the function morphemes in place. Moreover, at the phonological level, the intended word *an* changes to *a* in agreement with the initial consonant in *pack* and the pronunciation of "-ed" changes from /t/ in *packed* to /d/ in *appled* (Fromkin, 1971). How to handle this sensitivity to structure is a major challenge for connectionist models, particularly for models that learn structure indirectly from the statistics of linguistic sequences.

LEXICAL ACCESS

Lexical access is, relatively speaking, the easy part of production to model. It is simple pattern association: A pattern of activation corresponding to the meaning of a word needs to be mapped onto a pattern corresponding to the word's sounds. Moreover, lexical access is not a generative process. Aside from the productive use of morphology, the words that one seeks are stored in the lexicon.

Despite this seeming simplicity, lexical access poses a number of challenges. First, word choice must be made in the context of other retrieved words and the speaker's communicative goals. For example, one can refer to someone as a "person," a "woman," a "mother," a "female parent," "Sheila," or even "she." As Roelofs (1996) and Levelt (1989) point out, characterizing lexical access as just a mapping from the semantic features of a concept to a lexical item ignores the fact that such features do not uniquely identify a word. Second, words that have similar meanings do not necessarily have similar sounds; for example, the words *mother*, *father*, *man*, and *woman*. A semantic coding of these words in terms of FEMALE (1 or 0) and PARENT (1 or 0) and a phonological encoding of whether their initial sound is /m/ or not creates a mapping that is formally equivalent to exclusive-OR (see Dell et al., 1997). As a result, the mapping between meaning and sound is not linearly separable, and any network achieving this mapping would require a layer of nonlinear hidden units between semantics and sound. Third, as we have already mentioned, the output of lexical access is a sequence of sounds. Consequently, the mapping from meaning to sounds is one from a static (meaning) to a dynamic (phonological) representation. Finally, the output is more than just a sequence of phonological units. Rather, the retrieved phonological units are related to one another by the syllabic and metrical organization of the word's form.

Because of the complexity of the mapping from meaning to sound, theories of lexical access often assume that this mapping occurs in two steps. In the first step, lemma selection, a concept is mapped onto a lemma, a nonphonological representation of a word. Often the lemma is assumed to be associated with the grammatical properties of the word, its syntactic category, and features such as gender or number. The second step, phonological encoding, transforms the lemma into an organized sequence of speech sounds. Probably the most intuitive evidence for these two steps comes from the tip-of-the-tongue (TOT) phenomenon. A speaker knows that a word exists but cannot access its sounds. A simple interpretation is that lemma selection has succeeded, but phonological encoding has not. Recent support for this claim has come from studies showing that speakers in the TOT state know the grammatical properties of the word being sought, including, surprisingly, the word's grammatical gender (Miozzo & Caramazza, 1997; Vigliocco, Antonini, & Garrett, 1997; see Caramazza, 1997, for an alternative view).

There has been considerable debate regarding the relationship between lemma selection and phonological encoding. Some models assume that they are discrete, modular stages (Levelt, 1989; Levelt et al., 1999; Roelofs, 1996, 1997). Lemma selection is completed before any phonological information is activated, and during phonological encoding no semantic information is consulted. Support for the modular view has come from studies showing that the access of semantic information strictly precedes that of phonological information (van Turennout, Hagoort, & Brown, 1997; Schriefers et al., 1990). However, other studies have offered evidence that phonological encoding begins before lemma access is complete (Cutting & Ferreira, 1999; Peterson & Savoy, 1998). Furthermore, speech errors such as *Hungarian restaurant* for *Hungarian rhapsody* or *snake* for *snail* suggest the simultaneous activation of semantic or associative information and phonological information. The first connectionist model that we present, the aphasia model, preserves the distinction between lemma selection and phonological encoding, but denies that these are modular stages. Instead, it allows later levels to begin processing before earlier ones have finished (cascading), and for processing at later levels to influence that at earlier ones (feedback).

The Aphasia Model

The aphasia model (Dell et al., 1997) was developed to explain the error patterns of aphasic and nonaphasic speakers in picture-naming experiments. Twenty-three patients and sixty nonaphasic controls were given 175 pictures of simple objects and had to pronounce each object's name (which was a noun for all the pictures). Errors were placed in five categories. For example, assuming that *cat* is the target, errors could be semantic (*dog*), formal (*mat* or *cap*), mixed (*rat*, both formally and semantically related), unrelated (*pen* or *log*), or nonwords (*lat*, also including nonwords bearing no resemblance to the target, such as *lom*).

Figure 7.1 shows the architecture of the aphasia model. There are three layers of units: semantic features, words, and phonemes. Each word corresponds to a single unit in the word layer. Bidirectional excitatory connections link words to their semantic features and phonemes. In the implementation used by Dell et al. (1997), each word connected to ten semantic features and three phonemes.

Lexical access is achieved by interactive spreading activation. Semantic units are activated, this activation spreads throughout the network, and ultimately the sounds of the intended word are retrieved. However, the model differs from classic interactive activation models (e.g., McClelland & Rumelhart, 1981) in several respects. Most important, the aphasia model has two clear steps in the retrieval process, corresponding to lemma selection and phonological encoding. We briefly describe these two steps using *cat* as an example.

At the start of lemma selection, activation is added to the semantic features of the target word *cat*. The activation spreads for a fixed number of time steps according to a noisy linear-activation update rule. The bidirectional excitatory connections cause all three network levels to become active. In addition to the target word unit, *cat*, semantic neighbors such as *dog* become activated through shared semantic features. More interesting, words such as *mat* receive activation by feedback from phonemes shared with the target. When a mixed word such as *rat* exists, it gains activation from both shared semantics and shared phonemes. Consequently, a mixed word is usually more activated than a purely semantic or formal neighbor of the target. Lemma selection is concluded by a decision process. The most highly activated word of the appropriate grammatical category (here, noun) is chosen. However, the process is not perfect. Because of activation noise, there is some chance that a semantic, formal, or mixed neighbor of the target (or even an unrelated word) will be selected.

The second step, phonological encoding, begins with a large boost of activation to the chosen word unit. This boost introduces a nonlinearity into the model's activation process, which enables the network to handle the arbitrary mapping between semantic features and phonemes. After the boost,

Figure 7.1
The Aphasia Model

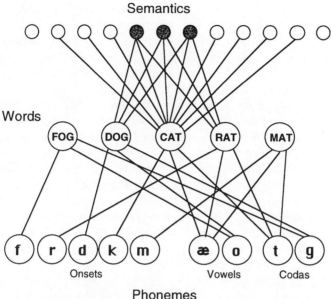

Connections are excitatory and bidirectional.

activation continues to spread for another fixed period of time. The most highly activated phonemes are then selected and linked to slots in a phonological frame, a structure that represents the number and kind of syllables in the word and its stress pattern. This linking concludes phonological encoding. Errors in phonological encoding occur when, due to noise, one or more wrong phonemes are more active than those of selected word. Typically, such errors result in nonwords (e.g., *lat* for *cat*), or, less often, form-related words (e.g., *mat* or *sat* for *cat*). In principle, the other error categories can also happen during phonological encoding, but the most common locus of these errors in the aphasia model is lemma selection.

In applying the model to aphasic naming errors, Dell et al. (1997) made two critical claims. First, they hypothesized that patient error patterns would fall between two extremes: the normal pattern produced by nonaphasic speakers and a random pattern defined by the error opportunities associated with the error categories. The normal pattern was estimated from the sixty control speakers' data in the picture-naming task: Correct responses (97%), semantic errors (1%), and mixed errors (1%) nearly exhausted all of the relevant responses. The random pattern is the probability of each error type happening if a person knew no words, only the rules of sound combination in English, and "randomly" produced legal phonological strings in the picture-naming task. Dell et al. estimated these error opportunities for English from a variety of sources. Roughly speaking, the random pattern is mostly nonwords (80%), with the remaining responses being, in order of likelihood, unrelateds, formals, semantic errors, and mixed errors. In claiming that the set of possible patient error patterns falls between the normal pattern and the random pattern, the aphasia model instantiated the continuity thesis, an idea that goes back at least to Freud (1891/1953). Under this thesis, normal speech errors and aphasic paraphasias reflect the same processes.

The second basic claim of the aphasia model concerns its mechanism for creating error patterns between the normal and random patterns. The model's lexicon was set up so that its error opportunities matched the error opportunities estimated for English, and its other parameters (noise, size of the activation boost to the selected word, connection weight, decay, and time) were selected to give an error pattern that matched the normal pattern (See Table 7.1). To create aphasic error patterns, the model was lesioned by limiting its ability to transmit activation (reducing the connection weight parameter, p), its ability to maintain its activation pattern (increasing the decay parameter, q), or both. The lesions create errors by reducing activation levels, which enhances the effect of noise. The greater the extent of the lesion, the more the model's error pattern approaches the random pattern. However, the weight and decay components to a lesion promote different kinds of errors. A pure decay lesion is associated with more semantic, formal, and mixed errors (related-word errors), while a pure weight lesion promotes nonword and unrelated word errors. For example, a weight lesion that reduces the model's correctness to 30 percent creates 41 percent nonwords, 10 percent unrelated, 12 percent formals, 7 percent semantic, and 1 percent mixed. In contrast, a decay lesion leading to 30 percent correct has an error pattern of 26 percent nonwords, 7 percent unrelated, 20 percent formals, 13 percent semantic, and 3 percent mixed. Reducing weight makes the activation patterns on each level less consistent with one another,

Table 7.1
Picture-Naming Error Proportions from Control Participants and Simulated Proportions from the Aphasia Model

	Response Category					
	Correct	Semantic	Formal	Nonword	Mixed	Unrelated
Controls	.97	.01	.00	.00	.01	.00
Aphasia Model	.97	.02	.00	.00	.01	.00

Connection weight (p) = .1; Decay (q) = .5. From Dell et al. (1997).

and leads to what Dell et al. (1997) call "stupid" errors. The production of a nonword reflects inconsistency between the word and phoneme layers, whereas an unrelated word reflects inconsistency between the semantic and word levels. When decay is increased without altering weight, errors tend to occur because noise dominates the decayed activation levels. But many of the errors reflect successful activation transmission among the levels because connection weights are still strong. These are "smart" errors (mixed, formal, and semantic errors) in which the word level is consistent with the semantic level or the phonological level is consistent with the word level.

The aphasia model gave a good account of patient error patterns. Dell et al. (1997) successfully fit the model to twenty-one of twenty-three fluent aphasic patients who were given the picture-naming test. Figure 7.2 illustrates the overall fit by plotting each predicted and obtained error proportion for all categories and patients. Table 7.2 shows the results for three patients, one fit with a pure decay lesion, I.G., one with a pure weight lesion, L.H., and one with a lower level of correctness, G.L.

Dell et al. (1997) then used the parameters assigned to the patients to make predictions. Here we mention two of these. First, if a patient's as-

Figure 7.2
A Comparison of Error Proportions from Twenty-One Patients and Predicted Proportion from the Aphasia Model

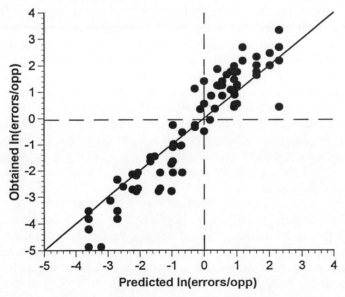

Proportions are transformed by the natural log of the ratio of the proportion and the error opportunities for each error category.

Table 7.2
Picture-Naming Error Proportions from Selected Patients and Simulated Proportions from the Aphasia Model

Patient/ Parameters	Response Category					
	Correct	Semantic	Formal	Nonword	Mixed	Unrelated
I.G.	.69	.09	.05	.02	.03	.01
$p=.1, q=.86$	.73	.13	.04	.05	.04	.01
L.H.	.69	.03	.07	.15	.01	.02
$p=.0057, q=.5$	.69	.07	.06	.14	.01	.03
G.L.	.28	.04	.21	.30	.03	.09
$p=.079, q=.85$	.27	.11	.20	.29	.03	.10

Source: From Dell et al. (1997).

signed connection weight was low they should not exhibit error phenomena that the model attributes to excitatory feedback between levels. The connection weights are just too low to support interaction between layers. According to the model, interactive feedback causes mixed errors (e.g., *rat* for *cat*) and formal errors that obey grammatical constraints (e.g., the noun *mat* replacing the noun *cat*). In support of the prediction, only the patients that the model assigned large weights to had significant tendencies to produce mixed errors and form-related nouns. The second prediction concerned recovery. Ten patients were retested on the naming test after one or more months. On average, the patients improved their performance by 16 percent. The model was able to fit these improved error patterns as well as the original ones. More important, recovery seemed to involve a movement of affected parameters toward normal values. Thus, recovery, or within-patient variation, takes place along the same dimensions as those that characterize between-patient variation.

The good points of the aphasia model arise from its interactive activation architecture. Interactive activation offers a natural mechanism for the error types and the model permits graceful degradation through parameter alterations. The fact that the model fits normal and patient error patterns provides support for both its general approach to lexical access and for the claim that brain damage entails disruption in the abilities to transmit and maintain activation. However, there are a number of limitations to the aphasia model. One is that it assumes that damage in the form of lower weights or greater decay is global; that is, damage cannot be confined to particular processing layers in the model. While this globality assumption was a useful starting point for the model, it is certainly false. More important, it is inconsistent with the two-step nature of the model. Recently, Foygel and Dell (in press) have shown that the two free global weight and global decay parameters of the Dell et al. (1997) model can be replaced with two others: lexical-semantic weight and lexical-phonological weight. Specifically, Foygel and Dell retained all of the characteristics of the original model except that they assumed that patients could vary only with respect to connection weight, instead of decay. But to account for the variation among patients, the weight parameter was allowed to differ between the "top" and "bottom" parts of the network. The resulting model fit the data presented in Dell et al. as well as the earlier model. In addition, the new model could better account for patients whose error patterns were more indicative of a dissociation between errors of lemma selection and errors of phonological encoding, and it was better able to predict patient performance in a word-repetition task.

Aside from the aphasia model's assumption of global damage, there are three other key limitations from our perspective. First, it is not sequential. The model's phonemes are retrieved all at once, contrary to data (e.g., Meyer, 1991). Second, the network structure is not learned. Finally, the model assumes the existence of prestored phonological frames that specify the syllabic and metrical structure of each word. While there may be considerable evidence for such frames (e.g., Sevald, Dell, & Cole, 1995), the aphasia model neither implements nor explains them. The next model that we present confronts these limitations.

The Phonological Error Model

The phonological error model (Dell, Juliano, & Govindjee, 1993) is an attempt to apply parallel distributed processing (PDP) principles specifically to phonological encoding. The model uses a simple recurrent network (Elman, 1990; Jordan, 1986) to map from a static representation of a word to a sequence of phonological features. Figure 7.3 shows the architecture.

The input layer represented the word to be spoken. In different versions of the model the input was either a random bit vector (which can be viewed as either a lemma or a semantic representation) or a vector that was correlated with the word's form (either an underlying phonological representation or the orthographic input from a reading-aloud task.) In both cases the input remained unchanged during the production of the word. The input activation passed through a hidden layer to an output layer of eighteen phonological features, one unit for each feature.

The phonological error model produces sequences of features by means of recurrent one-to-one connections from the output and hidden layers to layers of context units. One context layer is a copy of the hidden layer's

Figure 7.3
The Architecture of the Phonological Error Model

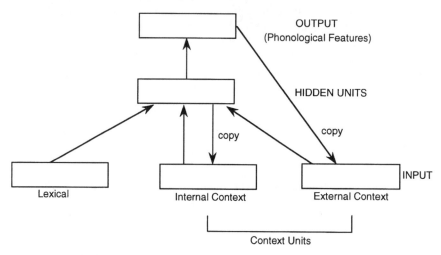

Each rectangle indicates a group of units.

activation on the previous pass through the network (internal context units), and the other corresponds to that for the output layer (external context units). Specifically, the production of a word (here, *cat*) goes like this: The input units are activated in the pattern designated for CAT. The internal context units are initialized to zero, and the external context units are set to a pattern that symbolizes a word boundary (0.5 on every unit). Activation spreads from the input and context units to hidden units and then to the output phonological features. The target activation pattern corresponds to the features of the first phoneme, /k/. To the extent that the output deviates from the target, weights are adjusted by back-propagation. The model's output and hidden-layer activations are then copied to the external and internal context units, respectively. The context units keep track of where the model is in the sequence. After the /k/ is produced, the context represents the state of already having produced that phoneme, instead of the word-boundary state. This change in the context allows for the production of /æ/ in the next forward pass of activation. The process continues for the remainder of the word, with the final target being the word-boundary pattern.

The model was trained by repeatedly presenting words and adjusting weights. Dell et al. (1997) trained several models on vocabularies of 50 to 412 short English words (one to three phonemes), and examined how performance differed with training vocabulary and architecture. Here our concern is with the model's ability to explain facts about phonological speech errors.

Some speech error effects have been interpreted as evidence for a *frame-and-slot* approach to word-form retrieval (Shattuck-Hufnagel, 1979). Frame-

and-slot models separate the retrieval of a word's sounds from the retrieval of a phonological frame. The frame represents the number of syllables in the word and the location of stress. Within the frame, each syllable is associated with slots that label the kind of sound (e.g., consonant or vowel) that the slot may hold. The word form is assembled by placing the retrieved sounds in the slots. Recall that the aphasia model used an activation-sensitive version of this mechanism; the phoneme units with the highest activation levels were selected by linking them to frame slots.

The speech error effects that support the idea of a separate frame include the following: the phonotactic regularity of errors, syllabic constituent effects, and the existence of sound exchanges. Here we define these and explain why they are supportive of separately representing sounds from the structures in which they occur. First, phonological errors have a strong tendency to follow the phonotactic patterns of the language. Thus, in English, one would not expect to see slips such as *king* to *nging* because syllable-initial /N/ does not occur in English. The phonotactic regularity of errors has been attributed to phonological rules that guide the insertion of retrieved sounds into frame slots. Presumably, in English, the insertion of /N/ into an onset slot would be blocked.

Syllabic constituent effects concern which parts of syllables are most likely to slip. Syllables are thought to have a hierarchical onset-rime structure in which, for example, a CVC syllable is composed of a C onset and a VC rime. Speech errors reflect this structure. For a CVC syllable, one is more likely to see a slip of either an onset (C) or a rime (VC) than other combinations, such as the CV part of a CVC syllable. For example, the error *Tup Kin* instead of *Tin Cup* involves the movement of rime constituents. Because the constituent structure of syllables is often assumed to be a property of phonological frames, these effects support phonological frames.

Some phonological errors involve the exchange of speech sounds (e.g., *heft lemisphere*). Although these are not very common—only 5 to 10 percent of phonological errors are exchanges—they are clearly not random events. Rather, an initial anticipatory substitution (*left* being spoken as *heft*) appears to cause another substitution, typically in the next word, in which the replaced sound replaces the anticipated sound (*lemisphere*). The existence of exchanges suggests the action of phonological frames. Each sound was erroneously placed in the other's frame slots.

The phonological error model accounts for some of the error effects attributed to separate phonological frames, although it lacks explicit frames. When noise is introduced into the model's weights, it produces realistic phonological errors. Specifically, erroneous phoneme sequences in the model have a strong tendency to be phonotactically regular. The percentage of errors that were phonotactically legal in the model ranged between 87 and 100 percent. Moreover, the errors tend to involve the hypothesized frame constituents. The model produces more syllable-onset than syllable-coda errors, and it produces more rime (VC) errors than CV errors. In general, the model's errors are sensitive to the structure of English words because it is trained on English words and it represents those words with linguistically motivated features (see Anderson, Milostan, & Cottrell, 1998). The superimposed weight changes associated with the training set creates sequential schemata, pathways in the model's activation space that reflect common sequences of features. When the model errs, it sticks close to these pathways. Thus, the errors obey English phonotactics. The reason that the model's errors tend to involve onsets rather than codas is a consequence of both the English vocabulary and the model's sequential nature. There is more variety in word and syllable onsets than in codas. Hence, there is more uncertainty about onsets, which makes them more error prone. This difference in uncertainty is enhanced by the sequential nature of the model. At the beginning of a word the context units' activation state is uninformative about the phoneme to be retrieved. However, as the model produces more of the word, the context units become more informative. For example, after having already retrieved /kæ/, the possible continuations are much fewer than before. That the model's errors tend to involve VC (rime) units more than CV units is also due to the vocabulary structure. English, like most languages, tends to have fewer VCs than CVs (Kessler & Treiman, 1997) and consequently must "reuse" the VCs that it does have. In the model, the VCs that are present thus become part of well-worn paths. When output jumps from one such path to another, a slip of an entire VC results.

The main problem with the phonological error model is that it has no mechanism for exchanges. The model could conceivably produce an anticipatory substitution such as *heft* for *left* in the context of *left hemisphere* through contamination from an upcoming word. But such an error would not naturally trigger a subsequent substitution to make the exchange *heft lemisphere*. The very fact that exchanges occur between structurally similar sounds points to a mechanism that binds values (retrieved sounds) to variables (slots in a frame). Specifically, in localist activation-based models with frames (e.g. Berg & Schade, 1992; Dell, 1986; Hartley & Houghton, 1996; Stemberger, 1985; MacKay, 1982), an exchange such as *heft lemisphere* can happen as follows: First, the activation of the /h/ node is greater than that of /l/, and so replaces it in the frame slot for the onset of the first syllable. The selected sound, /h/, then undergoes inhibition, which tends to prevent its reselection. When the onset slot of the next syllable is filled, the /l/, which did not undergo inhibition, may be more active than the inhibited /h/, and thus replace it, completing the exchange. The phonological error model does not have this kind of mechanism, or any other in which a substitution in one syllable triggers a corresponding substitution in a later syllable.

The phonological error model's failure to produce exchanges is a serious problem. It leads us to question its architecture. However, it does not cause us to abandon many of the principles present in the model. For example, the model attributes several error effects to the statistical structure of the word-form lexicon and to the fact that sounds are retrieved in sequence by means of a dynamic context. We believe that this attribution is correct. So, regardless of the architecture of the phonological access system, it should, in our view, embody mechanisms for sensitivity to sound statistics and sequence.

Before we turn to grammatical encoding, we should make a few observations about both of the lexical access models we have reviewed. The aphasia model and the phonological error model are, at least on the surface, quite different. The former is a two-step interactive activation model that retrieves position-specific phonemes in parallel and links them to slots in a frame. The latter is a PDP simple recurrent network that learns distributed representations, allowing for the sequential output of phonological features. Moreover, the phonological error model deals only with phonological processes, while the aphasia model does both lemma and phonological access.

Given these differences between the models, it is useful to consider how the phonological error model's approach could be extended to deal with the larger domain of the aphasia model. In fact, Plaut and Kello (1999) have constructed such a model. Their model learned to map from representations of word meaning to sequences of articulatory gestures by using error signals emerging from knowledge acquired during word comprehension. The resulting model has two key features of the aphasia model. First, connections run from semantics to phonology and in the reverse direction, making the activation flow interactive. Second, the model has something very much like two steps when it produces a word. This is because the intermediate layer must achieve its proper activation pattern before a sequential articulation process can begin. So, the first step involves retrieval of a static representation, and the second consists of turning that representation into a sequence.

The two steps in Plaut and Kello's (1999) model, however, are not the two steps of the aphasia model. The aphasia model's first step is retrieval of a word's lemma, while Plaut and Kello's model's first step is retrieval of a static phonological representation. It is difficult to tell whether these differences are fundamental or not, because Plaut and Kello made no claims about grammatical processes. It may turn out that the lemma is a static representation at an intermediate level that serves both as input to a sequential phonological output process and as output from processes that map from messages onto word sequences. If so, then there is a great deal of concordance between the models. More generally, we believe that models such as the aphasia model are high-level characterizations whose insights will be useful for understanding PDP implementations such as Plaut and Kello's model or the phonological error model. In the final section of this chapter we ask whether a PDP model of grammatical encoding, one that shares many characteristics with the Plaut and Kello and phonological error models, can handle facts about the production of sentences.

GRAMMATICAL ENCODING

Like phonological encoding, grammatical encoding has often been conceptualized in terms of frames and slots based on patterns found in speech errors. In frame-and-slot models of grammatical encoding (e.g., Bock, 1982; Dell, 1986; Garrett, 1975; MacKay, 1982), frames represent syntactic structures with slots labeled with the grammatical classes (e.g., noun or verb) of the lemmas that may fill them. Analogous to the phonotactic regularity of sound errors is the grammaticality of word substitutions. Word substitutions and exchanges tend to involve words of the same grammatical class, such as *please pass the FORK*, in which *fork* replaces *salt*, keeping the utterance grammatical while altering its meaning (Garrett, 1975). Within a frame-and-slot model, exchanges across grammatical classes such as *please SALT the PASS* are unlikely, because they involve two violations: a noun in a verb slot and a verb in a noun slot.

Recall that the phonological error model accounted for phonological structural effects by means of a learning mechanism that derived structure from the statistics of the training set rather than from explicit word frames. Perhaps an analogous approach to sentence learning could be used to study grammatical structure. However, there are many differences between sentence and word production that make grammatical encoding a more difficult process to model. Here we will review some of these differences as part of a summary of psycholinguistic research into sentence production, and then describe a new model of sentence production, the structural priming model (Chang, Griffin, Dell, & Bock, 1997), which attempts to explain some structural effects using a connectionist model of learning.

Most sentences are novel, while most words are not. One speaks of "retrieving" a word's form from memory, but of "generating" a sentence. Consequently, a greater emphasis must be placed on the generalization ability of a sentence-production model than on one that produces word forms. To get the right kind of generalization, one must first understand the nature of the input to production, the message, and then consider the mapping from the message to a word sequence. Because of the arbitrary but fixed mapping between a word's meaning and its sound, the input to phonological encoding can be a unique representation lacking internal structure, as in the aphasia model's word. In contrast, a message must logically possess internal structure to support generalization to novel utterances. The message must contain sufficient information about its elements to allow appropriate words to be selected and must express the relations among those elements: who did what to whom. The difficulty for the modeller lies in how to represent this information. Debates within linguistics have provided a wealth of ideas about what information is necessary in a representation of sentence meaning. But psycholinguistic research on the nature of message representation is scanty (see, however, Bock & Eberhard, 1993; Griffin & Bock, 1999; Slobin, 1996).

An important feature of the mapping between messages and grammatical forms is its variability. First, there is lexical variability. Unlike word forms, which are usually unambiguously associated with the same sounds, there may be many ways to map between message elements and words. A cat can be *cat, animal, Spot, it*, and so on. Second, a message can be realized by different syntactic structures without changing its core meaning. For example, when no particular element is in focus, the same proposition could be expressed with an active (*The horse kicked the cow*) or a passive sentence (*The cow was kicked by the horse*). When this syntactic flexibility is combined with flexibility in word choice, very similar statements can be made using very different syntactic structures, as in *Clinton defeated Dole, Dole lost to Clinton, Dole was defeated by the president*, and so on.

If messages do not determine word order, what does? In English, the assignment of lemmas to grammatical roles (e.g., subject, direct object) is the primary determinant of eventual word order, and grammatical role assignment depends on the ease of lexical encoding. Evidence comes from studies showing lexical priming effects on grammatical role assignments (Bock, 1986a, 1987b). The easier it was to select a word to express a substantive concept, the more likely it was to be encoded as a sentential subject. This result implies that noun phrases are assigned to grammatical roles in the order in which their lemmas are selected and in the order of grammatical role prominence (subject, then direct object, then object of preposition). Moreover, more conceptually available message elements (by virtue of being more topical, imageable, animate, or prototypical) are placed in more prominent grammatical roles than are less accessible elements (e.g., Bock & Warren, 1985; Ferreira, 1994). Such conceptual factors probably influence grammatical role assignment indirectly by taking priority in lemma selection. Together, these findings indicate that grammatical encoding is highly opportunistic; the most prominent message elements are the first to be lexicalized and the earliest lexicalized concepts are assigned to the earliest occurring grammatical roles, such as sentential subject.

However, more than conceptual and lexical accessibility affect word order and sentence structure. Studies conducted by Bock and colleagues (Bock, 1986b; Bock & Loebell, 1990) demonstrate the existence of *structural priming*: Speakers tend to repeat the structures of previously uttered sentences even when the sentences differ in prosodic, lexical, and conceptual content. For example, speakers are more likely to describe the event depicted in Figure 7.4 with a passive, such as *A policeman is being hit by an ambulance*, if they just produced a sentence that was passive rather than active. Furthermore, this increase in the use of one structure does not appear to be caused by strengthening links between grammatical role assignments and event roles (e.g., agent, patient) in the message (Bock & Loebell, 1990). Intransitive-locatives (*The 747 was landing by the control tower*) and passives (*The 747 was landed by the control tower*) differ primarily in the event roles that their constituents play (e.g., whether the sentential subject is the agent).

Figure 7.4
Example of a Target Picture and Active and Passive Prime Sentences

Transitive Primes

A. The jogger wasn't tripped by the chain (Passive)

B. The chain didn't trip the jogger. (Active)

Target Sentence

"The cop is getting hit by an ambulance."
(Passive)

From Bock (1986b).

Nevertheless, a speaker is as likely to use a passive structure after producing an intransitive-locative prime as after a passive prime. This suggests that the link between grammatical and event roles is not the locus of structural priming. Rather, the priming appears to be related to the constituent structure of the sentences (e.g., whether there is a prepositional phrase after the main verb). Furthermore, results of a study by Bock, Loebell, and Morey (1992) suggest that conceptual factors influence when elements are lexicalized and assigned grammatical roles, while structural accessibility has an independent influence by affecting the type of grammatical roles that are filled (e.g., subject and direct object for actives, or subject and object of preposition for passives and intransitive-locatives). Thus, grammatical encoding cannot be accomplished by blindly assigning lemmas to grammatical roles as concepts are lexicalized. Lemmas must be marked with event-related information to ensure that the relationship between message elements is not lost, otherwise an agent could easily become the subject of a passive sentence. This has been called the coordination problem (Bock, 1987a), and poses difficulties for all models of grammatical encoding.

In summary, grammatical encoding is a particularly challenging process to model for several reasons: (1) Little is known about its input representation, except that its internal structure must permit generalization; (2) the mapping between concepts and words is variable, as is the mapping between message relationships and grammatical roles; (3) the assignment of grammatical roles is constrained but not determined by message relationships; and (4) there are structural priming effects of a character that suggest structural frames. A connectionist learning model overcoming these challenges needs to demonstrate structural effects without possessing explicit structures and role binding without explicit tags or grammatical roles, and must make flexible and opportunistic decisions in the choice of words and structures.

Fortunately, some aspects of grammatical encoding may be readily accounted for within a connectionist framework. Recent studies indicate that the influence of a prime sentence persists across the production of up to ten structurally unrelated sentences (Bock, Dell, Griffin, Chang, & Ferreira, 1996; Bock & Griffin, in press). This result suggests that priming may be a type of implicit learning rather than the result of activation of structures in short-term memory. If so, connectionist-learning models associated with gradual weight change may be able to explain some features of priming. Furthermore, Elman (1993) demonstrated that a recurrent network could implicitly learn grammatical structure when trained to anticipate the next word in a sentence. The structural priming model (Chang et al., 1997), to which we now turn, employed a related architecture in an attempt to produce grammatical sequences from a message and mimic the structural priming effect.

Structural Priming Model

The central claim of the structural priming model is that structural priming is a form of implicit learning. In other words, the same mechanism through which the model learns to produce sentences causes the priming. To realize this claim, it was necessary to make the model accord with three basic assumptions about production. First, production starts with a message expressing propositional content. Second, message elements may differ in their accessibility and these differences contribute to structural choices. Third, words are selected one at a time, with earlier selections constraining later ones; that is, processing is incremental and left to right. To reflect these assumptions, the model used a type of simple recurrent network that learned to map from a static message to a sequence of words, and it allowed for differential activation levels among message elements to determine the target sequence.

In this framework, structural priming results from the learning algorithm, which was back-propagation. When a prime sentence is produced, weight changes take place that favor the production of that sentence from its message. Chang et al.'s (1997) hypothesis was that these changes would generalize to structurally related sentences. So, a subsequent message that may be associated with more than one structure, such as an active–passive or double-object–prepositional dative option, would be more likely to be encoded using the structure of the prime. This is possible because the weight changes associated with a particular message-sentence mapping are shared with other message-sentence combinations.

Figure 7.5 illustrates the general theory behind the model. Like some other connectionist treatments of language (e.g. Christiansen & Chater, 1999; Plaut & Kello, 1999), Chang et al. (1997) propose a close relationship between comprehension and production. In particular, they suggest that the context representations that guide sequential production arise during comprehension. For example, suppose that comprehension is carried out by a simple recurrent network that maps word sequences onto messages, and that this network uses the activation pattern of its hidden units as the context to facilitate this mapping. We know that the changes in the activation patterns of these hidden units would come to be sensitive to the structure of input sentences (Elman, 1993) and to the mapping of this structure onto meaning. Chang et al. hypothesize that these hidden-unit–context-activation patterns could be directly used during production in the following way: At the beginning of a sentence to be produced, the context units would be set to null values, indicating a sentence boundary. The production side of the model would then output the first word. This word would be fed into the input of the comprehension side of the model, thereby updating the context units' activations. These activations would then serve as contextual input to production, effectively signalling the system that it is now time to produce the second word, and so on until the end of the sentence.

We now describe Chang et al.'s (1997) implemented model and their simulations of the structural priming effect. As Figure 7.5 shows, Chang et al. did not actually implement the comprehension side of their model. Rather, they attempted to approximate the contribution from comprehension by creating a localist transition network and using it as context for production. This transition network will be described after we introduce other aspects of the implemented model.

The input to the model was a message, a set of localist semantic features representing a single proposition (see St. John & McClelland, 1990). The message was an eighty-seven-dimensional vector that represented concepts such as *boy*, actions such as *walking*, and the event roles, agent, patient, recipient, and location. The message remained activated throughout the production of the sentence. The relationships among the message participants involved associating blocks of features with event roles. So, within the agent

Figure 7.5
Comprehension Can Provide the Dynamic Context for Production

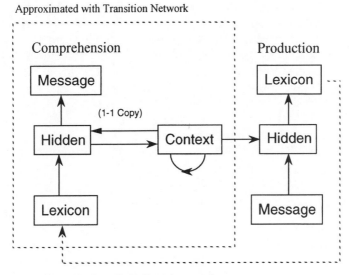

Copy back of previous word

From Chang et al. (1997).

block, there were eighteen units including units for CHILD, MALE, and UNITARY. The patient, recipient, and location blocks also had eighteen units each and these coded for the same features as the agent block. The action block had fifteen features. These included localist units for specific actions such as WALKING, GIVING, or CHASING, and their number of arguments. For example, the message CHASE (BOYS, DOG) would be associated with activated agent units CHILD, MALE, MULTIPLE; patient units BARKS, ANIMAL, UNITARY; and action units CHASING and 2-ARGUMENT.

Differences in conceptual accessibility were implemented by having the features of one role more activated than others. These differences determined the target structure of sentences during training. Given filled agent and patient roles and a transitive action, the model was trained to produce an active sentence if the agent was more activated than the patient, and a passive if the reverse was true. A message for the production of a double-object dative sentence, as opposed to a prepositional dative sentence, differed only in whether the patient or recipient was more highly activated.

The message units had learnable connections to fifty hidden units, which, in turn, had learnable connections to the model's output layer. In the output layer, there was one unit for each of the fifty-nine words in its vocabulary. These included singular and plural nouns (twelve of each), two obligatorily transitive verbs, *chase(s)* and *feed(s)*; two optionally transitive verbs, *see(s)* and *hear(s)*; two intransitive verbs, *walk(s)* and *live(s)*; and four dative verbs, *give(s)*, *make(s)*, *show(s)*, and *write(s)*. Each verb that could be used transitively also had a past-participle form (e.g., *heard*) and each verb that could be used intransitively had a present-participle form (e.g., *living*). There were also units for *is, are, by, near, for, to*, and *PERIOD* (end of sentence marker). Verbs had to agree with subject nouns in number. The following list gives examples of the sentences that the model was trained to produce:

Sentence Type	Percentage in Training	Structure Sequence
Intransitive	17	AGENT VERB.
		Girl walks.
Active Transitive	27	AGENT VERB PATIENT.
		Man chases dog.
Passive Transitive	9	PATIENT AUX PASTPART by AGENT.
		Dog is chased by man.
Double-Object Dative	17	AGENT VERB RECIPIENT PATIENT.
		Woman gives man dog.
Prepositional Dative	17	AGENT VERB PATIENT PREP RECIPIENT.
		Woman gives dog to man.
Intransitive Locative	4	AGENT AUX PRESPART PREP LOCATION.
		Boys are walking near bus.
Transitive Locative	9	AGENT VERB PATIENT PREP LOCATION.
		Girls chase dogs to car.

The transition network served as another input layer to the model. It reflected the current state of the sentence from the perspective of the comprehension system. This network contained ten localist nodes representing the following syntactic and event role categories: PERIOD, VERB, AUX, PastParticiple, PresentParticiple, PREP, AGENT, PATIENT, RECIPIENT, and LOCATION. Each of these nodes had connections with modifiable weights to each hidden unit. The activation of the transition network's nodes changes as the sentence progressed. The following list shows which nodes would activate and when they would activate for particular sentence types:

Intransitive: PERIOD → {AGENT PATIENT} → VERB → PERIOD

Active Transitive: PERIOD → {AGENT PATIENT} → VERB → PATIENT → PERIOD

Passive Transitive: PERIOD → {AGENT PATIENT} → AUX → PastP → PREP → AGENT → PERIOD

Double-Object Dative: PERIOD → {AGENT PATIENT} → VERB →
{RECIPIENT PATIENT} → PATIENT → PERIOD

Prepositional Dative: PERIOD → {AGENT PATIENT} → VERB → {RECIPIENT
PATIENT} → PREP → RECIPIENT → PERIOD

Transitive Locative: PERIOD → {AGENT PATIENT} → VERB → {RECIPIENT
PATIENT} → PREP → LOCATION → PERIOD

Intransitive Locative: PERIOD → {AGENT PATIENT} → AUX → PresP →
PREP → LOCATION → PERIOD

Consider, for example, the sentence, *Girls give man robot*. Before any
word has been produced, the sentence-boundary node PERIOD is the only
unit in the transition network that is on. (Note that this PERIOD is different
from the output layer unit for *PERIOD*). So, the input to the model consists
of just PERIOD plus the appropriate message representation. Under these
conditions the model should produce *girls*. The word *girls* is then assumed
to pass to the comprehension system, which would determine that it is likely
an agent or possibly a patient. This interpretation by the comprehension
system was implemented by turning on the nodes for AGENT and PA-
TIENT in the transition network. (See, in the list, that for double-object
datives the first transition is from PERIOD to {AGENT PATIENT}.) The
node for PERIOD would also remain partly on. Each transition-network
node retained half of its activation across the production of each additional
word. Notice that the ambiguity associated with the role assignment for
girls is only from the comprehension system's perspective. The message on
the production side knows that *girls* is the agent. The state of AGENT and
PATIENT on and PERIOD half on then signals for the production of the
next word, *give*. The comprehension of *give* turns on the VERB unit, which
then enables the production of *man*. Again, because of ambiguity, the comprehension system does not know whether *man* is RECIPIENT or PATIENT,
and so both of these units then turn on. The process continues with the
production of the final word *robot*, which is now unambiguously identified
as a PATIENT. Because the comprehension system is controlling the state
changes of the context, there is no need to relearn the sentence patterns
during production. However, the production system does have to learn how
to associate these patterns with messages to produce sequential output. An
important consequence of using a context derived from the comprehension
system is that the contextual states are associated with temporary ambiguity
(here, ambiguity about event roles of noun phrases). According to Chang et
al. (1997), this ambiguity contributes some error to the production side of
the model, which in turn makes for greater weight change on that side, and
ultimately leads to sizable structural priming due to those weight changes.

The model was trained using back-propagation. Weights were initialized
to normally distributed random values, with mean 0 and variance 0.5. The
training corpus consisted of 3,600 sentences reflecting the proportions of

sentence types shown earlier. Each of these was trained an average of thirty-one times. The learning rate for the first quarter of the training was 0.06, and 0.03 for the remainder. Momentum was 0.9.

The 3,600 training sentences represented a fraction of the 175,152 sentences that were possible given the vocabulary and sentence types. Aside from the fact that actives occurred more frequently than passives, the proportions of each sentence type in the training set were not designed to reflect the relative frequencies of the structures in natural language. After the model learned, it was tested on a random set of 400 sentences that preserved the proportion of sentence types in the corpus. Of these, 74 percent were novel sentences (66% of the nonnovel sentences were intransitives because there is less opportunity for variety with this type). The model accurately produced the correct word 94 percent of the time.

To test priming, the model was first given a priming trial consisting of a message that required either a simple active or a passive sentence (in the case of datives, a double-object or prepositional dative sentence). As in training, weights were adjusted as the sentence was produced, using a learning rate of 0.03. Then the model was given a target message that was neutral with respect to conceptual accessibility. For a transitive message, the agent and patient were equally activated, and correspondingly for the patient and recipient of a dative message. For the datives, each prime and target was a novel message, one that had not been previously trained. For transitives, one-fourth of the test messages had been trained before. Chang et al. (1997) recorded the percentage of times that each structure was produced as a function of the prime, the differences being the measure of priming.

The model exhibited a fair amount of structural priming. For example, *Boys chase dogs* as a prime would promote *Girl feeds cat* over *Cat is fed by girl*. Figures 7.6 and 7.7 show the magnitude of active–passive and dative priming from Bock et al. (1996) and from the model. The sizes of the priming effects in the model match up well with the data. The absolute percentage of propositional datives, though, is lower in the model than in the data. Pictures in the experiment were selected so that alternating structures were used equally often on average. No such constraint was applied to the model. The figures also show the model's successful simulation of the persistence of priming over ten intervening neutral sentences (Bock et al., 1996). Thus, the model exhibits the phenomenon that motivates an account of priming as implicit learning. The same type of weight changes used in learning caused persistent structural priming.

Chang et al. (1997) also investigated whether the model could simulate the effects of Bock and Loebell (1990), who showed that priming is centered on the surface syntactic structure of the prime, rather than its mapping from event to grammatical roles. Here, the model's success was more checkered. It showed priming between intransitive locatives such as *boys are walking near bus* and the thematically different but structurally similar pas-

Figure 7.6
Dative Priming over Intervening Sentences

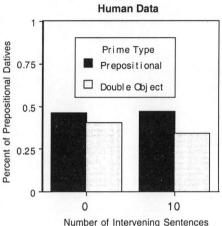

From Bock et al. (1996).

sive *dog is chased by man*, in agreement with Bock and Loebell. However, it failed to show priming between transitive locatives such as *girls chase dogs near car* and prepositional datives, which Bock and Loebell had found.

In summary, the structural priming model successfully realizes the hypothesis that priming is a form of implicit learning. Moreover, it shows that structural priming may be compatible with sequential connectionist models that derive structure from experience. Interestingly, Chang et al. (1997) believe that this structure must come from learning to comprehend, as well

Figure 7.7
Active–Passive Priming over Intervening Sentences

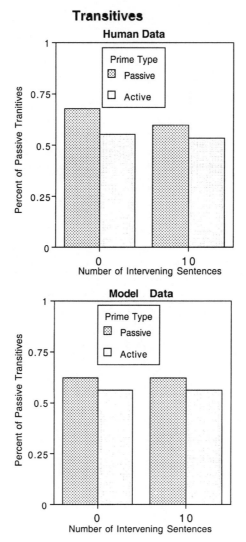

From Bock et al. (1996).

as learning to produce. The reasons that the model fails to account for the totality of the priming data are, of course, difficult to ascertain. However, we believe that its assumptions about message structure may be partly responsible. For example, the model assumes separate banks of message units for the four event roles that it uses. This assumption has some unrealistic consequences. First, it denies the possibility that roles have a similarity structure; for example, locations are like recipients (see Jackendoff, 1972). Second, it treats roles as categories that are independent of actions, contrary to some modern theories (e.g., Pollard & Sag, 1994). In general, connectionist models are ultimately only as good as their assumptions about input and output representations. Progress in models of grammatical encoding is therefore dependent on the development of knowledge about meaning and communication.

A recent model (Chang, Dell, Bock, & Griffin, 2000) has attempted to address two of the shortcomings of the structural priming model. First, the new model, unlike the original one, directly embodies Chang et al.'s (1997) assumption that knowledge gained from learning to comprehend is used in production. The transition network used by Chang et al. (1997) was replaced by states derived from a network that actually learned to comprehend. This was done by first training a simple recurrent network to map from a sequence of words to a static message representation. Then the model was trained to produce sentences, using the dynamic context representation from the comprehension network as part of the context that supports production. The second change involved the nature of the message representation. Making use of some ideas from Jackendoff (1987, 1990) and Dowty (1991), Chang et al. (2000) collapsed the thematic roles into a set of three "message roles," and added features to the role slots to distinguish among the characteristics of the participants in an event. With these changes, the new model showed priming in the condition examined by Bock and Loebell (1990) that was problematic for the earlier model (transitive locatives priming prepositional datives). This is because the new model's message representation recognizes that locations (*drove the Mercedes to* THE CHURCH) have something in common with recipients (*gave the Mercedes to* THE CHURCH).

Although these new results are encouraging, there is still some distance to go. Chang et al. (2000) found that there is much variability among replications of networks with respect to priming. Small changes in architectures, training experiences, and even initial random weights can have a large effect on the extent and distribution of priming. Clearly, there is a need for systematic model exploration with multiple replications, and, more generally, for a greater understanding of why models behave the way they do.

Before concluding, let us briefly consider how the structural priming model might relate to the two lexical access models. First, consider the structural priming model's relation to the aphasia model. The aphasia model has a layer of lemma nodes that are actively selected and inserted into syntactic frames. The hidden layer of structural priming model may be seen as approximating the result of this selection and insertion process, with the contribution of the frame being associated with the context representations. However, these similarities between the models should not be overstated.

For example, the context representations of the structural priming model are not pure syntactic frames, something that is made evident by the model's failure to show priming between the structurally identical prepositional datives and transitive locatives.

Next, consider the structural priming model in concert with the phonological error model. They are both recurrent network models and it is tempting to just link them up, the output of the structural priming model providing input to the phonological error model. Such a linkage, however, creates independent phonological and grammatical modules and hence does not allow for interaction between phonological and lexical representations, which we argued (through the aphasia model) was needed to explain interactive error effects. Another point about the two recurrent network models concerns exchanges. Recall that the phonological error model does not produce exchanges such as *cogs and dats* for *dogs and cats*. It turns out that the structural priming model does (rarely) produce word exchanges; for example, *Dog is chased by cat* as a blend of two possible correct sentences *Dog chases cat* and *Cat is chased by dog*. One can speculate that what is lacking in the phonological error model is an analogous mechanism at the phonological level—a conflict between two alternative correct outputs—along with a constraint that tries to have each intended output unit (word or phoneme) occur just once in the output sequence. Perhaps a combination phonological–grammatical model that is associated with alternations such as *cats and dogs* versus *dogs and cats* could produce *cogs and dats*. In fact, this conflict account of phonological exchanges is not new. It is the competing-plans hypothesis of Baars (1980), and is even similar to Freud's (1891/1953) ideas on speech errors.

CONCLUSIONS

Our review of connectionist models in production has focused on our recent work in lexical access and grammatical encoding. Our lexical access models, when considered together with other spreading-activation models (e.g., Roelofs, 1997), provide a fair coverage of the data. One would expect so, because these kinds of models have been around for some time. The main problem is that different models have different strengths and weaknesses, and so there is no unified approach that has been shown to do the job. Work on models of grammatical encoding, however, is just beginning, and so what has been accomplished is exciting (at least to us), although quite limited.

We consider two key features of production to be serial output and sensitivity to linguistic structure. In the PDP recurrent network models, structure and order are entwined in the sequential schemata that develop from the superimposed weight changes associated with the training set. It remains to be seen whether these schemata have the right characteristics to support generalization in grammatical encoding (e.g., the right kind of structural priming), or account for the sequential structure of word forms (e.g., exhibit phonological exchange errors).

Ultimately, we believe that connectionist models of the acquisition of the skills of speaking (and comprehending) will contribute to explanations of the nature of language—why it is the way it is (see, e.g., Christiansen & Devlin, 1997; Hare & Elman, 1995; Gupta & Dell, 1999). Moreover, we believe the PDP approach offers the best chance to explain production as a skill, as something that one learns to do over years of experience. Perhaps most important, a PDP approach to language production expresses its commonalities with other linguistic, and even nonlinguistic, skills.

FURTHER READINGS

Research into language production is not as plentiful as research dealing with comprehension. Over the last fifteen years, though, the study of speaking has emerged from obscurity and is now acknowledged to be a more or less equal partner to the study of language understanding. This is largely due to Levelt's (1989) book, which presented the first extensive theory of production. Levelt's theory was based in part on influential studies of speech errors by Garrett (1975), Fromkin (1971), Stemberger (1985), and MacKay (1982), who directed the attention of the psycholinguistic community to the richness of errors as a data source. Recent production research, however, has emphasized the use of controlled experimental techniques that measure the time course of production as opposed to the analyses of speech error collections (see Levelt et al., 1999).

The first sizable production theory that was implemented as a spreading-activation system was that of Dell (1986). The aphasia model presented here is one offspring of that theory (Dell et al., 1977; Foygel & Dell, in press). This model's interactive activation approach to lexical access in production can be contrasted with the two-stage noninteractive theory proposed by Levelt et al. (1999) and the independent-levels theory outlined in Caramazza (1997).

The structural priming phenomenon that is central to the Chang et al. (1997) model was first presented in Bock (1986b). A general introduction to research on grammatical encoding in production can be found in Bock (1990) and Levelt (1989). Recent discoveries in structural priming are reviewed in Bock and Griffin (in press).

NOTE

The authors thank Kay Bock, Vic Ferreira, Prahlad Gupta, Anita Govindjee, and Linda May for their assistance on this project, and Morten Christiansen and Nick Chater for helpful comments. The research was supported by NSF SBR 93-19368, NIH DC-00191, and HD 21011.

REFERENCES

Anderson, K., Milostan, J., & Cottrell, G. W. (1998). Assessing the contribution of representation to results. In *Proceedings of the Twentieth Annual Conference of the Cognitive Science Society* (pp. 48–53). Mahwah, NJ: Erlbaum.

Baars, B. J. (1980). The competing plans hypothesis: An heuristic viewpoint on the causes of errors in speech. In H. W. Dechert & M. Raupach (Eds.), *Temporal variables in speech* (pp. 39–49). The Hague: Mouton.

Berg, T., & Schade, U. (1992). The role of inhibition in a spreading activation model of language production. Part 1: The psycholinguistic perspective. *Journal of Psycholinguistic Research, 22*, 405–434.

Bock, J. K. (1982). Towards a cognitive psychology of syntax: Information processing contributions to sentence formulation. *Psychological Review, 89*, 1–47.

Bock, J. K. (1986a). Meaning, sound, and syntax: Lexical priming in sentence production. *Journal of Experimental Psychology: Learning, Memory and Cognition, 12*, 575–586.

Bock, J. K. (1986b). Syntactic persistence in language production. *Cognitive Psychology, 18*, 355–387.

Bock, J. K. (1987a). Coordinating words and syntax in speech plans. In A. Ellis (Ed.), *Progress in the psychology of language* (Vol. 3, pp. 337–390). London: Lawrence Erlbaum.

Bock, J. K. (1987b). An effect of accessibility of word forms on sentence structures. *Journal of Memory and Language, 26*, 119–137.

Bock, J. K. (1990). Structure in language: Creating form in talk. *American Psychologist, 45*, 1221–1236.

Bock, J. K., Dell, G. S., Griffin, Z. M., Chang, F., & Ferreira, V. S. (1996). *Structural priming as implicit learning*. Paper presented at the meeting of the Psychonomic Society, Chicago, Illinois.

Bock, J. K., & Eberhard, K. M. (1993). Meaning, sound, and syntax in English number agreement. *Language and Cognitive Processes, 8*, 57–99.

Bock, J. K., & Griffin, Z. M. (in press). The persistence of structural priming: Transient activation or implicit learning? *Journal of Experimental Psychology: General*.

Bock, J. K., & Loebell, H. (1990). Framing sentences. *Cognition, 35*, 1–39.

Bock, J. K., Loebell, H., & Morey, R. (1992). From conceptual roles to structural relations: Bridging the syntactic cleft. *Psychological Review, 99*, 150–171.

Bock, J. K., & Warren, R. K. (1985). Conceptual accessibility and syntactic structure in sentence formulation. *Cognition, 21*, 47–67.

Burke, D. M., MacKay, D. G., Worthley, J. S., & Wade, E. (1991). On the tip of the tongue: What causes word finding failures in young and older adults? *Journal of Memory and Language, 30*, 542–579.

Caramazza, A. (1997). How many levels of processing are there in lexical access? *Cognitive Neuropsychology, 14*, 177–208.

Chang, F., Dell, G. S., Bock, J. K., & Griffin, Z. M. (2000). Structural priming as implicit learning: A comparison of models of sentence production. *Journal of Psycholinguistic Research, 29*, 217–229.

Chang, F., Griffin, Z. M., Dell, G. S., & Bock, K. (1997, August). *Modelling structural priming as implicit learning*. Paper presented at Computational Psycholinguistics, Berkeley, California.

Christiansen, M. H., & Chater, N. (1999). Toward a connectionist model of recursion in human linguistic performance. *Cognitive Science, 23*, 157–205.

Christiansen, M. H., & Devlin, J. T. (1997). Recursive inconsistencies are hard to learn: A connectionist perspective on universal word order correlations. In *Proceedings of the Nineteenth Annual Conference of the Cognitive Science Society* (pp. 113–118). Mahwah, NJ: Lawrence Erlbaum.

Cutting, J. C., & Ferreira, V. S. (1999). Semantic and phonological information flow in the production lexicon. *Journal of Experimental Psychology: Learning, Memory, and Cognition, 25*, 318–344.

Dell, G. S. (1986). A spreading activation theory of retrieval in language production. *Psychological Review, 93*, 283–321.

Dell, G. S., Juliano, C., & Govindjee, A. (1993). Structure and content in language production: A theory of frame constraints in phonological speech errors. *Cognitive Science, 17*, 149–195.

Dell, G. S., & Reich, P. A. (1977). A model of slips of the tongue. In R. J. Dipietro & E. L. Blansitt (Eds.), *The third LACUS forum* (pp. 448–455). Columbia, SC: Hornbeam Press.

Dell, G. S., Schwartz, M. F., Martin, N., Saffran, E. M., & Gagnon, D. A. (1997). Lexical access in aphasic and nonaphasic speakers. *Psychological Review, 104*, 801–939.

Dowty, D. (1991). Thematic proto-roles and argument selection. *Language, 67*, 547–619.

Eikmeyer, H.-J., & Schade, U. (1991). Sequentialization in connectionist language-production models. *Cognitive Systems, 3*, 128–138.

Elman, J. L. (1990). Finding structure in time. *Cognitive Science, 14*, 179–211.

Elman, J. L. (1993). Learning and development in neural networks: The importance of starting small. *Cognition, 48*, 71–99.

Ferreira, F. (1994). Choice of passive voice is affected by verb type and animacy. *Journal of Memory and Language, 33*, 715–736.

Ferreira, V. (1996). Is it better to give than to donate? Syntactic flexibility in language production. *Journal of Memory and Language, 35*, 724–755.

Ferreira, V. (1997). *Syntactic and lexical choices in language production: What we can learn from "that."* Unpublished doctoral dissertation. University of Illinois at Urbana–Champaign.

Foygel, D., & Dell, G. S. (in press). Models of impaired lexical access in speech production. *Journal of Memory and Language.*

Freud, S. (1953). *On aphasia: A critical study.* New York: International Universities Press. (Original work published 1891.)

Fromkin, V. A. (1971). The non-anomalous nature of anomalous utterances. *Language, 47*, 27–52.

Garrett, M. F. (1975). The analysis of sentence production. In G. H. Bower (Ed.), *The psychology of learning and motivation* (pp. 133–175). San Diego: Academic Press.

Griffin, Z. M., & Bock, J. K. (1998). Constraint, word frequency, and the relationship between lexical processing levels in spoken word production. *Journal of Memory and Language, 38*, 313–338.

Griffin, Z. M., & Bock, J. K. (1999). *What the eyes say about speaking.* Manuscript submitted for publication.

Gupta, P. (1996). *Immediate serial memory and language processing: Beyond the articulatory loop* (Tech. Rep. No. CS-96-02). Urbana, IL: Beckman Institute Cognitive Science.

Gupta, P., & Dell, G. S. (1999). The emergence of language from serial order and procedural memory. In B. MacWhinney (Ed.), *Emergentist approaches to language*. Mahwah, NJ: Lawrence Erlbaum.

Hare, M., & Elman, J. L. (1995). Learning and morphological change. *Cognition, 56*, 61–98.

Harley, T. A. (1984). A critique of top-down independent levels models of speech production: Evidence from non-plan-internal speech errors. *Cognitive Science, 8*, 191–219.

Hartley, T., & Houghton, G. (1996). A linguistically-constrained model of short-term memory for nonwords. *Journal of Memory and Language, 35*, 1–31.

Houghton, G. (1990). The problem of serial order: A neural network model of sequence learning and recall. In R. Dale, C. Mellish, & M. Zock (Eds.), *Current research in natural language generation* (pp. 287–319). London: Academic Press.

Jackendoff, R. (1972). *Semantic interpretation in generative grammar*. Cambridge, MA: MIT Press.

Jackendoff, R. (1987). The status of thematic relations in linguistic theory. *Linguistic Inquiry, 18*, 369–411.

Jackendoff, R. (1990). *Semantic structures*. Cambridge, MA: MIT Press.

Jordan, M. I. (1986). Serial order: A parallel distributed processing approach (ICS Tech. Rep. No. 8604). La Jolla: University of California at San Diego.

Kempen, G., & Hoenkamp, E. (1987). An incremental procedural grammar for sentence formulation. *Cognitive Science, 11*, 201–258.

Kessler, B., & Treiman, R. (1997). Syllable structure and the distribution of phonemes in English syllables. *Journal of Memory and Language, 37*, 295–311.

Levelt, W.J.M. (1989). *Speaking: From intention to articulation*. Cambridge, MA: MIT Press.

Levelt, W.J.M., Roelofs, A., & Meyer, A. S. (1999). A theory of lexical access in speech production. *Behavioral and Brain Science, 22*, 1–75.

MacKay, D. G. (1982). The problems of flexibility, fluency, and speed-accuracy trade-off in skilled behaviors. *Psychological Review, 89*, 483–506.

MacKay, D. G. (1987). *The organization of perception and action: A theory for language and other cognitive skills*. New York: Springer-Verlag.

McClelland, J. L., & Rumelhart, D. E. (1981). An interactive activation model of context effects in letter perception: Part 1. An account of basic findings. *Psychological Review, 88*, 375–407.

Meyer, A. S. (1991). The time course of phonological encoding in language production: Phonological encoding inside a syllable. *Journal of Memory and Language, 30*, 69–89.

Miozzo, M., & Caramazza, A. (1997). The retrieval of lexical-syntactic features in tip-of-the-tongue states. *Journal of Experimental Psychology: Learning, Memory, and Cognition, 23*, 1–14.

Peterson, R. R., & Savoy, P. (1998). Lexical selection and phonological encoding during language production: Evidence for cascaded processing. *Journal of Experimental Psychology: Learning, Memory, & Cognition, 24*, 539–557.

Plaut, D. C., & Kello, C. T. (1999). The emergence of phonology from the interplay of speech comprehension and production: A distributed connectionist approach. In B. MacWhinney (Ed.), *The emergence of language*. Mahwah, NJ: Lawrence Erlbaum.

Pollard, C., & Sag, I. (1994). *Head-driven phrase structure grammar*. Stanford, CA: CSLI Publications.

Roelofs, A. (1996). Computational models of lemma retrieval. In T. Dijkstra & K. de Smedt (Eds.), *Computational psycholinguistics* (pp. 308–327). London: Taylor & Francis.

Roelofs, A. (1997). The WEAVER model of word-form encoding in speech production. *Cognition, 64*, 249–284.

Schriefers, H., Meyer, A. S., & Levelt, W.J.M. (1990). Exploring the time-course of lexical access in production: Picture-word interference studies. *Journal of Memory and Language, 29*, 86–102.

Sevald, C. A., Dell, G. S., & Cole, J. (1995). Syllable structure in speech production: Are syllables chunks or schemas? *Journal of Memory and Language, 34*, 807–820.

Shattuck-Hufnagel, S. (1979). Speech errors as evidence for a serial-order mechanism in sentence production. In W. E. Cooper & E.C.T. Walker (Eds.), *Sentence processing: Psycholinguistic studies presented to Merrill Garrett* (pp. 295–342). Hillsdale, NJ: Lawrence Erlbaum.

Slobin, D. I. (1996). From "thought and language" to "thinking for speaking." In J. Gumperz & S. C. Levinson (Eds.), *Rethinking linguistic relativity* (pp. 70–96). Cambridge: Cambridge University Press.

Stemberger, J. P. (1985) An interactive activation model of language production. In A. W. Ellis (Ed.), *Progress in the psychology of language* (Vol. 1, pp. 143–186). Hillsdale, NJ: Lawrence Erlbaum.

Stemberger, J. P. (1989). Speech errors in early child language production. *Journal of Memory and Language, 28*, 164–188.

St. John, M. F., & McClelland, J. L. (1990). Learning and applying contextual constraints in sentence comprehension. *Artificial Intelligence, 46*, 217–257.

van Turennout, M., Hagoort, P., & Brown, C. M. (1997). Electrophysiological evidence on the time course of semantic and phonological processes in speech production. *Journal of Experimental Psychology: Learning, Memory, and Cognition, 23*, 787–806.

Vigliocco, G., Antonini, T., & Garrett, M. F. (1997). Grammatical gender is on the tip of Italian tongues. *Psychological Science, 8*, 314–319.

Wheeldon, L. R., & Levelt, W.J.M. (1995). Monitoring the time course of phonological encoding. *Journal of Memory and Language, 34*, 311–334.

8

A Connectionist Approach to Word Reading and Acquired Dyslexia: Extension to Sequential Processing

David C. Plaut

Many researchers assume that the most appropriate way to express the systematic aspects of language is in terms of a set of rules. For instance, there is a systematic relationship between the written and spoken forms of most English words (e.g., *gave* ⇒ /geɪv/), and this relationship can be expressed in terms of a fairly concise set of grapheme–phoneme correspondence (GPC) rules (e.g., *g* ⇒ /g/, a_e ⇒ /eɪ/, *v* ⇒ /v/). In addition to being able to generate accurate pronunciations of so-called regular words, such rules also provide a straightforward account of how skilled readers apply their knowledge to novel items; for example, in pronouncing wordlike nonwords (e.g., *mave* ⇒ /meɪv/). Most linguistic domains, however, are only partially systematic. Thus, there are many English words whose pronunciations violate the standard GPC rules (e.g., *have* ⇒ /hæv/). Given that skilled readers can pronounce such exception words correctly, GPC rules alone are insufficient. More generally, skilled language performance at every level of analysis—phonological, morphological, lexical, syntactic—requires both effective handling of exceptional items and the ability to generalize to novel forms.

In the domain of reading there are three broad responses to this challenge. The first, adopted by dual-route theories (e.g., Coltheart, Curtis, Atkins, & Haller, 1993; Zorzi, Houghton, & Butterworth, 1998), is to add to the GPC system a separate, lexical system that handles the exceptions.

The second response, adopted by multiple-levels theories (e.g., Norris, 1994; Shallice & McCarthy, 1985), is to augment the GPC rules with more specific, context-sensitive rules, (e.g., *ook* ⇒ /uk/ as in *book*), including rules that apply only to individual exceptions (e.g., *have* ⇒ /hæv/). Both of these approaches retain the general notion that language knowledge takes the form of rules (although such rules may be expressed in terms of connections; see, e.g., Norris, 1994; Reggia, Marsland, & Berndt, 1988; Zorzi et al., 1998).

The third response to the challenge, adopted by distributed connectionist theories (Plaut, McClelland, Seidenberg, & Patterson, 1996; Seidenberg & McClelland, 1989; Van Orden, Pennington, & Stone, 1990) and elaborated in this chapter, is more radical. It eschews the notion that the knowledge supporting on-line language performance takes the form of explicit rules, and thus denies a strict dichotomy between "regular" items that obey the rules and "exception" items that violate them. Rather, it is claimed that language knowledge is inherently graded, and the language mechanism is a learning device that gradually picks up on the statistical structure among written and spoken words and the contexts in which they occur. In this way the emphasis is on the degree to which the mappings among the spelling, sound, and meaning of a given word are consistent with those of other words (Glushko, 1979).

To make this third perspective concrete, consider the connectionist–parallel distributed processing (PDP) framework for lexical processing depicted in Figure 8.1 (based on Seidenberg & McClelland, 1989). As the figure makes clear, the approach does not entail a complete lack of structure within the reading system. There is, however, uniformity in the processing mechanisms by which representations are generated and interact, and in this respect the approach is quite different from dual-route accounts. Orthographic, phonological, and semantic information is represented in terms of distributed patterns of activity over groups of simple neuronlike processing units. Within each domain, similar words are represented by similar patterns of activity. Lexical tasks involve transformations between these representations; for example, reading aloud requires the orthographic pattern for a word to generate the appropriate phonological pattern. Such transformations are accomplished via the cooperative and competitive interactions among units, including additional hidden units that mediate between the orthographic, phonological, and semantic units. In processing an input, units interact until the network as a whole settles into a stable pattern of activity—termed an *attractor*—corresponding to its interpretation of the input. Unit interactions are governed by weighted connections between them, which collectively encode the system's knowledge about how the different types of information are related. Weights that give rise to the appropriate transformations are learned on the basis of the system's exposure to written words, spoken words, and their meanings.

At a general level, the distributed connectionist approach to word reading is based on three general computational principles:

Figure 8.1
A Connectionist Framework for Lexical Processing Based on That of Seidenberg and McClelland (1989)

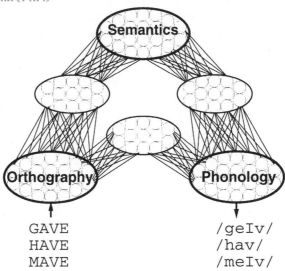

Reprinted from Plaut (1997).

Distributed representation. Orthography, phonology, and semantics are represented by distributed patterns of activity such that similar words are represented by similar patterns.

Gradual learning of statistical structure. Knowledge of the relationships among orthography, phonology, and semantics is encoded across connection weights that are learned gradually through repeated experience with words in a way that is sensitive to the statistical structure of each mapping.

Interactivity in processing. Mapping among orthography, phonology, and semantics is accomplished through the simultaneous interaction of many units such that familiar patterns form stable attractors.

Although these principles are general, the challenge is to demonstrate that, when instantiated in a particular domain—single-word reading—these principles provide important insights into the patterns of normal and impaired cognitive behavior. This chapter reviews a series of computational simulations of word reading based on the framework depicted in Figure 8.1. It then presents a new simulation that address some limitations of this work, relating to sequential processing and effects of orthographic length on the naming latencies of both normal and dyslexic readers. The simulation generates sequential phonological output in response to written input and has the ability to refixate the input when encountering difficulty. The normal model reads both words and nonwords accurately, and exhibits an effect of orthographic length and a frequency-by-consistency interaction in its naming latencies. When subject to peripheral damage, the model exhibits an increased length effect that interacts with word frequency, characteristic of letter-by-letter reading in pure alexia. Although the model is far from a fully adequate account of all the relevant phenomena, it suggests how connectionist models may be extended to provide deeper insight into sequential processes in reading.

BACKGROUND

Skilled Oral Reading

The distributed connectionist framework for word reading depicted in Figure 8.1 reflects a radical departure from traditional theorizing about lexical processing, particularly in two ways. First, there is nothing in the structure of the system that corresponds to individual words per se, such as a lexical entry, localist word unit (McClelland & Rumelhart, 1981), or logogen (Morton, 1969). Rather, words are distinguished from nonwords only by functional properties of the system—the way in which particular orthographic, phonological, and semantic patterns of activity interact (also see Plaut, 1997; Van Orden et al., 1990). Second, there are no separate mechanisms for lexical and sublexical processing (cf. Coltheart et al., 1993). Rather, all parts of the system participate in processing all types of input, although, of course, the contributions of different parts may be more or less important for different inputs.

In support of the general framework, Seidenberg and McClelland (1989) trained a connectionist network to map from the orthography of about 3,000 monosyllabic English words—both regular and exception—to their phonology. The network corresponded to the bottom portion of the framework in Figure 8.1 (referred to as the phonological pathway). After training, the network pronounced nearly all of the words correctly, including most exception words. It also exhibited the standard empirical pattern of an interaction of frequency and consistency in naming latency (see, e.g., Taraban & McClelland, 1987) when its real-valued accuracy in generating a response was taken as a proxy for response time. However, the model was much worse than skilled readers at pronouncing orthographically legal nonwords (Besner, Twilley, McCann, & Seergobin, 1990) and at lexical decision under some conditions (Besner et al., 1990; Fera & Besner, 1992). Thus, the model failed to refute traditional claims that localist, word-specific representations and separate mechanisms are necessary to account for skilled reading.

More recently, Plaut et al. (1996; also see Seidenberg, Plaut, Petersen, McClelland, & McRae, 1994) have shown that the limitations of the Seidenberg and McClelland (1989) model in pronouncing nonwords stem not from any general limitation in the abilities of connectionist networks in quasi-regular domains (as suggested by, e.g., Coltheart et al., 1993), but from its use of poorly structured orthographic and phonological representations. The original simulation used representations based on context-sensitive triples of letters or phonemic features. When more appropriately structured representations are used—based on graphemes and phonemes and embodying phonotactic and graphotactic constraints—network implementations of the phonological pathway can learn to pronounce regular words, exception words, and nonwords as well as skilled readers. Moreover, the networks exhibit the empirical frequency-by-consistency interaction pattern when trained on actual word frequencies. This remains true if naming latencies are modeled directly by the settling time of a recurrent attractor network (see Figure 8.2).

Plaut et al. (1996) also offered a mathematical analysis of the critical factors that govern why the networks (and, by hypothesis, subjects) behave as they do. The analysis was based on a network that, while simpler than the actual simulations—it had no hidden units and employed Hebbian learning—retained many of the essential characteristics of the more general framework (e.g., distributed representations and structure-sensitive learning). For this simplified network, it was possible to derive an analytic expression for how the response of the network to any input (test) pattern depends on its experience with every pattern on which the network is trained, as a function of its frequency of training, its similarity with the test pattern, and the consistency of its output with that of the test pattern. Specifically, the response $s_j^{[t]}$ of any output unit j to a given test pattern t is given by

$$s_j^{[t]} = \sigma \left(F^{[t]} + \sum_f F^{[f]} O^{[ft]} - \sum_e F^{[e]} O^{[et]} \right) \qquad (8.1)$$

in which the standard smooth, nonlinear sigmoidal input–output function for each unit, $\sigma(\cdot)$, is applied to the sum of three terms: (1) the cumulative frequency of training on the pattern t itself, $F^{[t]}$; (2) the sum of the frequencies $F^{[f]}$ of the *friends* of pattern t (similar patterns trained to produce the same response for unit j), each weighted by its similarity (overlap) with t, $O^{[ft]}$; and (3) minus the sum of the frequencies $F^{[e]}$ of the enemies of pattern t (similar patterns trained to produce the opposite response), each weighted by its similarity to t, $O^{[et]}$.

Many of the basic phenomena in word reading can be seen as natural consequences of adherence to this frequency–consistency equation. Factors that increase the summed input to units (e.g., word frequency, spelling–sound consistency) improve performance as measured by naming accuracy and/or latency, but their contributions are subject to "diminishing returns" due to the asymptotic nature of the activation function (see the lower panel of Figure 8.2). As a result, performance on stimuli that are strong in one factor is relatively insensitive to variation in other factors. Thus, regular

Figure 8.2
The Frequency-By-Consistency Interaction Exhibited in the Settling Time of an Attractor Network, and Its Explanation

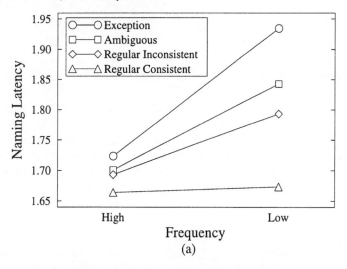

(a)

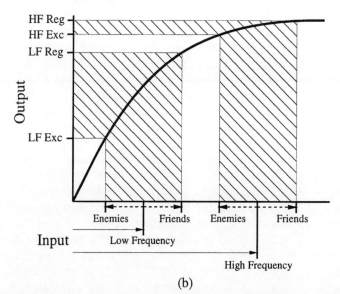

(b)

The top panel shows the frequency-by-consistency interaction exhibited in the settling time of an attractor network, implementation of the phonological pathway in pronouncing words of varying frequency and spelling–sound consistency (Plaut et al., 1996, Simulation 3); the bottom panel shows its explanation in terms of additive contributions of frequency and consistency subject to an asymptotic activation function (only the top of which is shown).

words show little effect of frequency, and high-frequency words show little effect of consistency, giving rise to the standard pattern of interaction between frequency and consistency, in which the naming of low-frequency exception words is disproportionately slow or inaccurate.

Surface Dyslexia

Although implementations of the phonological pathway on its own can learn to pronounce words and nonwords as well as skilled readers, a central aspect of Plaut et al.'s (1996) general theory is that skilled reading more typically requires the combined support of both the semantic and phonological pathways, and that individuals may differ in the relative competence of each pathway. A consideration of semantics is particularly important in the context of accounting for a pattern of reading impairment known as surface dyslexia (see Patterson, Coltheart, & Marshall, 1985), which typically arises from damage to the left temporal lobe. Surface dyslexic patients read nonwords and regular words with normal accuracy and latency, but exhibit an interaction of frequency and consistency in word-reading accuracy such that low-frequency exception words are pronounced disproportionately poorly, often eliciting a pronunciation consistent with more standard spelling–sound correspondences (e.g., sew read as "sue," termed a regularization error).

The framework for lexical processing depicted in Figure 8.1 (and the associated computational principles) provides an account of surface dyslexia based on the relative contributions of the semantic and phonological pathways in oral reading. At an abstract level, given that phonological units simply sum their inputs from the two pathways, the influence of the semantic pathway can be included in a straightforward manner by adding an additional term, $S^{[t]}$, to the summed input in Equation (8.1). Furthermore, if this term is assumed to increase with imageability, the equation produces the three-way interaction of frequency, consistency, and imageability found by Strain, Patterson, and Seidenberg (1995). When formulated explicitly in connectionist terms, however, this integration has important implications for the nature of learning in the two pathways. To the extent that the semantic pathway reduces performance error during training by contributing to the correct pronunciation of words, the phonological pathway will experience less pressure to learn to pronounce all of the words by itself. Rather, this pathway will tend to learn best those words high in frequency and/or consistency; on its own it may never master low-frequency exception words completely. On this account, the combination of the semantic and phonological pathways is fully competent in normal readers, but brain damage that impairs the semantic pathway reveals the latent limitations of an intact but isolated phonological pathway, giving rise to surface dyslexia.

Plaut et al. (1996) explored the viability of this account by extending their simulations of the phonological pathway to include influences from a putative semantic pathway. They approximated the contribution that a semantic pathway would make to oral reading by providing the output (phoneme) units of the phonological pathway with external input that pushed the activations of these units toward the correct pronunciation of each word during training. Plaut and colleagues found that, indeed, a phonological pathway trained in the context of support from semantics exhibited the central phenomena of surface dyslexia when the contribution of semantics was removed (see Figure 8.3). Moreover, individual differences in the severity of surface dyslexia could arise, not only from differences in the amount of semantic damage, but also from premorbid differences in the division of labor between the semantic and phonological pathways (Plaut, 1997). Thus, the few patients exhibiting mild to moderate semantic impairments without concomitant regularization errors (DRN, Cipolotti & Warrington, 1995; DC, Lambon Ralph, Ellis, & Franklin, 1995) may have, for various reasons, reading systems with relatively weak reliance on the semantic pathway.

Figure 8.3
Performance of Two Surface Dyslexic Patients (MP, Behrmann & Bub, 1992; Bub, Cancelliere, & Kertesz, 1985; and KT, McCarthy & Warrington, 1986) and the Plaut et al. (1996) Network for Two Levels of Semantic Impairment

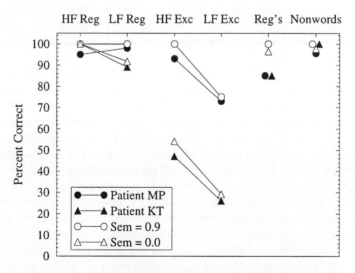

Correct performance is given for Taraban and McClelland's (1987) high-frequency (HF) and low-frequency (LF) regular consistent words (Reg) and exception words (Exc), and for Glushko's (1979) nonwords. "Reg's" is the approximate percentage of errors on the exception words that are regularizations. Adapted from Plaut et al. (1996).

Deep and Phonological Dyslexia

Patients with deep dyslexia (see Coltheart, Patterson, & Marshall, 1980) have reading impairments that are in many ways opposite to those with surface dyslexia, in that they appear to read almost entirely via semantics. Deep dyslexic patients are thought to have severe damage to the phonological pathway, as evidenced by their virtual inability to read even the simplest of pronounceable nonwords. They also have impairments in reading words that suggest additional partial damage to the semantic pathway. In particular, the hallmark symptom of deep dyslexia is the occurrence of semantic errors in oral reading (e.g., reading *cat* as "dog"). Interestingly, these semantic errors cooccur with pure visual errors (e.g., *cat* ⇒ "cot"), mixed visual-and-semantic errors (e.g., *cat* ⇒ "rat"), and even mediated visual-then-semantic errors (e.g., *sympathy* ⇒ "orchestra," presumably via *symphony*). Furthermore, correct performance depends on part of speech (nouns > adjectives > verbs > function words) and concreteness or imageability (concrete, imageable words > abstract, less imageable words). Finally, differences across patients in written and spoken comprehension, and in the distribution of error types, suggests that the secondary damage to the semantic pathway may occur before, within, or after semantics (Shallice & Warrington, 1980).

Deep dyslexia is closely related to another type of acquired dyslexia—so-called phonological dyslexia (Beauvois & Derouesné, 1979)—involving a selective impairment in reading nonwords compared with words (without concomitant semantic errors). Indeed, some authors (Friedman, 1996; Glosser & Friedman, 1990) have argued that deep dyslexia is only the most severe form of phonological dyslexia.

Hinton and Shallice (1991) reproduced the cooccurrence of visual, semantic, and mixed visual-and-semantic errors in deep dyslexia by damaging a connectionist network that mapped orthography to semantics. During training, the network learned to form attractors for forty word meanings across five categories, such that patterns of semantic features that were similar to a known word meaning were pulled to that exact meaning over the course of settling. When the network was damaged, the initial semantic activity caused by an input would occasionally fall within a neighboring attractor basin, giving rise to an error response. These errors were often semantically related to the stimulus, because words with similar meanings correspond to nearby attractors in semantic space. The damaged network also produced visual errors due to its inherent bias toward similarity: Visually similar words tend to produce similar initial semantic patterns, which can lead to a visual error if the basins are distorted by damage (see Figure 8.4).

Plaut and Shallice (1993) extended these initial findings in a number of ways. They established the generality of the cooccurrence of error types across a wide range of simulations, showing that it does not depend on

Figure 8.4
The Attractor Landscape for a Network That Maps Orthography to Semantics

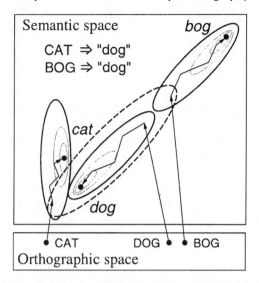

Damage to the network can distort the attractors (dashed oval) in a way that gives rise to both semantic errors (e.g., *cat* ⇒ "dog") and visual errors (e.g., *bog* ⇒ "dog"). Adapted from Plaut and Shallice (1993).

specific characteristics of the network architecture, the learning procedure, or the way responses are generated from semantic activity. A particularly relevant simulation in this regard involved an implementation of the full semantic pathway—mapping orthography to phonology via semantics—using a deterministic Boltzmann Machine (Hinton, 1989b; Peterson & Anderson, 1987). Lesions throughout the network gave rise to both visual and semantic errors, with lesions prior to semantics producing a bias toward visual errors and lesions after semantics producing a bias toward semantic errors. Thus, the network replicated both the qualitative similarities and quantitative differences among deep dyslexic patients. The network also exhibited a number of other characteristics of deep dyslexia not considered by Hinton and Shallice (1991), including the occurrence of visual-then-semantic errors, greater confidence in visual as compared with semantic errors, and relatively preserved lexical decision with impaired naming.

Plaut and Shallice (1993) carried out additional simulations to address the influence of concreteness on the reading performance of deep dyslexic patients. Another full implementation of the semantic pathway was trained to pronounce a new set of words consisting of both concrete and abstract words. Concrete words were assigned far more semantic features than were abstract words, under the assumption that the semantic representations of concrete words are less dependent on the contexts in which they occur (Jones, 1985; Saffran, Bogyo, Schwartz, & Marin, 1980; Schwanenflugel, 1991). As a result, the network developed stronger attractors for concrete than abstract words during training, giving rise to better performance in reading concrete words under most types of damage, as observed in deep dyslexia (see the top panel of Figure 8.5). Surprisingly, severe damage to connections implementing the attractors at the semantic level produced the opposite pattern, in which the network read abstract words better than concrete words (see the bottom panel of Figure 8.5). This pattern of performance is reminiscent of CAV, the single, enigmatic patient with concrete word dyslexia (Warrington, 1981). The double dissociation between reading concrete versus abstract words in patients is often interpreted as implying that there are separate modules within the cognitive system for concrete and abstract words. The Plaut and Shallice simulation demonstrates that such a radical interpretation is unnecessary: The double dissociation can arise from damage to different parts of a distributed network, in which parts process both types of items but develop somewhat different functional specializations through learning (see Plaut, 1995, for further results and discussion).

Taken together, the modeling work described provides strong support for a connectionist approach to normal and impaired word reading, embodying the computational principles outlined earlier: distributed representation, gradual learning of statistical structure, and interactivity in processing. There have, however, been recent empirical challenges to the specific models in particular, and the framework in general, which ultimately need to be addressed if the approach is to remain viable as an account of human performance. A number of these relate to the influence of orthographic length on the naming latencies of both normal and dyslexic readers.

CURRENT CHALLENGES: LENGTH EFFECTS

An aspect of the Seidenberg and McClelland (1989) and Plaut et al. (1996) models that has contributed substantially to their theoretical impact is that because they were trained on a sufficiently extensive corpus of words, their performance can be compared directly with that of human subjects on the very same stimuli. These comparisons have largely been successfully at the level of accounting for the effects of factorial manipulations (e.g., word frequency, spelling–sound consistency). More recently, however, the models have been found to be lacking when compared with human performance on an item-by-item basis. For instance, Spieler and Balota (1997) correlated the mean naming latencies of thirty-one subjects naming 2,820 words with the models' latencies for the same words and found that the models accounted for only about 3 to 10 percent of the variance associated with individual items. By contrast, the combination of the traditional measures of log frequency, orthographic length, and orthographic neighborhood size

Figure 8.5
Percent Correct Performance on Concrete versus Abstract Words of the Plaut and Shallice (1993) Simulation

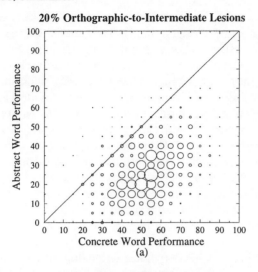

20% Orthographic-to-Intermediate Lesions

(a)

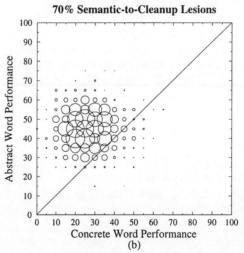

70% Semantic-to-Cleanup Lesions

(b)

After 1,000 lesions of 20 percent of orthographic-to-intermediate connections (top panel) and 1,000 lesions of 70 percent of semantic-to-cleanup connections (bottom panel). The radius of each circle is proportional to the number of lesions, yielding the performance levels indicated by the position of the circle. The diagonal lines correspond to equal levels of performance on concrete and abstract words. The advantage for concrete words in the top panel corresponds to the findings for deep dyslexia (Coltheart et al., 1980), whereas the advantage for abstract words in the bottom panel corresponds to the findings for concrete-word dyslexia (Warrington, 1981).

(Coltheart's N) collectively accounted for 21.7 percent of the variance; including an encoding of phonetic properties of the onset phoneme increased this figure to 43.1 percent.

In response, Seidenberg and Plaut (1998) carried out additional analyses with the Spieler and Balota (1997) data set, as well as another large naming data set (Seidenberg & Waters, 1989). They found that the models did not account well for effects of orthographic length, but when the model measures and length were entered first in a stepwise regression, there was little remaining variance accounted for by log frequency and orthographic neighborhood. Specifically, each traditional variable accounted for less than 1.7 percent of the remaining variance in all conditions, except that log frequency still accounted for 4.8 percent of the variance in the Spieler and Balota data set (but only 0.25% in the other data set) after length and the Plaut et al. (1996) reaction times were partialed out. Thus, the models provide a reasonably good (as well as mechanistic) account of the influence of these traditional factors on naming performance. With regard to orthographic length, Seidenberg and Plaut argued that the effects of this factor were due largely to visual and articulatory factors outside the domain of the existing models.[1]

More recently, Chris Kello (personal communication, January 1998) has provided some support for this claim. He hypothesized that some of the observed length effect might be due to the fact that longer monosyllabic words are more likely to have complex onset consonant clusters (e.g., /pr/, /str/), and the reduced acoustic amplitude at the beginning of such clusters introduces delay in tripping a standard voice key. For example, a voice key might register the /r/ in both *ring* and *string*, yielding an overly long reaction time in the latter case (extended by roughly the duration of the /st/). Kello repeated the Spieler and Balota (1997) stepwise regression analysis but used a more sophisticated encoding of the phonetic properties of word onsets, including the presence of certain consonant clusters. He found that, compared with the use of Spieler and Balota's encoding, the new encoding reduced the amount of residual variance accounted for by orthographic length by well over half, from 7.5 to 3.3 percent. These results indicate that a sizable amount of the effects of orthographic length can be accounted for by articulatory onset characteristics.

Although articulatory factors may contribute substantially to length effects, they cannot be the whole story. Recently, Weekes (1997) demonstrated differential effects of length for words versus nonwords matched for onset characteristics. Specifically, using three- to six-letter words and nonwords, Weekes found reliable length effects for nonwords and for low-but not high-frequency words. When he partialed out orthographic neighborhood size, the length effect was eliminated for words but not for nonwords. Weekes argued that these findings pose problems for any account in which words and nonwords are processed by a single mechanism.

Finally, length effects also play a prominent role in the analysis of acquired reading impairments, particularly in the context of the letter-by-letter (LBL) reading of pure alexic patients (Dejerine, 1892) and some nonfluent surface dyslexic patients (e.g., Patterson & Kay, 1982). Although the accuracy of these patients can be quite high, their naming latencies show an abnormally large word-length effect, sometimes on the order of one to three seconds per letter (cf. five to fifty msec per letter for normal readers; Henderson, 1982). One account of such patients (Patterson & Kay, 1982) is that they have a peripheral deficit that prevents adequate activation of letter representations in parallel; they thus must resort to a compensatory strategy of recognizing letters sequentially.

There is, in fact, considerable independent evidence for peripheral impairments in LBL readers (see Behrmann, Nelson, & Sekuler, 1998, for review). On the other hand, there is also evidence for the influence of lexical–semantic factors on LBL reading performance. There are two forms of this latter influence. First, when presented with words too briefly to allow overt naming, some LBL readers can nonetheless perform lexical decision and semantic categorizations tasks above chance (Coslett & Saffran, 1989; Shallice & Saffran, 1986). Quite apart from this type of "covert" reading, LBL readers also show lexical effects on their letter-by-letter reading latencies. For example, Behrmann, Plaut, and Nelson (1998) present data on seven LBL readers of varying severity, showing that the magnitudes of their length effects interacted both with frequency and with imageability. Moreover, these interactions were modulated by severity of the impairment, such that the most severe patients showed the strongest lexical–semantic effects. Behrmann and colleagues argue that these higher-level effects in LBL reading are consistent with a peripheral impairment given the interactive nature of processing with the reading system: Weakened (sequential) letter activation supports partial lexical–semantic activation that accumulates over time and feeds back to facilitate subsequent letter processing. They also propose that the sequential processing in LBL reading is not an abnormal strategy employed only following brain damage, but is the manifestation of the normal reading strategy of making additional fixations when encountering difficulty in reading text (Just & Carpenter, 1987; Reichle, Pollatsek, & Rayner, 1998). For example, in order to enhance stimulus quality, normal subjects make more fixations within long compared with short words. LBL readers also fixate more frequently; in fact, given the very poor quality of the visual input, they fixate almost every letter (Behrmann, Barton, Shomstein, & Black, 1999).

In summary, the effects of orthographic length on naming latency, both in normal and brain-damaged subjects, place important constraints on theories of word reading, and existing distributed models do not provide an adequate account of these effects. A fully adequate model of length effects in reading would need to incorporate considerably detailed perceptual and articulatory processes in addition to the more central processes relating orthography, phonology, and semantics. The intent of the simulation described in the following section is not so much to attempt such a comprehensive account, but rather to begin an exploration of the kinds of networks and processes that might provide deeper insight into length effects.

SIMULATION

Method

A simple recurrent network (Elman, 1990) was trained to produce a sequence of phonemes as output when given a string of position-specific letters as input. The training corpus consisted of the 2,998 monosyllabic words in the Plaut et al. (1996) corpus. The architecture of the network is shown in Figure 8.6. There are 26 letter units and a "blank" unit at each of ten positions. The third position from the left, indicated by the dark rectangle in the figure, corresponds to the point of fixation. These 270 letter units are fully connected to 100 hidden units, which, in turn, are fully connected to 36 phoneme units.[2] The hidden units also receive input from the previous states of phoneme units. In addition, there is a fourth group of position units, with connections both to and from the hidden units, that the network uses to keep track of where it is in the letter string as it is producing the appropriate sequence of phonemes, analogous to a focus of attention. Two copies of the position units and the phoneme units are shown in the figure simply to illustrate their behavior over time. Finally, there is a "done" output unit that the network uses to indicate that a pronunciation is complete. Including bias connections (equivalent to connections from an additional unit with a fixed state of 1), the network had a total of 45,945 connections that were randomized uniformly between ± 1.0 before training.[3]

In understanding how the network was trained, it will help to consider first its operation after it has achieved a reasonable level of proficiency at its task. First, a word is selected from the training corpus according to a logarithmic function of its frequency of occurrence (Kučera & Francis, 1967). Its string of letters is presented with the first letter at fixation by activating the appropriate letter unit at each corresponding position and the blank unit at all other positions.[4] Position information for internal letters is assumed to be somewhat inaccurate (see, e.g., Mozer, 1983), so that the same letter units at neighboring internal positions are also activated slightly (to 0.3). In Figure 8.6 the grey regions for letter units indicate the activations for the word *bay* when fixating the *b*. Initially, the position unit corresponding to fixation (numbered 0 by convention) is active and all others are inactive, and all phoneme units are inactive. (In the figure, the states of position and phoneme units show the network attempting $ay \Rightarrow$ /A/ after having generated $b \Rightarrow$ /b/.) Hidden-unit states are initialized to 0.2 at the beginning of processing the word.

Figure 8.6
The Network Architecture for the Refixation Network

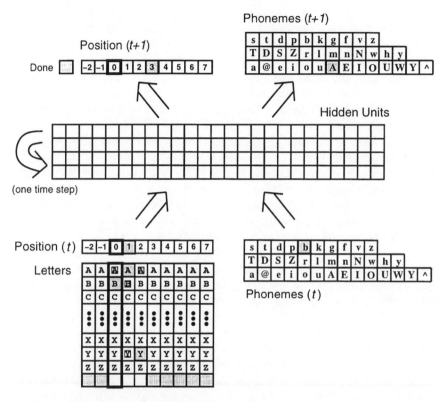

The arrows indicate full connectivity between groups of units. The recurrent connections among the hidden units only convey information about the last time step. The grey areas in the input and output units are intended to depict their activities at an intermediate point in processing the word *bay*, after the *b* ⇒ /b/ has been pronounced (with no refixation) and the *ay* ⇒ /A/ is being attempted.

The network then computes new states for the hidden units, phoneme units, and position units. The network has two tasks: (1) to activate the phoneme corresponding to the current grapheme, and (2) to activate the position of the next grapheme in the string (or, if the end of the string is reached, the position of the adjacent blank). For example, when attending to the letter *b* at fixation in *bay*, the network must activate the /b/ unit and position unit 1 (the position of *ay* in the input). Specifically, the target activations for the phoneme units consist of a 1 for the correct current phoneme and 0s elsewhere, and the targets for the position units consist of a 1 for the position of the next grapheme–blank in the string and 0s elsewhere. To the extent that the activations over the phoneme and position units are inaccurate (i.e., not within 0.2 of their target values), error is injected and back-propagated through the network. Performance error was measured by the cross-entropy (see Hinton, 1989a) between the correct and target activations.

Assuming that the network succeeds at generating the correct phoneme and position, this information is then used to guide the production of the next phoneme and position. For this purpose, the correct phoneme unit had to be activated above 0.7 and all others had to be below 0.3, and the correct position unit had to be more active than any other position unit. (During testing, this criterion applies to the most active phoneme unit rather than to the "correct" unit.) As shown in Figure 8.6 for *bay*, position unit 1 and the phoneme /b/ are now active, the letter input remains the same, and the network must activate /A/ (the phoneme corresponding to the indicated grapheme *ay*), position unit 3 (corresponding to the blank following the string), and the "done" unit (indicating a complete pronunciation). In general, when pronouncing a letter string the network is trained to activate the sequence of phonemes corresponding to its pronunciation while simultaneously keeping track of the position of the grapheme it is currently working on.

If, in pronouncing a letter string, every phoneme and position is generated correctly, the activations over the letter units remain fixed. If, however, the network fails at generating the correct phoneme or next position at some point, it refixates the input string and tries again. It does this by making the equivalent of a rightward saccade to fixate the problematic grapheme, using the position units as a specification of its position relative to fixation. This position information was generated over the position units on the previous time step, and thus is available to guide the appropriate saccade.[5] The actual saccade is implemented by shifting the input activation of the letter units to the left by the specified amount and resetting position unit 0 to be active. Following this, the network tries again to pronounce the (now fixated) grapheme, and then the remainder of the input string.

In general, the network pronounces as much of the static input as it can until it runs into trouble, then saccades to that part of the input and continues. Note that early on in training the network repeatedly fails at generating correct output, and so is constantly refixating. This means that essentially all of its training experience consists of pronouncing graphemes (in context) at fixation. As the network learns to pronounce these correctly, it begins to attempt to pronounce the graphemes in the near (right) periphery without refixating. If it fails, it will make a saccade and use its more extensive experience at fixation. Gradually, however, it will learn to pronounce these adjacent graphemes correctly, and will go on to attempt even more peripheral ones. In this way the network's competence extends gradually from fixation rightward to larger and larger portions of input strings, making fewer and fewer fixations per word as a result. However, the network can always fall back on its more extensive experience at fixation whenever it encounters difficulty. It is perhaps worth noting in this context that, although the network was trained only on monosyllabic words for convenience, it would be entirely straightforward to apply it to pronouncing polysyllabic words of arbitrary length.

To summarize, as the network is trained to produce the appropriate sequence of phonemes for a letter string, it is also trained to maintain a representation of its current position within the string. The network uses this position signal to refixate a peripheral portion of the input when it finds that portion difficult to pronounce. This repositions the input string so that the peripheral portion now falls at the point of fixation, where the network has had more experience in generating pronunciations. In this way the network can apply the knowledge tied to the units at the point of fixation to any portion of the string that is difficult for the network to read.

Results and Discussion

Normal Performance

The network was trained on 400,000 word presentations with a learning rate of 0.01, momentum of 0.9, and weight decay of 0.000001. The learning rate was then reduced to 0.001 and the network was trained on an additional 50,000 word presentations, in order to minimize the noise in the final weight values due to sampling error among training examples. The total number of presentations per word ranged from about 40 to 600, with a median of 130. Figure 8.7 shows, over the course of training, both the overall level of accuracy in pronouncing words as well as the mean number of fixations required. At the end of training, the network read 2,978 of 2,998 (99.3%) of the words correctly (where homographs were considered correct if they elicited either appropriate pronunciation). The network made an average of 1.32 fixations per word in generating correct pronunciations, with 2,290 (76.9%) involving a single fixation. Just under half (8 of 20) of the errors were regularizations of low-frequency exception words (e.g., *brooch* ⇒ "brewch," *sieve* ⇒ "seeve").

Given that the network essentially has a feed-forward architecture and outputs only a single phoneme at a time, it is not entirely clear what an appropriate measure of naming latency should be. The most natural analogue to the onset of acoustic energy that would trip a voice key in a standard empirical study would be the real-valued error on the first phoneme. This measure, however, fails to take into account the coarticulatory constraints on executing a fluent pronunciation that apply for subjects but not for the model. A more appropriate, albeit coarse measure in the current context is simply the number of fixations required to generate a correct pronunciation. This measure directly reflects the degree of difficulty that the system experiences in constructing a complete pronunciation.[6]

Figure 8.8 shows the mean number of fixations made by the model in generating correct pronunciations for words in the training corpus as a function of their length in letters. Using this measure as an analogue to naming

Figure 8.7
Percentage of Words Pronounced Correctly by the Network (top curve, left axis)
and the Mean Number of Fixations Required (bottom curve, right axis) as a
Function of the Number of Words Presented during Training

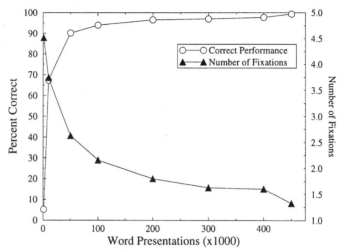

The improvement in performance from 400,000 to 450,000 is due to a reduction in learning rate.

latency, the model shows no latencies differences between three- and four-letter words (F < 1), but a steady increase in latency for four- to six-letter words and an overall length effect ($F_{3,2932} = 76.7$, $p < .001$), with a slope of 0.18 fixations per letter.

The network was tested for its ability to account for two sets of recent findings concerning length effects in normal readers. First, as mentioned earlier, Weekes (1997) found reliable effects of orthographic length in the naming latencies for both words and nonwords, but only the nonword effect remained reliable when orthographic neighborhood size was partialed out. In applying the current model to Weekes's stimuli, 24 of the words had to be eliminated because they are not in the model's training corpus; most of these are inflected forms (e.g., *boards, called*). Of the remaining items, the model correctly pronounced 86 of 86 of the high-frequency words, 89 of 90 of the low-frequency words, and 90 of 100 of the nonwords (where four of the ten errors were on pseudoinflected forms; e.g., *branks, loaked*). A nonword pronunciation was scored as correct if it matched the pronunciation of some word in the training corpus (e.g., *grook* pronounced to rhyme with *book*; see Plaut et al., 1996, for details).

Comparing four- versus six-letter stimuli, there was a reliable length effect in the mean number of fixations made by the model in correctly pronouncing high-frequency words (1.00 versus 1.25; $F_{1,34} = 7.56$, $p < .01$),

Figure 8.8
Mean Number of Fixations Made by the Network in Pronouncing Three- to Six-Letter Words

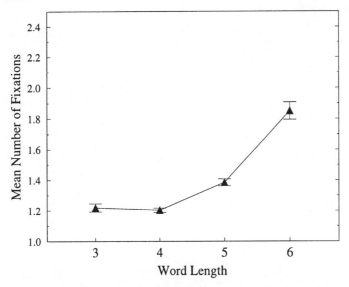

The y-axis scale is the same as that in Figure 8.11, for ease of comparison.

low-frequency words (1.38 versus 1.79; $F_{1,41} = 1.82$, $p < .05$), and nonwords (1.61 versus 2.38; $F_{1,42} = 6.55$, $p < .01$). When orthographic neighborhood size (calculated over the training corpus) was first partialed out of the data, the length effects for both high- and low-frequency words were eliminated ($F_{1,34} < 1$ and $F_{1,41} = 1.43$, $p > .2$, respectively), whereas the length effect for nonwords remained reliable ($F_{1,42} = 6.43$, $p < .05$). The only discrepancy between these findings and those of Weekes (1997) is that the small length effect for high-frequency words was reliable for the model but not for the human subjects.

The second length effect to which the model was applied was the recent finding of Rastle and Coltheart (1998) that among five-letter nonwords those with three-phoneme pronunciations (e.g., *fooph*) produce longer naming latencies than those with five-phoneme pronunciations (e.g., *frolp*); note that this is an effect of phonological rather than orthographic length. Certain aspects of Rastle and Coltheart's stimuli are problematic in the current context; namely, five of the twenty-four five-phoneme nonwords are pseudoinflected (e.g., *fruls*). If these and the matched three-phoneme nonwords are removed from the analysis, the mean number of fixations made by the model in pronouncing the three-phoneme nonwords is numerically larger than that for the five-phoneme nonwords, but the difference is

Figure 8.9
Mean Number of Fixations Required to Produce Correct Pronunciations for Words (Patterson & Hodges, 1992) as a Function of Their Frequency and Spelling–Sound Consistency

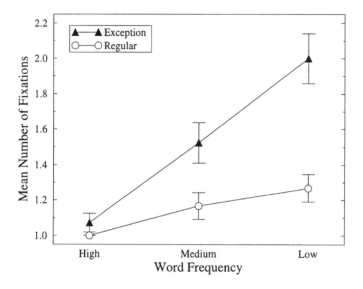

not reliable (2.95 versus 2.79, respectively; paired $t_{17} < 1$). The null result may stem in part from the small number of comparisons but also from the fact that under the model's phonological encoding the stimuli that Rastle and Coltheart considered to have three phonemes actually had a mean phonological length of 3.58, as a number of the nonwords have four or even five phonemes (e.g., *barch* ⇒ /bartS/).

The network was also tested for the standard effects of word frequency and spelling–sound consistency in its number of fixations, using a list of 126 matched pairs of regular and exception words falling into three frequency bands (Patterson & Hodges, 1992). The network mispronounced five of the words, producing regularization errors to four low-frequency exception words—*brooch, sieve, soot,* and *suede*—and an irregularization error to a low-frequency regular word—*sour* to rhyme with *pour* (see Patterson et al., 1996, for empirical evidence supporting the occasional occurrence of such errors). Figure 8.9 shows the mean number of fixations required to correctly pronounce the remaining words, as a function of their frequency and consistency. Overall, there was a main effect of frequency (means were high 1.04, medium 1.35, low 1.62; $F_{2,241} = 22.4$, $p < .001$) and a main effect of consistency (means were regular 1.14, exception 1.52; $F_{1,241} = 27.5$, $p < .001$), as well as a frequency-by-consistency interaction, with low-frequency exception words requiring disproportionately more fixations ($F_{2,241} = 7.67, p < .001$). These results are in accord with the relevant empirical findings on the naming latencies of skilled readers.

At the item level, the numbers of fixations made by the model was regressed against the mean naming latencies of Spieler and Balota's (1997) thirty-one subjects. Over the 2,812 of 2,820 words that the model pronounced correctly, its number of fixations accounted for 8.8 percent of the variance in the latency data ($t_{2810} = 16.5, p < .001$). This value is much better than that of the Plaut et al. (1996) model (3.3%) but not quite as good as the Seidenberg and McClelland (1989) model (10.1%).

Finally, the network was tested for its accuracy in pronouncing three sets of nonwords from two empirical studies: (1) forty-three nonwords derived from regular words (Glushko, 1979), (2) forty-three nonwords derived from exception words (Glushko, 1979), and (3) eighty nonwords used as controls for a set of pseudohomophones (McCann & Besner, 1987). As before, a nonword pronunciation was considered correct if it was consistent with some word in the training corpus. Figure 8.10 shows the performance of the network on this criterion, as well as the corresponding data for human subjects. The network was correct on 40 of 43 (93.0%) of the regular nonwords, 41 of 43 (95.3%) of the exception nonwords, and 73 of 80 (91.3%) of the control nonwords. By comparison, the corresponding levels of performance reported for human subjects were 93.8 percent on regular nonwords and 95.9 percent on exception nonwords (Glushko, 1979), and 88.6 percent on the control nonwords (McCann & Besner, 1987). Moreover, in pronouncing these nonwords the mean number of fixations produced by the network for correct pronunciations was 1.63 for the regular nonwords, 2.27 for the exception nonwords, and 1.92 for the control nonwords. The overall mean for nonwords, 1.94, is comparable to the value for low-frequency exception words (2.00; see Figure 8.9). Thus, the network's nonword reading accuracy and latency is comparable to that of skilled readers.

Performance Under a Peripheral Impairment

In order to model a peripheral deficit in letter perception of the sort postulated by Behrmann et al. (1998) to produce LBL reading, input letter activations were corrupted by Gaussian noise ($SD = .055$). When this was done, correct performance dropped from 99.3 to 90.0 percent correct (averaged across ten runs through the training corpus). Using a median split on frequency, accuracy was greater on high- versus low-frequency words (91.7% versus 88.7%, respectively; $F_{1,2983} = 18.0, p < .001$) and on short versus long words (e.g., 91.6% for four-letter words versus 86.8% for six-letter words; $F_{1,1523} = 14.1, p < .001$).

It was argued earlier that number of fixations can be used as a coarse approximation to naming latency for skilled readers because this measure reflects the degree of difficulty in constructing a coherent articulatory out-

Figure 8.10
Correct Performance of the Network and of Human Subjects in Pronouncing Three Sets of Nonwords

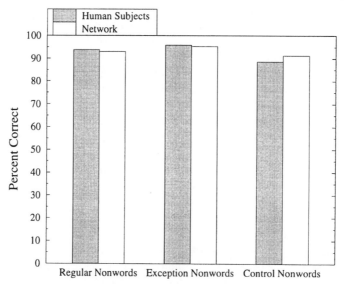

Regular and exception nonwords (N = 43 each) from Glushko (1979), and control nonwords (N = 80) from McCann and Besner (1987).

put. The situation is rather different in the context of LBL reading, because in this case it is more literally true that a pronunciation is constructed incrementally. For this reason, number of fixations in the model can be taken as a more direct analogue of the naming latency of LBL readers. Another plausible measure—the total number of processing steps required by the model in generating a pronunciation, including initial attempts and attempts after refixations—gives qualitatively equivalent results.

Among words pronounced correctly, the average number of fixations per word increased from 1.32 to 2.20 as a result of the introduction of input noise. Not surprisingly, this measure was strongly influenced by the length of the word. For example, the impaired model made an average of 2.00 fixations on four-letter words but 2.97 fixations on six-letter words ($F_{1,1522}$ = 380.1, $p < .001$), corresponding to a slope of 0.49 fixations per letter. The model also made fewer fixations on high- versus low-frequency words (means 2.10 versus 2.30, respectively; $F_{1,2973}$ = 50.5, $p < .001$). Finally, and most important for the Behrmann et al. (1998) account of LBL reading, there was a clear interaction of frequency and length. This was established by comparing performance on sets of four- and six-letter words matched for frequency (N = 100 for each cell). The average number of fixations per word

Figure 8.11
Mean Number of Fixations Made by the Model in Pronouncing Four- and Six-Letter Words as a Function of Their Frequency

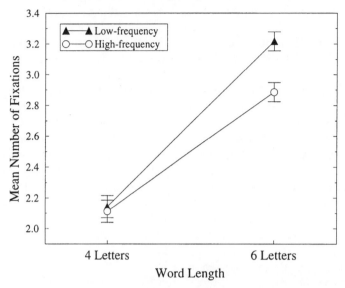

for these stimuli is shown in Figure 8.11. In addition to main effects of frequency ($F_{1,396} = 7.13$, $p < .01$) and length ($F_{1,396} = 186.6$, $p < .001$), frequency interacted with length such that the effect of frequency was larger for six- than for four-letter words ($F_{1,396} = 4.96$, $p < .05$). Thus, under peripheral damage the network exhibited the hallmark word-length effect characteristic of LBL reading, combined with the appropriate higher-level effects: a word frequency effect greater for long compared with short words.[7]

In summary, a simple recurrent network was presented with words as letter strings over position-specific units and was trained to generate the pronunciation of each word in the form of a sequence of phonemes. The model had the ability to refixate the input string when encountering difficulty. The network learned to pronounce correctly virtually all of the 2,998-word training corpus, including both regular and exception words, and also was capable of pronouncing nonwords as well as skilled readers. Moreover, if mean number of fixations was taken as an analogue of skilled naming latency, the model exhibited a length effect as well as the standard frequency-by-consistency interaction observed in empirical studies. Finally, peripheral damage to the model in the form of corrupted letter activations gave rise to the hallmark characteristics of letter-by-letter reading, including an increased length effect that interacts with lexical variables (e.g., word frequency).

GENERAL DISCUSSION

Connectionist modeling has made important contributions to a wide range of domains within cognitive science. Word reading, in particular, has received considerable attention because it is a highly learned skill that involves the rapid on-line interaction of a number of sources of information in an integrated fashion. There is also a wealth of detailed empirical data on normal reading acquisition and skilled performance, as well as patterns of reading impairments in developmental and acquired dyslexia, that play an essential role in evaluating and constraining explicit computational models. This chapter contributes to the development of a connectionist theory of normal and impaired word reading based on three general computational principles: distributed representation, gradual learning of statistical structure, and interactivity in processing. This endeavor has led to a number of important insights concerning the nature of the reading system, both in normal operation and when impaired by brain damage. These insights do not typically follow from alternative theoretical frameworks, although versions of them can be incorporated into these frameworks in a post hoc manner. Moreover, many of the insights have implications that extend beyond the specific domain of word reading.

First, the apparent dichotomy between "regular" versus "exception" items is a false one; rather, items vary along a continuum of consistency (Glushko, 1979), and a single mechanism can learn to process all types of items and yet also generalize effectively to novel items. This point was made first by Rumelhart and McClelland (1986) in the domain of inflectional morphology, and later by Seidenberg and McClelland (1989) in the domain of word reading. The impact of these early models was, however, undermined to a certain extent by limitations in the models' performance, particularly with respect to generalization. In the domain of word reading, these limitations were addressed in subsequent modeling work (Plaut et al., 1996) by incorporating more appropriately structured orthographic and phonological representations.

Apart from issues of parsimony, the importance of a single-mechanism account is that it provides insight into why there is so much shared structure between so-called regular and exception items. For instance, the exception word *pint* has regular correspondences for the *p, n,* and *t,* and even the exceptional *i* receives a pronunciation that it adopts in many other words (e.g., *pine, die*). Moreover, nonword pronunciation is influenced by exception as well as regular neighbors (Glushko, 1979). Accounts that invoke separate mechanisms for the regular-versus-exceptional aspects of language fail to explain or capitalize on this shared structure.

Second, skilled performance is supported by the integration of multiple sources of information; impaired performance following brain damage can reflect the underlying division of labor among these sources in the premorbid system. Patients with fluent surface dyslexia exhibit relatively normal reading of regular words and nonwords but produce regularization errors to many exception words, particularly those of low frequency. Dual-route theories explain surface dyslexia as partial damage to the lexical (nonsemantic) route that impairs low- more than high-frequency words, with the spared regular and nonword reading supported by the undamaged nonlexical route. There is, however, no explanation for why the lexical damage is always partial; the architecture provides equally well for complete elimination of the lexical route with complete sparing of the nonlexical route. This would yield an inability to pronounce any exception words with complete sparing of regular words and nonwords, a pattern that has never been observed empirically. As exception-word reading becomes very severely impaired, regular-word (and nonword) reading invariably begins to suffer (see Patterson et al., 1996).

By contrast, Plaut et al. (1996) provide an account of surface dyslexia in which it is impossible to eliminate exception-word reading without also impairing performance on regular words and nonwords. The reason is that normal performance is supported by the combination of both the phonological and semantic pathways. The contribution from semantics relieves the phonological pathway of having to learn to pronounce all types of words by itself. Rather, it becomes fully adequate only at those aspects of the task for which it is well suited: processing items that are high either in frequency or in spelling–sound consistency (see Equation [8.1]). Low-frequency exception words are processed to some degree, but typically require additional support from the semantic pathway to be pronounced correctly. Semantic damage, then, reveals the limitations of the undamaged phonological pathway, which manifest as surface dyslexia. Even complete elimination of semantics spares many exception words, particularly those with high frequency. The only way to completely eliminate exception-word reading is to damage the phonological pathway as well, but this also impairs regular-word and nonword reading (as observed empirically).

Third, the cooccurrence of different types of errors can arise from single lesions within a distributed system that learns to map among the different types of information. The error patterns of brain-damaged patients can place strong constraints on theoretical accounts of cognitive processes. The traditional account of the cooccurrence of visual and semantic errors in deep dyslexia (Morton & Patterson, 1980) assumes an impairment to visual access of (abstract) semantics to explain the visual errors, and a second impairment to semantic access of phonology to explain the semantic errors. The problem is that this account explains the occurrence of visual errors and of semantic errors, but not their cooccurrence: It is perfectly feasible within the framework to introduce only one of the lesions—say, the second—and predict patients who produce only semantic errors. While such cases have been reported (e.g., KE; Hillis, Rapp, Romani, & Caramazza, 1990), the vast majority of deep dyslexic patients make both visual and semantic errors (see Coltheart, Patterson, & Marshall, 1987), and the traditional account fails to explain this. An appeal to chance anatomic proximity of the related brain structures fails because the cooccurrence is not symmetric; many dyslexic patients make visual errors but no semantic errors.

On the connectionist account (Hinton & Shallice, 1991; Plaut & Shallice, 1993), the cooccurrence of visual errors with semantic errors is a natural consequence of the nature of learning within a distributed attractor network that maps orthography to semantics. Essentially, the layout of attractor basins must be sensitive to both visual and semantic similarity, and so these metrics are reflected in the types of errors that occur as a result of damage.

Fourth, a double dissociation in performing two tasks does not implicate separate modules dedicated to performing each of the tasks, but can arise from graded functional specialization with a distributed system that performs both tasks. Cognitive neuropsychologists have traditionally used double dissociations as a means of inferring the structure of the cognitive system (Teuber, 1955). If each of two tasks can be selectively impaired by brain damage while leaving the other relatively intact, it seems reasonable to assume that the two tasks are subserved by separate mechanisms. Unfortunately, this logic is often applied under the assumption that the cognitive system is composed of a set of distinct modules, but various types of nonmodular systems can also give rise to double dissociations (for discussion, see Farah, 1994; Shallice, 1988).

As a case in point, deep dyslexic patients are much worse at reading aloud abstract words compared with concrete words, whereas concrete-word dyslexic CAV (Warrington, 1981) showed the reverse pattern. This double dissociation prompted Warrington and others (e.g., Morton & Patterson, 1980) to assume that the semantics for abstract words was represented separately from those for concrete words. By contrast, Plaut and Shallice (1993; also see Plaut, 1995) developed an extension of the Hinton and Shallice (1991) deep dyslexia simulation in which there is no separation of the representations and processes subserving abstract and concrete word reading. The network does, however, develop stronger attractors for concrete words because they have much richer semantic representations (i.e., many more semantic features). This difference leads to a degree of functional specialization in the system. Damage between orthography and phonology produces a greater impairment on abstract words because these items benefit much less from the cleanup provided by the semantic attractors. Severe damage to sets of connections that implement these attractors, by contrast, impairs concrete words the most because they have come to rely on the cleanup, whereas many abstract words can be read without this support. Thus, the abstract–concrete double dissociation does reveal something important about the underlying organization of the system, but this organization does not correspond directly to the empirically manipulated stimulus dimension (concreteness).

These four points illustrate ways in which a distributed connectionist approach has provided new insights into both normal and impaired word reading. It must be acknowledged, however, that the existing implemented models have a number of basic limitations that ultimately prevent them from collectively constituting a comprehensive account of the domain. These limitations stem largely from the fact that all of them have very restricted temporal behavior: Single static monosyllabic words are presented as input, and a single static semantic and/or phonological pattern is generated as output. Naturalistic reading is, of course, a far more fluid and temporally complex activity, involving sequences of attentional shifts and eye movements over lines of text as input, sequences of articulatory gestures as spoken output, and interactions among multiple levels of linguistic structure in both comprehension and production (see Just & Carpenter, 1987).

This chapter presents a simulation that can be seen as a first step toward incorporating some of these complexities into connectionist models of reading. The model is still applied only to single monosyllabic words, but this limitation reflects more the choice of training corpus than any intrinsic limitation of the architecture. The network generates sequences of phonemes as output in response to letter strings as input. Critically, it maintains a focus of attention within the word as it is being pronounced; this focus is used to refixate the input string when the network encounters difficulty in generating a pronunciation. The model learned to pronounce virtually all of the 2,998-word training corpus, and pronounced nonwords as well as skilled readers. It also exhibited a length effect and the standard interaction of word frequency and spelling–sound consistency, if the number of fixations it makes in pronouncing a word was taken to reflect its naming latency.

Consideration of sequential processing for both visual input and articulatory output is critical for a full account of a number of empirical phenomena, particularly those related to the effects of the length of the input string. The current model is applied only to a small subset of these effects, relating to differential effects for words versus nonwords (Weekes, 1997), and the exaggerated length effect of letter-by-letter readers and its interaction with lexical variables (Behrmann, Plaut, et al., 1998). In the latter case, the empirical adequacy of the model is somewhat limited, in that the magnitudes of the length effects relative to normal performance are much smaller than for most letter-by-letter readers. Nonetheless, the model illustrates how letter-by-letter reading can be interpreted as reflecting the operation of the normal reading system following peripheral damage (see Behrmann, Plaut, et al., 1998b, for discussion).

Given that the current model is, in many respects, very different from previous models (Plaut et al., 1996; Seidenberg & McClelland, 1989), it is important to consider how they are related. With regard to the orthographic input, the models are relatively similar in that all of them are presented with an entire word as input. The current model differs in the use of position-specific letter units and a refixation mechanism. However, most words are processed in a single fixation in skilled performance, which corresponds to the static presentation of input in the previous models. In this way, even though the current model produces a single phoneme at a time, the fact that it does so based on the entire orthographic input at every step makes it fully consistent with evidence suggesting a considerable degree of parallel visual processing during word reading (see, e.g., Reichle et al., 1998). This property also distinguishes it from other sequential models in which the orthographic input is shifted leftward one letter each time a phoneme is generated (e.g., Bullinaria, 1997; Sejnowski & Rosenberg, 1987). In fact, these models are very similar to the current model when it is refixating every grapheme.

The more substantial difference between the model and the previous parallel ones concerns the generation of phonological output. The previous models generated a static representation of the pronunciation of an entire (monosyllabic) word, whereas the current model generates a pronunciation phoneme by phoneme. An intermediate case would be a model that derived a representation of an entire word (or at least a syllable) and then used this representation as input to generate sequential articulatory output. Plaut and Kello (1998) describe such a system in the context of modeling phonological development, although the phonological representation is generated from acoustic rather than orthographic input. A reading model that adopted the current model's treatment of orthographic input but Plaut and Kello's treatment of articulatory output would combine the strengths of the current sequential model and previous parallel models, and should be able to model effects on naming latencies, including those relating to orthographic length, directly in its temporal behavior. While such an approach appears promising for addressing the full range of empirical phenomena in normal and impaired word reading, it remains for future work to bring it to fruition.

FURTHER READINGS

Sejnowski and Rosenberg's (1987) NETtalk model was one of the first attempts to apply connectionist networks to realistic tasks. The subsequent highly influential modeling work by Seidenberg and McClelland (1989) was more psychologically oriented, making detailed contact with specific patterns of empirical data. Plaut et al. (1996) elaborated the approach taken by Seidenberg and McClelland by developing models that provided a better match to some empirical findings and by providing a more systematic treatment of the computational principles underlying the approach. Other recent connectionist models of word reading include Bullinaria (1997), Zorzi et al. (1998), and Harm (1998). The most influential nonconnectionist implementation of word reading is the Dual-Route Cascaded (DRC) model of Coltheart et al. (1993). These models focus largely on the mapping from print to sound; Hinton and Shallice (1991) carried out an important investigation of how networks can be applied to the task of mapping print to meaning. This work was followed up extensively by Plaut and Shallice (1993).

For background on some of the relevant empirical phenomena in normal and impaired word reading, see the following: normal skilled reading (Balota, 1994), surface dyslexia (Patterson et al., 1985), deep dyslexia (Coltheart et al., 1980), phonological dyslexia (Coltheart, 1996), length effects (Henderson, 1982), and pure alexia–letter-by-letter reading (Coltheart, 1998).

NOTES

This work was supported financially by the National Institute of Mental Health (grants MH47566 and MH55628). The simulation was run on a Silicon Graphics 4D/440 Challenge with eight R4400/150MHz CPUs, using an extended version of the Xerion simulator developed by Tony Plate, Drew van Camp, and Geoff Hinton at the University of Toronto. Some basic aspects of the simulation were first reported in Plaut, McClelland, and Seidenberg (1995). I thank Dave Balota, Marlene Behrmann, John Bullinaria, Jay McClelland, Karalyn Patterson, Mark Seidenberg, and Tim Shallice for helpful comments and discussions.

1. In their reply to Seidenberg and Plaut (1998), Balota and Spieler (1998) question whether length effects fall outside the scope of the models, given that Plaut et al. (1996, p. 85) actually demonstrated a small but reliable effect of length on the settling times of their attractor model. However, the fact that the model shows some sensitivity to length does not entail that it should be expected to account for all or even most of the effects of length on performance; the underlying theory may still ascribe length effects to other (unimplemented) parts of the reading system.

2. The encoding of words and nonwords as sequences of phonemes was based on the phonological representation employed by Plaut and McClelland (1993), which differs slightly from that used by Plaut et al. (1996).

3. Given the composition of the training corpus and all possible refixations, sixty-two of the letter units would never be activated during training. Therefore, to reduce the computational demands of the simulation slightly, all 6,200 outgoing connections from these units were removed, leaving an actual total of 39,745 connections in the network.

4. A more empirically accurate positioning would have placed the string so that fixation falls at or just to the left of the center of the word, corresponding to the "optimal" or "convenient" viewing position (see O'Regan, 1981). This distinction has no functional consequences for the current model, however, as it does not incorporate variation in visual acuity with eccentricity.

5. If the network fails on the first grapheme of a string, or immediately after refixating, the target for the position units is used during training as the location of the next fixation; during testing, the most active position unit is used. Also note that the network's rightward saccades are different than the regressive (leftward) saccades that subjects sometimes make when encountering difficult text (see Just & Carpenter, 1987). The current network cannot make regressive saccades.

6. There is emerging evidence that subjects can initiate their articulation prior to computing the entire pronunciation of a word (Kawamoto, Kello, Jones, & Bame, 1998). Note, however, that the most difficult aspect of mapping orthography to

phonology in English relates to inconsistency in vowel pronunciations, and the fixation measure used in the current simulation is sufficiently sensitive to reflect this property.

7. Given that the network contains no semantic representations, it cannot be used to account for the effects of imageability on LBL reading, nor the relatively preserved lexical decision and semantic categorization performance of these patients.

REFERENCES

Balota, D. A. (1994). Visual word recognition: The journey from features to meaning. In M. A. Gernsbacher (Ed.), *Handbook of psycholinguistics* (pp. 303–358). New York: Academic Press.

Balota, D. A., & Spieler, D. H. (1998). The utility of item-level analyses in model evaluation: A reply to Seidenberg and Plaut. *Psychological Science, 9*, 238–240.

Beauvois, M.-F., & Derouesné, J. (1979). Phonological alexia: Three dissociations. *Journal of Neurology, Neurosurgery, and Psychiatry, 42*, 1115–1124.

Behrmann, M., Barton, J. J., Shomstein, S., & Black, S. E. (1999). *Eye movements reveal the sequential processing in letter-by-letter reading.* Manuscript submitted for publication.

Behrmann, M., & Bub, D. (1992). Surface dyslexia and dysgraphia: Dual routes, a single lexicon. *Cognitive Neuropsychology, 9*, 209–258.

Behrmann, M., Nelson, J., & Sekuler, E. (1998). Visual complexity in letter-by-letter reading: "Pure" alexia is not pure. *Neuropsychologia, 36*, 1115–1132.

Behrmann, M., Plaut, D. C., & Nelson, J. (1998). A literature review and new data supporting an interactive account of letter-by-letter reading. *Cognitive Neuropsychology, 15*, 7–51.

Besner, D., Twilley, L., McCann, R. S., & Seergobin, K. (1990). On the connection between connectionism and data: Are a few words necessary? *Psychological Review, 97*, 432–446.

Bub, D., Cancelliere, A., & Kertesz, A. (1985). Whole-word and analytic translation of spelling-to-sound in a non-semantic reader. In K. E. Patterson, J. C. Marshall, & M. Coltheart (Eds.), *Surface dyslexia: Neuropsychological and cognitive studies of phonological readings* (pp. 15–34). London: Lawrence Erlbaum.

Bullinaria, J. A. (1997). Modeling reading, spelling, and past tense learning with artificial neural networks. *Brain and Language, 59*, 236–266.

Cipolotti, L., & Warrington, E. K. (1995). Semantic memory and reading abilities: A case report. *Journal of the International Neuropsychological Society, 1*, 104–110.

Coltheart, M. (Ed.). (1996). Special issue on phonological dyslexia. *Cognitive Neuropsychology, 13*, 749–934.

Coltheart, M. (Ed.). (1998). Special issue on pure alexia. *Cognitive Neuropsychology, 15*, 1–238.

Coltheart, M., Curtis, B., Atkins, P., & Haller, M. (1993). Models of reading aloud: Dual-route and parallel-distributed-processing approaches. *Psychological Review, 100*, 589–608.

Coltheart, M., Patterson, K. E., & Marshall, J. C. (Eds.). (1980). *Deep dyslexia*. London: Routledge & Kegan Paul.

Coltheart, M., Patterson, K. E., & Marshall, J. C. (1987). Deep dyslexia since 1980. In M. Coltheart, K. E. Patterson, & J. C. Marshall (Eds.), *Deep dyslexia* (pp. 407–451). London: Routledge & Kegan Paul.

Coslett, H. B., & Saffran, E. M. (1989). Evidence for preserved reading in "pure alexia." *Brain, 112*, 327–359.

Dejerine, J. (1892). Contribution à l'étude anatomoclinique et clinique des differentes variétés de cécité verbale. *Mémoires del la Société de Biologie, 4*, 61–90.

Elman, J. L. (1990). Finding structure in time. *Cognitive Science, 14*, 179–211.

Farah, M. J. (1994). Neuropsychological inference with an interactive brain: A critique of the locality assumption. *Behavioral and Brain Sciences, 17*, 43–104.

Fera, P., & Besner, D. (1992). The process of lexical decision: More words about a parallel distributed processing model. *Journal of Experimental Psychology: Learning, Memory, and Cognition, 18*, 749–764.

Friedman, R. B. (1996). Recovery from deep alexia to phonological alexia. *Brain and Language, 52*, 114–128.

Glosser, G., & Friedman, R. B. (1990). The continuum of deep/phonological alexia. *Cortex, 26*, 343–359.

Glushko, R. J. (1979). The organization and activation of orthographic knowledge in reading aloud. *Journal of Experimental Psychology: Human Perception and Performance, 5*, 674–691.

Harm, M. W. (1998). *Division of labor in a computational model of visual word recognition*. Unpublished doctoral thesis, Los Angeles: Department of Computer Science, University of Southern California.

Henderson, L. (1982). *Orthography and word recognition in reading*. London: Academic Press.

Hillis, A. E., Rapp, B., Romani, C., & Caramazza, A. (1990). Selective impairments of semantics in lexical processing. *Cognitive Neuropsychology, 7*, 191–243.

Hinton, G. E. (1989a). Connectionist learning procedures. *Artificial Intelligence, 40*, 185–234.

Hinton, G. E. (1989b). Deterministic Boltzmann learning performs steepest descent in weight-space. *Neural Computation, 1*, 143–150.

Hinton, G. E., & Shallice, T. (1991). Lesioning an attractor network: Investigations of acquired dyslexia. *Psychological Review, 98*, 74–95.

Jones, G. V. (1985). Deep dyslexia, imageability, and ease of predication. *Brain and Language, 24*, 1–19.

Just, M. A., & Carpenter, P. A. (1987). *The psychology of reading and language comprehension*. Boston: Allyn and Bacon.

Kawamoto, A. H., Kello, C., Jones, R., & Bame, K. (1998). Initial phoneme versus whole word criterion to initiate pronunciation: Evidence based on response latency and initial phoneme duration. *Journal of Experimental Psychology: Learning, Memory, and Cognition, 24*, 862–885.

Kučera, H., & Francis, W. N. (1967). *Computational analysis of present-day American English*. Providence, RI: Brown University Press.

Lambon Ralph, M., Ellis, A. W., & Franklin, S. (1995). Semantic loss without surface dyslexia. *Neurocase, 1*, 363–369.

McCann, R. S., & Besner, D. (1987). Reading pseudohomophones: Implications for models of pronunciation and the locus of the word-frequency effects in word naming. *Journal of Experimental Psychology: Human Perception and Performance, 13*, 14–24.

McCarthy, R., & Warrington, E. K. (1986). Phonological reading: Phenomena and paradoxes. *Cortex, 22*, 359–380.

McClelland, J. L., & Rumelhart, D. E. (1981). An interactive activation model of context effects in letter perception: Part 1. An account of basic findings. *Psychological Review, 88*, 375–407.

Morton, J. (1969). The interaction of information in word recognition. *Psychological Review, 76*, 165–178.

Morton, J., & Patterson, K. (1980). A new attempt at an interpretation, or, an attempt at a new interpretation. In M. Coltheart, K. E. Patterson, & J. C. Marshall (Eds.), *Deep dyslexia* (pp. 91–118). London: Routledge & Kegan Paul.

Mozer, M. C. (1983). Letter migration in word perception. *Journal of Experimental Psychology: Human Perception and Performance, 9*, 531–546.

Norris, D. G. (1994). A quantitative multiple-levels model of reading aloud. *Journal of Experimental Psychology: Human Perception and Performance, 20*, 1212–1232.

O'Regan, K. (1981). The "convenient viewing position" hypothesis. In D. F. Fisher, R. A. Monty, & J. W. Senders (Eds.), *Eye movements: Cognition and visual perception* (pp. 289–298). Hillsdale, NJ: Lawrence Erlbaum.

Patterson, K. E., Coltheart, M., & Marshall, J. C. (Eds.). (1985). *Surface dyslexia.* Hillsdale, NJ: Lawrence Erlbaum.

Patterson, K. E., & Hodges, J. R. (1992). Deterioration of word meaning: Implications for reading. *Neuropsychologia, 30*, 1025–1040.

Patterson, K. E., & Kay, J. (1982). Letter-by-letter reading: Psychological descriptions of a neurological syndrome. *Quarterly Journal of Experimental Psychology, 34A*, 411–441.

Patterson, K. E., Plaut, D. C., McClelland, J. L., Seidenberg, M. S., Behrmann, M., & Hodges, J. R. (1996). Connections and disconnections: A connectionist account of surface dyslexia. In J. Reggia, R. Berndt, & E. Ruppin (Eds.), *Neural modeling of cognitive and brain disorders* (pp. 177–199). New York: World Scientific.

Peterson, C., & Anderson, J. R. (1987). A mean field theory learning algorithm for neural nets. *Complex Systems, 1*, 995–1019.

Plaut, D. C. (1995). Double dissociation without modularity: Evidence from connectionist neuropsychology. *Journal of Clinical and Experimental Neuropsychology, 17*, 291–321.

Plaut, D. C. (1997). Structure and function in the lexical system: Insights from distributed models of word reading and lexical decision. *Language and Cognitive Processes, 12*, 765–805.

Plaut, D. C., & Kello, C. T. (1998). The interplay of speech comprehension and production in phonological development: A forward modeling approach. In B. MacWhinney (Ed.), *The emergence of language.* Mahwah, NJ: Lawrence Erlbaum.

Plaut, D. C., & McClelland, J. L. (1993). Generalization with componential attractors: Word and nonword reading in an attractor network. In *Proceedings of the Fifteenth Annual Conference of the Cognitive Science Society* (pp. 824–829). Hillsdale, NJ: Lawrence Erlbaum.

Plaut, D. C., McClelland, J. L., & Seidenberg, M. S. (1995). Reading exception words and pseudowords: Are two routes really necessary? In J. P. Levy, D. Bairaktaris, J. A. Bullinaria, & P. Cairns (Eds.), *Connectionist models of memory and language* (pp. 145–159). London: UCL Press.

Plaut, D. C., McClelland, J. L., Seidenberg, M. S., & Patterson, K. E. (1996). Understanding normal and impaired word reading: Computational principles in quasi-regular domains. *Psychological Review, 103*, 56–115.

Plaut, D. C., & Shallice, T. (1993). Deep dyslexia: A case study of connectionist neuropsychology. *Cognitive Neuropsychology, 10*, 377–500.

Rastle, K., & Coltheart, M. (1998). Whammies and double whammies: The effect of length on nonword reading. *Psychonomic Bulletin & Review, 5*, 277–282.

Reggia, J. A., Marsland, P. M., & Berndt, R. S. (1988). Competitive dynamics in a dual-route connectionist model of print-to-sound transformation. *Complex Systems, 2*, 509–547.

Reichle, E. D., Pollatsek, A., & Rayner, K. (1998). Toward a model of eye movement control in reading. *Psychological Review, 105*, 125–157.

Rumelhart, D. E., & McClelland, J. L. (1986). On learning the past tenses of English verbs. In J. L. McClelland & D. E. Rumelhart (Eds.), *Parallel distributed processing: Explorations in the microstructure of cognition.* Vol. 2: *Psychological and biological models* (pp. 216–271). Cambridge, MA: MIT Press.

Saffran, E. M., Bogyo, L. C., Schwartz, M. F., & Marin, O.S.M. (1980). Does deep dyslexia reflect right-hemisphere reading? In M. Coltheart, K. E. Patterson, & J. C. Marshall (Eds.), *Deep dyslexia* (pp. 381–406). London: Routledge & Kegan Paul.

Schwanenflugel, P. J. (1991). Why are abstract concepts hard to understand? In P. J. Schwanenflugel (Ed.), *The psychology of word meanings.* Hillsdale, NJ: Lawrence Erlbaum.

Seidenberg, M. S., & McClelland, J. L. (1989). A distributed, developmental model of word recognition and naming. *Psychological Review, 96*, 523–568.

Seidenberg, M. S., & Plaut, D. C. (1998). Evaluating word-reading models at the item level: Matching the grain of theory and data. *Psychological Science, 9*, 234–237.

Seidenberg, M. S., Plaut, D. C., Petersen, A. S., McClelland, J. L., & McRae, K. (1994). Nonword pronunciation and models of word recognition. *Journal of Experimental Psychology: Human Perception and Performance, 20*, 1177–1196.

Seidenberg, M. S., & Waters, G. S. (1989). Word recognition and naming: A mega study [Abstract 30]. *Bulletin of the Psychonomic Society, 27*, 489.

Sejnowski, T. J., & Rosenberg, C. R. (1987). Parallel networks that learn to pronounce English text. *Complex Systems, 1*, 145–168.

Shallice, T. (1988). *From neuropsychology to mental structure.* Cambridge: Cambridge University Press.

Shallice, T., & McCarthy, R. (1985). Phonological reading: From patterns of impairment to possible procedures. In K. E. Patterson, M. Coltheart, & J. C. Marshall (Eds.), *Surface dyslexia* (pp. 361–398). Hillsdale, NJ: Lawrence Erlbaum.

Shallice, T., & Saffran, E. (1986). Lexical processing in the absence of explicit word identification: Evidence from a letter-by-letter reader. *Cognitive Neuropsychology, 3*, 429–458.

Shallice, T., & Warrington, E. K. (1980). Single and multiple component central dyslexic syndromes. In M. Coltheart, K. E. Patterson, & J. C. Marshall (Eds.), *Deep dyslexia* (pp. 119–145). London: Routledge & Kegan Paul.

Spieler, D. H., & Balota, D. A. (1997). Bringing computational models of word naming down to the item level. *Psychological Science, 8*, 411–416.

Strain, E., Patterson, K. E., & Seidenberg, M. S. (1995). Semantic effects in single-word naming. *Journal of Experimental Psychology: Learning, Memory, and Cognition, 21*, 1140–1154.

Taraban, R., & McClelland, J. L. (1987). Conspiracy effects in word recognition. *Journal of Memory and Language, 26*, 608–631.

Teuber, H. L. (1955). Physiological psychology. *Annual Review of Psychology, 9*, 267–296.

Van Orden, G. C., Pennington, B. F., & Stone, G. O. (1990). Word identification in reading and the promise of subsymbolic psycholinguistics. *Psychological Review, 97*, 488–522.

Warrington, E. K. (1981). Concrete word dyslexia. *British Journal of Psychology, 72*, 175–196.

Weekes, B. S. (1997). Differential effects of number of letters on word and nonword latency. *Quarterly Journal of Experimental Psychology, 50A*, 439–456.

Zorzi, M., Houghton, G., & Butterworth, B. (1998). Two routes or one in reading aloud? A connectionist dual-process model. *Journal of Experimental Psychology: Human Perception and Performance, 24*, 1131–1161.

PART **II** ————————————————

FUTURE PROSPECTS

9

Constraint Satisfaction in Language Acquisition and Processing

Mark S. Seidenberg and
Maryellen C. MacDonald

The question of how children acquire language plays a central role in modern theorizing about language and raises broader issues about the neural representation of knowledge and the interplay between biological and experiential factors in determining behavior. Research within the generative approach has been seen as providing compelling evidence that children are born with grammatical knowledge and that languages could not be learned as rapidly and accurately as they are without it.[1] The "poverty of the stimulus" argument (Chomsky, 1965, 1986) is a cornerstone of the approach; for many years it has guided researchers toward certain types of explanations for how language is acquired (e.g., Universal Grammar) and away from others (e.g., learning based on experience). Over the past few years an alternative approach to language acquisition has begun to emerge as an outgrowth of several developments outside of the linguistic mainstream. The sources for this new approach include the renewed interest in the statistical and probabilistic aspects of language on the part of many language researchers; the connectionist approach to knowledge representation, learning, and processing; and research on learning in infants and young children. We will call this the "probabilistic constraints" approach, because its central idea is that acquisition and processing involve the use of multiple, simultaneous, probabilistic constraints defined over different types of linguistic and nonlinguistic information. This chapter will provide an overview of the approach, focusing on the relationship between language acquisition and adult language processing. Instead of asking how the child acquires grammar, we view acquisition in terms of how the child converges on adultlike performance in comprehending and producing utterances. This performance orientation changes the picture considerably with respect to classic issues about language learnability and provides a unified framework for studying acquisition and processing.[2]

GENERATIVE GRAMMAR AND PROBABILISTIC CONSTRAINTS

The questions that have been the focus of modern research on language are, What is knowledge of a language? How is this knowledge acquired? and How is this knowledge used in comprehension and production (Chomsky, 1986)?[3] The generative paradigm entails assumptions about how to find the answers to these questions and provides provisional answers to them (see Lightfoot, 1982, Atkinson, 1992 for reviews):

- Knowing a language involves knowing a grammar, a domain-specific form of knowledge representation that permits the creation of a nearly infinite set of well-formed utterances. The grammar specifies how language is structured at different levels of representation and provides a basis for distinguishing well-formed from ill-formed sentences.

- The grammar is a characterization of the knowledge of an idealized speaker–hearer. This "competence" assumption means that grammatical theory abstracts away from many of the factors that govern language use, including memory limitations, individual differences, facts about the computational system that implements the grammar, and so on.

- Poverty of the stimulus arguments suggest that this knowledge cannot be derived solely or even largely from experience. The input is impoverished insofar as children's knowledge of language eventually extends far beyond the range of utterances to which they are exposed; the input is overly rich insofar as it affords incorrect inductive generalizations that children never make; hence, the input cannot be the source of core grammatical knowledge. Results from Gold (1967) and others suggest that grammar identification cannot be achieved unless there are strong constraints on the possible forms of grammatical knowledge.

- The view that children are born with knowledge of Universal Grammar is compatible with the results of behavioral studies indicating that various types of knowledge about linguistic structure (e.g., empty categories; the binding principles) are present in children as young as they can be tested. It is also compatible with the observation that languages exhibit structures for which there is simply no evidence in the input (see Crain & Thornton, 1998, for review of both claims).

- This view will simultaneously account for facts about linguistic universals and it is compatible with other converging evidence (concerning, e.g., creolization and language acquisition under atypical circumstances; see Bickerton, 1984, and Landau & Gleitman, 1985, respectively).

AN ALTERNATIVE FRAMEWORK

The probabilistic constraints framework provides an alternative perspective on all of these issues.

An Alternative to Grammar

In the approach that we are advocating, knowing a language is not equated with knowing a grammar. Rather, we adopt the functionalist assumption of knowledge of language as something that develops in the course of learning how to perform the primary communicative tasks of comprehension and production (see, e.g., Bates & MacWhinney, 1982). As a first approximation, we view this knowledge as a neural network that maps between form and meaning and vice versa. Other levels of linguistic representation (e.g., syntax, morphology) are thought to be emergent structures that the network develops in the course of learning to perform these tasks. We discuss morphology in greater detail later in this chapter; Allen and Seidenberg (1999) provide an illustration of this approach as applied to syntactic structure (for related studies, see Christiansen & Chater, 1999, Chapter 5, this volume; Elman, 1990). Allen and Seidenberg implemented an attractor network that was trained on two tasks: It was given a sequence of words as input and had to compute their semantics (comprehension), or it was given semantic patterns as input and had to compute a sequence of words (production). The network was trained on sentences that exhibited a fairly broad range of syntactic structures; these sentences were based on ones that had been used by Linebarger, Schwartz, and Saffran (1983) in a classic study of aphasic language. The model was trained on ten examples of each of ten sentence types using a vocabulary of ninety-seven words. It was then tested on novel examples of these structures using the same words. Allen and Seidenberg show that the model generalized to these novel forms quite accurately.

Even though the Allen and Seidenberg (1999) network's coverage of the grammar of English is quite limited, it serves to illustrate several components of the probabilistic constraints approach. The network developed a representation of (some aspects of) the structure of English in the course of learning to produce and comprehend utterances, on the basis of exposure to well-formed examples. The representation of this knowledge—by the weights on connections between units—is not a grammar; it does not have the form of rewrite rules or constraints on tree structures that are seen in standard symbolic grammars or compute the same types of representations. Moreover, it encodes statistical aspects of the input that are excluded from standard generative grammars, information that in our view plays critical roles in language acquisition and use.

Grammars also provide a basis for distinguishing well- from ill-formed sentences, a task that assumes considerable importance because it has provided the main data for constructing grammatical theories. Allen and

Seidenberg's (1999) model illustrates how this task can be construed within our framework. As part of their assessment of the model's capacity to generalize, Allen and Seidenberg tested it on novel grammatical and ungrammatical sentences, such as *He came to my house at noon* and *He came my house at noon*, respectively. The model performed qualitatively differently on these types of sentences, computing the semantic representations for words less accurately in ungrammatical ones. Allen and Seidenberg also reported the results of testing the model on sentences that are comparable to Chomsky's (1957) classic *Colorless green ideas sleep furiously*. The network's responses to such sentences patterned more closely with performance on other grammatical sentences than with ungrammatical ones.[4] Thus, within the limited fragment of English grammar on which the model was trained, it treated grammatical and ungrammatical sentences differently. These differences provide a basis for labeling sentences as well- or ill-formed, even though the network itself is not a grammar.

An Alternative to "Competence"

Our approach does not share the competence orientation that is central to generative linguistics. We think that the competence–performance distinction encourages disregarding data that are actually essential to understanding basic characteristics of language. The competence approach uncontroversially excludes performance mishaps such as false starts, hesitations, and speech errors from the characterization of linguistic knowledge. However, it also excludes aspects of linguistic performance that are more central to the structure of utterances. It is assumed, for example, that language should be characterized independently of the perceptual and motor systems employed in language use, memory capacities that limit the complexity of utterances that can be produced or understood, and reasoning capacities used in comprehending text or discourse. Following the *Colorless green ideas sleep furiously* example, the competence theory also systematically excludes information about statistical and probabilistic aspects of language. How often particular structures are used and in what combinations are not seen as relevant to characterizing the essential nature of language.

It is clear from recent studies, however, that these aspects of language play enormously important roles in acquisition and processing (see, for example, MacDonald, Pearlmutter, & Seidenberg, 1994; Tanenhaus & Trueswell, 1995; Kelly, 1992; Saffran, Aslin, & Newport, 1996; Morgan & Demuth, 1996). The apparent complexity of language and its uniqueness vis-à-vis other aspects of cognition, which are taken as major discoveries of the standard approach, may derive in part from the fact that these performance factors are not available to enter into explanations of linguistic structure. Partitioning language into competence and performance and then treating the latter as a separate issue for psycholinguists to figure out has the effect of excluding many aspects of language structure and use from the data on which the competence theory is developed. What is left as a basis for characterizing language are the various abstract, domain-specific, theory-internal kinds of knowledge structures that are characteristic of grammatical theory. Linguists then ask how a grammar of this sort could be acquired. Given this approach to theory construction, it is not surprising that the resulting characterization of linguistic knowledge seems only remotely related to the child's experience.

The competence approach also promotes systematic overattributions about the nature of linguistic knowledge. It is well known that competence grammar is overly powerful relative to people's actual capacities to comprehend and produce utterances. The classic example is that the grammar permits unlimited amounts of center-embedding, as in the following examples. People's capacities to comprehend or produce such structures are quite limited: Only a single embedding (1) is easily processed, and multiple levels of embedding are difficult or impossible to comprehend or produce.

(1) *The cat [that the dog chased] is now sitting on the window sill.*

(2) *The cat that [the dog [that the girl bought] chased] is now sitting on the window sill.*

(3) *The cat that [the dog [that the girl [who Willard loves] bought] chased] is now sitting on the window sill.*

How to address the discrepancy between what the grammar allows and what people can comprehend or produce has been an issue since the earliest days of generative grammar (Chomsky, 1957). The standard solution is to allow such structures to be generated by the grammar but introduce extrinsic "performance constraints" to account for the difficulty of (2) and (3) (see Gibson, 1998, for a recent example). Our approach is different: We are attempting to characterize a performance system that handles all and only those structures that people can. Performance constraints are embodied in the system responsible for producing and comprehending utterances, not extrinsic to it (MacDonald & Christiansen, in press; Christiansen & Chater, 1999, Chapter 5, this volume). This approach obviates the paradox created by a characterization of linguistic knowledge that generates sentences that people neither produce nor comprehend.

The fact that we are trying to account for people's attested capacities rather than the ones assumed by the competence approach is important. Our methodology involves implementing connectionist models that simulate detailed aspects of performance. In the past, some of the criticism of such models has focused on whether they can capture one or another aspect of grammatical competence characterized in the usual idealized manner (e.g., Fodor & Pylyshyn, 1988). However, the appropriate way to assess our models is in terms of people's performance, not the idealized characterization of linguistic knowledge that is competence grammar.

An Alternative to Grammar Identification

The probabilistic constraints approach also differs from generative grammar with regard to how the task confronting the language learner is characterized. The generative approach assumes that the task is *grammar identification*: Armed with Universal Grammar and positive examples, the child has to converge on the knowledge structures that constitute the grammar of the language to which he or she has been exposed. Questions about acquisition are framed in terms of problems in acquiring grammar (e.g., how the child could set parameters of the grammar based on limited experience, or how the child could recover from grammatical overgeneralizations in the absence of negative evidence). The alternative view is that the task the child is engaged in is learning to use language (see Seidenberg, 1997; see Bates & MacWhinney, 1982, for an earlier statement of this view). In the course of mastering this task, children develop various types of knowledge representations. The primary function of this knowledge is producing and comprehending utterances. A derived function is allowing the child to distinguish grammatical from ungrammatical sentences, even though a competence grammar is not the target of the acquisition process.

This change in orientation from grammar identification to learning to use language has important consequences for standard poverty of the stimulus arguments. In brief, it turns out that many of the classic arguments for the innateness of grammar rest on the assumption that the child's task is grammar identification, and these arguments simply no longer apply if the task is instead acquiring the performance system underlying comprehension and production. For example, the fact that the input contains both grammatical and ungrammatical utterances that are not labeled as such is far more problematic for the task of grammar identification than it is for learning to comprehend and produce utterances. Given that the target is no longer construed as a grammar, our approach does not entail the assumptions that underlie the analyses of learnability by Gold (1967) and others. Other classic arguments concern how the child copes with noisy or variable input, issues for which connectionist learning principles provide a potential solution. One of the important properties of the algorithms used in training such models is their capacity to derive structural regularities from noisy or variable input. Similarly, the claim that "negative facts cannot be learned" (Crain, 1991) is contradicted by the behavior of even very simple networks, such as the Allen and Seidenberg (1999) model described earlier. A network is trained on the basis of exposure to examples. Adjustments to the weights in response to these attested forms simultaneously provide evidence against structures that have not been observed because they do not occur in the language (e.g., because they are ungrammatical). The network nonetheless supports generalization because novel grammatical sentences share structure with previously encountered sentences. Thus, the Allen and Seidenberg model treated ungrammatical sentences such as *John came my house* differently than grammatical sentences such as *John came to my house* the first time it was exposed to them.

Evidence from Studies of Young Children

Two aspects of children's performance have been taken as particularly strong evidence for the innateness of grammatical principles. One is that children exhibit sensitivity to grammatical constraints at the youngest ages at which they can be tested. The other is that children show sensitivity to structures for which there is no evidence in the input (see Crain, 1991, for summaries of both arguments). With our change in theoretical orientation there is a need to reexamine these kinds of arguments. The validity of both claims depends on the theory of what is being learned (i.e., the target) and the theory of how children learn. The notion of what constitutes important evidence for learning a particular structure is not theory-neutral. Poverty of the stimulus arguments have been developed within a framework in which the target was grammar and the learning mechanism involved testing hypotheses about grammatical rules. Because these arguments have been very persuasive, research on language acquisition within the generative tradition has not examined relevant aspects of children's learning capacities very closely.

We have already suggested that our approach entails a different perspective on the nature of the target: The characterization of the target changes if we abandon the assumption that it is a grammar and various performance factors are permitted to enter into explanations of linguistic structure. Our approach also entails a different account of children's learning. Rather than involving hypothesis testing about grammatical rules, learning involves accumulating information about statistical and probabilistic aspects of language. We now know that learning about these aspects of language is very robust and begins at a very early age. For example, Saffran et al. (1996) demonstrated such learning in eight-month-olds. Other studies suggest that this kind of learning begins in utero: Newborns already show a preference for listening to speech in their mother's language (Moon, Panneton-Cooper, & Fifer, 1993). Results such as these raise questions about the extent to which children could have learned various aspects of language by the time they reach the age at which experimenters are able to test them (in studies such as Crain's, 1991, around 2.6 to 3.0 years old). Claims about what cannot be learned by the child (and must therefore be innately endowed) need to be assessed in terms of the kinds of statistical information available to the child and learning mechanisms that are able to extract nonobvious regularities from it.

In pointing out the potentially important role for statistical learning in language acquisition, we do not mean to assert that claims about the innateness of all aspects of linguistic knowledge are necessarily wrong. Our assertion is only that the probabilistic constraints framework provides strong motivation for reexamining claims about acquisition that are taken as givens within the generative approach. The same holds for other sorts of converging evidence thought to support the conclusion that grammar is innate. Linguistic universals, for example, are standardly explained by placing universal grammar in the brain of the child. However, there are other sources of constraint on the forms of languages that need to be considered. Languages may exhibit the properties they do because otherwise they could not be processed (given the nature of human perceptual and memory capacities), could not be learned (given the nature of human learning), would not fulfill particular communicative functions, or would not have evolved in the species. Together these considerations suggest a need to reexamine both the nature of the biological endowment relevant to language and the evidence for it (see also Elman et al., 1996, who reach similar conclusions).

CONTINUITY BETWEEN ACQUISITION AND PROCESSING

In the generative approach the target for the acquisition process is competence grammar, the idealized characterization of linguistic knowledge. In our approach the target is provided by adult performance. Skilled users of language possess knowledge of how to comprehend and produce language, not just constraints on the well-formedness of utterances. The probabilistic constraints approach emphasizes the essential continuity between acquisition and processing, and the goal is to develop an integrated theory in which the same principles apply to both. This view suggests that it will be important for acquisition researchers to understand the nature of the adult processing system in order to understand how the child converges on it (e.g., Trueswell, Sekerina, Hill, & Logrip, in press). Similarly, research on adult performance should benefit from an understanding of the acquisition process, particularly how constraints on learning shape the nature of the adult system. The observation that there is continuity between acquisition and processing may seem obvious, but in fact the generative approach has tended to treat the issues separately and to explain them by different principles. Acquisition is explained in terms of concepts such as the "maturation" of grammar (Wexler, 1990) or the setting of grammatical parameters (Lightfoot, 1991), whereas processing is explained in terms of a "parser" endowed with heuristics to aid ambiguity resolution (e.g., Frazier, 1987). This division is also seen in the interpretation of empirical results. Whereas accuracy on a task such as pointing to a picture that matches an auditory sentence is typically thought to reflect grammar development in the child, the identical task, when performed by adults, is generally taken as reflecting performance mechanisms rather than grammatical competence.

We do not have a comprehensive theory of all aspects of adult performance in hand, but a picture of the general character of the system is provided by recent constraint-based theories of adult language comprehension

(MacDonald et al., 1994; Tanenhaus & Trueswell, 1995). The essential idea of the constraint-based approach is that comprehending or producing an utterance involves interactions among a large number of probabilistic constraints over different types of linguistic and nonlinguistic information.[5] In much of this work, knowledge of language is represented in terms of a complex lexical network. MacDonald et al. review arguments for an enriched conception of the lexicon, in which it encodes not merely the spellings, sounds, and meanings of words, but also information such as the argument structures associated with verbs. This enriched view of the lexicon is broadly consistent with developments in syntactic theory, in which the lexicon has also assumed increasing importance. However, the use of a network representation also permits the encoding of information about the frequencies of occurrence for different types of information, as well as higher-order statistics concerning combinations of elements. The representation that the network computes in comprehending a sentence is that which best satisfies the constraints of the language, which are encoded by the weights on connections between units. Comprehensive computational models are not yet available, but a number of researchers have developed simulations that implement small parts of the system (McRae, Spivey-Knowlton, & Tanenhaus, 1998; Pearlmutter, Daugherty, MacDonald, & Seidenberg, 1994; Tabor & Tanenhaus, Chapter 6, this volume; Elman, 1990; Kim, Bangalore, & Trueswell, in press). In an interesting parallel development, recent work in computational linguistics has emphasized the importance of probabilistic lexical information in the construction of machine parsers (e.g., Charniak, 1997; Collins & Brooks, 1995). Although these parsers differ in fundamental ways from the kind of parallel-constraint satisfaction networks that we take as the model for the human sentence processor, the shared interest in the role of probabilistic lexical constraints on the part of researchers holding very different theoretical orientations underscores the importance of this type of information.

To illustrate the general character of the constraint-based approach, we will focus here on a few important aspects of it that are particularly relevant to acquisition. First, a network of this sort is both a representation of linguistic knowledge and a processing mechanism. As in other connectionist models, there is no strong distinction between the two. As a result, "performance constraints" (e.g., limits on the complexity of sentences that can be processed) are encoded by the same machinery as knowledge of language itself. This situation contrasts with other approaches, in which knowledge of the language (grammar) is represented separately from the performance systems that make use of this knowledge (e.g., the parser, working memory). Second, the constraints that the model encodes are probabilistic rather than absolute. For example, a noun phrase (NP) at the start of a sentence is typically the agent of the action specified by the verb, but not always. Third, the interactions among constraints are nonlinear. Types of information that are not very constraining in isolation become highly constraining when considered together. For example, the probability that a sentence-initial NP is an agent goes up substantially if the NP is animate. Fourth, the levels of linguistic representation over which these computations occur are thought to emerge in the course of acquisition. For example, we think of morphological structure as an interlevel representation that emerges in a multilayer connectionist network that is computing relations among semantics, phonology, and the contexts in which words occur. Similarly, grammatical categories derive from several sources of correlated information, including meanings, phonological structure, and syntactic context (Kelly, 1992; Mintz, Newport, & Bever, 1998; Redington, Chater, & Finch, 1998; Schuetze, 1997).

These principles have been explored in a number of recent studies of syntactic ambiguity resolution during language comprehension (see MacDonald et al., 1994, for review). Much of this research has focused on how semantic and syntactic properties of individual verbs affect the production and comprehension of syntactic structure. A simple example concerns the interpretation of prepositional phrases (PPs) in sentences such as *The spy saw the cop with the binoculars*, in which the PP *with the binoculars* can be interpreted as modifying either the verb, such that it is an instrument of seeing, or the direct-object NP, such that the spy saw the cop who had the binoculars, rather than some other cop. This ambiguity is syntactic because the uncertainty of interpretation focuses not on the individual words but rather on the relationships between phrases, namely whether the phrase *with the binoculars* modifies a noun or verb.

Traditional accounts of syntactic ambiguity resolution have assumed that the fact that language comprehension is essentially immediate is incompatible with the use of multiple probabilistic constraints, which were thought to be too weak or not available early enough in processing to yield useful information. Instead, an initial interpretation of an ambiguity was thought to be computed based on a single metric, such as the complexity (e.g., Frazier, 1987) or frequency (Mitchell, Cuetos, Corley, & Brysbaert, 1995) of the alternative structures. These simple decision processes predict that people's initial interpretations of the PP ambiguity will frequently be wrong, as corpus data suggest that about 60 percent of the PPs modify the direct-object NP, and the remaining 40 percent modify the verb (Hindle & Rooth, 1993; Collins & Brooks, 1995). Thus, any simple structural metric will make errors in the initial interpretation of this ambiguity on the order of 40 percent of the time at best, and the Minimal Attachment metric favored by the best known structural account, the Garden Path model (Frazier, 1987), initially chooses the verb modification and therefore makes about 60 percent errors. It is hard to reconcile these predictions with the observation that comprehenders resolve this ambiguity quite easily. It is also hard to understand why the human sentence-processing mechanism would have converged on so inefficient a strategy.

Research within the constraint-based approach suggests that comprehenders avoid making errors 40 to 60 percent of the time by using other information that sentences provide. For example, many prepositions do not modify nouns and verbs with equal frequency (e.g., *of* almost exclusively modifies noun phrases, as in *glass of wine, president of the company*), and Collins and Brooks (1995) report that choosing the verb-versus-noun attachment based solely on the bias of the preposition to modify nouns or verbs will resolve the ambiguity correctly about 72 percent of the time. This is substantially better than the accuracy of any purely structural decision, and when several of these probabilistic lexical constraints are combined, the ambiguity resolution problem narrows greatly. Some other key lexical information comes from the verb in the sentence. Action verbs, which typically cooccur with a PP expressing the instrument or manner of the action (e.g., *cut with a knife, ate in a hurry*) promote the interpretation in which the PP modifies the verb, whereas perception verbs (*see, hear*, etc.) are not typically modified with manners or instruments, and they promote the noun-modification interpretation of the PP (Spivey-Knowlton & Sedivy, 1995; Taraban & McClelland, 1988). Spivey-Knowlton and Sedivy showed that an additional, weaker constraint is provided by the direct-object NP: Indefinite NPs (e.g., *a dog*) promote the noun-modification interpretation of the PP, whereas definite NPs (*the dog*) promote the verb-modification interpretation. The verb and noun constraints combine in a nonlinear manner: The weaker noun-definiteness constraint has little effect when a verb strongly promotes the verb-modification interpretation, but its effects can be clearly seen when the verb is one of perception. Finally, information from the surrounding discourse context also exerts some constraint, so that when the discourse creates a context in which more information is needed about the direct object NP (as when several cops were previously mentioned so that *The spy saw the cop* does not pick out a unique referent in the discourse), the noun-modification interpretation is promoted (Altmann & Steedman, 1988). Thus, the system is one that is strongly guided by verb- and preposition-based constraints, which are in turn modulated by constraints from other lexical items and from the broader discourse context.

Other syntactic ambiguities have been shown to have a similar character. For example, the main verb–reduced relative ambiguity, which has a strong asymmetry in the frequencies of its alternative interpretations, is shown in the following sentences:

(4) Temporary main verb–reduced relative ambiguity: *The three men arrested . . .*

(5) Main verb interpretation: *The three men arrested the fugitives who had escaped from the county jail.*

(6) Reduced relative interpretation: *The three men arrested in the parking lot had just escaped from the county jail.*

The ambiguity centers on the role of an ambiguous verb, in this case *arrested*. In one interpretation, shown in (5), *arrested* is the main verb of the sentence, and the preceding NP (*The three men*) is the agent of the action. In (6), however, this NP is the patient of the action, and the verb *arrested* introduces a passive relative clause (called a "reduced" relative because the optional words *who were* are omitted from the start of the relative clause). A number of researchers have observed that interpretation of this ambiguity is strongly constrained by the frequency with which the ambiguous verb occurs in transitive and passive structures, of which reduced relative clauses are a special type (MacDonald, 1994; MacDonald et al., 1994; Trueswell, 1996). Interpretation of this structure is also constrained by combinatorial lexical information, such as the plausibility of the prenominal noun phrase (e.g., *The three men*) filling the agent or patient role of the verb (MacDonald, 1994; McRae et al., 1998; Pearlmutter & MacDonald, 1992; Tabossi, Spivey-Knowlton, McRae, & Tanenhaus, 1994; Trueswell, Tanenhaus, & Garnsey, 1994). Additional constraints are provided by discourse context (e.g., Spivey-Knowlton, Trueswell, & Tanenhaus, 1993; Altmann & Steedman, 1988). Again, combination of constraints is nonlinear, in that manipulations of noun agency or discourse context can successfully promote the rarer reduced relative interpretation only when properties of the ambiguous verb make this interpretation a viable one (MacDonald et al., 1994).

The picture that emerges from these and other studies of adult language comprehension is that adults have a vast amount of statistical information about the behavior of lexical items in their language, and that, at least for English, verbs provide some of the strongest constraints on the resolution of syntactic ambiguities. Comprehenders know the relative frequencies with which individual verbs appear in different tenses, in active versus passive structures, and in intransitive versus transitive structures. Comprehenders also know the typical kinds of subjects and objects that a verb takes and many other such facts. This information is acquired through experience with input that exhibits these distributional properties. A verb's behavior is also closely related to its semantics and other properties specific to it. For example, part of the essence of the verb *arrested* includes the fact that it is frequently used in passive contexts in which the person arrested is the subject of the sentence. In our approach, this information is not some idiosyncratic fact in the lexicon isolated from "core" grammatical information; rather, it is relevant at all stages of lexical, syntactic, and discourse comprehension.

Bootstrapping versus Constraint Satisfaction

Given this view of the adult system, one of the central questions in acquisition concerns how knowledge of probabilistic constraints is acquired. In fact, there is a significant body of acquisition research relevant to this question: studies of children's acquisition of verbs. This research (e.g., Gleitman,

1990; Pinker, 1989) has not been framed in terms of adult performance or connectionist models, but in fact it is quite compatible with our approach; a recent paper by Gillette, Gleitman, Gleitman, and Lederer (1998) makes the connection between this acquisition research and constraint satisfaction mechanisms explicit. Children learning English eventually come to know both the meanings of verbs and a complex set of conditions governing their occurrence in sentence structures (in some theories these are termed "conditions on subcategorization"). Consider, for example, some differences among the three common, semantically related verbs *load, pour,* and *fill.* *Load* can appear in both of the locative constructions given in (7) and (8). *Pour* and *fill,* in contrast, are each limited to one of the alternatives (9) through (12).

(7) *I loaded the bricks onto the truck.*

(8) *I loaded the truck with bricks.*

(9) *I poured the water onto the ground.*

(10) **I poured the ground with water.*

(11) **I filled the bricks onto the truck.*

(12) *I filled the truck with bricks.*

The behavior of these verbs is not idiosyncratic; each of them is representative of a class of semantically similar verbs that behave alike with respect to their participation in the two locative constructions:

load: *pile, cram, scatter,* . . .
pour: *drip, slop, spill, slosh,* . . .
fill: *blanket, cover, flood, clog, coat,* . . .

Thus, there are systematic relationships between the syntax and semantics of verbs (Levin, 1993). Errors such as *fill the salt into the bear* (Bowerman, 1982) make it clear that it takes time for the child to learn how verbs can be used. Exactly how the child exploits the correlations between syntax and semantics in acquiring this knowledge has been the subject of considerable controversy, however.

Pinker's (1989) theory emphasizes hypothesis testing and observational learning, in which the child observes the consistencies across situational contexts in which a verb is used to derive the verb's meaning. Aspects of a situation that are not consistent across uses of the verb would be expunged from a verb's lexical entry. The verb *pour*, for instance, would be observed in many contexts, including those in which a substance moves from a container into another container (pouring water into a bucket or a glass), as well as those in which a liquid moves from a container but not into another container (pouring water onto the ground). Since the end point of the liquid's motion is inconsistent across situations, the child would expunge any concrete specification of the endpoint of pouring events from the lexical entry for *pour*. Innate "linking rules," which specify the relation between an argument's place in a semantic representation and its place in a syntactic representation, would then allow a verb's syntactic privileges to be deduced directly from the resulting lexical entry. What will be consistent about events described by *pour* in the child's environment will be a liquid that moves from a container by the force of gravity, and this notion will form the basis of the word's lexical entry. Since this description includes an element (the liquid) that can be mapped to the innate notion "undergoer" or "patient," innate linking rules that map undergoers to grammatical direct-object position will tell the child that the direct object of *pour* will be the liquid that undergoes movement. In this way, the child comes to know how to use *pour* (as *pour* and not as *fill*) because of what it means. This scenario assumes a probabilistic learning mechanism capable of keeping track of the similarities across situations, allowing the child to deduce which aspects of the local situation are relevant to the meaning of the verb, and relies on the existence of innate linking rules to explain how the child knows how to use the verb once its meaning is known.

Gleitman and colleagues (e.g., Fisher, Gleitman, & Gleitman, 1991; Naigles, Gleitman, & Gleitman, 1993) have argued that this observational procedure is too weak. Many verbs with opposite meanings can be used to describe the same situation, so paying attention only to the situation in which a verb is used will not tell the child which argument is subject and which object. For example, because every chasing event is also a fleeing event, the child has no way of knowing, from the situation alone, whether *chase* means "chase" or "flee." With pouring events there may be only one element of the situation that undergoes a change of location, and that will be the argument mapped onto direct-object position. With *chase* and *flee*, however, there are two moving entities. Which will be the patient and thus linked to the direct object? It could be the chaser, if the child views the event as one in which the fox is attempting to move to the location of the rabbit, or it could be the chasee, in which case the rabbit is attempting to distance himself from the fox.

Gleitman and colleagues' syntactic bootstrapping theory is that the forms in which a verb appears direct the child toward the correct meaning. Hearing a verb in a transitive frame, the child utilizes the linking rule that maps undergoers to direct-object positions in reverse, such that the knowledge that an argument is the direct object tells the child that the argument is a patient, and that the verb's meaning is one that includes an undergoer of the type expressed by the argument. Other constructions provide other aspects of meaning. Hearing a verb in an intransitive frame, the child can deduce that the verb describes an action on the part of the subject. Hearing a dative construction (such as *The girl gave the dog a bone,* or *The girl gave a bone to the dog*) provides information that the verb contains the meaning of transfer. In other words, the child learns what a verb means because of how it is used.

Criticism of Gleitman's proposal has focused on the sufficiency of the syntactic bootstrapping mechanism. Pinker (1994), for example, has observed there are many more verbs than there are distinct syntactic contexts (subcategorization frames). Many aspects of verb meaning are not associated with difference in syntactic structure. For example, walking, strolling, and sashaying differ semantically but behave the same way syntactically. This critique is based on a reading of Gleitman's proposal in which the child's use of syntactic information to bootstrap meaning restricts the use of other available sources of information, such as observation; however, the theory clearly does not limit the child in this way. Rather, it holds that the conjunction of information provided by the syntactic and discourse contexts in which verbs occur provides a basis for establishing their meanings. As Naigles et al. (1993) observed,

We hold, with many others, that the information available from inspection of real-world contingencies for verb use, taken alone, is too variable and degenerate to fix the construals. Therefore there must be an additional convergent source of evidence that the child exploits in constructing a mental lexicon. One such potential source resides in the structural privileges of occurrence for the meaningfully distinct verb items. (p. 135)

Thus, the syntactic contexts in which a verb occurs constrain its meaning to a limited range of alternatives that can then be further disambiguated by observational data concerning the discourse context. In this way the use of syntactic information provides the necessary basis for overcoming the limits of observational learning, rather than replacing it in toto.

Similarly, Grimshaw (1990) has argued that because adjuncts cannot be distinguished from arguments, using syntax to learn the semantics of verbs will be an unreliable procedure. However, this kind of observation overlooks perhaps the central characteristic of constraint satisfaction mechanisms, which is that they rely on conjunctions of multiple sources of information that may indeed be only partially constraining when taken in isolation.

Our view is that the bootstrapping mechanisms that have figured centrally in discussions of verb learning are components of a more general constraint satisfaction processing system that exploits correlations between different sources of information, wherever they are found in the input. The view that lexical acquisition involves multiple kinds of bootstrapping is gaining currency among child-language researchers (e.g., Morgan, 1986; Jusczyk, 1997; Morgan & Demuth, 1996; Gillette et al., 1998; Mintz et al., 1998), and there is also a growing body of work that examines the extent to which children are attending to and learning from various statistical and probabilistic aspects of the input (see Morgan & Demuth, 1996). It is becoming quite clear that acquiring multiple types of probabilistic linguistic information is not an impossible task for the child; rather, even very young infants are picking up considerable information concerning distributional and sequential aspects of linguistic signals. The extent to which this type of learning provides the basis for various aspects of linguistic structure is unknown, but the similarity between these studies of learning and studies of adult processing is striking: "Bootstrapping" in acquisition is "constraint satisfaction" in adult processing; the former involves using correlations among different types of information to infer structure; the latter involves using such correlations to comprehend sentences.[6]

An illustration of the close theoretical linkage between the acquisition and adult processing can be found in a connectionist model of verb acquisition developed by Allen (1997). This model acquired verb semantics from the pairing of child-directed speech taken from the CHILDES corpus, particularly verb argument structure information, and information concerning the set of events accompanying the speech. For example, for the transitive sentence *Cathy broke the cup*, the model received the argument structure information that there were two arguments, one before the verb and one after, and that the verb was *break*. This information was paired with the interpretation that there were two participants, one the agent and one the patient, and that the event consisted of a breaking event. The goal of the modeling effort was to use knowledge acquired from exposure to these pairings to activate both appropriate argument-role interpretations and the verb semantics for each utterance, including constructions on which the model had not been trained, such as *the toy broke*. Allen's model performed well, exhibiting both the ability to supply role interpretations for novel constructions and to activate appropriate verb semantics for novel verbs when given information about both the argument structure and the semantics of the noun arguments in the utterance. In other words, the model encoded the partial regularities of the system and bootstraps from incomplete data, enabling it to generalize to novel instances.

Allen (1997) showed that the model took advantage of a great deal of distributional information in the input to acquire its verb representations. This information included, in approximately descending order of importance, the frequency with which a verb was used, the set of constructions the verb appeared in, the frequency with which a verb was used in particular constructions, the semantic relation between a verb and other verbs used in similar constructions, the combined frequencies of related verbs, and the size of the set of semantically related verbs. These factors combined to form neighborhoods of verbs with semantically mediated privileges of cooccurrence. Allen's model did not simply use syntactic information to acquire semantic information or information from the world to acquire syntactic information; rather, it simultaneously performed syntactic and semantic bootstrapping, using probabilistic constraints from multiple sources to converge on syntactic and semantic representations of verbs. Moreover, though this process might be termed "bootstrapping" in the acquisition literature, it is equally an example of constraint-based language processing; the distributional information that the model acquired looks very similar to the constraints that are used in adult performance (MacDonald, 1999). This relationship is not accidental, because the task of the model was not acquisition per se but rather a simplified version of what human adult comprehenders do; namely, assign a representation to each input sentence. In the course of assigning these representations, Allen's model passed activation across various levels of representation, and each utterance affected the weights between connections in the network. In this system, encoding of distributional information does not stem from some specialized acquisition mechanism, but is rather an inevitable consequence of this kind of processing architecture when applied to the task of comprehension or production.

In summary, the characteristic of the adult system we take to be crucial is the rapid integration of multiple probabilistic constraints involving different types of information. This aspect of processing has been explored extensively in studies of syntactic ambiguity resolution and other aspects of language comprehension. The acquisition problem is how the child acquires this system. Specific issues that need to be addressed include how structures ("levels of linguistic representation") emerge in the course of acquisition; the properties of these representations, which may deviate from classical accounts; and which kinds of statistical information are acquired from experience.

We have described one area, verbs and their argument structures, in which this approach has been explored in some detail. Related work includes studies of the word-segmentation problem (i.e., how children identify spoken words in continuous speech; Aslin, Woodward, LaMendola, & Bever 1996; Christiansen, Allen, & Seidenberg, 1998), and how children identify the grammatical categories of words (Kelly, 1992; Mintz et al., 1998; Redington et al., 1998). All of these problems share important characteristics. In each case, researchers have identified a variety of sources of information in the input that might contribute to solving the problem. Using these cues to linguistic structure raises classic learnability questions: How does the child know which cues are the relevant ones? The cues are probabilistic rather than absolute; if a cue is not entirely reliable, how could it be useful? Moreover, what benefit could arise from combining several unreliable cues?

Answers to these questions are provided by coupling these observations about probabilistic cues with computational mechanisms that explain how cues can be identified and combined. Connectionist networks provide a useful tool in this regard. A network that is assigned a task such as identifying the boundaries between words acts as a discovery procedure: It will make use of whatever information in the input facilitates mastering the task. This property is simply a consequence of using a learning algorithm that minimizes a cost function. From our perspective, the question "how does the child know which statistics to compute" is ill-formed. Certain information will be acquired given the nature of the architecture, the learning rule, and the input data. We can attempt to quantify this information statistically, but the best characterization of what the child knows will be provided by examining the behavior of a network that simulates the child's behavior in appropriate detail. Examining the behavior of such networks also provides insights about the cue-reliability question. These networks are not restricted to using a single type of information in solving a problem; their power derives from the capacity to combine multiple probabilistic cues efficiently. Individual cues that are not highly informative when taken in isolation may be highly constraining when taken in conjunction with each other.

MORPHOLOGY

Morphology, the aspect of language related to the structure and formation of words, provides another example of our approach. Our theory emphasizes the role of the lexicon in language acquisition and processing, and one of the important aspects of lexical systems is that they exhibit internal structure. Morphology is a major area of linguistic research, which mainly focuses on explaining universal and language-specific aspects of word formation and its relationship to other components of grammar (e.g., syntax, phonology). Morphology has also provided a domain in which to explore the role of connectionist concepts in explaining linguistic phenomena. Pinker and his colleagues (Pinker, 1991, 1994) have argued that some morphological processes implicate rules and other types of knowledge representations that are not compatible with connectionism. Our theory draws heavily on connectionist concepts such as distributed representations, multilayer networks, and learning through incremental weight adjustment; such networks provide a way of implementing the constraint satisfaction mechanisms already described. Thus, the asserted limitations of the approach vis-à-vis morphology raise serious questions about attempts to apply it to other aspects of language. Although we cannot discuss all aspects of this controversy here, we can explain how morphological phenomena fit within our general approach and indicate why the existing critiques should not discourage further research along these lines. We first discuss derivational morphology, the formation of words through combinations of stems and affixes (e.g., *bake* + *er*, *like* + *ness*, etc.). We then turn to inflectional morphology, particularly the controversy surrounding theoretical accounts of the formation of the English past tense, which has proved to be a testing ground for several very disparate accounts of human lexical knowledge.

Derivational Morphology

Derivational morphology concerns the formation of words through processes such as affixing (see Spencer, 1991, for an overview). Linguistic theories of derivational morphology attempt to provide a principled account of the universal and language-specific aspects of morphological systems. Psycholinguistic studies have addressed more performance-related issues concerning the representation of morphological information in memory and how it is used in reading (e.g., Murrell & Morton, 1974), writing (e.g., Badecker, Hillis, & Caramazza, 1990), spoken language comprehension (e.g., Tyler, Marslen-Wilson, Rentoul, & Hanney, 1988), and production (e.g., Bock & Eberhard, 1993). The basic issue is this: Words such as *baker* and *photograph* seem to consist of components (e.g., *bake, er, photo*, and *graph*), standardly called morphemes, which recombine to form other words (e.g., *photographer*). There are constraints on the possible forms of words that apparently operate over these units; thus, *photographer* is a word in English but *photoergraph* is not a legal sequence of morphemes. That language users are aware of the internal structure of words is indicated by their ability to form and understand novel words (i.e., to generalize). Derivational morphology is quasi-regular, in that the system has systematic, productive aspects but there are many degenerate cases that deviate from central tendencies in different ways and degrees. For example, there are units that seem to function as morphemes but make little semantic contribution to the words in which they appear (e.g., *-mit* in *permit* and *remit*, *-turb* in *disturb* and *perturb*, *-cede* in *precede* and *recede*; Aronoff, 1976). There are words such as *cranberry* that appear to consist of two morphemes, one of which (*cran-*) has no independent meaning. There are cases such as *relax* or *return* in which a stem morpheme (*lax, turn*) is combined with other material that is not obviously morphemic (the *re-* in these words is not the prefix that occurs in *rewrite*). There are also anomalous forms, such as *sweetbreads*, in which the meaning of the word is unrelated to the meanings of the components. See Aronoff for discussion and many other examples.

From our perspective, these phenomena seem ideally suited to the probabilistic constraints approach (Seidenberg & Gonnerman, 2000). Traditional linguistic and psycholinguistic theories have assumed that words consist of discrete units out of which other words are formed, but because of the quasi-regular character of the system, there has been little agreement about the nature of the units or how they might be recovered in the course of processing. Consider again a word such as *cranberry*: Is it morphologically complex or simple? Intuitively it appears to have an internal structure that is absent in a word such as *kangaroo*, despite the fact that *cran-* has no meaning for most users of the language. *Cranberry* is less puzzling if its etymology is considered: *cran-* derives from the Low German *kraan*, meaning "crane," apparently in reference to the beaklike shape of the plant's stamens. Whether the decision about how to treat *cranberry* should turn on such historical facts depends on the goals of one's theory, and linguists have taken a number of different positions on this issue (e.g., Anderson, 1992; Bybee, 1985). The morphological structure of words in present-day English depends in part on events in the history of the language, including lexical borrowing and diachronic change, that create what appear to be irregularities from the point of view of the language user.

Despite these uncertainties about the nature of morphological units, psycholinguists have pursued the idea that the representations of words in lexical memory include information about their morphological structure, and that this information plays a role in word recognition (see, e.g., Feldman, 1991). The studies are technically challenging because morphological structure is correlated with other types of information. Consider a morphologically complex word such as *government*. The word can be treated as consisting of two morphemes, each of which participates in other words (e.g., *governor, amusement*). Some studies have been taken as providing evidence for a distinct level in lexical memory at which these components of the word are represented (see Caramazza, Laudanna, & Romani, 1988, Taft, 1994, Marslen-Wilson, Tyler, Waksler, & Olden, 1994, for proposals of this type). However, these units might be perceptually salient not because there is a distinct morphological level but because they all happen to be familiar conjunctions of orthographic, phonological, and semantic information. Thus, the fact that *governor* facilitates responses to *govern* in various experimental paradigms (Napps, 1989; Marslen-Wilson et al., 1994) might be due to overlap in terms of these other factors, rather than shared morphological structure per se.

A number of studies have attempted to show that there are effects of morphological structure above and beyond those that are attributable to these other factors. The logic of the studies involves using various control conditions intended to assess effects due to nonmorphological factors. In a classic study, for example, Murrell and Morton (1974) examined the priming of words that were morphologically related (e.g., *cars–car*) and ones that were merely related in form (*card–car*), compared to an unrelated baseline condition (e.g., *book–car*). Because they found priming for pairs such as *cars–car*, but not *card–car*, Murrell and Morton concluded that the effect was due to morphological overlap rather than formal (orthographic-phonological) overlap. However, the effects could also be due to the fact that the *cars–car* pairs are semantically related, whereas the *card–car* items are not. Other studies attempted to address this issue by including items that are semantically but not formally related. If *government–govern* produces larger priming effects than *bread–cake*, this might be taken as evidence for an effect of morphological structure beyond that due to semantic overlap. The problem with this comparison is that *government–govern* exhibit more formal overlap than *bread–cake*. The comparison controls for one confounding factor (semantic overlap) but introduces another (formal overlap).

As another example, consider the studies of "prefix stripping" by Taft and colleagues (e.g., Taft, 1979; Taft & Forster, 1975), which were interpreted as indicating that comprehenders recognized prefixed words by first removing the prefix and then accessing the stem in the lexicon. The original studies in this series were criticized for introducing numerous confounding factors (e.g., Smith & Sterling, 1982). Acknowledging these problems, Taft (1994) attempted to conduct a perfected version of the Taft and Forster (1975) experiment that examined lexical decision latencies for nonwords like *peccable* (from *impeccable*) compared to *tuccable* (which does not occur in any word). The stimuli were carefully equated in terms of factors such as length and bigram (that is, letter pair) frequency that had varied in earlier studies. Nonwords like *peccable* were harder to reject as words than nonwords like *tuccable*. Taft concluded (like Taft & Forster) that *peccable* is a morpheme listed in the lexicon and that words like *impeccable* are recognized by prefix-stripping. However, the stimuli in the two conditions differ on other grounds; stimuli like *peccable* are more familiar letter strings than ones like *tuccable* by virtue of their occurrence in one or more words, even though the bigram frequencies were equated. Differences in the perceived familiarity of the letter string would be expected to influence lexical decision latencies (Seidenberg, 1985). Hence, it cannot be concluded that *peccable* itself is represented as a unit in memory.

The nature of morphological information makes it very difficult for researchers to create conditions that differ only with respect to this aspect of word structure. The usual strategy of designing a factorial experiment that manipulates all of the relevant factors runs into difficulty when the factors are intrinsically highly correlated, as is the case for semantics, orthography, phonology, and morphology. Moreover, it is difficult but necessary to include conditions that examine the interactions between different types of information. For example, it is clear that mere phonological overlap is not sufficient to produce priming under some conditions; thus, in a cross-modal priming study, Marslen-Wilson et al. (1994) found that words that are only formally related (e.g., *tinsel–tin*) did not yield a significant priming effect compared to an unrelated control condition. However, this same kind of overlap may have an effect when words are also semantically related. Thus, there may be an effect of a given type of relatedness only at a certain level of another type of relatedness. The language makes it difficult to create all of the conditions that would assess the independent and joint effects of different aspects of word structure, holding other aspects constant.

Whereas the goal of most existing studies has been to establish morphological effects with these other factors "controlled," our approach entails the opposite idea: that morphological structure is the *result* of confluences among these factors; therefore, morphological effects in word recognition should be predictable from them. The basic idea is that morphology is an intermediate level of representation that develops in the course of acquiring lexical knowledge. Morphological structure represents the convergence of phonological, semantic, and (in literate people) orthographic information and some aspects of syntax. This newer theory replaces the idea of morphemes as minimal units of meaning or "access units" with the idea that morphology is a representation of relationships among words that overlap along different dimensions and in different degrees. The lexicon encodes information about the spellings, sounds, and meanings of words and the mappings between them, plus additional information derived from the contexts in which words occur (e.g., data about the distributions of words in sentences, and grammatical category). The problem of lexical learning is framed in terms of a connectionist network employing distributed representations of these types of information. The lexical network supports computations from orthography to phonology, phonology to meaning, meaning to phonology, and so on, which are utilized in performing tasks such as reading or pronouncing a word.

Figure 9.1 provides a schematic illustration of this approach. The network is a modified version of the Seidenberg and McClelland (1989) model, in which semantic, phonological, and orthographic information are represented by pools of units representing featural primitives and a single set of hidden units mediates the computations between codes. Learning a lexicon involves learning to use these codes to perform different tasks. Listening and reading, for example, involve taking a phonological or orthographic code as input, respectively, and computing meaning; speaking involves taking a semantic code and generating phonology; and so on for other tasks. Connections between the units carry weights that govern the spread of activation through the system; weights are adjusted using a learning algorithm such as back-propagation.

A network trained to perform mappings between codes using standard connectionist learning techniques will pick up on the structure that is implicit in the training corpus with respect to these types of information (subject to limitations imposed by the quality of the input and output representations and other architectural variables). In English, the codes are related in different ways. Previous research has focused on the strong though imperfect correlations between orthography and phonology in monosyllabic words and their role in pronouncing letter strings aloud, another example of a quasiregular system. Reading normally involves computing the meanings of words, however, and in monosyllabic words the correspondences between orthography and semantics are largely arbitrary (as is also true of phonology–semantics, ignoring sound symbolism). However, these correspondences are not arbitrary in complex words; the units we think of as classical morphemes make similar semantic contributions to neighborhoods of related words (e.g., *drink, drinker, drinking, drinkable*). Note that *drink* also makes consistent orthographic and phonological contributions to these words. Importantly, the degree of consistency in the contributions of orthography, phonology, and semantics to related words—the degree to which these codes converge—varies across neighborhoods of words. *Drink* makes highly similar orthographic, phonological, and semantic contributions to different words

Figure 9.1
Lexical Processing Network in Which Interlevel Hidden Units Represent the
Convergence of Codes

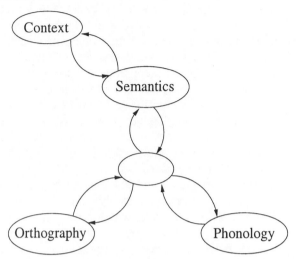

and so behaves like a classical morpheme. In contrast, there is less phonological overlap between *divine* and *divinity* because a vowel change called trisyllabic laxing has applied to the derived form; this difference is also reflected (weakly) in the orthography. Other partial overlaps between words have been created by diachronic changes in pronunciation and meaning. For example, *return* is no longer a prefixed word meaning "to turn again," a fact that is also reflected in the destressing of the initial syllable *re-* (compare to *reload*). However, *return* is not semantically unrelated to the word *turn*, either. *Deliver*, in contrast, is structurally similar to *return* but semantically unrelated to *liver*. In the *-mit* cases (*permit*, etc.), there is a high degree of orthographic and phonological similarity across words, but *-mit* makes only a weak contribution to their meanings. These and other classic morphological phenomena can be seen in terms of degrees of convergence among different types of information across words. Typically, orthography, phonology, and semantics are highly correlated, but the system admits many partial deviations for a variety of reasons.

As described earlier, traditional linguistic and psycholinguistic approaches to these phenomena invoked a discrete notion of morphemic compositionality, involving the nature of morphological rules and exceptions in linguistics and factorial manipulations of morphological complexity in psycholinguistic studies. These approaches miss the broader generalization about the quasi-regular character of the lexicon. *Turn* is very related to *turned* and very unrelated to *retain; turn*'s relationship to *return* falls somewhere in-between.

It would be desirable to have a knowledge representation that reflects these different degrees of relatedness. Thus, the newer approach views the issues in terms of acquiring the knowledge that allows a person to perform tasks such as computing the meaning of a word or generating a pronunciation. Being able to perform such tasks requires acquiring the several codes that constitute knowledge of a word. We use an architecture that encodes this information in terms of mappings between codes. Because it is a connectionist network employing distributed representations, the same weights are used to encode the mappings for many different words. Hence, the weights come to encode different degrees of similarity across words. If the architecture includes an intermediate level of hidden units, it will come to represent convergences between different types of information across words. Thus, a "morphological" level of representation will emerge in the course of learning to perform different language tasks.

This new approach to derivational morphology has begun to be explored in recent empirical work. Gonnerman, Devlin, Anderson, & Seidenberg (1999) describe the results of a study in which a large number of subjects (over 100 per item) were given prefixed or suffixed word pairs such as *head–behead* and *half–behalf* and asked to decide how related they are in meaning using a 9-point scale. Examples of clearly related (e.g., *bake–baker*) and clearly unrelated (e.g., *corn–corner*) pairs were provided, and subjects were encouraged to use the whole scale if appropriate. As in these examples, the stimuli were chosen to neutralize the contribution of phonological factors (thus, items such as *return* were excluded). Subjects' ratings suggested that the complex words differed in the degree to which the stem words (e.g., *bake*) contributed to their meanings; results for a sample of items are presented in Table 9.1. Whereas *rebuild* was rated as closely related to *build*, subjects said there was no *corn* in *corner*. More important, items such as *belittle* and *backer* received intermediate ratings. In general, the ratings formed a continuum, with no obvious discontinuity between morphologically related and morphologically unrelated pairs, consistent with the graded notion of morphological structure. Gonnerman et al. used these ratings of semantic similarity combined with a measure of phonological similarity to account for priming effects in an experiment by Marslen-Wilson et al. (1994) that had been taken as evidence for a discrete level of morphological structure. They also implemented a simple connectionist network that simulated these effects.

Gonnerman, Anderson, and Seidenberg (1999) present four experiments using the cross-modal priming paradigm that examined the contributions of phonological and semantic information to morphological priming effects. One study examined the effects of semantic relatedness holding phonology constant, using pairs that varied in semantic relatedness, such as *baker–bake* (high), *backer–back* (medium), and *corner–corn* (low); unrelated trials such as *backer–corn* and semantically related trials such as *bread–cake*

Table 9.1
Mean Relatedness Ratings

Suffixed			Prefixed		
Stem	Related Word	Rating	Stem	Related Word	Rating
teach	teacher	6.62	build	rebuild	7.45
coward	cowardly	6.64	view	preview	6.98
back	backer	3.21	set	onset	3.46
public	publication	3.26	way	subway	3.02
corn	corner	1.07	tail	retail	1.96
custom	customer	1.70	appoint	disappoint	1.90

Ratings were on a 9-point scale, 1 = unrelated, 9 = highly related.

were also included. Another study examined the effects of phonological relatedness holding degree of semantic overlap constant, as in pairs such as *acceptable–accept* (no change in stem phonology), *criminal–crime* (vowel change), and *introduction–introduce* (vowel and consonant change). In both studies the magnitude of priming effects was a function of the degree of overlap between prime and target. Gonnerman, Anderson, et al. (1999b) also examined pairs such as *jubilant–jubilee* and *glisten–glitter*, which are morphologically unrelated but rated as semantically and phonologically similar. These items produced priming effects similar in magnitude to morphologically related pairs with the same degree of semantic and phonological similarity. This work is still preliminary and has been applied to only limited aspects of morphological structure in English, but the results we have described are consistent with the graded, emergent notion of morphological structure discussed earlier. In the next section, we discuss how a similar approach should capture phenomena in inflectional morphology, particularly formation of the English past tense.

Inflectional Morphology

Inflectional morphology in English consists of the marking of verbs for tense and nouns and verbs for number. This knowledge is acquired in the course of learning the lexicon. In the course of acquisition, the child learns to produce and comprehend many words based on examples, including verbs in their various conjugations. Some of the regularities that the child learns include the past-tense rule in which the morpheme spelled -*ed* is pronounced either /d/, /t/, or /id/, depending on the properties of the prior phoneme, as in *baled, baked,* and *baited.* The past-tense system also includes irregular forms such as *took* and *made*.

Like spelling–sound correspondences and derivational morphology, the English past-tense system is quasi-regular, and therefore is a natural target for connectionist modeling. On this approach a lexical network encodes a complex set of constraints that hold among orthographic, phonological, and semantic codes. The output that the model produces is that which best fits these many simultaneous constraints, given a particular input. The workings of the model can be made clearer by considering the generation tasks that are typically used to assess knowledge of the past tense. Normal speech production involves taking a specification of the semantics of a verb (e.g., *take*) and a specification of pastness (typically represented in implemented models as one or more bits in the distributed semantic representation) and computing phonological output. Behavioral studies dating from Berko (1958) have employed a variant of this task, in which the subject is given a present-tense form and must generate its past tense. If the stimulus is a word (e.g., *take*) and the subject knows its meaning, the input consists of its phonological and semantic codes and the past-tense bit; the output is whatever satisfies these constraints given the settings of the weights. If the stimulus is a nonword (e.g., *wug*), the output must be computed based on a conjunction of its phonological code and the past-tense bit. In another variant of the task, the subject reads rather than hears the present tense of a verb, providing an additional source of information. Thus, past-tense generation is a constraint satisfaction task in which the subject is given different types of information and produces the best-fitting output. Generalization, on this view, simply involves using the weights that were set on the basis of exposure to positive examples to process novel strings. A number of connectionist models have been developed to account for acquisition and adult knowledge of the past tense, including MacWhinney and Leinbach (1991), Plunkett and Marchman (1991), Daugherty and Seidenberg (1992), and Joanisse and Seidenberg (1999).

There is some controversy about the adequacy of this approach to the past tense and other aspects of inflectional morphology. In a series of books and articles, from Pinker and Prince (1988) through Pinker (1999), Pinker and his colleagues have suggested that the past tense involves a different type of knowledge, a symbolic rule. Pinker has proposed a dual-mechanism theory in which a past-tense production rule is supplemented by a connectionist network to handle the irregular cases (such as *sing–sang* and *take–took*). A considerable body of data has been amassed in support of this theory. The evidence principally concerns dissociations between rule-governed forms and exceptions. The basic logic is that any differences between regulars and exceptions count against the connectionist approach in which a single network is used to process both. At the same time, Pinker and colleagues have pointed out various limitations of the connectionist approach, claiming, for example, that linguistic phenomena exhibit properties that cannot be captured by such nets or could be captured only by "implementing" the rule-based theory. These claims have elicited a number of critical responses over the years (e.g., MacWhinney & Leinbach, 1991; Seidenberg, 1992; Seidenberg & Hoeffner, 1998).

We cannot provide a detailed review of this controversy in the space available, but a summary of the main issues follows. Our general view is that there are close correspondences between the past tense and the spelling–sound phenomena investigated previously (Seidenberg & McClelland, 1989), that the principles that were used in the reading models extend gracefully to the past tense, that the kinds of data and arguments used to support the dual-mechanism past-tense model have already been addressed in the spelling–sound domain, and that the limitations of the connectionist approach have been greatly overstated. Thus, there is a strong basis for developing a theory that provides a better account of the detailed aspects of the phenomena, using general principles rather than ones specific to the past tense.

Dissociations Do Not Demand Separate Mechanisms

The assumption underlying much of the debate is that because the connectionist approach uses a single mechanism for both regulars and exceptions it predicts that they should always behave alike. This claim has set off a vigorous hunt for ways in which they differ. The assumption is wrong, however. Forms that are nominally "rule-governed" or "exceptions" according to the dual-mechanism theory differ in ways that affect network performance. The kinds of dissociations that have been identified do not distinguish between the theories because they arise for different reasons in our nets. For example, Prasada and Pinker (1993) noted that frequency has a bigger effect on the generation of irregular past tenses than regular. This "dissociation" was taken as evidence for two mechanisms, one frequency sensitive (the associative net) and the other not (rule application). However, this is merely the frequency by regularity interaction that has been prominent in research on spelling–sound conversion; it was simulated by the Seidenberg and McClelland (1989) model, and Plaut, McClelland, Seidenberg, and Patterson (1996) provided a mathematical and computational analysis of it.

This situation, in which differences between regulars and exceptions said to favor the dual-mechanism theory are already understood within connectionist theory, recurs throughout the large literature on the past tense. To take one other example, Marslen-Wilson and Tyler (1997) presented data concerning patients who exhibited impaired knowledge of verbs, with some more impaired on exceptions and others on regulars. This "double dissociation" suggested that brain injury can selectively impair the routes in the dual-route model. However, these impairments are closely related to acquired forms of dyslexia in which patients are more impaired on reading either exception words (surface dyslexia) or rule-governed forms (phonological dyslexia). Plaut et al. (1996) provided an account of these impairments in terms of damage to semantic versus phonological representations, which have different effects on exceptions versus regulars, respectively; the same account has been extended to the verb impairments. Joanisse and Seidenberg (1999) describe a connectionist network that, when lesioned in different ways, produces the patterns of impaired performance seen in patient studies such as Ullman et al. (1997). Thus, connectionist research has strongly called into question the traditional approach to the interpretation of double-dissociation data that Marslen-Wilson and Tyler (1997) employ (for additional discussion, see Plaut, 1995).

There Are Unresolved Empirical Questions

Pinker and colleagues have reported data drawn from domains including acquisition, skilled performance, and language breakdown, and two languages (English, German), and so the sheer amount of evidence presented as favoring their position is enormous. As noted, some of these phenomena can be explained by existing models. In other areas, questions have been raised about how accurately the phenomena have been characterized (see, e.g., Hoeffner's, 1997, re-examination of the Marcus et al., 1992, acquisition data; similar controversies have arisen in other areas, e.g., claims about selective developmental impairments in inflectional morphology; Gopnik & Crago, 1991; Leonard, McGregor, & Allen, 1992; Joanisse & Seidenberg, 1998).

Methodological Problems with Particular Experiments

As we observed in the case of prefix stripping, experimental investigation of morphological processes is extraordinarily difficult, and the literature contains many cases that fail to test the issues as intended. As an example, Seidenberg and Hoeffner (1998) discuss the PET neuroimaging study by Jaeger et al. (1996) that appeared to provide decisive evidence for the dual-mechanism approach. They observed that this study, like others in the literature, was designed to provide evidence consistent with the dual-mechanism theory but did not test valid predictions derived from the connectionist alternative.

Overgeneralizations from the Limitations of a Single Model to the Entire Connectionist Approach

Pinker focuses his critique of connectionist models on an early attempt to model the acquisition of the English past tense by Rumelhart and McClelland (1986a) (see Pinker, 1999), but he conflates the limitations of this model with limitations of the entire approach. For example, the Rumelhart and McClelland model was limited to phonological representations and therefore could not handle homophones such as *ring–rang* and *ring–ringed*. This limitation does not apply in the Joanisse and Seidenberg (1999) model described earlier, which incorporates Rumelhart and McClelland's basic insights about the nature of the problem but includes orthography and semantic representations in addition to phonology. Pinker and Prince (1988) noted that "adding semantics" to the Rumelhart and McClelland model would not solve its problems; they asserted that a model that used semantic information would err on items such as *slap, hit*, and *strike*, which are semantically related but form their past tenses three different ways. The assertion is false, however. If the semantics of verbs are not predictive of the past tense and the training set accurately reflects this fact, the model cannot learn the opposite, incorrect generalization. It is trivial to compute one or the other past tense of *ring* based on a conjunction of its phonological form and meaning. Pinker and Prince made several valid points about the limitations of the Rumelhart and McClelland model, but their broader assertions about how networks behave in general and about their intrinsic limitations do not follow.

We intend to address other issues that have arisen in this controversy elsewhere. In closing this discussion we should point out that further progress is likely to be made by pursuing the similarities between the past-tense and spelling–sound problems. The Pinker (1994) model is a variant of Coltheart, Curtis, Atkins, and Haller's (1993) dual-route model of reading; both involve a rule component and an associative net. Both systems are quasi-regular: They are systematic and productive but also admit many exceptions that deviate from central tendencies in differing degrees. In both cases the irregular forms are not arbitrary; they share structure with the rule-governed forms. There are phonological similarities between regular and irregular past tenses (e.g., *stepped* versus *slept*), and between present and past tenses of both regulars and irregulars (e.g., in both *bake–baked* and *take–took* the past tense retains the onset and coda of the present tense). Even the suppletive form *went* shares structure with rule-governed past tenses insofar as it ends in /t/, one of the allomorphs of the regular past-tense suffix.[7] In addition, there are phonological similarities among subpools of exceptions (e.g., *sing–sang, ring–rang*). Analogous phenomena occur in the spelling–sound case: *Have* is irregularly spelled, but its spelling shares structure with the rule-governed forms *hat* and *hive*; the irregulars form nonarbitrary pools such as *done–none–does*, *sweat–threat–death*, and so on. As is true of the past tense, the irregular spelling forms tend to cluster among the higher-frequency words in the language. Because the same weighted connections are used in producing all forms, connectionist networks provide a natural way to represent these partial regularities. Dual-mechanism models, in which rule-governed forms and exceptions are handled by separate, unrelated mechanisms, do not. This may explain why the dissociations between regular and irregular forms tend to be partial rather than complete (Joanisse & Seidenberg, 1999).

The theoretical links between this account of inflectional morphology and the previous discussion of derivational morphology should be apparent. Inflectional and derivational morphology are different aspects of the knowledge encoded by the lexical network. We view both in terms of acquiring and representing lexical knowledge that permits people to perform specific tasks. The primary tasks are producing and comprehending words, but other tasks include generating morphologically related forms, creating new words, or deciding if a letter string is a word in the language or not. In both areas the critical issues concern relationships among related forms and the treatment of items that deviate from central tendencies. In both cases we exploit the capacity of the network to encode differing degrees of overlap between forms, and use this to explain facts about performance.

This approach is schematic in its present form and will need further development and testing. There is an obvious need to implement models like the one in Figure 9.1 and train them on the realistic corpora needed in order to develop humanlike generalizations about the structure of the lexicon. Moreover, the lexical processing system we have been describing needs to be integrated with a sequential network that processes sentences. To this point, models of the lexicon and models of sentence processing have tended to be pursued independently, using somewhat different architectures (e.g., attractor networks, simple recurrent networks). We think the link between the two is provided by the concept of a lexical processing system capable of tracking multiple types of probabilistic information. Although the technical challenges to mating these two approaches are considerable, the theoretical motivation for pursuing this effort seems clear.

PROSPECTS

Researchers within the generative tradition often assume that the goal of this work is to show that language is not innate or highly structured; thus, it represents a return to a form of empiricism that most linguists thought was conclusively refuted years ago (see, for example, Pinker, 1991; Wexler, 1991). Our assumption is that modern cognitive neuroscience and developmental neurobiology provide alternatives to both the Chomskian version of nativism and *tabula rasa* empiricism. It seems obvious that children are born with capacities to think, perceive, and learn that allow them to acquire language, whereas other animals, such as chimpanzees, do not. However, the hypothesis that children are born with knowledge of Universal Grammar may not be the only way to explain the facts about acquisition. At this point we do not have confidence in the validity of various arguments in support of innate Universal Grammar, but this does not mean the hypothesis is necessarily wrong. Our assumption is that we cannot validly infer what is innate without thoroughly investigating what can be learned. It is already clear that much more can be learned on the basis of the input available to the child, using simple and general learning mechanisms, than the generative approach has assumed. How far these mechanisms take the child toward the adult steady state is not known, but needs to be investigated thoroughly.

FURTHER READINGS

The classical arguments concerning the innateness of grammar and the poverty of the stimulus are summarized in every linguistics textbook or monograph on language acquisition; see Crain and Thornton (1998) and Lightfoot (1999) for recent examples. Pinker (1999) provides an accessible overview and argument for the innateness position with many humorous touches. For an alternative position, see Elman et al. (1996).

A breakthrough in the study of language acquisition was achieved with the development of experimental methods that can be used with infants; Jusczyk (1997) summarizes his own important contributions in this area and related work.

The classic texts in connectionist theory are the PDP volumes (Rumelhart & McClelland, 1986b; McClelland & Rumelhart, 1986), which include the famous verb-learning paper that elicited such a strong response from linguists and psycholinguists of the generative persuasion. Elman et al. (1996) provide an overview of basic connectionist concepts, but more important, their book articulates a view of innate capacities that is based on evidence about brain structure and development, rather than inferences about what must be innate given a set of behavioral facts (e.g., about acquisition).

The series of connectionist models of visual word recognition (Seidenberg & McClelland, 1989; Plaut et al., 1996; Harm & Seidenberg, 1999) provides perhaps the best-worked-out example of a connectionist theory of behavior. Many of the ideas about knowledge representation, learning, and processing discussed in this chapter were developed in the course of work on word recognition. This work is clearly relevant to constraint satisfaction processes at other levels of language comprehension. MacDonald et al. (1994) and Tanenhaus and Trueswell (1995) review the role of probabilistic constraints in sentence processing. Though many of the ideas are the same at the word and sentence level, the probabilistic constraints have received a much greater degree of implementation in word recognition than in sentence processing. This pattern is slowly changing, and Tabor and Tanenhaus (Chapter 6, this volume) is one such example.

NOTES

Preparation of this chapter was supported by grants NIMH MH PO1-47566, NIMH MH KO2 01188, and NSF SBR95-11270. We thank Morten Christiansen and Joseph Allen for helpful discussions.

1. Although Chomsky (1986, p. 3) remarks that "generative" means nothing more than "explicit," we use the term to identify the body of linguistic and psycholinguistic research inspired by his thinking.

2. This chapter provides a brief overview of a theoretical framework that has emerged out of the work of many people. Space limitations preclude a comprehensive review of the literature (see MacWhinney, 1998; MacWhinney & Chang, 1995;

Chater & Christiansen, 1999; Christiansen & Chater, Chapter 2, this volume). We have attempted to develop an integrated framework that, while not sui generis, casts the issues in a particular way, one that derives in large part from considering language acquisition from the perspective provided by what is known about adult performance.

3. To this list we would now add What is the neurobiological basis of language? and How did language evolve in the species?

4. Allen and Seidenberg (1999) discuss why this result obtained. In brief, the crucial fact is that although the words in a sentence like *Colorless* have very low transition probabilities, they contain familiar sequences of semantic types, such as < PROPERTY PROPERTY THING ACTION MANNER >. At this level they are comparable to grammatical sentences with higher word-transition probabilities. In contrast, ungrammatical sentences such as < IDEAS COLORLESS SLEEP FURIOUSLY GREEN > do not contain such sequences (thus, < THING PROPERTY ACTION MANNER PROPERTY > does not occur in the language). The model was sensitive to both types of sequential information and therefore treated grammatical and ungrammatical sentences differently.

5. For early statements of this general idea, see Marslen-Wilson and Welsh (1978) and Rumelhart (1977).

6. Pinker (1987) discussed bootstrapping mechanisms in language acquisition in terms of constraint satisfaction principles drawn from artificial intelligence. This is a symbolic notion of constraint satisfaction somewhat different than the one discussed here (see Macworth, 1977). However, Pinker's description of the verb-learning problem as one involving multiple simultaneous constraints was rather accurate. He closed his article by noting that connectionist models were said to be able to efficiently compute complex interactions among constraints, but that a connectionist researcher had told him that this was a difficult problem.

7. This observation is due to Jay McClelland.

REFERENCES

Allen, J. (1997). Probabilistic constraints in acquisition. In A. Sorace, C. Heycock, & R. Shillcock (Eds.), *Proceedings of the GALA '97 Conference on Language Acquisition* (pp. 300–305). Edinburgh: University of Edinburgh.

Allen, J., & Seidenberg, M. S. (1999). The emergence of grammaticality in connectionist networks. In B. MacWhinney (Ed.), *The emergence of language* (pp. 115–151). Mahwah, NJ: Lawrence Erlbaum.

Altmann, G.T.M., & Steedman, M. (1988). Interaction with context during human sentence processing. *Cognition, 30*, 191–238.

Anderson, S. R. (1992). *A-Morphous morphology*. New York: Cambridge University Press.

Aronoff, M. (1976). *Word formation in generative grammar*. Cambridge, MA: MIT Press.

Aslin, R. N., Woodward, J. Z., LaMendola, N. P., & Bever, T. G. (1996). Models of word segmentation in fluent maternal speech to infants. In J. L. Morgan & K. Demuth (Eds.), *From signal to syntax* (pp. 117–134). Mahwah, NJ: Lawrence Erlbaum.

Atkinson, M. (1992). *Children's syntax: An introduction to principles and parameters theory*. Oxford: Blackwell.

Badecker, W., Hillis, A., & Caramazza, A. (1990). Lexical morphology and its role in the writing process: Evidence from a case of acquired dysgraphia. *Cognition, 35*, 205–243.

Bates, E., & MacWhinney, B. (1982). Functionalist approaches to grammar. In E. Wanner & L. Gleitman (Eds.), *Language acquisition: The state of the art*. New York: Cambridge University Press.

Berko, J. (1958). The child's learning of English morphology. *Word, 14*, 150–177.

Bickerton, D. (1984). The language bioprogram. *Behavioral and Brain Sciences, 7*, 173–221.

Bock, J. K., & Eberhard, K. M. (1993). Meaning, sound and syntax in English number agreement. *Language and Cognitive Processes, 8*, 57–99.

Bowerman, M. (1982). Evaluating competing linguistic models with language acquisition data: Implications of developmental errors with causative verbs. *Quaderni di Semantica, 3*, 5–66.

Bybee, J. L. (1985). *Morphology: A study of the relation between meaning and form*. Philadelphia: John Benjamins.

Caramazza, A., Laudanna, A., & Romani, C. (1988). Lexical access and inflectional morphology. *Cognition, 28*, 297–332.

Charniak, E. (1997). Statistical techniques for natural-language parsing. *AI Magazine, 18*, 33–43.

Chater, N., & Christiansen, M. H. (1999). Connectionism and natural language processing. In S. Garrod & M. Pickering (Eds.), *Language processing* (pp. 233–279). Cambridge, MA: MIT Press.

Chomsky, N. (1957). *Syntactic structures*. The Hague: Mouton.

Chomsky, N. (1965). *Aspects of the theory of syntax*. Cambridge, MA: MIT Press.

Chomsky, N. (1986). *Knowledge of language*. New York: Praeger.

Christiansen, M. H., Allen, J., & Seidenberg, M. S. (1998). Learning to segment speech using multiple cues: A connectionist model. *Language and Cognitive Processes, 13*, 221–268.

Christiansen, M. H., & Chater, N. (1999). Toward a connectionist model of recursion in human linguistic performance. *Cognitive Science, 23*, 157–205.

Collins, M., & Brooks, J. (1995). Prepositional phrase attachment through a backed-off model. In *Proceedings of the Third Workshop on Very Large Corpora*.

Coltheart, M., Curtis, B., Atkins, P., & Haller, M. (1993). Models of reading aloud: Dual-route and parallel-distributed-processing approaches. *Psychological Review, 100*, 589–608.

Crain, S. (1991). Language acquisition in the absence of experience. *Behavioral and Brain Sciences, 14*, 597–650.

Crain, S., & Thornton, R. (1998). *Investigations in universal grammar: A guide to experiments on the acquisition of syntax and semantics*. Cambridge, MA: MIT Press.

Daugherty, K., & Seidenberg, M. S. (1992). Rules or connections? The past tense revisited. In *Proceedings of the Fourteenth Annual Conference of the Cognitive Science Society* (pp. 259–264). Hillsdale, NJ: Lawrence Erlbaum.

Elman, J. L. (1990). Finding structure in time. *Cognitive Science, 14*, 179–211.

Elman, J. L., Bates E. A., Johnson M. H., Karmiloff-Smith, A., Parisi, D., & Plunkett, K. (1996). *Rethinking innateness: A connectionist perspective on development*. Cambridge, MA: MIT Press.

Feldman, L. (Ed.). (1991). *Morphological aspects of language processing*. Hillsdale, NJ: Lawrence Erlbaum.

Fisher, C., Gleitman, H., & Gleitman, L. (1991). On the semantic content of subcategorization frames. *Cognitive Psychology, 23, 331–392.*

Fodor, J. A., & Pylyshyn, Z. W. (1988). Connectionism and cognitive architecture: A critical analysis. *Cognition, 28*, 3–71.

Frazier, L. (1987). Sentence processing: A tutorial review. In M. Coltheart (Ed.), *Attention and performance 12: The psychology of reading* (pp. 559–586). Hillsdale, NJ: Lawrence Erlbaum.

Gibson, E. (1998). Linguistic complexity: Locality of syntactic dependencies. *Cognition, 68*, 1–76.

Gillette, J., Gleitman, H., Gleitman, L., & Lederer, A. (1998). *Human simulations of vocabulary learning*. Manuscript submitted for publication.

Gleitman, L. (1990). The structural sources of verb meanings. *Language Acquisition, 1*, 3–55.

Gold, E. M. (1967). Language identification in the limit. *Information and Control, 16*, 447–474.

Gonnerman, L. M., Andersen, E. A., & Seidenberg, M. S. (1999). *Graded semantic and phonological effects in lexical priming: Evidence for a distributed connectionist approach to morphology*. Manuscript submitted for publication.

Gonnerman, L. M., Devlin, J. T., Andersen, E. S., & Seidenberg, M. S. (1999). *Derivational morphology as an emergent interlevel representation*. Unpublished manuscript.

Gopnik, M., & Crago, M. B. (1991). Familial aggregation of a developmental language disorder. *Cognition, 39*, 1–50.

Grimshaw, J. (1990). *Argument structure*. Cambridge, MA: MIT Press.

Harm, M. W., & Seidenberg, M. S. (1999). Phonology, reading acquisition, and dyslexia: Insights from connectionist models. *Psychological Review, 106*, 491–528.

Hindle, D., & Rooth, M. (1993). Structural ambiguity and lexical relations. *Computational Linguistics, 19*, 103–120.

Hoeffner, J. (1997). *Are rules a thing of the past? A connectionist approach to inflectional morphology*. Unpublished doctoral dissertation, Department of Psychology, Carnegie Mellon University.

Jaeger, J. J., Lockwood, A. H., Kemmerer, D. L., VanValin, R. D., Murphy, B. W., & Khalak, H. G. (1996). Positron emission tomographic study of regular and irregular verb morphology in English. *Language, 72*, 451–497.

Joanisse, M., & Seidenberg, M. S. (1998). Specific language impairment: A deficit in grammar or in processing? *Trends in Cognitive Science, 2*, 240–246.

Joanisse, M., & Seidenberg, M. S. (1999). Impairments in verb morphology following brain injury: A connectionist model. *Proceedings of the National Academy of Sciences, 96*, 7592–7597.

Jusczyk, P. W. (1997). *The discovery of spoken language*. Cambridge, MA: MIT Press.

Kelly, M. H. (1992). Using sound to resolve syntactic problems: The role of phonology in grammatical category assignments. *Psychological Review, 99*, 349–364.

Kim, J., Bangalore, S., & Trueswell, J. C. (in press). The convergence of lexicalist perspectives in psycholinguistics and computational linguistics. In P. Merlo & S. Stevenson (Eds.), *Lexical basis for sentence processing*. Philadelphia: John Benjamins.

Landau, B., & Gleitman, L. (1985). *Language and experience: Evidence from the blind child.* Cambridge, MA: Harvard University Press.

Leonard, L. B., McGregor, K. K., & Allen, G. D. (1992). Grammatical morphology and speech-perception in children with specific language impairment. *Journal of Speech and Hearing Research, 35,* 1076–1085.

Levin, B. (1993). *English verb classes and alternations: A preliminary study.* Chicago: University of Chicago Press.

Lightfoot, D. (1982). *The language lottery.* Cambridge, MA: MIT Press.

Lightfoot, D. (1991). *How to set parameters: Arguments from language change.* Cambridge, MA: MIT Press.

Lightfoot, D. (1999). *The development of language.* Oxford: Blackwell.

Linebarger, M. C., Schwartz, M. F., & Saffran, E. M. (1983). Sensitivity to grammatical structure in so-called agrammatic aphasics. *Cognition, 13,* 361–392.

MacDonald, M. C. (1994). Probabilistic constraints and syntactic ambiguity resolution. *Language and Cognitive Processes, 9,* 157–201.

MacDonald, M. C. (1999). Distributional information in language comprehension, production, and acquisition: Three puzzles and a moral. In B. MacWhinney (Ed.), *The emergence of language.* Mahwah, NJ: Lawrence Erlbaum.

MacDonald, M. C., & Christiansen, M. H. (in press). Reassessing working memory: A comment on Just & Carpenter (1992) and Waters & Caplan (1996). *Psychological Review.*

MacDonald, M. C., Pearlmutter, N. J., & Seidenberg, M. S. (1994). The lexical nature of syntactic ambiguity resolution. *Psychological Review, 101,* 676–703.

MacWhinney, B. (1998). Models of the emergence of language. *Annual Review of Psychology, 49,* 199–227.

MacWhinney, B., & Chang, F. (1995). Connectionism and language learning. In N. C. Alexander (Ed.), *Basic and applied perspectives on learning, cognition, and development. The Minnesota Symposia on Child Psychology* (Vol. 28, pp. 33–57). Mahwah, NJ: Lawrence Erlbaum.

MacWhinney, B., & Leinbach, J. (1991). Implementations are not conceptualizations: Revising the verb learning model. *Cognition, 40,* 121–157.

Macworth, A. (1977). Consistency in networks of relations. *Artificial Intelligence, 8,* 99–118.

Marcus, G. F., Pinker, S., Ullmen, M., Hollander, J., Rosen, T., & Xu, F. (1992). Overregularization in language acquisition. *Monographs of the Society for Research in Child Development, 57* [Serial No. 228].

Marslen-Wilson, W. D., & Tyler, L. K. (1997). Dissociating types of mental computation. *Nature, 387,* 592–594.

Marslen-Wilson, W. D., Tyler, L. K., Waksler, R., & Older, L. (1994). Morphology and meaning in the English mental lexicon. *Psychological Review, 101,* 3–33.

Marslen-Wilson, W. D., & Welsh, A. (1978). Processing interactions and lexical access during word recognition in continuous speech. *Cognitive Psychology, 10,* 29–63.

McClelland, J. L., & Rumelhart, D. E. (Eds.). (1986). *Parallel distributed processing: Explorations in the microstructure of cognition.* Vol. 2: *Psychological and biological models.* Cambridge, MA: MIT Press.

McRae, K., Spivey-Knowlton, M. J., & Tanenhaus, M. K. (1998). Modeling the influence of thematic fit (and other constraints) in on-line sentence comprehension. *Journal of Memory and Language, 38,* 283–312.

Mintz, T. H., Newport, E. L., & Bever, T. G. (1998). *The distributional structure of grammatical categories in speech to young children*. Manuscript submitted for publication.

Mitchell, D. C., Cuetos, F., Corley, M.M.B., & Brysbaert, M. (1995). Exposure-based models of human parsing: Evidence for the use of coarse-grained (non-lexical) statistical records. *Journal of Psycholinguistic Research, 24*, 469–488.

Moon, C., Panneton-Cooper, R. P., & Fifer, W. P. (1993). Two-day infants prefer their native language. *Infant Behavior Development, 16*, 495–500.

Morgan, J. (1986). *From simple input to complex grammar*. Cambridge, MA: MIT Press.

Morgan, J., & Demuth, K. (Ed.). (1996). *Signal to syntax: Bootstrapping from speech to grammar in early acquisition*. Mahwah, NJ: Lawrence Erlbaum.

Murrell, G. A., & Morton, J. (1974). Word recognition and morphemic structure. *Journal of Experimental Psychology, 102*, 963–968.

Naigles, L. G., Gleitman, H., & Gleitman, L. (1993). Children acquire word meaning components from syntactic evidence. In E. Dromi (Ed.), *Language and cognition: A developmental perspective*. Norword, NJ: Ablex.

Napps, S. E. (1989). Morphemic relationships in the lexicon: Are they distinct from semantic and formal relationships? *Memory & Cognition, 17*, 729–739.

Pearlmutter, N. J., Daugherty, K. G., MacDonald, M. C., & Seidenberg, M. S. (1994). Modeling the use of frequency and contextual biases in sentence processing. In *Proceedings of the Sixteenth Annual Conference of the Cognitive Science Society* (pp. 699–704). Hillsdale, NJ: Lawrence Erlbaum.

Pearlmutter, N. J., & MacDonald, M. C. (1992). Plausibility and syntactic ambiguity resolution. In *Proceedings of the Fourteenth Annual Conference of the Cognitive Science Society* (pp. 498–503). Hillsdale, NJ: Lawrence Erlbaum.

Pinker, S. (1987). The bootstrapping problem in language acquisition. In B. MacWhinney (Ed.), *Mechanisms of language acquisition* (pp. 339–441). Hillsdale, NJ: Lawrence Erlbaum.

Pinker, S. (1989). *Learnability and cognition*. Cambridge, MA: MIT Press.

Pinker, S. (1991). Rules of language. *Science, 253*, 530–535.

Pinker, S. (1994). How could a child use verb syntax to learn verb semantics. In L. Gleitman & B. Landau (Eds.), *The acquisition of the lexicon* (pp. 377–410). Cambridge, MA: MIT Press.

Pinker, S. (1999). *Words and rules: The ingredients of language*. New York: Basic Books.

Pinker, S., & Prince, A. (1988). On language and connectionism: Analysis of a parallel distributed processing model of language acquisition. *Cognition, 28*, 73–193.

Plaut, D. C. (1995). Semantic and associative priming in a distributed attractor network. *Proceedings of the Seventeenth Annual Conference of the Cognitive Science Society* (pp. 37–42). Hillsdale, NJ: Lawrence Erlbaum.

Plaut, D. C., McClelland, J. L., Seidenberg, M. S., & Patterson, K. E. (1996). Understanding normal and impaired word reading: Computational principles in quasi-regular domains. *Psychological Review, 103*, 56–115.

Plunkett, K., & Marchman, V. (1991). U-shaped learning and frequency effects in a multilayered perceptron: Implications for child language-acquisition. *Cognition, 38*, 43–102.

Prasada, S., & Pinker, S. (1993). Generalization of regular and irregular morphological patterns. *Language and Cognitive Processes, 8*, 1–56.

Redington, M., Chater, N., & Finch, S. (1998). Distributional information: A powerful cue for acquiring syntactic categories. *Cognitive Science, 22*, 425–469.

Rumelhart, D. E. (1977). Toward an interactive model of reading. In S. Dornic (Ed.), *Attention and performance VI* (pp. 220–235). Hillsdale, NJ: Lawrence Erlbaum.

Rumelhart, D. E., & McClelland, J. L. (1986a). On learning the past tenses of English verbs. In J. L. McClelland & D. E. Rumelhart (Eds.), *Parallel distributed processing: Explorations in the microstructure of cognition*. Vol. 2: *Psychological and biological models* (pp. 216–271). Cambridge, MA: MIT Press.

Rumelhart, D. E., & McClelland, J. L. (Eds.). (1986b). *Parallel distributed processing: Explorations in the microstructure of cognition*. Vol. 1: *Foundations*. Cambridge, MA: MIT Press.

Saffran, J. R., Aslin, R. N., & Newport, E. L. (1996). Statistical learning by 8-month-old infants. *Science, 274*, 1926–1928.

Schuetze, H. (1997). *Ambiguity resolution in language learning: Computational and cognitive models*. Stanford, CA: CSLI.

Seidenberg, M. S. (1985). The time course of information activation and utilization in visual word recognition. In D. Besner, T. Waller, & G. Mackinnon (Eds.), *Reading research: Advances in theory and practice* (Vol. 5, pp. 200–252). New York: Academic Press.

Seidenberg, M. S. (1992). Connectionism without tears. In S. Davis (Ed.), *Connectionism: Advances in theory and practice* (pp. 84–122). Oxford: Oxford University Press.

Seidenberg, M. S. (1997). Language acquisition and use: Learning and applying probabilistic constraints. *Science, 275*, 1599–1603.

Seidenberg, M. S., & Gonnerman, L. (2000). Explaining derivational morphology as the convergence of codes. *Trends in Cognitive Science, 4*, 353–361.

Seidenberg, M. S., & Hoeffner, J. H. (1998). Evaluating behavioral and neuroimaging data on past tense processing. *Language, 74*, 104–122.

Seidenberg, M. S., & McClelland, J. L. (1989). A distributed, developmental model of word recognition and naming. *Psychological Review, 96*, 523–568.

Smith, P. T., & Sterling, C. M. (1982). Factors affecting the perceived morphemic structure of written words. *Journal of Verbal Learning and Verbal Behavior, 21*, 704–721.

Spencer, A. (1991). *Morphology*. Oxford: Basil Blackwell.

Spivey-Knowlton, M. J., &. Sedivy, J. (1995). Resolving attachment ambiguities with multiple constraints. *Cognition, 55*, 227–267.

Spivey-Knowlton, M. J., Trueswell, J. C., & Tanenhaus, M. K. (1993). Context effects in syntactic ambiguity resolution: Discourse and semantic influences in parsing reduced relative clauses. *Canadian Journal of Experimental Psychology, 47*, 276–309.

Tabossi, P., Spivey-Knowlton, M. J., McRae, K., & Tanenhaus, M. K. (1994). Semantic effects on syntactic ambiguity resolution: Evidence for a constraint-based resolution process. In C. Umilta & M. Moscovitch (Eds.), *Attention and performance XV* (pp. 589–616). Cambridge, MA: MIT Press.

Taft, M. (1979). Lexical access via an orthographic code: The basic orthographic syllable structure (BOSS). *Journal of Verbal Learning and Verbal Behavior, 18,* 21–40.

Taft, M. (1994). Interactive-activation as a framework for understanding morphological processing. *Language and Cognitive Processes, 9,* 271–294.

Taft, M., & Forster, K. (1975). Lexical storage and retrieval of prefixed words. *Journal of Verbal Learning and Verbal Behavior, 14,* 638–647.

Tanenhaus, M. K., & Trueswell, J. C. (1995). Sentence comprehension. In J. L. Miller & P. Eimas (Eds.), *Handbook of perception and cognition 11: Speech, language, and communication* (pp. 217–262). New York: Academic Press.

Taraban, R., & McClelland, J. L. (1988). Constituents attachment and thematic role assignment in sentence processing: Influences of content-based expectations. *Journal of Memory and Language, 27,* 597–632.

Trueswell, J. C. (1996). The role of lexical frequency in syntactic ambiguity resolution. *Journal of Memory and Language, 35,* 566–585.

Trueswell, J. C., Sekerina, I., Hill, N. M., & Logrip, M. L. (in press). The kindergarten-path effect: Studying on-line sentence processing in young children. *Cognition.*

Trueswell, J. C., Tanenhaus, M. K., & Garnsey, S. M. (1994). Semantic influences on parsing: Use of thematic role information in syntactic ambiguity resolution. *Journal of Memory and Language, 33,* 285–318.

Tyler, L. K., Marslen-Wilson, W. D., Rentoul, J., & Hanney, P. (1988). Continuous and discontinuous access in spoken-word recognition: The role of derivational prefixes. *Journal of Memory and Language, 27,* 368–381.

Ullman, M. T., Corkin, S., Coppola, M., Hickok, G., Growdon, J. H., Koroshetz, W. J., & Pinker, S. (1997). A neural dissociation within language: Evidence that the mental dictionary is part of declarative memory, and that grammatical rules are processed by the procedural system. *Journal of Cognitive Neuroscience, 9,* 266–276.

Wexler, K. (1990). Innateness and maturation in linguistic development. *Developmental Psychobiology, 23,* 645–660.

Wexler, K. (1991). On the argument from the poverty of the stimulus. In A. Kasher (Ed.), *The Chomskyan turn.* Oxford: Blackwell.

10

Grammar-Based Connectionist Approaches to Language

Paul Smolensky

This chapter is addressed to basic methodological issues arising in connectionist research on language. I will attempt to briefly sketch a lengthy argument begun in Smolensky, Legendre, and Miyata (1992) and presented in detail in Smolensky and Legendre (2001). In many places I will try to articulate personal viewpoints and, to a very limited degree, justify them. The focus is on two main claims. The first is that there are two general styles of research that both deserve a central place in connectionist approaches to language. The first, model-based research, is well-established. The second, grammar-based research, is less so. Each approach, I will argue, has important strengths that are lacking in the other. The second main claim is that the time has come to stop regarding generative grammar and connectionist approaches to language as incompatible research paradigms. Each has significant potential for contributing to the other. I will suggest a view of the core theoretical commitments of the two paradigms, connectionism and generative linguistics, and argue that these commitments combine to support a coherent and fruitful research program in connectionist-grounded generative grammar. It is my belief, although I will not attempt to justify it in detail here, that the core commitments I identify are indeed consensus beliefs of the connectionist and generative linguistics research communities.

Going beyond the core commitments, individual researchers have further commitments that are often not mutually compatible, and these competing scientific hypotheses must of course be adjudicated by theoretical and empirical arguments. But at this level, competition between incompatible hypotheses is readily found among generative grammarians themselves, or among connectionists themselves, as well as between generative linguists and connectionists. Thus, it seems to me more accurate to regard the current scientific debates about language as individual conflicts between individual hypotheses, rather than a war between two unified paradigms, Connectionism and Generative Grammar.

COMMITMENTS OF CONNECTIONISM

The parallel distributed processing (PDP) school of connectionism is founded, it seems to me, on the following general principles (Rumelhart & McClelland, 1986b):

(1) Fundamental commitments of connectionism: The PDP principles
  a. Mental representations are distributed patterns of numerical activity.
  b. Mental processes are massively parallel transformations of activity patterns by patterns of numerical connections.
  c. Knowledge acquisition results from the interaction of
    i.   innate learning rules.
    ii. innate architectural features.
    iii. modification of connection strengths with experience.

Testing the implications of these fundamental principles is a challenge in part because of their great generality: Depending on how they are instantiated, they can be used to support a number of contradictory claims concerning fundamental issues, such as modularity and nativism. This diversity of potential implications of the PDP principles was already rather clearly in evidence in the earliest PDP models, as the representative citations in the following paragraphs show.

Consider the first PDP principle: Mental representations are distributed patterns of numerical activity. This can easily be seen as entailing that mental representations are crucially graded (nondiscrete). Indeed, this is the default case illustrated by many connectionist models, including the majority of the early ones discussed in Rumelhart and McClelland (1986b) and McClelland and Rumelhart (1986).

However, this same PDP principle is consistent with the claim that mental representations are discrete, as seen in a number of classes of connectionist model. Most obviously, representations are discrete in networks with discrete-valued units (e.g., the original Boltzmann Machine—Hinton and Sejnowski, 1983—and Harmony Theory—Smolensky, 1983—architectures).

But discreteness also plays a crucial role in the important class of models with continuous units that converge to discrete representations (e.g., Anderson, Silverstein, Ritz, & Jones, 1977; Rumelhart, Smolensky, McClelland, & Hinton, 1986), including models with "winner-take-all" subnetworks (e.g., Grossberg, 1976; Feldman & Ballard, 1982; Rumelhart & Zipser, 1985; Mozer, 1991). And, of course, discreteness of representations is also a central property of a number of connectionist techniques for embedding symbolic structures as patterns of activity (e.g., Touretzky, 1986; Touretzky & Hinton, 1988; Dolan, 1989; Pollack, 1990; Smolensky, 1990). The conclusion must be that the PDP principle concerning representations, (1)a, is consistent with both crucial discreteness and crucial non-discreteness of mental representations.

In similar vein, consider the second PDP principle, (1)b: Mental processes are massively parallel transformations of activity patterns by patterns of numerical connections. This can readily be viewed as entailing that mental processing is highly interactive, nonmodular, and nonsequential. Indeed, this is the case for "classic" PDP models (e.g., Sejnowski & Rosenberg, 1987), in which one layer of input units, containing information of many types, projects directly to one output layer of units (possibly through a hidden layer), with connectivity unrestricted.

But clearly this PDP principle is also consistent with the claim that mental processing is modular or sequential. Modularity of a certain type is central to connectionist models in which different types of information are represented over different groups of units, and in which restricted connectivity between groups of units allows only certain types of information to interact directly (e.g., Mozer, 1991; Plaut & Shallice, 1994). Modularity is the heart of networks that learn to specialize different subnetworks for different subtasks (e.g., Jacobs, Jordan, Nowlan, & Hinton, 1991). And sequentiality is crucial for many applications of simple recurrent networks (Elman, 1990) and related recurrent architectures, including the early model of Jordan (1986).

Again, we must conclude that the PDP principle governing processing, (1)b, is consistent with modular or nonmodular processing, and processing with or without essential sequentiality.

Finally, consider the most controversial of the PDP principles, (1)c: Knowledge acquisition results from the interaction of innate learning rules, innate architectural features, and modification of connection strengths with experience. On first glance, this principle would seem to imply that knowledge acquisition consists entirely in the statistical associations gathered through experience with some task. And this does characterize those early connectionist *tabula rasa* models with simple Hebbian-like learning rules (e.g., Kohonen, 1977; Stone, 1986) and input–output representations that have no built-in domain structure (e.g., local representations, as in Hinton, 1986).

However, much of the most noteworthy progress in connectionist learning is more appropriately characterized by another claim: Connectionist knowledge acquisition consists in fitting to data the parameters of task-specific knowledge models. To varying degrees, this describes somewhat more recent networks (e.g., Rumelhart, Durbin, Golden, & Chauvin, 1996; Smolensky, 1996c), in which more sophisticated error functions that embody Occam's Razor force simplicity of knowledge to compete with closeness of fit to data. It also describes networks with specialized activation functions, connectivity patterns, and learning rules that provide task-appropriate biases to the learning process (e.g., McMillan, Mozer, & Smolensky, 1992), and models in which input–output representations reflect, even implicitly, task-specific regularities (e.g., see Lachter & Bever, 1988, and Pinker & Prince, 1988, on Rumelhart & McClelland, 1986a).

Thus, a commitment to the PDP principles of (1) does not per se constitute a commitment regarding the degree to which discreteness, modularity, or innate learning bias apply to human cognition. This conclusion is no surprise to the practicing connectionist, of course, but it seems to deserve considerably more recognition than it tends to get in polemical debates between pro- and anticonnectionists. The reason for bringing it up here, however, is to point out that the indeterminism of the basic connectionist commitments toward most central issues of cognitive theory forces a major choice of research strategy. The most popular choice is this.

(2) Model-based strategy for connectionist research on language:

Because the basic connectionist principles are too general to have definitive consequences for key theoretical issues, less vague connectionist proposals are needed. These can be achieved as follows:

a. Choose a *particular* set of cognitive data on which these issues bear (a set of specific input–output pairs).

b. Propose a *specific connectionist model* in which, for the particular data in question, choices are made of a specific input–output representations, specific activation functions and learning algorithms, specific numbers of internal layers of specific sizes and connectivity, and so on.

c. Evaluate the proposed model based on the closeness of fit to the data achieved by a computer simulation of the model, and on the internal structure in the model that allows it to achieve its performance.

As I will discuss later, there are many advantages to this research strategy, and it has produced many important results. The main point of this chapter is to argue that there is, however, another strategy available within PDP connectionism, and while this new approach has significant limitations, it also has certain advantages lacking in the model-based strategy. This alternative strategy could be formulated at various levels of generality, but given the topic of this volume I will use a formulation directed at the study of language. (For another cognitive domain—say, reasoning—a description of the analogous strategy results from replacing "grammar formalism" with "formal theory of human reasoning," and so on.)

(3) Grammar-based strategy for connectionist language research:

Because the basic connectionist principles are too general to have definitive consequences for key theoretical issues, less vague connectionist proposals are needed. These can be achieved as follows:

a. Choose a mathematically precise formulation of the PDP principles in (1).

b. Derive from these principles a precise but general grammar formalism (or grammatical theory).

c. To evaluate the proposed formalism, choose a particular class of target empirical generalizations concerning human language.

d. Apply the grammar formalism to language data instantiating the target generalizations, defining a formal "account" of the target phenomena.

e. Compare the degree of explanation of the target generalizations that can be achieved with the new account with that achieved with previous grammar formalisms ("explanation" here means deduction of generalizations and particular data from the principles defining the proposed account).

I would not argue that all, or even most, connectionist research on language should pursue this grammar-based strategy; my claim is only that a central place in connectionist language research should be reserved for a certain amount of such work, because the model- and grammar-based strategies are nicely complementary. What the grammar-based strategy seeks to provide is a way of pursuing the explanatory goals of linguistic theory while incorporating computational insights from connectionist theory concerning mental representation, mental processing, and learning.

In the remainder of this chapter I will briefly illustrate the grammar-based strategy with Harmonic Grammar and Optimality Theory; identify some of the central goals and commitments of one approach to linguistic theory, generative grammar, and illustrate how Optimality Theory addresses these goals while introducing certain general connectionist insights; and discuss the complementary strengths and weaknesses of the model- and grammar-based strategies for connectionist research on language.

CONNECTIONIST GRAMMAR ILLUSTRATED

If we believe that a mind is an abstract, higher-level description of a brain—as I presume most cognitive scientists do—and if we believe that connectionist networks provide a useful stand-in for a solid theory of neural computation yet to be constructed—as I presume most connectionists do—then it follows that abstract, higher-level descriptions of connectionist computation should provide the basis for theories of mind (Smolensky, 1988). The nature of the abstract, higher-level descriptions of connectionist computation will depend on which types of connectionist networks we adopt: some more discrete than others, some more modular than others, some containing more innate knowledge than others, and so forth. Among many such possibilities, here is one:

(4) The Symbolic Approximation

> In the domain of language, the patterns of activation constituting mental representations admit abstract, higher-level descriptions that are closely approximated by the kinds of discrete, abstract structures posited by symbolic linguistic theory.

That this is indeed a possibility is suggested by research over the past decade showing how distributed patterns of activity can possess the same abstract properties as symbolic structures like syntactic trees. (One such proposal, tensor product representations, Smolensky, 1990, is mentioned later; for related proposals, see Dolan, 1989, Pollack, 1990, and Plate, 1991; see also Tesar & Smolensky, 1994, for relations to temporal-synchrony schemes such as Hummel & Biederman, 1992, and Shastri & Ajjaganadde, 1993.) That the Symbolic Approximation is the correct possibility is, of course, a working hypothesis; indeed, it seems to me that it must be the hypothesis underlying all symbolic language research that takes linguistic representations to be psychologically real. Evidence for the correctness of this hypothesis comes from the successes of symbolic linguistic theory in explaining the overall structure of human language, successes I take to be most impressive.

The relevant hypothesis, to be somewhat more precise, is that some—not all—aspects of the mental representation of linguistic information are well-approximated by the abstract symbolic structures posited by linguistic theory. It is agreed by everyone that such representations do not capture all that cognitive theory wants to capture. The claim is that what they do capture has great explanatory power.[1]

The approaches to connectionist grammar I will now briefly describe both assume the Symbolic Approximation. This assumption is not required by the grammar-based strategy for connectionist research outlined in (3); indeed, it would be extremely interesting to develop a connectionist grammar based on an alternative formal higher-level description of linguistic representations (for example, less discrete, more imagelike, representations, perhaps along the lines of certain proposals of cognitive linguistics; e.g., Lakoff, 1987; Langacker, 1987; Talmy, 1988).

Harmonic Grammar

As a first illustration of the connectionist grammar strategy, I indicate explicitly for each step of the strategy in (3) how that step is instantiated in Harmonic Grammar. The presentation here is brief and informal; more formal versions may be found in Legendre, Miyata, and Smolensky (1990a, 1990b). We will step through the five parts of the grammar-based strategy outlined in (3).

Choose a Mathematically Precise Formulation of the PDP Principles

The first principle, (1)a, is made more precise via the Symbolic Approximation: Linguistic representations are assumed to be patterns of activity in a connectionist network that are well-approximated by tensor product realizations of the types of symbolic structures proposed in symbolic theories. Tensor product representations are a general class of schemes by which structured information is encoded in distributed representations. The distributed pattern realizing a symbolic structure is the sum or superposition of distributed patterns realizing its constituent parts, each of which is a distributed pattern realizing a symbolic filler bound by the tensor (generalized outer) product operation to a distributed pattern realizing its structural role.

The second principle, (1)b, is more precisely rendered as follows: Linguistic processing is performed by a connectionist network with a "harmonic" architecture, which entails that network outputs maximize harmony; that is, optimally satisfy the simultaneous soft constraints encoded in the connections. (The connectionist principle of harmony maximization, or "energy" minimization, and an appreciation of its significance and generality, emerged from a body of research, including Hopfield, 1982, 1984, Cohen & Grossberg, 1983, Hinton & Sejnowski 1983, 1986, Smolensky, 1983, 1986, Golden, 1988. For recent review articles, see Hirsch, 1996, and Smolensky, 1996a.)

The final principle is (1)c. More precisely, we assume that the connections in the language-processing network have been adjusted so that the higher the harmony of a linguistic structure, the more well-formed it is in the language; specifically, the harmony-to-well-formedness function is assumed to be a monotonically increasing logistic function.

Derive from These Principles a Precise but General Grammar Formalism (Or Grammatical Theory)

Given the assumptions in the previous section, it can be shown that the language-processing network has the following property. At a higher level of description, the output of the network corresponds to a symbolic structure that optimally satisfies a set of soft constraints of the following form: If a structure contains a constituent of type i, then it must (or must not) contain a constituent of type j (strength $= H_{i,j}$). A particular set of such constraints defines a Harmonic Grammar.

*To Evaluate the Proposed Formalism, Choose a Particular Class
of Target Generalizations Concerning Human Language*

In a wide range of languages, intransitive verbs divide into two classes according to whether their argument noun phrase displays objectlike or subjectlike properties (e.g., in *the river froze,* the argument of *froze, the river*, displays objectlike syntactic properties relative to the more subjectlike argument of *flowed* in *the river flowed*). Which type of behavior is displayed by the arguments of a verb correlate in problematic ways with various syntactic and semantic properties of the verb and argument, but precisely characterizing these correlations as grammatical principles often proves problematic.

*Apply the Grammar Formalism to Linguistic Data
Instantiating the Target Generalizations, Defining
a Formal "Account" of the Target Phenomena*

A variety of French intransitive verbs and sentence structures illustrate the correlations referred to in the previous section. A set of soft constraints defining a Harmonic Grammar is developed to account for the overall acceptability pattern of the French sentences. A typical soft constraint is, "If a structure contains a verb describing an event with an inherent endpoint, then it must not contain a subjectlike argument." These rules, with their strengths, capture the correlations of interest; the Harmonic Grammar formalism defines formally how the conflicting demands of these rules are combined to make precise predictions of sentence well-formedness.

*Compare the Degree of Explanation of the Target
Generalizations That Can Be Achieved with the New Account
with That Achieved with Previous Grammar Formalisms*

The Harmonic Grammar account allows a complexity of interaction between syntactic and semantic constraints that better fits the French data, while elucidating the nature and grammatical role of the general correlations. The proposed soft constraints provide the means for precise prediction of the well-formedness of particular sentences, as well as deductive links to the general correlations to be explained.

Optimality Theory

A grammar formalism conceptually related to Harmonic Grammar, Optimality Theory (OT) (Prince & Smolensky, 1991, 1993, 1997), is considerably more restrictive, and, as we see in the next section, therefore better suited to the explanatory goals of linguistic theory. The relevant principles of the theory are summarized using the traditional generative concept of the input and output of a grammar; for current purposes, we can roughly take the input to be the intended interpretation a speaker wishes to convey, and the output to be the actual linguistic structure that expresses that interpretation in the language (for a more accurate characterization, see Legendre, Smolensky, & Wilson, 1998).

(5) Optimality Theory

    a. Given an input, the grammar produces as output the linguistic structure that maximizes harmony.

    b. The harmony of a potential output is the degree to which it simultaneously satisfies a set of violable constraints on linguistic well-formedness (including constraints requiring that the output faithfully express the input).

    c. The constraints have different strengths, determining which take priority when constraints conflict.

    d. The grammar of a language is a ranking of constraints from strongest to weakest; a higher-ranked constraint has absolute priority over all lower-ranked constraints.

    e. The set of possible outputs, and the set of constraints, is the same in all languages; grammars of languages differ only in the way constraints are ranked.

The additional restrictiveness of Optimality Theory over Harmonic Grammar comes from restricting the interactions among constraints to those that can be achieved by ranking (as opposed to arbitrary numerical strengths), and from the principle that the grammatical constraints, and the possible outputs, are the same in all languages. These additional restrictions reflect important empirical facts about language, some of which are long-standing observations of linguists, others of which were discovered in the process of developing OT (more on this in the next section).

In (6), connectionism is related to the fundamental principles that define OT and differentiate it from other generative theories of grammar (see also Prince & Smolensky, 1993, ch. 10).

(6) Fundamental defining principles of OT, and their relation to connectionism:

    Principles deriving from connectionism:

    a. *Optimality*. The correct output representation is the one that maximizes harmony.

    b. *Containment*. Competition for optimality is between outputs that include the given input. (Clamping the input units restricts the optimization in a network to those patterns including the input.)

    c. *Parallelism*. Harmony measures the degree of simultaneous satisfaction of constraints. (Connectionist optimization is parallel: The constraints encoded in the connections all apply simultaneously to a potential output.)

    d. *Interactionism*. The complexity of patterns of grammaticality comes not from individual constraints, which are relatively simple and general, but from the mutual interaction of multiple constraints. (Each connection in a network is a simple, general constraint on the coactivity of the units it connects; complex behavior emerges only from the interaction of many constraints.)

e. *Conflict.* Constraints conflict: It is typically impossible to simultaneously satisfy them all. (Positive and negative connections typically put conflicting pressures on a unit's activity.)

f. *Domination.* Constraint conflict is resolved via a notion of differential strength: Stronger constraints prevail over weaker ones in cases of conflict.

g. *Minimal violability.* Correct outputs typically violate some constraints (because of conflicts), but do so only to the minimal degree needed to satisfy stronger constraints.

h. *Learning requires determination of constraint strengths.* Acquiring the grammar of a particular language requires determining the relative strengths of constraints in the target language.

Principles not deriving from connectionism:

i. *Strictness of domination.* Each constraint is stronger than all weaker constraints combined. (This corresponds to a strong restriction on the numerical constraint strengths, and makes it possible to determine optimality without numerical computation.)

j. *Universality.* The constraints are the same in all human grammars. (This corresponds to a strong restriction on the content of the constraints, presumably to be explained eventually by the interaction of certain innate biases and experience.)

The OT conception of grammar embodied in (6)a–h directly reflects basic connectionist computational principles. The last two principles, (6)i–j, however, are unexpected from a connectionist perspective. These two principles reflect empirical discoveries about the similarities and differences among human grammars, to be discussed in the next section. These surprising principles would appear to have strong implications for the connectionist foundations of OT, but these potentially important implications remain to be explored in future research.

In the final section I will briefly consider the relative strengths and weaknesses of the model-based and grammar-based strategies for connectionist language research. But the strengths of the grammar-based connectionist strategy are closely tied to the goals of grammar-based research more generally, so I digress to discuss these in the next section. In the process, I will argue that generative grammar and connectionism are not incompatible research paradigms, the second main claim of this chapter.

OPTIMALITY THEORY AND GENERATIVE GRAMMAR

Within generative linguistics, a grammar is taken to be a mathematical function: Given an input—for us, roughly, an intended interpretation—the grammar determines an output—the linguistic structure that expresses that interpretation. The grammar in the mind of an English speaker is the knowledge that entails that *Which theory did Noam trash?* is the English formulation of a particular question in a particular discourse context, a question that would be rendered in other languages (with appropriate substitution of the corresponding words): *Noam which theory trashed? Noam trashed which theory? Which theory trashed Noam?* and so on. A speaker uses his or her grammar every time he or she utters or hears a sentence; popular misconceptions notwithstanding, grammars are for producing and comprehending words and sentences, they are not for producing metalinguistic grammaticality judgments (although they can be indirectly pressed into service for that purpose).

Among the most basic generalizations molding the enterprise of generative grammar are those listed in Table 10.1; shown also are the roles generative grammar assigns to grammatical theory in response to these generalizations (see Archangeli, 1997, for a recent pedagogical exposition). The right column of Table 10.1 indicates schematically how Optimality Theory meets the demands of a generative theory of grammar. By using optimal satisfaction of simultaneous conflicting violable constraints as the computational mechanism, OT offers novel proposals for solving the basic problems of grammatical theory, and new types of explanations of the central generalizations of linguistics.

The central column of Table 10.1 constitutes, I believe, the core of the central commitments defining generative grammar. None of these seems to me inconsistent with connectionist principles. Indeed, in addition to Optimality Theory, other connectionist-based approaches to generative grammar can be identified; for example, the Linear Dynamic Model (Goldsmith & Larson, 1990; see also Touretzky & Wheeler, 1990, a connectionist implementation of a proposal by Lakoff, 1993). The Linear Dynamic Model is a framework proposed for syllabification and stress assignment based on a particular connectionist architecture. This framework was used to argue the importance of graded linguistic representations and of numerical weights for encoding phonological grammars; yet this model received serious consideration within generative linguistics. Indeed, Alan Prince—known to most connectionists for his critical evaluation with Steven Pinker of early claims about grammar based on connectionist modeling (Pinker & Prince, 1988)—has studied this model in great mathematical detail in order to evaluate its linguistic implications (Prince, 1993). The name "Linear Dynamic Model" derives in fact from Prince's formal analysis of the linear dynamics of these networks. As part of his analysis, Prince proposes an alternative version of the model, which is radically more continuous. It should not be surprising that the Linear Dynamic Model was taken seriously by generative linguists, because, despite the major breaks with mainstream phonology concerning the nature of linguistic representations and grammatical knowledge, this work nonetheless attempts to address the central issues identified in Table 10.1.

The commitments of generative grammar are not inconsistent with graded

Table 10.1
Some Central Generalizations Shaping the Generative Approach to Grammatical Theory

Generalizations	Role of theory	Optimality Theory
Grammars of widely-scattered languages of the world share a tremendous amount of commonality.	Grammatical theories must identify these common principles.	All human grammars share a specified set of well-formedness constraints.
With respect to some particular aspect of linguistic structure, the grammars of languages differ, but in a remarkably limited number of ways.	Grammatical theories must identify exactly the possible modes of variation across languages.	Language-particular grammars are different rankings of the same constraints.
The principles common across languages are connected to the observed data in complex ways.	Grammatical theories must provide formal accounts of the complex connection between general linguistic principles and the data of a particular language.	The structures of a language are those that maximize Harmony, i.e., those that optimally satisfy the constraints as ranked by the language's grammar.
Relative to the astronomical number of generalizations children *could* draw based on the data of their language, they converge remarkably quickly toward a correct grammar.	Grammatical theories must provide formal accounts of how a correct grammar can be efficiently learned.	The space of possible OT grammars is sufficiently restricted and well-structured that algorithms for identifying a correct ranking can be formulated, and efficiency results obtained.

representations, grammars encoded as numerical weights, or, indeed, probabilistic models, nonmodular architecture, or theories in which all language-specific knowledge is acquired by induction. The commitments of generative grammar are to explain the overarching generalizations about human language summarized in Table 10.1, and if there is in the generative literature a strong preponderance of grammatical formalisms that rely on discrete representations, sequential symbol manipulation, modular nonprobabilistic rule systems, and a highly constrained role for learning from the environment, it is because those working assumptions have enabled substantial progress in addressing the issues of Table 10.1. Other proposals that also do so—be they based in numerical representations and knowledge like the Linear Dynamic Model, or parallel satisfaction of soft constraints like Optimality Theory—will be seriously considered and evaluated on the quality of the explanations that they provide for the key generalizations in Table 10.1 and their many particular manifestations in the world's languages.

In this section I have tried to explain why generative grammar and connectionism should not be considered incompatible research paradigms. The practice of generative grammar requires addressing a certain body of generalizations and providing precise theories of grammatical knowledge that offer some explanation of these generalizations. Connectionism provides proposals for the computational architecture underlying grammar, proposals concerning representation, processing, and learning. The grammar-based strategy for connectionist research on language provides a way of integrating connectionism with generative grammar. In the final section I give reasons why such an integrated research program is a valuable complement to model-based connectionism.

COMPLEMENTARITY OF MODEL- AND GRAMMAR-BASED STRATEGIES FOR CONNECTIONIST LANGUAGE RESEARCH

Two criteria are useful for bringing out the complementary strengths and weaknesses of the model- and grammar-based strategies for connectionist language research. The first criterion concerns the feasibility of incorporating connectionist computational proposals into language research; the second, the feasibility of providing explanations of empirical generalizations about language.

Feasibility of Incorporating Connectionist Computational Proposals into Language Research

It will not have escaped anyone's attention that while Optimality Theory replaces generative grammar's previous computational architecture—sequential rule application and hard constraints—with parallel optimization over soft constraints, OT fails to incorporate many other central features of connectionism: graded representations, probabilistic processing, and associationist learning, to name a few. That OT lacks these features is not per se a virtue, although what I find most striking is the impact on grammatical theory that can result from incorporating even a single connectionist conception, parallel optimization over soft constraints. It is my hope that the grammar-based strategy for connectionist language research will develop further grammatical theories that successfully incorporate more features of the connectionist computational architecture, but one has to start somewhere.

The real point here is that incorporating connectionist computational features into grammar-based research is difficult, because what is needed is a precise characterization of the higher-level consequences of these connectionist features that is precise enough that these consequences can be used as the fundamental principles of a formal grammatical theory. The connections between Optimality Theory and connectionist theory arise from two connectionist features, the higher-level consequences of which can be connected to grammar: tensor product representations, connecting the low-level structure of certain distributed patterns of activity to their higher-level structure as symbolic representations, and harmony maximization, connecting the low-level structure of certain activation-spreading rules to their higher-level structure as parallel optimization over soft constraints. I believe there are many more such connections to be exploited, linking lower- and higher-level structure in neural networks (indeed, hopes of furthering this aspect of connectionist theory was my primary motivation in assembling a book; see Smolensky, Mozer, & Rumelhart, 1996).

The model-based strategy suffers from no such limitation on the incorporation of features of connectionist computation into language research. Not relying on a mathematical characterization of the higher-level consequences of lower-level network assumptions, the model-based strategy uses computer simulation to explore the consequences for specific linguistic data of specific computational proposals. This has opened up new ways of conceptualizing linguistic representations via distributed representations, suggested new ways of computing linguistically relevant functions using massively parallel processing, and deepened our perspective on language learning, for example, by providing provocative glimpses into the self-organizing capacities of sophisticated inductive systems. This work is still in the exploratory stage, with the main issues remaining open: Can connectionist networks capture real linguistic knowledge without, to a considerable extent, implementing symbolic representations and rules? Can connectionist learning provide an account of linguistic acquisition that is not an implementation of innate knowledge triggered by experience? While I consider these questions largely unresolved by modeling research to date, our understanding of the issues has been significantly sharpened and deepened by modeling work.

It seems likely that model-based research will always play a central role in connectionist approaches to cognition because the computer-simulation-based study of various features of connectionist computation will likely continue to be decades ahead of strong mathematical results concerning those features. (At the same time, it seems clear that mathematical results, for their part, have frequently precipitated the development of many new connectionist techniques.)

Feasibility of Providing Explanations of
Empirical Generalizations about Language

What, then, is the relative advantage of grammar-based connectionist research? The principal advantage concerns scientific explanation. Since this is a notoriously controversial topic, I will attempt to ground my argument in a (very) concrete little example.

Consider the French word for small (masculine), *petit*. Oversimplifying slightly, it is pronounced with a final *t* (/pətit/) only when it is followed by a vowel-initial word; otherwise, the pronunciation is (/pəti/). How are we to understand this quite typical example of context-sensitive phonological alternation?

It might well prove interesting to build a connectionist model that learned the contextually appropriate pronunciation of this word—and others like it—from examples. Suppose this done. We are now positioned to address some very interesting questions about data-driven acquisition of phonology. What kind of initial structure in the representations and architecture of the network, and what kind of data, allow learning procedures to master this pattern of alternation?

Another kind of question is extremely important, however: Putting aside questions about the learning process itself, we pass to questions of exactly what knowledge the network has acquired. That is, we now want an explanation of how the word *petit* is represented (in the model's lexicon), and how the network's connections (its grammar) manage to produce the right pronunciation at the right time.

Why is this type of question important? Isn't it enough to show that the trained network generalizes correctly to, say, 96 percent of unfamiliar words? Do we really need to characterize the lexicon and grammar that the network has learned?

Perhaps not. But in that case, we can't conclude that connectionism has provided an alternative way to explain linguistic knowledge and its acquisition. This is so for at least the following three reasons. First, the network may not provide an "explanation" in an acceptable sense of the word because the degree of success that it does achieve may be due to aspects of the simulation that are not actually theoretical commitments of the implicit connectionist theory of language being proposed (McCloskey, 1992). For example, aspects of the input–output representations may provide important biases, reflecting principles of symbolic linguistic theory, and these biases may be more crucial than any general connectionist principles in allowing the network to perform reasonably well. Thus, it is important to understand what knowledge the network actually has and what the critical sources of that knowledge are.

Second, for all we know, whatever correct performance the network displays, or whatever explanation of the phenomena the account provides, may arise because the network partially implements some symbolic system of linguistic representations and rules. Proponents of symbolic theories believe that symbolic rules and representations are somehow implemented in neural networks—perhaps they're right, and our network has managed to perform just such an implementation, at least to the limited degree required to achieve a 96-percent success rate on its limited data. Unless we have adequate understanding of the network's knowledge at the higher, more abstract levels, where symbolic rules and representations could possibly reside, we have no grounds to argue that the network's success counts as evidence against symbolic theory.

Third (and most likely), it is possible that what the network has learned has little or no relevance to any general conclusions about linguistics knowledge. Surely it would be a staggering modeling feat to develop a network capable of learning the full phonology of any known human language. In the imaginable future, all models will confront an infinitesimal fraction of these data. The important point to note is that, in contrast, theories of linguistic knowledge developed in theoretical linguistics are informed by, and responsible to, an overwhelmingly larger body of cross-linguistic data than any feasible connectionist model.

When a theoretical linguist analyzes a set of data D of the scope that might feasibly be presented to a network for training, the linguist's analysis is shaped by a huge mass of implicit data in addition to the particular data D explicitly under scrutiny. This point will be developed further later, but to briefly illustrate with the case of *petit*, the data informing contemporary symbolic linguistic analysis of the pronunciation of *petit* includes other phonological processes in French that have little superficial relation to the issue of final-consonant pronunciation, the pronunciation of final consonants in Australian languages, the syllabification of word-internal consonants in all known languages, the pronunciation of certain vowels in Slavic languages, and much more. All this is the implicit data that inform the linguist's analysis of *petit*; a proposed analysis is responsible for generalizing, in the relevant respects, to all these implicit data. Thus, a large number of logically possible analyses of D are rejected by the linguist because such analyses would have no hope of generalizing beyond D to other phonological phenomena and other languages. Successfully accounting for D in isolation is usually quite easy; what is hard is accounting for D in a way that employs representations and processes that might conceivably generalize beyond D.

Now it is imaginable that we have in our heads one network for handling one data set D, a separate network for another data set D', yet another for D'', and so on. Such an approach to linguistic knowledge is hypermodular, in a sense favored by no proponent of modularity within linguistics; the burden of proof is on the connectionist modeler to show that it could conceivably work and, if so, that it provides the best explanation. Theoretical linguistic methodology, by contrast, imposes the constant methodological constraint that proposed analyses exploit every means of generalization possible, and thus the burden of generality is borne within each analysis, and not by splicing together a collection of separate analyses, each employing knowledge of highly restricted generality. Thus, unless we have some understanding of what knowledge a network is using to cope with a very limited body of data D, we have no basis for believing that this knowledge will generalize beyond D, and indeed no reason to believe the network has solved a relevantly difficult problem: accounting for the data D in a way that generalizes well beyond D. Furthermore, what makes these problems difficult is often a relatively small set of challenging cases; which cases are the challenging ones depends on the analysis. Thus, unless we understand how the network is analyzing D, for all we know the challenging cases amount to only 4 percent of the data, and these are just the cases our network gets wrong; that is, the network has simply failed to handle the pattern that makes D difficult in the first place.

Thus, it seems that the model-based strategy provides a researcher two options. The first is to be content with a model that accounts for 96 percent of its data, and with only very fragmentary understanding of what knowledge the network has that allows it to exhibit this performance. In this case, for the reasons outlined in the previous paragraphs, the model cannot be seen as providing strong evidence one way or the other concerning the question of whether connectionism provides a viable alternative to symbolic linguistic theory.

The second option is to determine what knowledge the network has, and to show (1) that this knowledge derives from genuine principles of a connectionist theory of language, and not from arbitrary implementation details of the simulation; (2) that it is not the case that this knowledge is (partially) successful only because it (partially) implements a symbolic linguistic theory; and (3) that this knowledge encodes regularities of considerable (cross-)linguistic generality, and correctly explains the patterns in the data that make the data interestingly challenging. Armed with such a characterization of the knowledge in the network, we could take its success as evidence that connectionist principles lead to linguistic knowledge that is not an implementation of a symbolic theory, and is of sufficient generality to be significant; that is, as evidence that connectionist principles can provide an alternative to symbolic accounts of linguistic knowledge.

But achieving such a strong understanding of the knowledge residing in a network that is sophisticated enough to perform linguistically complex tasks is a very tall order, well beyond the current state of the art. Unfortunately, while some significant progress has been made over the past decade, our ability to understand the knowledge in networks of any sophistication remains quite rudimentary. So suppose we have trained a network to pronounce *petit* and related French words, achieving 96 percent generalization to novel words. It seems reasonable to expect—based on the past decade's experience with such experiments—that with a great deal of insight, skill, and persistence (and a bit of luck), a researcher *might* be able to analyze the trained network to the point of being able to explain why, given the connection weights and the representation of individual words like *petit* in various contexts, the correct pronunciation behavior mathematically follows. It does not seem at all likely, however, that a researcher could produce more than highly fragmentary explanations at any greater level of generality about the lexical and grammatical knowledge of the network and its consequent behavior.

How does such depth and breadth of explanation of this tiny bit of phonology compare with that provided by basic linguistic theory? To provide some perspective on this question, Table 10.2 summarizes some aspects of an explanation of *petit*'s behavior that emerge from contemporary generative phonology.

Starting with row a of Table 10.2, /pətit/ ~ /pəti/ means that the two pronunciations of *petit* are alternants; we have already stated a generalization concerning the contexts in which each form appears. In beginning the generative explanation, the first thing to note is that this behavior is not a phenomenon peculiar to French; in as far-flung a language as Lardil, an Australian aboriginal language, we discover that the noun stem for *story* is pronounced /ŋaluk/ when followed by a vowel-initial suffix, but /ŋalu/ otherwise: The final *k* behaves like the final *t* of *petit* (row b). (Indeed, even English has a tiny vestige of such behavior, in the indefinite article *an* ~ *a*.) The next observation is that in French this behavior is not limited to *petit*; the final *t* in many—but not all—French words behaves the same way. In row c, this is written: "*t* ~ $\emptyset]_{Wd}$"; that is, *t* alternates with silence before the right word-boundary, denoted "$]_{Wd}$." Again, the situation in Lardil is parallel: Before a stem-boundary, *k* alternates with silence; this time, for all words.

The next observation (row d) is that in French this behavior is not limited to *t*: There is a class of final consonants that all behave the same way. Again, in Lardil, *k* is merely one member of a class of consonants that can appear only before a vowel. In Lardil, this class can be loosely characterized as all consonants specifying a place of articulation different from that of a *simple coronal*, a single occlusion created by the tongue tip in the general area of the alveolar ridge (see Prince & Smolensky, 1993, ch. 7, and the literature cited therein).

The next step (row e) is to observe that the behavior of French final consonants like *t* in *petit* is part of a much more general pattern of "defective segments" seen in a number of the world's languages; for example, Slavic languages have vowels that come and go. The general pattern is that defective segments provide phonological material that can be present or absent, depending on whether the resulting phonological structure would be "better" with or without that material. In the case of final consonants, the relevant notion of "better" is this: A consonant is better placed at the beginning of a syllable (the onset), rather than the end of a syllable (the coda).

Table 10.2
A *Petit* Explanation

	Level of Generality	French	Lardil
a.	word in target language	pətit ~ pəti	
b.	word in other language		ŋaluk ~ ŋalu
c.	segment in language	t ~ ∅]$_{Wd}$ (certain words)	k ~ ∅]$_{Stem}$ (always)
d.	segment class in language	C ~ ∅]$_{Wd}$ (certain words)	C ~ ∅]$_{Stem}$ (certain Cs)
e.	universal	Patterns of 'defective segments' cross-linguistically; C ~ ∅ in syllable coda cross-linguistically, especially 'worse' Cs	
f.	markedness	Cs avoided in syllable coda in: adult inventories, adult phonology, child language, language change ...	

French defective final consonants appear when they would start a syllable (including the initial vowel of the following word); they disappear when they would fall into a syllable coda. In Lardil, the syllable coda (unlike the onset) can never contain the "worst" consonants, those specifying a place of articulation different from that of a simple coronal.

The general notion that certain linguistic structures are better than others was developed in the 1930s by Jakobson, Trubetzkoy, and others of the Prague Linguistics Circle under the name "markedness," the worse structures being called "marked" (as by a scarlet letter; Trubetzkoy, 1939/1969; Jakobson, 1941/1968). Thus, syllable codas are marked relative to syllable onsets; simple coronal consonants are unmarked relative to other consonants. The Praguian view is that markedness pervades all aspects of language (row f). Marked structures are avoided altogether in certain languages; that is, entirely absent from their inventories of possible structures (e.g., languages in which no syllables have codas; Blevins, 1995). In other languages, these same marked structures may appear, but only under strongly restricted conditions (e.g., in Lardil, codas can appear only if they contain unmarked consonants). In such languages, marked structures are avoided "when possible" through phonological alternations (e.g., the final *t* of *petit*). Furthermore, marked structures are avoided by changes across time to the language itself (in Old French, the final *t* of *petit* was pronounced even in coda position). Moreover, Jakobson believed marked structures to be acquired later by children; first to be lost in aphasia; and, presumably, harder to process on-line.

Exploiting the notion of markedness, the explanation suggested in Table 10.2 weaves the tiny thread of *t*'s behavior in *petit* into a web of cross-linguistic empirical generalizations. The behavior of *t* is explained as the avoidance of syllable codas; this, in turn, is then woven together with the tendency of children to avoid syllable codas, an instance of how avoidance of markedness of all sorts—from syllable codas and noncoronal consonants in phonology through plural number in morphology to passive voice in syntax—pervades all of language: intact and disordered, adult and child.

The notion of linguistic markedness parallels in important respects the notion of (negative) Harmony (or energy) in connectionist networks. Optimality Theory's basic hypothesis, that the output of the grammar is the structure that maximizes Harmony relative to the given input, can be viewed as a formalization of the notion that languages avoid more marked—less harmonic—structures. Optimality Theory's formal calculus of markedness—a version of parallel soft constraint satisfaction, Harmony maximization—has for the first time enabled markedness to provide the very core of a generative theory of grammar.

At all the levels of explanation identified in Table 10.2, OT analyses have provided a formal means to deduce from the basic principles of the theory both detailed language-particular patterns and overarching empirical generalizations. In OT, a marked linguistic structure is formalized as one that violates one or more universal well-formedness constraints. To express the universal markedness of syllable codas, a universal constraint on the well-formedness of syllables is posited: NoCODA, "Syllables do not have codas" (Prince & Smolensky, 1993, Ch. 6). Similarly, universal constraints express the universal unmarkedness of simple coronal consonants relative to other consonants (Prince & Smolensky, 1993, Ch. 9; Smolensky, 1993). The possible phonetic bases of such constraints in articulation and perception is one facet of OT research, but what concerns us now is not what gives rise to these constraints, but rather, what the constraints give rise to: precise accounting of the forms of particular words in particular contexts in particular languages (rows a–d), and the universal generalizations of which language-particular facts are instances (rows e–f).

Along with other hypothesized universal constraints, NoCODA enables correct prediction of the different context-dependent phonological forms of *petit* and other French words with final defective consonants (Tranel, 1994).

Such analysis formally captures the explanation that such consonants are present or absent depending on which option gives the better—more harmonic, less marked—form, entailing avoidance of harmony-lowering violations of NoCODA. NoCODA plays a formally parallel role in the prediction of the context-dependent forms of Lardil words like *faluk* (Prince & Smolensky, 1993, Ch. 7), formally capturing the commonness shared by final consonants in French and Lardil (rows a–d of Table 10.2).

Moving to a still more universal level (row e of Table 10.2), an OT analysis of the property that distinguishes defective French consonants from ordinary consonants makes it possible to formally deduce a universal typology that spells out the cross-linguistic possibilities for the behavior of defective material (Zoll, 1996). This typology situates French defective consonants in a universal picture that connects them to the defective vowels of Slavic and even to defective material in African languages, consisting only in a pitch tone. The Lardil prohibition against placing the least harmonic consonants in the least harmonic syllable position (coda) is seen as one instance of a formal pattern of harmony maximization—"banning the worst of the worst"—which is evident in many linguistic contexts, including, for example, requirements in African languages that vowels in the same word have the same tongue-root configuration (Prince & Smolensky, 1993, p. 180; Smolensky, 1993, 1997).

At a yet more general level, the overarching generalizations concerning markedness summarized in row f of Table 10.2 can be formally deduced within OT. Once any markedness-defining constraint C (e.g., NoCODA) is recognized as a universal constraint, the general computational principles of OT take over and many logical consequences follow.

According to the general OT theory of cross-linguistic variation, languages will differ in how highly ranked C is in their grammars. There will be some languages in which C is very highly ranked, with the effect that marked structures violating C will never be most harmonic; they will never appear in the language. Thus, there will be languages that ban C-violating structures from their inventories of possible structures, but no languages that ban C-satisfying structures. (For the case $C = $ NoCODA, this derives the typological fact that among the world's languages there are some that prohibit syllable codas but none that require them, and just the opposite for syllable onsets; Jakobson, 1962; Prince & Smolensky, 1993, Ch. 6.)

In other languages, C will be less dominant; C will be outranked by other conflicting constraints that are relevant in some contexts but not in others. In such a language, C violations will be possible in the language in some contexts, but avoided in others by phonological alternations: marked, C-violating structures will not be optimal, except in those limited contexts where conflicting constraints outranking C are relevant.

Furthermore, according to a general OT learning theory (Tesar & Smolensky, 1996, 1998; Tesar, 1998; Smolensky, 1996b, in press), markedness-defining constraints C are initially highly ranked, so children's early grammars allow only unmarked structures to be produced; only after such a constraint has been demoted in rank during learning can children produce marked, C-violating structures. (When C = NoCoda, this derives the tendency of children's initial syllables to lack codas.)

OT analysis of language change as reranking of constraints over time (e.g., Zubritskaya, 1997) predicts that when a constraint C assumes higher rank, the language loses C-marked structures. And at the frontier of current OT research, in studies of on-line sentence processing, an incremental-optimization theory of parsing connects processing difficulty to relative harmony or markedness of syntactic structures (Stevenson & Smolensky, 1997), and current studies of phonological errors by aphasic patients seek to model damage as relative promotion of markedness constraints, so aphasic productions lack certain marked structures produced by the intact grammar (Goldrick, Rapp, & Smolensky, 2000).

It will be a long time, surely, before our ability to analyze specific connectionist models trained on specific linguistic data reaches the depths and breadths necessary to deduce from basic principles the range of generalizations summarized in Table 10.2. But a product of grammar-based connectionist research, Optimality Theory, is already able to do so. And that is the primary reason why—despite the significant limitations on the aspects of connectionist theory that can today be successfully exploited—it seems the grammar-based strategy is a valuable complement to the model-based strategy in the arsenal of connectionist approaches to language.

SUMMARY

Debates about the relation of connectionism to language often seem to take it for granted that it is possible to identify two broad theories of language, connectionism and generative grammar, and that these theories are locked in deep scientific conflict. I believe this to be quite false. It is not difficult to identify a particular connectionist proposal about language that conflicts with a particular generative proposal about the same aspect of language: The classic debate about the acquisition of the English past tense (Rumelhart & McClelland, 1986a; Pinker & Prince, 1988; Lachter & Bever, 1988) may be such a case. But it is equally easy to identify two connectionist proposals that conflict as accounts of a common phenomenon, and even easier to identify pairs of conflicting generative proposals. There are plenty of disagreements about language to go around; the question is, do the theories divide into two camps, connectionism and generative grammar, with fundamentally incompatible commitments?

The basic commitments of PDP connectionism are often taken to entail commitments about modularity, nativism, and other Big Issues, but it seems to me that brief inspection reveals that while a particular PDP proposal may entail such commitments, the broad class of PDP models encompasses proposals that span the spectrum of possible positions on the Issues. Equally, the basic commitments of generative grammar entail no commitments on the Big Issues, despite the fact that prominent generative linguists, speaking for themselves, have expressed such commitments.

The view I have tried to sketch here is that PDP connectionism is a commitment to fundamental computational mechanisms, and generative grammar is a commitment to certain types of explanations of certain types of empirical generalizations. These commitments are not in conflict. As recent research shows, it is possible to deploy the computational mechanisms of PDP connectionism to advance the explanatory goals of generative grammar.

Doing so is not possible using the standard model-based strategy for developing concrete proposals within the broad compass of PDP connectionism, at least for the foreseeable future. This is because the types of explanations demanded by generative grammar are not currently feasible within this strategy. Of course, the model-based strategy has produced important advances in cognitive science, and will continue to do so for a long time to come. While it may not advance the goals of generative grammar, model-based research serves other scientific goals that seem to me at least as important.

But the goals of generative grammar can in fact be advanced by a different, grammar-based strategy for developing PDP proposals concerning language. In this strategy, new grammatical theories based upon fundamental PDP computational mechanisms are developed, and replace traditional grammatical theories based upon computational mechanisms such as serial symbol manipulation and hard-constraint satisfaction.

In these early days of exploring the potential of the grammar-based strategy for connectionist linguistics, we have succeeded in developing new grammatical formalisms that incorporate only a small part of the full arsenal of connectionist computational principles. But such is the power of the approach that even a small amount of connectionist input, that embodied in Optimality Theory, has already had a major impact on the practice of generative grammar (many OT papers and an extensive OT bibliography can be accessed electronically at the Rutgers Optimality Archive, http://ruccs. rutgers.edu/roa.html).

Looking to the future, two types of prospect can now be discerned. One is the development of new grammatical theories that incorporate additional PDP principles (including theories going beyond the Symbolic Approximation). The other is the advancement of connectionist theories of higher cognition. For Optimality Theory has led to empirical discoveries about universal grammar that are a surprise from the current PDP perspective, and these discoveries seem to be telling us that current PDP computational principles are missing something, something quite important for language, at least. It will be most interesting to see what this turns out to be.

FURTHER READINGS

The seminal exchange on the topic of connectionism and linguistic theory is the classic paper by Rumelhart and McClelland (1986a) and the responses published in a special issue of *Cognition*, reprinted in Pinker and Mehler (1988), most important, the paper by Pinker and Prince (1988). Pinker and Prince address many points on several levels, but one issue permeating much of the discussion is the question of exactly what theory is being proposed via the connectionist network simulated by Rumelhart and McClelland. This issue is most explicitly addressed in McCloskey (1992), which addresses another important connectionist model proposed by Seidenberg and McClelland (1989). McClelland has also been explicitly concerned with the development of connectionist principles for cognitive theory; see, for instance, McClelland (1993). Further development of connectionist principles usable for cognitive theory depends on advances in mathematical analysis; foundations for such work are presented in Smolensky, Mozer, and Rumelhart (1996), which contains contributed chapters introducing and applying sixteen different areas of mathematics, along with four chapters summarizing and integrating these disparate approaches to the formalization of neural computation.

An introduction to generative linguistics couched explicitly in Optimality Theory may be found in Archangeli (1997). The classic articulation of markedness as the central organizing principle for all of language is Jakobson (1941/1968). For a number of accessible, self-contained introductions to elements of (mostly pre-OT) phonological theory, see Goldsmith (1995). The founding document of OT is Prince and Smolensky (1993); another classic source crucial for the development of the theory is McCarthy and Prince (1993). Information on how to obtain these book manuscripts is available electronically at the Rutgers Optimality Archive site (http://ruccs. rutgers.edu/roa.html), home to numerous OT articles, a bibliography, and software. Prince and Smolensky (1997) is an introduction to OT and its relation to neural networks.

NOTES

I am grateful to Géraldine Legendre and Bob Frank for very helpful comments on earlier drafts, to Alan Prince for insightful discussion of the issues, and to NSF for financial support through the Learning and Intelligent Systems Initiative.

1. The situation seems highly parallel to what I see as the relation of connectionism to neuroscience. To the criticism that connectionism ignores a tremendous amount of knowledge about the brain, I would respond thus: The hypothesis justifying connectionism is that some—not all—cognitively relevant aspects of neural structure are well-approximated by the abstract computational systems posited by connectionist theory. It is agreed by everyone that such systems do not capture all that cognitive theory wants to capture. The claim is that what they do capture has great explanatory power.

REFERENCES

Anderson, J. A., Silverstein, J. W., Ritz, S. A., & Jones, R. S. (1977). Distinctive features, categorical perception, and probability learning: Some applications of a neural model. *Psychological Review, 84*, 413–451.

Archangeli, D. (1997). Optimality theory: An introduction to linguistics in the 1990s. In D. Archangeli & D. T. Langendoen (Eds.), *Optimality theory: An overview* (pp. 1–32). Malden, MA: Blackwell.

Blevins, J. (1995). The syllable in phonological theory. In J. A. Goldsmith, (Ed.), *The handbook of phonological theory*. Cambridge, MA: Blackwell.

Cohen, M. A., & Grossberg, S. (1983). Absolute stability of global pattern formation and parallel memory storage by competitive neural networks. *IEEE Transactions on Systems, Man, and Cybernetics, 13*, 815–825.

Dolan, C. P. (1989). *Tensor manipulation networks: Connectionist and symbolic approaches to comprehension, learning, and planning.* Unpublished doctoral thesis. Los Angeles: Department of Computer Science, University of California.

Elman, J. L. (1990). Finding structure in time. *Cognitive Science, 14*, 179–211.

Feldman, J. A., & Ballard, D. H. (1982). Connectionist models and their properties. *Cognitive Science, 6*, 205–254.

Golden, R. M. (1988). A unified framework for connectionist systems. *Biological Cybernetics, 59*, 109–120.

Goldrick, M., Rapp, B., & Smolensky, P. (2000). *Markedness, optimality, and phonological errors in aphasia.* Manuscript in preparation.

Goldsmith, J. A. (Ed.). (1995). *The handbook of phonological theory.* Cambridge, MA: Blackwell.

Goldsmith, J. A., & Larson, G. (1990). Local modeling and syllabification. In K. Deaton, M. Noske, & M. Ziolkowski (Eds.), *Papers from the Twenty-Sixth Annual Regional Meeting of the Chicago Linguistic Society* (Part 2). Chicago: Chicago Linguistic Society.

Grossberg, S. (1976). Adaptive pattern classification and universal recoding: Part I. Parallel development and coding of neural feature detectors. *Biological Cybernetics, 23*, 121–134.

Hinton, G. E. (1986). Learning distributed representations of concepts. In *Proceedings of the Eighth Annual Conference of the Cognitive Science Society* (pp. 1–12). Hillsdale, NJ: Lawrence Erlbaum.

Hinton, G. E., & Sejnowski, T. J. (1983). Optimal perceptual inference. In *Proceedings of the IEEE Computer Society Conference on Computer Vision and Pattern Recognition* (pp. 448–453).

Hinton, G. E., & Sejnowski, T. J. (1986). Learning and relearning in Boltzmann machines. In D. E. Rumelhart & J. L. McClelland (Eds.), *Parallel distributed processing: Explorations in the microstructure of cognition.* Vol. 1: *Foundations* (pp. 282–317). Cambridge, MA: MIT Press.

Hirsch, M. W. (1996). Dynamical systems. In P. Smolensky, M. C. Mozer, & D. E. Rumelhart (Eds.), *Mathematical perspectives on neural networks* (pp. 271–323). Mahwah, NJ: Lawrence Erlbaum.

Hopfield, J. J. (1982). Neural networks and physical systems with emergent collective computational abilities. *Proceedings of the National Academy of Sciences USA, 79*, 2554–2558.

Hopfield, J. J. (1984). Neurons with graded response have collective computational properties like those of two-state neurons. *Proceedings of the National Academy of Sciences USA, 81*, 3088–3092.

Hummel, H. E., & Biederman, I. (1992). Dynamic binding in a neural network for shape recognition. *Psychological Review, 99*, 480–517.

Jacobs, R. A., Jordan, M. I., Nowlan, S. J., & Hinton, G. E. (1991). Adaptive mixtures of local experts. *Neural Computation, 15*, 219–250.

Jakobson, R. (1941/1968). *Child language, aphasia and phonological universals.* The Hague: Mouton.

Jakobson, R. (1962). *Selected writings I: Phonological studies.* The Hague: Mouton.

Jordan, M. I. (1986). Attractor dynamics and parallelism in a connectionist sequential machine. In *Proceedings of the Eighth Annual Conference of the Cognitive Science Society* (pp. 10–17). Hillsdale, NJ: Lawrence Erlbaum.

Kohonen, T. (1977). *Associative memory: A system theoretical approach.* New York: Springer.

Lachter, J., & Bever, T. G. (1988). The relation between linguistic structure and associative theories of language learning: A constructive critique of some connectionist learning models. *Cognition, 28*, 195–247.

Lakoff, G. (1987). *Women, fire, and dangerous things.* Chicago: University of Chicago Press.

Lakoff, G. (1993). Cognitive phonology. In J. Goldsmith (Ed.), *The last phonological rule.* Chicago: University of Chicago Press.

Langacker, R. W. (1987). *Foundations of cognitive grammar: Vol. 1. Theoretical prerequisites.* Stanford, CA: Stanford University Press.

Legendre, G., Miyata, Y., & Smolensky, P. (1990a). Harmonic grammar—A formal multi-level connectionist theory of linguistic well-formedness: An application. In *Proceedings of the Twelfth Annual Conference of the Cognitive Science Society* (pp. 884–891). Hillsdale, NJ: Lawrence Erlbaum.

Legendre, G., Miyata, Y., & Smolensky, P. (1990b). Harmonic grammar—A formal multi-level connectionist theory of linguistic well-formedness: Theoretical foundations. In *Proceedings of the Twelfth Annual Conference of the Cognitive Science Society* (pp. 388–395). Hillsdale, NJ: Lawrence Erlbaum.

Legendre, G., Smolensky, P., & Wilson, C. (1998). When is less more? Faithfulness and minimal links in *wh*-chains. In P. Barbosa, D. Fox, P. Hagstrom, M. McGinnis, & P. Pesetsky (Eds.), *Is the best good enough? Optimality and competition in syntax.* Cambridge, MA: MIT Press and MIT Working Papers in Linguistics. Available as Tech. Rep. No. JHU-CogSci-96-7, Department of Cognitive Science, Johns Hopkins University, 1996. Rutgers Optimality Archive, ROA-117.

McCarthy, J. J., and Prince, A. S. (1993). *Prosodic morphology I: Constraint interaction and satisfaction* (Tech. Rep. No. TR-3). New Brunswick, NJ: Rutgers Center for Cognitive Science, Rutgers University.

McClelland, J. L. (1993). Toward a theory of information processing in graded, random, and interactive networks. In D. E. Meyer & S. Kornblum (Eds.), *Attention and performance XIV: Synergies in experimental psychology, artificial intelligence, and cognitive neuroscience* (pp. 655–688). Hillsdale, NJ: Lawrence Erlbaum.

McClelland, J. L., & Rumelhart, D. E. (1986). *Parallel distributed processing: Explorations in the microstructure of cognition.* Vol. 2: *Psychological and biological models.* Cambridge, MA: MIT Press.

McCloskey, M. (1992). Networks and theories: The place of connectionism in cognitive science. *Psychological Science, 2,* 387–395.

McMillan, C., Mozer, M., & Smolensky, P. (1992). Rule induction through integrated symbolic and subsymbolic processing. In J. Moody, S. Hanson, & R. Lippman, (Eds.), *Advances in neural information processing systems 4* (pp. 969–976). San Mateo, CA: Morgan Kaufmann.

Mozer, M. C. (1991). *The perception of multiple objects: A connectionist approach.* Cambridge, MA: MIT Press/Bradford Books.

Pinker, S., & Mehler, J. (Eds.). (1988). *Connections and symbols.* Cambridge, MA: MIT Press/Bradford Books.

Pinker, S., & Prince, A. (1988). On language and connectionism: Analysis of a parallel distributed processing model of language acquisition. *Cognition, 28,* 73–193.

Plate, T. (1991). Holographic reduced representations: Convolution algebra for compositional distributed representations. In J. Mylopoulos & R. Reiter (Eds.), *Proceedings of the Twelfth International Joint Conference on Artificial Intelligence* (pp. 30–35). San Mateo, CA: Morgan Kaufmann.

Plaut, D. C., & Shallice, T. (1994). *Connectionist modeling in cognitive neuropsychology: A case study.* Hillsdale, NJ: Lawrence Erlbaum.

Pollack, J. B. (1990). Recursive distributed representations. *Artificial Intelligence, 46,* 77–105.

Prince, A. (1993). *In defense of the number i: Anatomy of a linear dynamical model of linguistic generalizations* (Tech. Rep. No. RuCCS-TR-1). New Brunswick, NJ: Rutgers Center for Cognitive Science, Rutgers University.

Prince, A., & Smolensky, P. (1991). *Notes on connectionism and Harmony Theory in linguistics* (Tech. Rep. No. CU-CS-533-91). Boulder: Department of Computer Science, University of Colorado.

Prince, A., & Smolensky, P. (1993). *Optimality theory: Constraint interaction in generative grammar* (Tech. Rep. No. CU-CS-696-93). Boulder: Department of Computer Science, University of Colorado; (Tech. Rep. No. TR-2). New Brunswick, NJ: Rutgers Center for Cognitive Science, Rutgers University.

Prince, A., & Smolensky, P. (1997). Optimality: From neural networks to universal grammar. *Science, 275,* 1604–1610.

Rumelhart, D. E., Durbin, R., Golden, R., & Chauvin, Y. (1996). Backpropagation: The basic theory. In P. Smolensky, M. C. Mozer, & D. E. Rumelhart (Eds.), *Mathematical perspectives on neural networks* (pp. 533–566). Mahwah, NJ: Lawrence Erlbaum.

Rumelhart, D. E., & McClelland, J. L. (1986a). On learning the past tenses of English verbs. In J. L. McClelland & D. E. Rumelhart (Eds.), *Parallel distributed processing: Explorations in the microstructure of cognition.* Vol. 2: *Psychological and biological models* (pp. 390–431). Cambridge, MA: MIT Press.

Rumelhart, D. E., & McClelland, J. L. (Eds.). (1986b). *Parallel distributed processing: Explorations in the microstructure of cognition.* Vol. 1: *Foundations.* Cambridge, MA: MIT Press.

Rumelhart, D. E., Smolensky, P., McClelland, J. L., & Hinton, G. E. (1986). Schemata and sequential thought processes in parallel distributed processing. In J. L. McClelland & D. E. Rumelhart (Eds.), *Parallel distributed processing: Explorations in the microstructure of cognition.* Vol. 2: *Psychological and biological models* (pp. 7–57). Cambridge, MA: MIT Press.

Rumelhart, D. E., & Zipser, D. (1985). Feature discovery by competitive learning. *Cognitive Science, 9*, 75–112.

Seidenberg, M. S., & McClelland, J. L. (1989). A distributed, developmental model of word recognition and naming. *Psychological Review, 96*, 523–568.

Sejnowski, T. J., & Rosenberg, C. R. (1987). Parallel networks that learn to pronounce English text. *Complex Systems, 1*, 145–168.

Shastri, L., & Ajjanagadde, V. (1993). From simple associations to systematic reasoning: A connectionist representation of rule, variables and dynamic bindings using temporal synchrony. *Behavioral and Brain Sciences, 16*, 417–494.

Smolensky, P. (1983). Schema selection and stochastic inference in modular environments. In *Proceedings of the National Conference on Artificial Intelligence* (pp. 378–382).

Smolensky, P. (1986). Information processing in dynamical systems: Foundations of harmony theory. In D. E. Rumelhart & J. L. McClelland (Eds.), *Parallel distributed processing: Explorations in the microstructure of cognition.* Vol. 1: *Foundations* (pp. 194–281). Cambridge, MA: MIT Press.

Smolensky, P. (1988). On the proper treatment of connectionism. *Behavioral and Brain Sciences, 11*, 1–23.

Smolensky, P. (1990). Tensor product variable binding and the representation of symbolic structures in connectionist networks. *Artificial Intelligence, 46*, 159–216.

Smolensky, P. (1993). *Harmony, markedness, and phonological activity*. Paper presented at the Rutgers Optimality Workshop 1, Rutgers University, New Brunswick, NJ. Rutgers Optimality Archive ROA-87.

Smolensky, P. (1996a). Dynamical perspectives on neural networks. In P. Smolensky, M. C. Mozer, & D. E. Rumelhart (Eds.), *Mathematical perspectives on neural networks* (pp. 245–270). Mahwah, NJ: Lawrence Erlbaum.

Smolensky, P. (1996b). On the comprehension/production dilemma in child language. *Linguistic Inquiry, 27*, 720–731.

Smolensky, P. (1996c). Statistical perspectives on neural networks. In P. Smolensky, M. C. Mozer, & D. E. Rumelhart (Eds.), *Mathematical perspectives on neural networks* (pp. 453–495). Mahwah, NJ: Lawrence Erlbaum.

Smolensky, P. (1997). *Constraint interaction in generative grammar II: Local conjunction* (or, *Random rules in Universal Grammar*). Paper presented at the Hopkins Optimality Theory Conference/University of Maryland Mayfest, Baltimore, Maryland.

Smolensky, P. (in press). The initial state and "richness of the base" in Optimality Theory. *Linguistic Inquiry*.

Smolensky, P., & Legendre, G. (2001). *Toward a calculus of the mind/brain: Neural network theory, optimality, and universal grammar.* Manuscript in preparation.

Smolensky, P., Legendre, G., & Miyata, Y. (1992). *Principles for an integrated connectionist/symbolic theory of higher cognition* (Tech. Rep. No. CU-CS-600-92). Boulder: Department of Computer Science, and 92-8, Institute of Cognitive Science, University of Colorado.

Smolensky, P., Mozer, M. C., & Rumelhart, D. E. (Eds.). (1996). *Mathematical perspectives on neural networks*. Mahwah, NJ: Lawrence Erlbaum.

Stevenson, S. & Smolensky, P. (1997). *Extending Optimality Theory to comprehension: Competence and performance*. Paper presented at the Architectures and Mechanisms for Language Processing Conference, Edinburgh.

Stone, G. O. (1986). An analysis of the delta rule and the learning of statistical associations. In D. E. Rumelhart & J. L. McClelland (Eds.), *Parallel distributed processing: Explorations in the microstructure of cognition. Vol. 1: Foundations* (pp. 444–459). Cambridge, MA: MIT Press.

Talmy, L. 1988. Force dynamics in language and cognition. *Cognitive Science, 12*, 49–100.

Tesar, B. (1998). Error-driven learning in Optimality Theory via the efficient computation of optimal forms. In P. Barbosa, D. Fox, P. Hagstrom, M. McGinnis, & D. Pesetsky (Eds.), *Is the best good enough? Optimality and competition in syntax* (pp. 421–435). Cambridge, MA: MIT Press and MIT Working Papers in Linguistics.

Tesar, B., & Smolensky, P. (1994). Synchronous-firing variable binding is spatiotemporal tensor product representation. In *Proceedings of the Sixteenth Annual Conference of the Cognitive Science Society*. Hillsdale, NJ: Lawrence Erlbaum.

Tesar, B., & Smolensky, P. (1996). *Learnability in Optimality Theory* (long version) (Tech. Rep. No. JHU-CogSci-96-3). Department of Cognitive Science, Johns Hopkins University, Baltimore, MD. Rutgers Optimality Archive ROA-156.

Tesar, B., & Smolensky, P. (1998). Learnability in Optimality Theory. *Linguistic Inquiry, 29*, 229–268.

Touretzky, D. S. (1986). BoltzCONS: Reconciling connectionism with the recursive structure of stacks and trees. In *Proceedings of the Eighth Annual Conference of the Cogntiive Science Society* (pp. 522–530). Hillsdale, NJ: Lawrence Erlbaum.

Touretzky, D. S., & Hinton, G. E. (1988). A distributed connectionist production system. *Cognitive Science, 12*, 423–466.

Touretzky, D. S., & Wheeler, D. W. (1990). A computational basis for phonology. In D. S. Touretzky (Ed.), *Advances in neural information processing systems 2* (pp. 372–379). San Mateo, CA: Morgan Kaufmann.

Tranel, B. (1994). *French liaison and elision revisited: A unified account within Optimality Theory*. Rutgers Optimality Archive ROA-15.

Trubetzkoy, N. (1939/1969). *Principles of phonology*. Berkeley and Los Angeles: University of California Press.

Zoll, C. C. (1996). *Parsing below the segment in a constraint based framework*. Unpublished doctoral thesis, Linguistics Department, University of California, Berkeley. Rutgers Optimality Archive ROA-143.

Zubritskaya, K. (1997). Mechanism of sound change in Optimality Theory. *Language Variation and Change, 9*, 121–148.

11

Connectionist Sentence Processing in Perspective

Mark Steedman

As many chapters in this book attest, an active and constructive dialogue about processing at the level of spoken and written words, and about the acquisition of related systems such as phonology, morphology and the lexicon, is going on between symbolic or rule-oriented theorists and connectionist or neurally oriented theorists. There seems to be much less dialogue between symbolic and rule-based approaches to syntactic analysis, despite genuine efforts to reconcile these positions on the connectionist side; for example, by Hinton (1990c), Smolensky (1990), and here, and others collected in Hinton (1990a). This chapter is a reciprocal attempt from the symbolist side to get such a dialogue going on the basis of the contributions collected here.

The traditional rule-based view of syntactic processing divides the problem among various modules. One fairly generally applicable way of doing this is to distinguish a grammar, characterized by syntactic and semantic rules of certain classes and a related characteristic automaton; an algorithm, characterized by properties like the order in which rules are applied to the string, whether bottom-up or top-down, and by certain memory resources, such as those used in building structure and the charts or tables used in parsers based on dynamic programming; and an oracle or decision criterion for deciding which rule to apply the algorithm to in cases where there is more than one possibility.

In any given theoretical presentation or implementation, these modules may be combined, but in rule-based theories they can usually be distinguished in functional terms. The fact that they are in that sense distinct modules does not of course imply that the corresponding computations must be carried out in a series of chronologically distinct phases: For example, it is quite possible to construct systems in which the oracle can call on the results of semantic interpretation in mid-parse, while grammatical analysis and the algorithm are still under way.

Connectionism is no more intrinsically nonmodular than any other approach, and many connectionists including some represented here have explicitly endorsed modular architectures of various kinds. Nevertheless, the emphasis in the connectionist literature on distributed representation and "emergence" of rulelike behavior from such systems has sometimes made it hard for connectionists and symbolists alike to recognize the often close relations between their respective systems.

Part of the difficulty in reconciling the two stems from the involvement of two rather different views of the role of grammar in processing. The "performance" grammar used by the three-module processor described earlier can in theory be quite different from the grammar that linguists identify as the "competence" grammar. The linguists' grammar is usually one whose derivation structures are closely related to their intuitions about the interpretation of sentences. (Since we have no direct access to interpretations, the practical criteria for choosing one linguistic analysis over another are usually described in rather different terms by linguists like Chomsky, but in fact this is what it comes down to.)

Interpretations, and hence the linguistic competence grammars that (however imperfectly) reflect them, have a number of important properties. Most important, interpretations are *compositional*, which means that they are recursively defined solely in terms of the interpretations of their parts. This means that to know the meaning–grammatical category of a predicate like *walks* is to know the meaning–grammaticality of the proposition that results from applying that predicate to any argument of the appropriate type. Similarly, to know the meaning–grammatical category of a verb like *deny* is to know the meaning–grammaticality of denying any proposition in the language, including those involving the verb *deny*. Compositionality entails a property that Fodor and Pylyshyn (1988) proposed as a test for grammar induction or emergence that they called "systematicity," which means that a system cannot be claimed to embody a grammar unless it can recognize the grammaticality and ultimately the interpretation of any sentence of the language, whether it has been encountered before (see Hadley, 1994a, 1994b, on definitions of this property of increasing levels of strictness up to "semantic" systematicity).

If a grammar accepts all and only the strings that some other grammar accepts, then the two are said to be weakly equivalent. Some early parsing programs used algorithms requiring grammars in a normal form that was not particularly congenial to linguists. They therefore used a weakly equivalent normal-form "covering grammar" to build structures that could be transduced into the structural representation required by the linguists. Modern parsers often compile large grammars into finite-state covering grammars (whose coverage must necessarily be incomplete) for reasons of efficiency (see Black, 1989).

For reasons of evolutionary simplicity that will be elaborated later, it would actually be rather surprising to find that human processors used a covering grammar. Nevertheless, it is possible in theory, and there are some properties of human processors that might appear to suggest that they do. In particular, there are well-known (if poorly understood) limitations on human abilities to process sentences involving center-embedding. Since center-embedding is one of the properties of natural grammars that led Chomsky (1957) to claim that context-free grammars represented a lower bound on expressive power, it has sometimes been claimed that these limitations are evidence that human processors work with an incomplete finite-state covering grammar. Of course, other explanations are possible. It might be the algorithm that is incomplete, perhaps because of memory limitations, or even that there is something about these constructions that irrevocably misleads the oracle.

However, if a covering grammar is involved, it must be one that is capable of specifying the interpretation. That is not the same as saying that the derivations themselves must correspond to traditional syntactic structure. Linguists tend to think of syntactic derivation as surface structure-building, but it is equally possible to think of such structures (as computational linguists tend to) as implicit in the flow of control in a parser that incrementally builds the interpretation directly (the early Augmented Transition Network [ATN] parser of Woods, 1970, had this character). Such derivations can be structurally quite unlike traditional grammarians' analyses.

Linguists (especially computational linguists) also usually think of interpretations as structures or logical forms, but as a matter of fact this is not strictly necessary either. As in the work of Montague (1970, 1974), it is possible, in principle, to regard logical form as no more than the flow of control in computing models, in the sense of that term used in model-theoretic semantics. However, it is important not to get carried away by this possibility. Model theory is really only good for proving very general properties of formal systems, such as soundness and completeness. In artificial intelligence (AI) and natural language understanding we are usually interested in the form of a constructive proof that we can get to New York City, rather than the mere truth of that proposition, because such a proof tells us how to actually get there. This means that practical knowledge-representation systems are almost always proof-theoretic, involving manipulation of formulae, rather than model-theoretic. The significance of this point is that when faced with a connectionist processor one must not only ask what grammar is implicit in it, but how it can be made to deliver logical forms of a kind that can be manipulated by the equivalent of rules like *Modus Ponens*.

A second source of difficulty in comparing connectionist and rule-based systems lies in the tendency of certain kinds of connectionist architecture to combine the roles of grammar and oracle or ambiguity-resolution device in a single representation distributed over a single set of hidden units. This can make it hard to know whether one should compare the systems as a whole, or regard the connectionist system as merely a disambiguating device; for example, as the analog of a Markovian part-of-speech (POS) filter in a standard parsing architecture. I shall argue later that some devices that have presented as sentence processors should be thought of in this more restricted sense, and that (if the problems of reliability and scalability inherent in mechanisms based on back-propagation can be overcome), this view offers a way forward to a kind of system that embodies both rules and subsymbolic representations in a principled way.

RECURRENT NETWORKS AND FINITE-STATE DISAMBIGUATORS

The recurrent networks proposed by Jordan (1989) and Elman (1990) use an auxiliary bank of "state" or "context" units to store information about the previous state of an otherwise standard three-level feed-forward network using back-propagation to adjust a hidden layer of units. The recurrence consists of copying either the output units or the hidden units to the context units. The context units then provide some of the inputs to the hidden units. Jordan applies such a device to the coarticulation problem in speech, and uses context units to represent the preceding items directly by copying the output units from the previous cycle. Copying the hidden units, as in Elman's simple recurrent network (SRN) shown in Figure 11.1, can represent more abstract properties of the preceding sequence. Interestingly, the context units can come to carry "echoes" of earlier states of the computation, and can thereby be used to represent quite distant dependencies between string elements. Elman applies SRNs to the problem of supervised grammar induction in a rather indirect sense in which the device (since it does not build structure or exhibit internal states) can only reveal the implicit grammar indirectly, by predicting the next word or word category. This, of course, is a test related to weak equivalence of the implicit grammar.

Elman's (1990) early work was criticized by Hadley (1994a) for nonsystematicity in the selection of test materials with respect to the claimed implicit grammar, so that in some cases the implicit grammar was not even proved weakly equivalent to the one that was initially claimed. However, Christiansen and Chater (1994), Niklasson and van Gelder (1994), and the work by Allen (1997) discussed by Seidenberg and MacDonald (Chapter 9,

Figure 11.1
Architecture of the Simple Recurrent Network

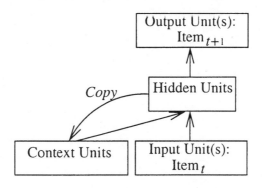

this volume) show that SRNs can achieve systematicity in acquiring implicit grammars weakly equivalent to phrase structure fragments. Elman's work is also extended by Cleeremans (1993) and by Christiansen and Chater (1999, Chapter 5, this volume), among many others. In particular, Christiansen has shown that SRNs can cover (finitely bounded sublanguages of) small context-free grammars with center-embedding, and (similarly bounded sublanguages of) small trans-context-free grammars, including crossing dependencies of the kind notoriously characteristic of Germanic verb raising constructions (Bresnan, Kaplan, Peters, & Zaenen, 1982; Huybregts, 1984; Shieber, 1985). There is no doubt that SRNs and other recurrent nets can approximate covering finite-state machines (FSM) of this kind (see Cleeremans, 1993; Cleeremans, Servan-Schreiber, & McClelland, 1995; Casey, 1996). The only obvious limitation on the approximation is that it appears to rapidly become less reliable for a given number of hidden units as the distance of the dependency increases. For this reason the precise place of such "graded-state" automata in the automata–theoretic hierarchy is not entirely clear, but in practice they seem to be limited to finite-state machines.

It is important to recall that the sole task that the SRN is required to do is to predict the next word or word category at each point in the string. We know from work on symbolic finite-state models, such as Hidden Markov Models (HMM) and part-of-speech taggers (Jelinek, 1976; Church, 1988; Merialdo, 1994; Brill, 1992), that such approximations can achieve very high accuracy—around 97 percent—without having any claim whatsoever to embody the grammar itself. (To put this number in perspective, one should, however, recall that prediction of category on the basis of simple unigram frequency alone yields around 91 percent accuracy.) One of the surprising things about the recurrent network literature is that there is very little link to statistical computational linguistics, despite some early identifications of an equivalence relation by Williams and Hinton (1990) and Bridle

(1992). Nevertheless, the comparison with finite-state POS taggers seems to be a relevant one.

The resemblance is even closer among versions like that presented by Tabor and Tanenhaus (Chapter 6, this volume), in which a principal-components analysis of the hidden units is used to reveal implicit grammatical categories. It has even been suggested that the trajectory that a sequence of such categories defines through the high-dimensional space defined by the hidden units and/or principal components can be thought of as defining a meaning (Elman, 1995), a claim that would begin to address the issue of semantic systematicity.

Although we shall see later that hidden units can legitimately be viewed as encoding certain kinds of semantic information, this last claim seems too strong. A mere sequence of words, even a sequence that is successfully disambiguated as to syntactic category and even word sense (as is reasonable to expect from a stochastic tagger), is not a sentence meaning, as is evident from the fact that the following string remains structurally and semantically globally ambiguous even when the lexical categories are unambiguously identified:

(1) *Put the block in the box on the table.*

We will defer until later the discussion of whether the further information that is needed to resolve the ambiguity is probabilistic or inferential, and whether the special graded nature of SRNs can capture the probabilistic alternative. The relevant point is that a significant component of the grammar induction and parsing problems as they are usually understood remains to be dealt with once n-gram-based POS taggers have done their work, and the same appears to be true for the SRN as it is used in these experiments.

This observation should not be taken to deny that SRNs are useful as a component of sentence processors. SRNs and related devices may be a very good way of building stochastic part-of-speech disambiguators as an input to parsing proper. This seems to be the role that the SRN plays in the modular architectures of St. John and McClelland (1990), Berg (1992), Sharkey and Sharkey (1992), and Mikkulainen (1993, 1995), discussed later. Interestingly, Srinivas (1997) and Srinivas and Joshi (1994) have shown that increasing the set of POS tags to include the subcategorization or domain of government information implicit in the lexicalist grammars, discussed later, may increase the effectiveness of such devices (although it decreases tagging accuracy by increasing the number of POS categories), because by the same token the categories make more information available to the parser itself. Kim, Srinivas, and Trueswell (1998) show that SRNs can induce a tagger for such extended category sets. We shall also see below that SRNs can in principle be used to look at string contexts that extend beyond the sentential boundary. But none of these undoubted virtues suggest that it is correct to regard grammar itself as in any sense an emergent property of these devices as presently used.

It is also worth noting that distributed representations potentially allow exponentially greater efficiency in representation of stochastic finite-state machines over those induced by HMMs (Williams & Hinton, 1990) (although to the extent that SRNs seriously exploit the potential of hidden units for efficiently distributing the representation of the FSM they approximate, it becomes correspondingly harder to see how to associate structure-building operations of any kind with them directly). It is not likely that the SRN itself will achieve such efficiency, because of the trade-off that it makes between full back-propagation through time and on-line computation (see Pearlmutter, 1995, for relevant discussion). But if finite-state POS tagging is what an SRN is actually doing, then we may not want to interpret hidden-unit states, but may rather prefer to exploit the efficient way in which they and some of the other devices discussed by Williams and Hinton can exploit information-theoretic redundancy in text quite independently of grammar. For example, the Latent Semantic Analysis (LSA) program of Landauer and Dumais (1997), when trained on large volumes of text and tested on similarity judgments between words and passages, showed very high correlations with human similarity judgments. More recent work in the framework, using similarity measures between student essays (which LSA treats as unordered bags of words) and instructional text for the relevant domain, yielded correlations with grades assigned to the essays by human assessors comparable to the correlation across human graders themselves (Landauer, Laham, Rehder, & Schreiner, 1997). However, despite its name and its very interesting performance, this result cannot be equated with the delivery of a meaning, as anyone who does the thought experiment of running the theory in the opposite direction to generate the student essays will agree.

PSYCHOLOGICAL RELEVANCE OF SRN

A number of studies have investigated the fit of SRNs to human parsing performance. The studies by Dell, Chang, and Griffin (Chapter 7, this volume), and Tabor and Tanenhaus (Chapter 6, this volume), are examples of this kind of work. Tabor and Tanenhaus advance the theoretical model via an elaboration of the copying mechanism the SRN uses to approximate back-propagation through time (BTT, Rumelhart, Hinton, & Williams, 1986; Pearlmutter, 1995), and by a "gravitational" analysis using attractors obtained from a principal components analysis of the patterns of activation on the hidden units to interpret them as FSM states. The authors point out that these can be viewed as parse hypotheses that can be mapped onto more traditional symbolic models (although, as we have seen, the close relation between finite-state POS tagging and SRNs makes it likely that such a translation will in general be nontrivial, and that it may be seriously incomplete).

Tabor and Tanenhaus (Chapter 6, this volume) also provide a detailed comparison with the experimental findings of McRae, Spivey-Knowlton, and Tanenhaus (1998) concerning the influence of "thematic fit" of verbs and arguments in on-line sentence comprehension for minimal pairs of sentences like (2) and (3), in which the misleadingly better thematic fit of *cop* as agent than as patient in an indicative reading of *arrested* in comparison to *crook* causes a temporary increase in processing load later in sentence (2), when that reading leads to no grammatical analysis.

(2) *The cop arrested by the detective was guilty.*

(3) *The crook arrested by the detective was guilty.*

The fit of the model in terms of predicting word-by-word processing effort as revealed by increased reading times is impressive. The authors are justified in their claim that the SRN can cover the same phenomenon as the structure-invoking "garden path" model (whose most recent incarnation is Frazier & Clifton, 1996), without building any structure at all.

However, the claim that this amounts to the "emergence" of grammar from the SRN model seems premature. It remains the case that the only thing the SRN is doing is predicting the next category in the sentence. It is actually not in the least surprising that the SRN can do at least as well as the structural model. It is learning a finite-state machine, and we have seen that FSMs can do very well at category prediction for homogeneous corpora. Earlier work by Tanenhaus's own group has shown that structural properties of sentences are confounded with frequency effects, and that when frequency is properly controlled, there is no evidence for any residual purely structural preference (see Trueswell & Tanenhaus, 1992; Trueswell, Tanenhaus, & Kello, 1993; Trueswell, Tanenhaus, & Garnsey, 1994; Spivey-Knowlton, Trueswell, & Tanenhaus, 1993). Nor does the success of the SRN in predicting processing difficulty on the basis of frequency information alone justify any claim that the human processor works on the same basis. Frequency is even more strongly confounded with semantic and pragmatic plausibility, since word-transition probabilities are compiled from coherent text corpora. As Tanenhaus and colleague's earlier papers are careful to point out, their results therefore do not distinguish between a model of the processor-like SRN that resolves ambiguity entirely probabilistically and one where ambiguity is resolved on the basis of active computation of semantic and/or pragmatic plausibility via inference.

There is evidence that favors the latter interpretation. First, the performance of low-level Markovian POS taggers is actually not very good by the standards of human sentence processing. The average length of the sentences in the *Wall Street Journal* corpus is around 23.5 words. An accuracy rate of 97 percent means an error in over half the sentences of average length in this type of written text, as Church and Mercer (1993) point out.

Ratnaparkhi (1998) shows that in practice this is about the proportion for all sentences in the corpus. (Using a 96.3% accurate tagger he finds only 47.7% of sentences in the *Wall Street Journal* corpus are error free). While de Marcken (1990), Elworthy (1994), and Carroll and Briscoe (1996) show that by allowing sets of POS tags to go forward when the top candidates are close in probability, 99.9-percent accuracy can be attained for a mean set size of around 1.3 tags per word, both of these results mean something other than *n*-gram frequency must be doing some of the work in humans. If something else is doing some of the work, then it may be doing all of it.

There is also experimental evidence in work by Crain, Altmann, and Steedman (see Crain, 1980; Crain & Steedman, 1985; Altmann, 1988; Altmann & Steedman, 1988; and Steedman & Altmann, 1989, for discussion) that shows that parsing decisions are sensitive to the relative plausibility of the semantic interpretations of rival analyses, which may depend on quite transient and rapidly changing properties of the referential context. This fact has implications even for sentences presented in isolation. They showed, for example, that the mention of a single policeman or a set of policemen in the discourse immediately preceding examples like sentence (3) can effect the tendency to assume that the verb is indicative rather than participial. The authors argued that this was because the presence of multiple individuals or tokens of a given type in a hearer's mental model of the situation under discussion makes use of a restrictive relative clause or other modifier pragmatically felicitous, whereas the presence of a single individual of a given type makes it redundant and infelicitous. Moreover, they argued that in the null context where no policeman at all has been mentioned, so that a referent and attendant presuppositions must be "accommodated" or added to the contextual model, the accommodation of one individual is less effortful than the accommodation of several together, with further distinguishing properties presupposed by the modifier.

If preferences for parsing decisions can be reversed by a few preceding context-setting sentences, then it becomes implausible to argue that the human parser's decision is made on the basis of global frequencies collected over large volumes of input. While finite-state approximation techniques can be quite immediately generalized to sequences of words and categories that cross sentence boundaries, as Seidenberg and MacDonald (Chapter 9, this volume) propose, it is dangerous to assume that this will capture transient referential effects of the kind established by these experiments. Since definite expressions can refer to entities that are merely inferable from the things that have actually been mentioned, there seem to be simply too many ways of getting sets of policemen into the context for it to be possible to collect appropriate statistics based on words and word senses alone. The only alternative seems to be to assume that interpretations are incrementally computed for rival analyses, which are then compared, leading to rapid elimination of less plausible alternatives. But it it is hard to believe that this can be done without a fuller grammatical analysis than that implicit in the SRN.

The study of syntactic priming (Bock, 1986) in Dell et al. (Chapter 7, this volume) might appear at first glance to encourage a more optimistic view. It uses a variant of the simple recurrent network architecture linking the context units of an SRN trained to associate words in sequence with content vectors (or, rather, a simulation using a transition network of the successive states of such context units) to those of a production network producing sequences from content. Crucially, pairs of sequences corresponding to active versus passive surface forms are associated with the same content. Having trained the network, the authors are able to show that a further presentation of a string in active voice biases immediately subsequent productions toward that pattern, even for different content, with results comparable to Bock's subjects. As the authors claim, this shows that apparently syntactic priming effects can emerge from implicit learning rather than from rule activation or structures in short-term memory.

However, this observation is entirely compatible with the idea that the nature of this implicit learning lies in a change to the probabilities in an implicit finite state machine. As we have seen, it does not follow that the rules themselves are implicit, or that interpretation can be done on the basis of the probabilities alone. It merely shows that syntactic priming is not necessarily syntactic at all. Nor does it follow that the analogous priming effects in humans are mediated by actual probabilities, because of the confounding of probability with actively computed semantics and pragmatic inference discussed in connection with Tabor and Tanenhaus's (Chapter 6, this volume), and Crain and Altmann's (1985) experiments.

The relation of recurrent networks to finite-state machines of a more traditional sort, such as POS taggers and HMMs (which is, of course, evident in Jordan's [1989] elegant application of recurrent networks to model coarticulation in speech and other motor-control problems), suggests a further direction in which connectionist models of syntactic processing might evolve. The trend in symbolic stochastic language processing is away from grammar-independent POS tagging and toward a greater integration of probabilistic information with the grammar and recursive parsing algorithms, and in particular with the lexicon. This requires a rather different kind of mechanism.

RECURSIVE AUTO-ASSOCIATIVE MEMORY AND GRAMMAR

A number of connectionist processors have used nets as distributed representations of structure, and such networks can be viewed as encoding the thematic roles of propositions. Early versions of the idea, such as McClelland and Kawamoto (1986), were nonrecursive, but Pollack (1990) showed how recursively embedded structure could be built into such rulelike nets, in an architecture called the recursive auto-associative memory (RAAM). This was a more efficient version of an even simpler device called the associative net (Willshaw, Buneman, & Longuet-Higgins, 1969; Willshaw, 1981). An associative net acts as a distributed memory associating pairs of input and output vectors, as in Figure 11.2, which represents a grid of horizontal input lines and vertical output lines with binary switches (triangles) at the intersections. To store an association between the input vector on the left and the output vector along the top, switches are turned on (black triangles) at the intersection of lines that correspond to a 1 in both input and output patterns. To retrieve the associate of the input, a signal is sent down each horizontal line corresponding to a 1 in the input. When such an input signal encounters an "on" switch, it increments the signal on the corresponding output line by one unit. These lines are then thresholded at a level corresponding to the number of on-bits in the input. With such thresholding, an associative memory can store a number of associations in a distributed fashion, with interesting properties of noise and damage resistance. The point of the device for present purposes is that the association of an input vector with an output vector can be regarded as analogous to storing one or more pointers between addresses. Since the output can in turn be used as an input and associated with a further output, an associative memory can be used to store recursive structures of any depth, subject only to information-theoretic limits dependent upon size. Smolensky's (1990) tensor-product representation is a generalization of the same idea.

Figure 11.2
An Associative Net Storing a Single Pointer

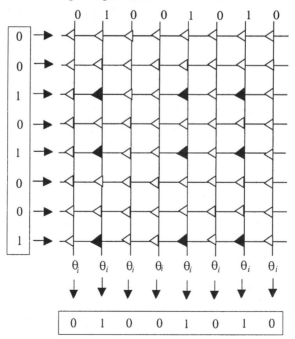

The RAAM mainly differs from the primitive associative net in using hidden units rather than observable switches to encode the association more efficiently. This is achieved by realizing the device as a three-level feed-forward network with the input and output units structured into n sectors, each large enough to copy the hidden units into, where n is the maximum branching factor of the nodes in the structure. Alternatively, as in the case of the associative net, we could regard each pointer as the responsibility of n separate associative devices. We shall see that we do not actually need the ordering information implicit in the standard RAAM. A binary version of the device is sketched in Figure 11.3.

A recursive structure can be stored bottom-up in the RAAM, starting with the leaf elements by recursively auto-associating vectors comprising up to n hidden-unit activation patterns that resulted from encoding their daughters. The activation pattern that results from each auto-association of the sets of daughters can then be treated as the address of the parent. Since by including finitely many further units on the input and output layers, we can associate node-label or content information with the nodes (a variant that is sometimes referred to as a labelling RAAM, or LRAAM). This device can store recursive parse structures, thematic representations, or other varieties of logical forms of sentences.

The device should not be confused with a parser: It is trained with fully articulated structures that it merely efficiently stores. However, the hidden units can be regarded as encoding to some approximation the context-free productions that defined those structures, in a fashion similar to the way Hinton (1990b) encoded part–whole relations. In that sense the device has been claimed to be capable of inducing the corresponding grammar from the trees (Pollack, 1990, pp. 88–89). It is also the basis for a very limited degree of generalization (p. 94; also of a corresponding tendency to decode novel trees as members of the training set). In theory this generalization could be recursively productive, but in practice this does not seem to have been achieved, possibly because of severe practical limitations on RAAM,

Figure 11.3
Architecture of a Binary Recursive Auto-Associative Memory

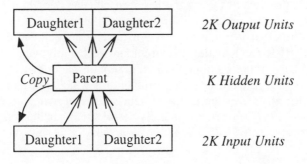

which is slow to train and inherits poor scaling properties from its use of back-propagation. Associative devices more closely related to Willshaw nets, such as the holographic reduced representations (HRR) proposed by Plate (1991, 1994, 1997), are a promising alternative for both recursive-structure building and grammar representation.

Niklasson and van Gelder (1994) make the interesting claim that rules that transform RAAM representations of structures of this kind in ways that are analogous to the operations of grammatical transformations or simple logical equivalences, such as the replacement of $p \to q$ by $\neg p \lor q$, can be automatically induced via a three-layer back-propagation network. Significantly, such rules are claimed to operate holistically, without the recursive process of dereferencing pointers that would be standard in the corresponding symbolic representations. Plate (1994) makes a related claim, showing that similar transformation vectors can be constructed by hand for HRR representations of logical formulae. Recently, Neuman (2000a, 2000b) has presented methods for automatically acquiring such transformation vectors for HRR representations of formulae, and has shown that they generalize both to structures containing novel elements and to structures of higher complexity than the training examples, extending the degree of systematicity attained by connectionist representations of structure. One important open question about such representations is whether they can carry out operations equivalent to inference rules that reduce two formulae to one, such as *Modus Ponens*. If they can then they are equivalent to rule systems of considerable expressive power.

Pollack (1990) proposed to augment the trained RAAM with a variant of the recursive network parsers discussed in the last section to make a parser-interpreter, along lines suggested by St. John and McClelland (1990) for its nonrecursive predecessor, and there have been many related proposals since, including Berg (1992), Sharkey and Sharkey (1992), and Mikkulainen (1993, 1995). The earlier remarks about limitations on the sense in which SRNs can be said to represent grammars, as opposed to more primitive notions like current state of the FSM or corresponding part-of-speech, show up in the extent to which such devices generalize to truly novel sentence structures. Some authors mentioned augment the SRN–RAAM with further modules, but to the extent that these duplicate the standard finite-state control and stack architecture of the symbolic approach, they lack both the simple virtues of the RAAM and the wild romance of the pure SRN.

This suggests that it might be better to reserve associative devices like RAAM and HRR for inducing the grammar in the following sense. Linguists and other symbolists often think of grammar induction as the problem of inducing structure from strings, a problem for which an exact solution is impossible for all interesting cases without some external source of information (Gold, 1967). For interesting classes of grammar the task can technically be approximated to any degree of exactness, as is shown by the work considered here and much work in statistical language-learning theory since Horning (1969; see Manning & Schütze, 1999, for a review). However, the amounts of data and the computational resources that are required for realistically sized cases are psychologically quite daunting. This has led to symbolist claims of innate linguistic knowledge that any red-blooded empiricist is bound to bridle at. However, the only plausible source for such pregrammatical knowledge has always been semantics, under the assumption that the child comes to language learning equipped with universal conceptual structures on which language-specific grammar is rather directly hung by pairing words and sentences with conceptual structures describing the situation of utterance (see Chomsky, 1965, although Chomsky has always insisted that our access to the detailed nature of conceptual structures, other than via syntax itself, is so inadequate as to make the observation empirically useless).

Gleitman (1990) and Fisher, Hall, Rakowitz, and Gleitman (1994) have rightly pointed to the dangers of identifying "situation of utterance" with "instantaneous state of the physical world," and warned against the assumption that the situation uniquely identifies the relevant conceptual structure or proposition. But Siskind (1996) has shown that under more reasonable assumptions about the nature of the mental representations and the nature of the ambiguity, the information needed for verb learning is available.

The relevance of this point for the present discussion is that conceptual structures can reasonably be regarded as the structural input to a device such as RAAM for purposes of induction of the underlying grammar. Of course, this is not the whole of language acquisition, because conceptual structure represents Universal Grammar rather than any specific language; indeed, conceptual structures should properly be regarded as unordered. However, if we regard the RAAM or related device as storing word meanings as logical forms rather than sentences, then we can pair those logical forms with language-specific categories. In any of the lexicalist frameworks discussed in the next section, such categories amount to a specification of most if not all of the language-specific grammar.

Such categories could provide the input to a standard-architecture modular symbolist parser using RAAM, HRR, or some other associative device to build interpretable structure, the distinctively connectionist contribution lying in the distributed lexical entries and logical form. The interesting point of such a representation is that we might assume that during training conceptual structures are available prelinguistically, and result relatively directly from the structure of connections to the sensorium, short-term memory, and the like. Much of this structure is undoubtedly the result of biological evolution over a very long period, as Wilkens and Wakefield (1995) have pointed out. At higher levels, such structure may arise from nonlinguistic network concept learning of the kind discussed by Hinton (1990b), without mediating symbolic forms.

NETWORKS AND THE LEXICON

The representations that would be built by RAAM or related distributed associative memory under these assumptions would embody the traditional local domain defined by lexical entities like verbs and their arguments, including the subject. There is a growing consensus across linguistic theories that the lexicon is the main locus of language-specific grammatical information, and that what we might loosely call "heads" are lexically specified as controlling such a local domain, as in Lexical-Functional Grammar (LFG; see Bresnan, 1982), Combinatory Categorial Grammar (CCG; see Steedman, 1985, 1986), Head-Driven Phrase-Structure Grammar (HPSG; see Pollard & Sag, 1987, 1994), Lexical Tree-Adjoining Grammar (LTAG; see Joshi & Schabes, 1992), and certain versions of the Government-Binding theory (GB; see, e.g., Hale & Keyser, 1993, and Grimshaw, 1997).

The advantage of such theories lies in a closer integration of the lexicon, syntax, semantics, and phonology, including intonation, as called for by Kelly (1992), Kelly and Martin (1994), and Christiansen, Allen, and Seidenberg (1998). For example, in CCG each word and constituent is associated with a directional syntactic type, a logical form, and a phonological type. "Combinatory" syntactic rules combine such entities to produce not only standard constituents associated with the same three components, such as predicates or verb phrases, but also nonstandard constituents corresponding to substrings such as *I have found*. The latter are involved in phenomena such as coordination and intonational phrasing, as in (4) and (5) (in which % marks an intonational phrase boundary marked by a rise and/or lengthening, and capitals indicate pitch accent or stress).

(4) *You have lost, and I have found, a quarter.*

(5) [Q:] *I know you lost a DIME, but what have you FOUND?*
   [A:] *I have FOUND% a QUARTER.*

The intonational phrasing in the latter example is related in Steedman (1991) to discourse-information structural notions like theme–topic, rheme–comment, and focus–new information. Such nonstandard constituents are also claimed by Crain and Steedman (1985) and Altmann and Steedman (1988) to provide direct grammatical support for the fine-grain incremental interpretation by the processor that is implicated by Crain's and Altmann's experimental results.

Within such frameworks, grammar acquisition reduces to decisions such as whether the syntactic type corresponding to, say, the *walking* concept looks for its subject to the left or to the right in the particular language that the child is faced with; in CCG terms, whether it is $S\backslash NP$ or S/NP. Since directionality can be represented as a value on an input unit, and since the categories themselves can be defined as finite-state machines, this can be handled by network lexicon learning using devices like RAAM, SRN, and the like. Part of the interest of this proposal lies in the possibility that such learning might capture word-order generalizations over the lexical categories, a point that is made by Christiansen and Devlin (1997). It is also important to note once more that any assumption of a covering grammar not transparent to semantics in this way, such as the FSM implicit in the SRN, complicates the task of associating meanings with categories very greatly, and appears to pose equivalent difficulties for any attempt to explain the evolution of the language faculty.

These observations suggest that there might be a closer relation between the connectionist and symbolist theories than is usually assumed. Grimshaw (1997), in particular, relates the forms that categories can take to a constraint-satisfaction problem that can be elegantly solved within Optimality Theory (Prince & Smolensky, 1997), a branch of the neural network literature discussed by Smolensky (Chapter 10, this volume). Since this process of ordered constraint satisfaction is best seen as a definition of the notion "possible human lexicon," rather than as a process that the parser goes through, the connection is likely to be at the level of language acquisition and machine learning, rather than processing as such, as in the work discussed by Seidenberg (1997) and Seidenberg and MacDonald (Chapter 9, this volume). Constraints such as semantically related categories (such as tensed transitive verbs) tend to have the same directionality in a given language (such as the English SVO order), and are "soft" constraints, which can have exceptions (such as English auxiliary verbs), one of the main motivations behind Optimality Theory. Since Optimality-Theoretic constraint systems can be regarded (under some assumptions at least) as defining finite-state transducers (Eisner, 1997), it seems likely that the associative-memory-based lexical-acquisition device sketched earlier might be suited to acquiring such soft-constraint-based lexicons, as an interesting alternative to the learning mechanisms proposed by Tesar (1998). If so, then the claim that the form of possible lexicons was "emergent" from the neural mechanism would have some force.

A similar tendency toward lexical involvement is evident in current statistical computational-linguistic research as well. Much recent work in probabilistic parsing, including proposals by Jelinek et al. (1994), Magerman (1994), Collins (1997), and Charniak (1997), moves away from autonomous Markovian POS tagging and prefiltering, and toward a greater integration of probabilities with grammar (see Manning & Schütze, 1999, for a review). Collins, in particular, uses a standard dynamic-programming-based parsing algorithm under the guidance of a probabilistic language model based on dependencies between heads, such as those between main verbs and the nouns that head their arguments. This architecture is quite directly compatible with lexicalized grammars such as CCG, HPSG, and LTAG, a line of research that is being pursued by Baldridge, Bierner, and Hockenmaier (2000) and Xia (1999).

SEMANTICS AND NEURAL NETWORKS

To observe that both resolution of syntactic nondeterminism by human parsers and language acquisition appear to depend upon a structurally explicit semantics manipulated by stack automata might appear to be a sort of underhand appeal for capitulation to the symbolist view. Instead, I want to argue that the most important contribution of subsymbolic theories to the problem of language understanding may be at the level of semantics, rather than syntax, for the following reason.

The conclusion that the decisions of the human sentence processor depend on semantics is quite depressing for those of us who need to build practical computational parsers, because we know that the semantics in question is very poorly understood, and that there are no knowledge representation systems that can support it affordably for other than small restricted domains. For that reason, we can expect applied computational linguists to keep on using statistics instead, despite the fact that we can be pretty sure that this tactic will never be entirely successful.

However, there is no reason for connectionists to be inhibited in this way, and there is a good reason for them to concentrate their attention elsewhere. The reason our grasp of semantics is so inadequate is undoubtedly that the conceptual primitives that underlie language are grounded in very obscure ways in our physical, social, and intellectual interactions with the real world. It is likely that in many cases the forms they take are directly related to the physical structure of the sensory–motor apparatus. In most cases it seems likely that, as Fodor (1975) has claimed, there really is very little decomposition of meaning below the level of the morpheme. That is, even if one believes (pace Fodor, whose arguments to the contrary do not really apply to lexicalized grammars of the kind assumed here) that the logical form of the verb *kill* involves the composition of a CAUSE predicate and a DIE predicate, that is about as far as it goes. The CAUSE primitive doesn't seem to want to decompose any further, and in fact shows signs of being distinct from the translation of the word *cause*. In fact, all one seems to be able to do is to define the inference system directly in terms of meaning postulates relating these morpheme- or near-morpheme-level primitives directly, as Fodor proposed. This nondecomposability of lexical meaning shows itself in many ways, from the nonexistence of a concept that means exactly the same thing as *waterproof* but applies to nonphysical entities such as integers, to the fuzziness of the verb classification schemata of Levin (1993), discussed by Dang, Rosenzweig, and Palmer (1997). The latter looks more like the result of a principal-components or factor analysis than a semantically interpretable set of features, despite its strong syntactic foundation.

This again seems to be exactly the kind of system that the subsymbolic approach is best suited to analyze. If this analysis is correct, then we would not expect a principal-components analysis to be interpretable in the way that we expect the results of parsing to be, and would be happy to tolerate a high degree of cognitive impenetrability in return for the efficiency and learnability of distributed representation. This again would really be emergence worthy of the name.

CONCLUSION:
PROJECT FOR A SCIENTIFIC PSYCHOLINGUISTICS

A project of the kind outlined in this chapter for the development of a grounded semantics will require starting at a much earlier stage than the onset of language learning. It is likely that it will have to recapitulate in neural computational terms the kind of program of sensory–motor development outlined in Piaget (1952) (though much theoretical baggage can be dispensed with, particularly in light of more recent research on the status of "preoperational" and "formal operational" components). Work along these lines has already been sketched in more symbolic computational terms by Drescher (1991) and Siskind (1995).

It is likely that such a research program would proceed by first conceptualizing primary bodily actions and sensations; then coordinating perception and primary actions like reaching; and then conceptualizing identity, permanence, and location of objects, first independent of their percepts, then of the particular actions they are involved in, amounting to the internalization of the components of a stable world independent of the child's actions. Later stages would have to include the conceptualization of more complex events, including intrinsic actions of objects themselves (such as falling), translations and events involving multiple participants, intermediate participants including tools, and goals. At this final stage of purely sensory–motor development most of the prerequisites for language learning would be established, perhaps embedded in RAAM or some other associative memory, and could be used to support a program of inducing a similarly layered sequence of linguistic categories such as deictic terms based on a proximal-distal dimension (whose central place in language development with respect to reference and definiteness is discussed by Lyons, 1977; cf. Freud, 1920, pp. 11–16, for a revealing case study), markers of topic, comment and contrast, common nouns, spatial and path terms, causal verbs, modal and propositional attitude verbs, and temporal terms. It is likely that the semantic theory that would emerge from this work would be rather unlike anything proposed so far within standard logicist frameworks. Such a semantics would be likely to make us view phenomena like quantification, modality, negation, and variable binding in new ways, within a unified theory combining symbolic and neurally grounded levels.

It is probably too soon to tell whether the distributed computational devices of the connectionist approach make such an ambitious research program any more feasible than it was at the time of Freud's (1895/1954) unpublished *Project for a Scientific Psychology*, arguably the first manifesto for a cognitive neuroscience (albeit a localist one), which he abandoned forever in 1895 in favor of the symbolic approach. The success of the present project is likely to depend crucially on the involvement of more reliable and biologically plausible network models than the three simple types of feed-forward networks considered in this chapter. In particular, in order to concentrate on the general relation of this class of models to symbolist alternatives, I have only referred in passing to some well-known problems with techniques specifically based on back-propagation, which include poor scaling of data-set size and learning times as the number of connections increases (Hinton & Gharamani, 1997, present an interesting recent alternative). Nevertheless, the chapters collected here make a convincing case that the attempt must be made, and has already begun.

FURTHER READING

An important source for several important early papers on connectionist approaches to symbolic processing discussed here is Hinton (1990a). An introduction to parallel distributed processing is to be found in the two-volume handbook edited by McClelland and Rumelhart (1986), along with several other early language-related papers using the approach. Smolensky, Mozer, and Rumelhart (1996) present mathematical results concerning learning and generalization by neural nets. Manning and Schütze (1999) is an excellent recent review of the (almost totally nonoverlapping) literature on statistical natural language processing. For both connectionist and computational linguistic approaches, the Internet has become the primary source for current developments. Most of the authors discussed here maintain home pages from which their latest work is continually available.

NOTE

This chapter is a revised and extended version of Steedman (1999). Thanks to Gerry Altmann, Ted Briscoe, Nick Chater, Morten Christiansen, Michael Collins, Geoff Hinton, Julia Hockenmaier, Mark Liberman, Jane Neumann, and the referees for *Cognitive Science* for comments and advice. The research was supported in part by ESRC Award Number M/423/28/4002 and EPSRC grant GR/M96889.

REFERENCES

Allen, J. (1997). Probabilistic constraints in acquisition. In A. Sorace, C. Heycock, & R. Shillcock (Eds.), *Proceedings of the GALA '97 Conference on Language Acquisition* (pp. 300–305). Edinburgh: University of Edinburgh.

Altmann, G.T.M. (1988). Ambiguity, parsing strategies, and computational models. *Language and Cognitive Processes, 3*, 73–98.

Altmann, G.T.M., & Steedman, M. (1988). Interaction with context during human sentence processing. *Cognition, 30*, 191–238.

Baldridge, J., Bierner, G., & Hockenmaier, J. (2000). *Providing robustness for a ccg system*. Unpublished manuscript, University of Edinburgh. Available at < http://grok.sourceforge.net/ > .

Berg, G. (1992). A connectionist parser with recursive sentence structure and lexical disambiguation. In *Proceedings of the Tenth National Conference on Artificial Intelligence* (pp. 32–37). Cambridge, MA: MIT Press.

Black, A. (1989). Finite state machines from feature grammars. In *Proceedings of the 1989 International Parsing Technologies Workshop*, Pittsburgh, August (pp. 277–285).

Bock, J. K. (1986). Syntactic persistence in language production. *Cognitive Psychology, 18*, 355–387.

Bresnan, J. W. (Ed.). (1982). *The mental representation of grammatical relations*. Cambridge, MA: MIT Press.

Bresnan, J. W., Kaplan, R. M., Peters, S., & Zaenen, A. (1982). Cross-serial dependencies in dutch. *Linguistic Inquiry, 13*, 613–636.

Bridle, J. (1992). Neural networks or hidden markov models for automatic speech recognition: Is there a choice? In P. Laface & R. De Mori (Eds.), *Speech recognition and understanding: Recent advances, trends and applications* (pp. 225–236). NATO Advanced Science Institutes Series F: Computer and Systems Sciences, No. 75. Springer.

Brill, E. (1992). A simple rule-based part-of-speech tagger. In *Proceedings of the Third Conference on Applied Natural Language Processing*, Trento (pp. 152–155). San Francisco: Morgan Kaufmann.

Carroll, J., & Briscoe, E. (1996). Apportioning development effort in a probabilistic lr parsing system through evaluation. In *Proceedings of the Second ACL SIGDAT Conference on Empirical Methods in Natural Language Processing*, Philadelphia (pp. 92–100).

Casey, M. (1996). The dynamics of discrete-time computation, with application to recurrent neural networks and finite state machine extraction. *Neural Computation, 8*, 1135–1178.

Charniak, E. (1997). Statistical parsing with a context-free grammar and word statistics. In *Proceedings of the Fourteenth National Conference of the American Association for Artificial Intelligence*, Providence, RI (pp. 598–603).

Chomsky, N. (1957). *Syntactic structures*. The Hague: Mouton.

Chomsky, N. (1965). *Aspects of the theory of syntax*. Cambridge, MA: MIT Press.

Christiansen, M. H., Allen, J., & Seidenberg, M. S. (1998). Learning to segment speech using multiple cues: A connectionist model. *Language and Cognitive Processes, 13*, 221–268.

Christiansen, M. H., & Chater, N. (1994). Generalization and connectionist language learning. *Mind and Language, 9*, 273–287.

Christiansen, M. H., & Chater, N. (1999). Toward a connectionist model of recursion in human linguistic performance. *Cognitive Science, 23*, 157–205.

Christiansen, M. H., & Devlin, J. T. (1997). Recursive inconsistencies are hard to learn: A connectionist perspective on universal word order correlations. In *Proceedings of the Nineteenth Annual Conference of the Cognitive Science Society* (pp. 113–118). Mahwah, NJ: Lawrence Erlbaum.

Church, K. (1988). A stochastic parts program and a noun phrase parser for unrestricted text. In *Proceedings of the Second Conference on Applied Natural Language Processing*, Austin, TX (pp. 136–143). Cambridge, MA: MIT Press.

Church, K., & Mercer, R. (1993). Introduction to the special issue on computational linguistics using large corpora. *Computational Linguistics, 19*, 1–24.

Cleeremans, A. (1993). *Mechanisms of implicit learning*. Cambridge MA: MIT Press.

Cleeremans, A., Servan-Schreiber, D., & McClelland, J. L. (1995). Graded state machines: The representation of temporal contingencies in feedback. In Y. Chauvin & D. E. Rumelhart (Eds.), *Backpropagation: Theory, architectures, and applications* (pp. 274–312). Hillsdale, NJ: Lawrence Erlbaum.

Collins, M. (1997). Three generative lexicalized models for statistical parsing. In *Proceedings of the Thirty-Fifth Annual Meeting of the Association for Computational Linguistics*, Madrid (pp. 16–23). San Mateo, CA: Morgan Kaufmann.

Crain, S. (1980). *Pragmatic constraints on sentence comprehension*. Unpublished doctoral dissertation, University of California, Irvine.

Crain, S., & Steedman, M. (1985). On not being led up the garden path: The use of context by the psychological parser. In L. K. David Dowty & A. Zwicky (Eds.), *Natural language parsing: Psychological, computational and theoretical perspectives* (pp. 320–358). Cambridge: Cambridge University Press.

Dang, H. T., Rosenzweig, J., & Palmer, M. (1997). Associating semantic components with levin classes. In *Proceedings of Interlinga Workshop, MTSUMMIT97*, San Diego, CA (pp. 11–18).

Drescher, G. (1991). *Made-up minds*. Cambridge, MA: MIT Press.

Eisner, J. (1997). Efficient generation in primitive optimality theory. In *Proceedings of the Thirty-Fifth Annual Meeting of the Association for Computational Linguistics and the Eighth Conference of the European Association for Computational Linguistics*, Madrid (pp. 313–320). San Mateo, CA: Morgan Kaufmann.

Elman, J. L. (1990). Representation and structure in connectionist models. In G. Altmann (Ed.), *Cognitive models of speech processing* (pp. 345–382). Cambridge, MA: MIT Press.

Elman, J. L. (1995). Language as a dynamical system. In R. Port & T. van Gelder (Eds.), *Mind as motion: Explorations in the dynamics of cognition* (pp. 195–225). Cambridge, MA: MIT Press.

Elworthy, D. (1994). Automatic error detection in part of speech tagging. In *Conference on New Methods in Language Processing*, Manchester.

Fisher, C., Hall, G., Rakowitz, S., & Gleitman, L. (1994). When it is better to receive than to give: Syntactic and conceptual constraints on vocabulary growth. *Lingua, 92*, 333–375.

Fodor, J. A. (1975). *The language of thought*. Cambridge, MA: Harvard University Press.

Fodor, J. A., & Pylyshyn, Z. W. (1988). Connectionism and cognitive architecture: A critical analysis. *Cognition, 28*, 3–71.

Frazier, L., & Clifton, J. C. (1996). *Construal*. Cambridge, MA: MIT Press.

Freud, S. (1895/1954). A project for a scientific psychology. In *The origins of psychoanalysis: Letters to William Fliess* (Standard Ed., Vol. 1, pp. 295–343). London: Imago.

Freud, S. (1920). *Beyond the pleasure principle* (Standard Ed., Vol. 18, pp. 7–64). London: Hogarth Press.

Gleitman, L. (1990). The structural sources of verb meanings. *Language Acquisition, 1*, 1–55.

Gold, E. M. (1967). Language identification in the limit. *Information and Control, 16*, 447–474.

Grimshaw, J. (1997). Projection, heads, and optimality. *Linguistic Inquiry, 28*, 373–422.

Hadley, R. F. (1994a). Systematicity in connectionist language learning. *Mind and Language, 9*, 247–272.

Hadley, R. F. (1994b). Systematicity revisited: Reply to Christiansen & Chater and Niklasson & van Gelder. *Mind and Language, 9*, 431–444.

Hale, K., & Keyser, S. J. (1993). On argument structure and the lexical expression of syntactic relations. In K. Hale & S. J. Keyser (Eds.), *The view from building 20* (pp. 53–109). Cambridge, MA: MIT Press.

Hinton, G. E. (Ed.). (1990a). *Connectionist symbol processing*. Cambridge, MA: MIT Press/Elsevier.

Hinton, G. E. (1990b). Mapping part–whole hierarchies into connectionist networks. *Artificial Intelligence, 46*, 47–75.

Hinton, G. E. (1990c). Preface to the special issue on connectionist symbol processing. *Artificial Intelligence, 46*, 1–4.

Hinton, G. E., & Gharamani, Z. (1997). Generative models for discovering sparse distributed representations. *Philosophical Transactions of the Royal Society of London, B, 352*, 1177–1190.

Horning, J. (1969). *A study of grammatical inference*. Unpublished doctoral dissertation, Stanford.

Huybregts, R. (1984). The weak inadequacy of context-free phrase-structure grammars. In G. de Haan, M. Trommelen, & W. Zonneveld (Eds.), *Van Periferie naar Kern*. Dordrecht: Foris.

Jelinek, F. (1976). Continuous speech recognition by statistical methods. *Proceedings of the Institute for Electronic and Electrical Engineers, 64*, 532–556.

Jelinek, F., Lafferty, J. D., Magerman, D., Mercer, R. L., Ratnaparkhi, A., & Roukos, S. (1994). Decision tree parsing using a hidden ferivation model. In *Proceedings of the 1994 DARPA Human Language Technology Workshop* (pp. 272–277). San Francisco: Morgan Kaufmann.

Jordan, M. I. (1989). Serial order: A parallel distributed processing approach. In J. L. Elman & D. E. Rumelhart (Eds.), *Advances in connectionist theory*. Hillsdale, NJ: Lawrence Erlbaum.

Joshi, A. K., & Schabes, Y. (1992). Tree-adjoining grammars and lexicalized grammars. In M. Nivat & A. Podelski (Eds.), *Definability and recognizability of sets of trees*. Princeton, NJ: Elsevier.

Kelly, M. H. (1992). Using sound to solve syntactic problems: The role of phonology in grammatical category assignments. *Psychological Review, 99*, 349–364.

Kelly, M. H., & Martin, S. (1994). Domain-general abilities applied to domain-specific tasks: Sensitivity to probabilities in perception, cognition, and language. *Lingua, 92*, 105–140.

Kim, A., Srinivas, B., & Trueswell, J. (1998). The convergence of lexicalist perspectives in psycholinguistics and computational linguistics. In P. Merlo & S. Stevenson (Eds.), *Papers from the special section on the lexicalist basis of syntactic processing*, CUNY Conference, Rutgers. Amsterdam: John Benjamins.

Landauer, T. K., & Dumais, S. T. (1997). A solution to Plato's problem: The latent semantic analysis of the acquisition, induction, and representation of knowledge. *Psychological Review, 104*, 211–240.

Landauer, T. K., Laham, D., Rehder, B., & Schreiner, M. (1997). How well can passage meaning be derived without using word order? In *Proceedings of the Nineteenth Annual Conference of the Cognitive Science Society*. Mahwah, NJ: Lawrence Erlbaum.

Levin, B. (1993). *English verb-classes and alternations: A preliminary study*. Chicago: University of Chicago Press.

Lyons, J. (1977). *Semantics* (Vol. 2). Cambridge: Cambridge University Press.

Magerman, D. (1995). Statistical decision tree models for parsing. In *Proceedings of the Thirty-Third Annual Meeting of the Association for Computational Linguistics*, Cambridge, MA (pp. 276–283). San Francisco: Morgan Kaufmann.

Manning, C., & Schütze, H. (1999). *Foundations of statistical natural language processing*. Cambridge, MA: MIT Press.

de Marcken, C. (1990). Parsing the lob corpus. In *Proceedings of the Twenty-Eighth Annual Meeting of the Association for Computational Linguistics*, Pittsburgh (pp. 243–251). San Mateo, CA: Morgan Kaufmann.

McClelland, J. L., & Kawamoto, A. H. (1986). Mechanisms of sentence processing. In J. L. McClelland & D. E. Rumelhart (Eds.), *Parallel distributed processing: Explorations in the microstructure of cognition*. Vol. 2: *Psychological and biological models* (pp. 272–325). Cambridge, MA: MIT Press.

McClelland, J. L., & Rumelhart, D. E. (Eds.). (1986). *Parallel distributed processing: Explorations in the microstructure of cognition*. Vol. 2: *Psychological and biological models*. Cambridge, MA: MIT Press.

McRae, K., Spivey-Knowlton, M. J., & Tanenhaus, M. K. (1998). Modeling the influence of thematic fit (and other constraints) in on-line sentence comprehension. *Journal of Memory and Language, 38*, 283–312.

Merialdo, B. (1994). Tagging English text with a probabilistic model. *Computational Linguistics, 20*, 155–171.

Mikkulainen, R. (1993). *Subsymbolic natural language processing*. Cambridge, MA: MIT Press.

Mikkulainen, R. (1995). Subsymbolic parsing of embedded structures. In R. Sun & L. Bookman (Eds.), *Computational architectures integrating neural and symbolic processes* (pp. 153–186). Dordrecht: Kluwer.

Montague, R. (1970). English as a formal language. In B. Visentini (Ed.), *Linguaggi nella Società e nella Technica* (pp. 189–224). Milan: Edizioni di Communità.

Montague, R. (1974). *Formal philosophy: Papers of Richard Montague* (Richmond H. Thomason, Ed.). New Haven, CT: Yale University Press.

Neuman, J. (2000a). Holistic transformation of holographic reduced representations. MS. Division of Informatics, University of Edinburgh.

Neuman, J. (2000b). Learning holistic transformations of hrr from examples. MS. Division of Informatics, University of Edinburgh.

Niklasson, L., & van Gelder, T. (1994). On being systematically connectionist. *Mind and Language, 9*, 288–302.

Pearlmutter, B. A. (1995). Gradient calculations for dynamic recurrent neural networks: A survey. *IEEE Transactions on Neural Networks, 6*, 1212–1228.

Piaget, J. (1952). *The origins of intelligence in children*. New York: Norton.

Plate, T. (1991). Holographic reduced representations: Convolution algebra for compositional distributed representations. In J. Mylopoulos & R. Reiter (Eds.), *Proceedings of the Twelfth International Joint Conference on Artificial Intelligence* (pp. 30–35). San Mateo, CA: Morgan Kaufmann.

Plate, T. (1994). *Distributed representations and nested compositional structure*. Unpublished doctoral dissertation, University of Toronto.

Plate, T. (1997). Structure matching and transformation with distributed representations. In R. Sun & F. Alexandre (Eds.), *Connectionist–symbolic integration*. Hillsdale, NJ: Lawrence Erlbaum.

Pollack, J. B. (1990). Recursive distributed representations. *Artificial Intelligence, 46*, 77–105.

Pollard, C., & Sag, I. (1987). *Information-based syntax and semantics* (Vol. 1). Stanford, CA: CSLI Publications.

Pollard, C., & Sag, I. (1994). *Head-driven phrase structure grammar*. Stanford, CA: CSLI Publications.

Prince, A., & Smolensky, P. (1997). Optimality: From neural networks to universal grammar. *Science, 275*, 1604–1610.

Ratnaparkhi, A. (1998). *Maximum entropy models for natural language ambiguity resolution*. Unpublished doctoral dissertation, University of Pennsylvania.

Rumelhart, D. E., Hinton, G. E., & Williams, R. J. (1986). Learning internal representations by error propagation. In D. E. Rumelhart & J. L. McClelland (Eds.), *Parallel distributed processing: Explorations in the microstructure of cognition*. Vol. 1: *Foundations* (pp. 318–362). Cambridge, MA: MIT Press.

Seidenberg, M. S. (1997). Language acquisition and use: Learning and applying probabilistic constraints. *Science, 275*, 1599–1603.

Sharkey, N., & Sharkey, A. (1992). A modular design for connectionist parsing. In A. Nijholt & M. Drossaers (Eds.), *Twente workshop on language technology 3: Connectionism and natural language processing* (pp. 87–96). Enschede, The Netherlands: Dept. of Computer Science, University of Twente.

Shieber, S. (1985). Evidence against the context-freeness of natural language. *Linguistics and Philosophy, 8*, 333–343.

Siskind, J. (1995). Grounding language in perception. *Artificial Intelligence Review, 8*, 371–391.

Siskind, J. (1996). A computational study of cross-situational techniques for learning word-to-meaning mappings. *Cognition, 61*, 39–91.

Smolensky, P. (1990). Tensor product variable binding and the representation of symbolic structures in connectionist systems. *Artificial Intelligence, 46*, 159–216.

Smolensky, P., Mozer, M. C., & Rumelhart, D. E. (Eds.). (1996). *Mathematical perspectives on neural networks*. Mahwah, NJ: Lawrence Erlbaum.

Spivey-Knowlton, M. J., Trueswell, J. C., & Tanenhaus, M. K. (1993). Context effects in syntactic ambiguity resolution: Discourse and semantic influences in parsing reduced relative clauses. *Canadian Journal of Psychology, 47*, 276–309.

Srinivas, B. (1997). *Complexity of lexical descriptions and its relevance to partial parsing*. Unpublished doctoral dissertation, University of Pennsylvania.

Srinivas, B., & Joshi, A. (1994). Disambiguation of super parts of speech (or supertags): Almost parsing. In *Proceedings of the International Conference on Computational Linguistics (COLING 94)*, Kyoto University, Japan. San Mateo, CA: Morgan Kaufmann.

St. John, M. F., & McClelland, J. L. (1990). Learning and applying contextual constraints in sentence comprehension. *Artificial Intelligence, 46*, 217–257.

Steedman, M. (1985). Dependency and coordination in the grammar of Dutch and English. *Language, 61*, 523–568.

Steedman, M. (1991). Structure and intonation. *Language, 67*, 262–296.

Steedman, M. (1996). *Surface structure and interpretation*. Cambridge, MA: MIT Press.

Steedman, M. (1999). Connectionist sentence processing in perspective. *Cognitive Science, 23*, 615–634.

Steedman, M., & Altmann, G. (1989). Ambiguity in context: A reply. *Language and Cognitive Processes, 4*, 105–122.

Tesar, B. (1998). An iterative strategy for language learning. *Lingua, 104*, 131–145.

Trueswell, J. C., & Tanenhaus, M. K. (1992). Consulting temporal context in sentence comprehension: Evidence from the monitoring of eye movements in reading. In *Proceedings of the Fourteenth Annual Conference of the Cognitive Science Society* (pp. 492–499). Hillsdale, NJ: Lawrence Erlbaum.

Trueswell, J. C., Tanenhaus, M. K., & Garnsey, S. M. (1994). Semantic influences on parsing: Use of thematic role information in syntactic ambiguity resolution. *Journal of Memory and Language, 33*, 285–318.

Trueswell, J. C., Tanenhaus, M. K., & Kello, C. (1993). Verb-specific constraints in sentence processing: Separating effects of lexical preference from garden-paths. *Journal of Experimental Psychology: Learning, Memory and Cognition, 19*, 528–553.

Wilkins, W., & Wakefield, J. (1995). Brain evolution: Neurolinguistic preconditions. *Behavioral and Brain Sciences, 18*, 161–182.

Williams, C., & Hinton, G. E. (1990). Mean field networks that learn to discriminate temporally distorted strings. In D. Touretsky, J. L. Elman, T. Sejnowski, & G. E. Hinton (Eds.), *Connectionist models: Proceedings of the 1990 summer school*. Hillsdale, NJ: Lawrence Erlbaum.

Willshaw, D. (1981). Holography, association and induction. In G. E. Hinton & J. Anderson (Eds.), *Parallel models of associative memory* (pp. 83–104). Hillsdale, NJ: Lawrence Erlbaum.

Willshaw, D., Buneman, P., & Longuet-Higgins, C. (1969). Non-holographic associative memory. *Nature, 222*, 960–962.

Woods, W. (1970). Transition network grammars for natural language analysis. *Communications of the Association for Computing Machinery, 18*, 264–274.

Xia, F. (1999). Extracting tree adjoining grammars from bracketed corpora. In *Proceedings of the Fifth Natural Language Processing Pacific Rim Symposium* (NLPRS-99).

Index

About the Editors
and Contributors

Franklin Chang is a graduate student in cognitive psychology at the University of Illinois. He is working on his dissertation with his advisor, Gary Dell, on a computational model of sentence production.

Nick Chater is Professor of Psychology and Director of the Institute for Applied Cognitive Science at the University of Warwick. His research focuses on computational and mathematical models of cognitive processes, including language processing, reasoning, and perception. He was an undergraduate at Cambridge and has a Ph.D, in Cognitive Science from University of Edinburgh. He has held lecturing appointments at University College London, University of Edinburgh and Oxford University.

Morten H. Christiansen is an Assistant Professor of Psychology at University. His research integrates connectionist modeling, statistical analyses, behavioral experimentation, and event-related potential (ERP) methods in the study of the learning and processing of complex sequential structure, in particular as related to language. He received his Ph.D. in Cognitive Science from the University of Edinburgh and has subsequently been a McDonnell Postdoctoral Fellow at the Philosophy, Neuroscience and Psychology Program at Washington University, an Advanced Postdoctoral Research Associate in the Neural, Informational and Behavioral Sciences Program at the University of Southern California, an Assistant Professor in the Departments of Psychology and Linguistics at Southern Illinois University, and Assistant Professor of Psycholgy at Cornell University.

Gary S. Dell is Professor of Psychology at the University of Illinois at Urbana-Champaign, where he is also the head of the cognitive science group of the Beckman Institute for Advanced Science and Technology. He is the author of many articles concerning language production and connectionist models.

M. Gareth Gaskell is a Senior Lecturer in Psychology at the University of York, U.K. His research combines connectionist, statistical, and human experimental research methods in the study of spoken language, and much of his work has focused on understanding the word recognition process in speech perception.

Zenzi M. Griffin received a Ph.D. in cognitive psychology from University of Illinois at Urbana-Champaign in 1998. After three years on the faculty of Stanford University's psychology department, she moved to her current position on the psychology faculty at Georgia Tech. Her research focuses on the time course of word selection as part of explaining how speakers produce grammatical utterances.

Patrick Juola is an Assistant Professor of Computer Science at Duquesne University, as well as an affiliated researcher at the Computer Emergency Response Team/Coordination Center, both in Pittsburgh, PA. His research interests include psycholinguistics and information theory.

Maryellen C. MacDonald is Professor of Psychology at the University of Wisconsin, Madison. Her work investigates sentence comprehension and production. She is the editor of *Lexical Representations and Sentence Processing* (1997) and the author of a number of articles and papers on the role of distributional information on comprehension and production processes.

William D. Marslen-Wilson is director of the Medical Research Council Cognition and Brain Sciences Unit, in Cambridge, U.K. His research focuses on the cognitive and neural systems underlying human language comprehension, and he has published more than 125 articles and chapters on this topic.

David C. Plaut is Associate Professor of Psychology and Computer Science at Carnegie Mellon University with a joint appointment in the Center for the Neural Basis of Cognition. His research involves using connectionist modeling, complemented by empirical studies, to extend our understanding of normal and impaired cognitive processing in the domains of reading, language, and semantics. He received an NIH FIRST award in 1997 and a Fulbright Scholarship in 2000, and has contributed to more than 70 scientific publications.

Kim Plunkett is Professor of Cognitive Neuroscience at Oxford University. He is the author of nine books and has contributed articles or chapters to more than 100 scholarly publications.

Mark S. Seidenberg is Professor in the Department of Psychology and in the Neuroscience Program at the University of Wisconsin-Madison. His research addresses a broad range of issues concerning language and cognitive neuroscience, using experimental methods and computational modeling. He currently holds a Research Scientist Development Award from NIMH and is writing a book with Maryellen C. MacDonald about language and connectionism.

Paul Smolensky is Professor in the Department of Cognitive Science at Johns Hopkins University, where he directs a major NSF graduate training program in the Cognitive Science of Language. His research addresses how the high-level properties of neural computation enable an integration of connectionism with symbolic cognitive theory, especially, the theory of universal grammar. His work focuses on Optimality Theory, a connectionist-based grammar formalism he developed with Alan Prince. He has been President of the Society for Philosophy and Psychology and twice President of the Cognitive Science Society.

Mark Steedman is Professor in the Division of Informatics at the University of Edinburgh. He is a Fellow of the American Association for Artificial Intelligence. His research interests cover issues in computational linguistics, artificial intelligence, computer science, and cognitive science—including syntax and semantics of natural language, parsing, and comprehension of natural language discourse by humans and by machine, natural language generation and spoken discourse, and computational analysis of music. Much of his current NLP research is addressed to issues in spoken discourse and dialogue, especially the meaning of intonation and prosody.

Whitney Tabor received his PhD in Linguistics from Stanford University in 1994, under the advisorship of Elizabeth Closs Traugott. He did postdoctoral research in psycholinguistics at the University of Rochester, MIT, and Cornell before becoming an Assistant Professor of Psychology at the University of Connecticut. His research interests include self-organization phenomena in sentence processing, change in structured systems (e.g., languages), and the formal relationship between symbolic and dynamical computation.

Michael K. Tanenhaus is Professor of Brain and Cognitive Sciences at the University of Rochester, where he has served as chair of the Department of Psychology and the Department of Linguistics and as codirector of the Center for Language Sciences. He has contributed more than 100 articles or chapters on a wide variety of topics in language comprehension, including spoken and visual word recognition, syntactic processing and reference resolution.